The Battle o

The Battle of Britain
The fight for survival in 1940
Michael JF Bowyer

Crécy Publishing Limited

The Battle of Britain
The fight for survival in 1940

First published by Patrick Stephens Limited in 1990
This revised and enlarged edition published in 2010 by Crécy Publishing
Limited

A CIP record for this book is available from the British Library

ISBN 9 780859 791472

Printed in Malta by
Melita Press

Crécy Publishing Limited
1a Ringway Trading Estate, Shadowmoss Road, Manchester M22 5LH
www.crecy.co.uk

CONTENTS

Acknowledgements
and suggestions for further reading

S urely 1940 will always be the most outstanding year in Britain's history. Since 1066 an invasion of our homeland had been unlikely, but in June 1940 it became for the first time a very serious possibility – once the mighty Royal Navy had been sunk and the RAF shot out of the sky. Although neither was achieved, everyone around at the time was provided with indelible memories of the attempts to achieve them through events great and small, while existing in a style now seemingly implausible. Recalled here are many events from that troubled time, the accent being placed upon those with an aeronautical flavour.

The year fell into four distinct phases: uncertain times, German conquests, the Battle of Britain, and the German night-bombing campaign. The Battle of Britain period is the core of this volume.

A 1941 official publication priced 6d, prepared by two official historians and entitled *The Battle of Britain* (HMSO), the first published account of the Battle, was followed by an hour-long radio programme. In security-strict days it amazingly revealed details of the assaults upon Croydon, Biggin Hill, Hawkinge, Kenley and Tangmere. Those two productions form the basis of this account and arguably all others. It also includes content from my 1940 diary.

In 1946 a skilled report outlining the Battle of Britain and written by Air Chief Marshal Sir Hugh Dowding appeared as a Supplement to *The London Gazette*. Not until 1953 did the next major account of the 1940 fighting appear. It was *The Fight at Odds*, the first volume of an official trilogy entitled *The Royal Air Force 1939-1945* (HMSO), of which a paperback edition followed in 1975. The author, Denis Richards, Principal of Morley College, had worked with one-time Librarian of The House of Commons, the late Hilary St George Saunders, on the 1941 publication. Skilfully, concisely, Volume 1 of the series describes many events of the 1940 war.

Basil Collier's *The Defence of the United Kingdom* (HMSO), reviewing land, sea and aerial aspects of UK wartime defence, appeared in 1957 as part of the extensive *Official History of the Second World War*, prepared under Professor J. R. M. Butler's leadership. Major L. F. Ellis's *The War in France and Flanders 1939-1940* (HMSO 1953) and *The War at Sea* Volume 1 by Captain S. W. Roskill, devoted to naval actions in 1940 and within the series, cover those fields. Detailed reports of attacks on FS/FN convoys are held in the National Archives within Class ADM199, in which reports by survivors appear in pieces 2130-2135.

In 1945 a very detailed search through captured enemy documents was ordered, to establish an accurate record of German aircraft losses during the Battle of Britain .It was an extremely difficult task. From the German Quartermaster General's record of losses, serviceability returns, casualty and POW records, and from many British, German and foreign documents – some never likely to be made public – a highly able Air Ministry Air Historical Branch team produced, after very extensive study, the required official record of losses. Their conclusions are drawn upon in official histories. Confirmed adjustments have been and still are made, but only after exhaustive checks.

Many official 1940 documents used by the official historians may now be consulted in the National Archives at Kew. Grouped within Classes, the most pertinent RAF records are Operations Record Books (Forms 540 and 541). These squadron records are held on microfilm within Class AIR 27. Fighter Command ORBs may be found within AIR 24 and fighter policy files in AIR 16. Combat reports appear in AIR 50, statistical and intelligence surveys in AIR 22 and AIR 40. Bomber and Coastal Command ORBs can be found in Class AIR 24. Individual histories of RAF aircraft (not classified as historical documents) are on microfilm, which the RAF Museum, Hendon, has available. In an astonishing twist, the Data Protection Act (rather historian-unfriendly) now restricts access to aircraft accident records at Hendon because of personal/personnel content, although for decades the material has been open to public scrutiny.

Details of anti-aircraft activity are available at Kew in Class WO and results of bombing raids in Class HO 198-202.

The Narrow Margin by Derek Wood and Derek Dempster (Hutchinson), which appeared in 1961, remains one of the most extensive and authoritative volumes devoted to the Battle. Air Chief Marshal Lord Dowding GCB GCVO CMG wrote the Foreword, and the book received widespread acclaim and the C. P. Robertson Memorial Trophy for its superb presentation of the RAF at war. The basis of the 1968 film *The Battle of Britain*, it appeared in 1969 as a paperback.

Later excellent books include Frank Mason's 1969 *Battle over Britain* (McWhirter Twins), the first to publicly include information from Luftwaffe loss records. Ten years later came *The Battle of Britain – Then and Now* (After the Battle) edited by Winston G. Ramsey, which placed much emphasis upon personnel involved. Later, After the Battle produced a three-volume series, *The Blitz – Then and Now*, along similar lines. Volume 1 covered fighting to 6 September 1940, the main night attacks featuring in Volume 2. *Most Secret War* (Hamish Hamilton) by Professor R. V. Jones details brilliantly the intelligence work he and others conducted in respect of German use of radio beams for navigation purposes.

All of these volumes influence other published works relating to 1940 and the Battle of Britain, although it is from official material (the Crown Copyright of which is acknowledged), and material gathered by myself in 1940 and since, that I have mainly worked.

To the Imperial War Museum I express thanks for photographs and permission to reproduce them. The Bundesarchiv in Koblenz helpfully supplied pictures of German forces, and rare photographs of Me 109s have been contributed by Michael Payne. To the Cambridgeshire Collection I am indebted for help as and when needed. Private sources are credited alongside pictures with particular thanks to Gerrit Zwanenburg. Thanks in profusion are due to a large number of people who, over very many years, have provided me with help, influence and companionship abundant over the last seven decades, contributing so much to fascinate and bring pleasure.

There is one to thank most specially, dear friend Laurence Haylock, so suddenly, unexpectedly taken from us. With very great skill mixed with some merriment, 'Lol' produced all the really superb artwork illustrating our book.

Abbreviations

Bf 109, 110	Generally accepted as the correct designation of the wartime Messerschmitt 109 and 110
CE	Channel convoy eastward-bound
CH	Chain Home radar station
CW	Channel convoy westward-bound
Establishment	Number of aircraft/personnel, etc, approved as total unit/squadron strength but not necessarily held
FN	East coast convoy sailing north to Forth
FS	East coast sailing south from Forth
FTR	Failed to return from operational sortie
GP	General-purpose HE bomb – SAP/AP bombs were for hardened targets
grt	Gross registered tonnage
HE	High-explosive bomb
He	Heinkel (111)
JG	Jagdeschwader (Luftwaffe fighter group)
KG	Kampfgeschwader (Luftwaffe bomber group), consisting of three or four Gruppen subdivided usually into three Staffel and denoted by Roman numerals, eg I, II, III, with a Stab or HQ Flight
KIA	Killed in action
PM	Parachute mine
SAP/AP	Semi armour piercing bombs
UX	Unexploded bomb

Chapter 1

The hard life

Ah yes! I remember them so well, those sights, sounds, worries and sorrows, the exhilaration and even the smells of 1940. What an incredible year, packed with so much impressive, unpredictable and unforgettable. All that and much more, it remains as vivid in memory now as if it was just yesterday.

Blackout total, multitudes of sandbags – weeping thanks to little fingers – at a time when every able-bodied man seemed to be joining something. In ARP posts – wondrous citadels of pomposity – their occupants were overseeing stirrup pumps that wouldn't work (although amazingly mine still does). Are they all 70 years away? Is it that long since swarming sirens swooned mournfully, competitively, warbled their warning in personal style, and often after an 'um-pahing' nasty Heinkel had, like our umbrella man, gone on 'his' way? Can it be seven decades since 'the ARP HQ' was ordered to issue its purple or red warning to keep us on edge hour upon hour for no evident reason? Is it so long since the window frames rattled alarmingly and, even more frighteningly, neighbour ARP Warden Mr Clark seemed to secretly hope that he would have to wear his even more ugly better-than-ours gas mask? Caped like a Phantom of the Opera, crowned with an oversized tin hat, whistle dangling and gas rattle desperate for trade, I once caught him flat on his tum-tum peering under our front door seeking a non-existent light.

Is it a few moments ago, or a bit longer, since that familiar cry 'It's one of ours' was promptly followed by a nasty bang or two, then the call 'Where's the RAF?'? The BBC soon told us – it had gone, yet again, to catch a train in the marshalling yard at Hamm. OK, we'd just have to put up with another rattling old Dornier. More encouragingly, a know-all would inevitably emerge, show off, proclaim that the secret aerodrome about to open nearby was to have a squadron of very secret fighters, Westland Whippets. How do we survive in 2010 without delectable rumourmongers frequenting the entire Kingdom? Yes, it was a wonderful world, gone – well, almost.

When King George VI radioed us in 1939, after we'd had the last proper Christmas dinner for the next ten years, he revealed that he'd been chatting to some guy he'd come across leaning on the gate of the year, that he'd been doing some hand-holding, and also that he'd been told where to go. Home-front life, as experienced in 1940, is a world so far removed from that of today that it is almost impossible to believe how harsh it was.

New Year's Day arrived wrapped in ice and snow. Without the luxury of any form of heating, and nothing remotely like double-glazing, the intense cold penetrated my unheated bedroom where I was lying on a feather mattress snug beneath layers of sheets, blankets, heavy bedspread (which cost 1s 11d at top shop 'the Belfast') and coats to make sure. I was almost certainly wearing a thick, cream-coloured woolly vest – and probably flannelette pyjamas. The New Year's Day overture was indeed a miserable experience, and there were millions of others similarly experiencing it.

Rubber hot water bottles becoming scarce, we were experimenting with stone ginger beer bottles, wrapped for insulation in old socks or stockings. Home-knitted bedsocks were plentiful for icy-cold feet, a national problem. By next winter chilblains, very widespread, excruciatingly painful, were unfortunately enhanced if, to keep warm, one sat close – as usual – to an open coal fire. For anyone shivering in the bitter cold concrete air raid shelters, chilblains were a particularly unpleasant side effect, but maybe not as disturbing as the suggested remedies, including placing one's feet in snow, or even worse immersing them in the contents of the chamber pot commonly nestling beneath most beds. Thermogene – orange in colour, and like cotton wool in texture – reclined upon many a chest to cure a common cold should inhalation of Friar's Balsam – or the sore nasal effect of Vick – be unacceptable. Uncomfortable as it was, January's cold as experienced on earth was insignificant by comparison with that being encountered by Whitley crews flying over Europe as high as 20,000 feet. They faced an incredible -70°F.

Irksome was the blackout strictly enforced until dawn. It demanded nightly dangling of thick curtains or positioning of shutters over all windows. Annoyance knew few bounds when the nation discovered that our closest allies, the French, were not bothering with it. Gas still used for lighting brought the constant problem of broken cotton mantles. Fortunately, many living in town houses were supplied with mains electricity. Ours, installed in 1936, dramatically changed our lives by providing instant bright lighting, revealing even the tiniest cobweb. A high proportion of houses featured fixed lighting downstairs only. Upstairs meant using a torch or even a candle, with paraffin stoves also being used for heating. In blackout conditions torches were very useful, especially in upstairs rooms. Unlikely as it may seem, oil lamps were the norm for home lighting in the countryside, and paraffin for heating by means of Valor stoves. Both produced unavoidable, irremovable, unforgettable aromas. Gas cookers were common in town, whereas in the country kitchen ranges burning wood and coal were general items.

Water was tap-supplied in towns, but it may seem unbelievable that in the countryside most still obtained their supply by using the village pump, or even a bucket dipped in a well. The authorities were deeply concerned should fractured water mains in cities fast become polluted.

Tea – rarely coffee – was mostly sipped from a cup on a saucer, not the modern mug. Shortage of bone china meant that broken items had to be replaced with clumsy, thick, white crockery. Middle-aged folk, remembering WWI sugar rationing (only a week away), took tea muttering 'zaccharin'.

As rationing day approached, some tried delaying its effect by hoarding. The poor, unable to do so, were also limited by available storage space! Some commodities still familiar by name remained available, off-ration: 'delicacies' such as Bisto, Bovril, Bournville cocoa, Burdell's gravy salt, Horlicks, Marmite, Oxo, Chiver's jam, Ovaltine, Kelloggs cornflakes, All Bran, Quaker Oats and Shredded Wheat. The latter was produced in what then was regarded as an ultra-modern-looking building at Welwyn Garden City.

A little known 1940 addiction, for many, was Horlicks tablets. The little creamy discs, in small, blue-and-cream tubular 3d packets, came from chemists' shops. Amazing was their popularity, especially at night in cold air raid shelters, wherein billions of them must have been consumed.

What the papers say: 8 January 1940

The arrival of 'Coupon Monday' is welcomed in many parts of the country. Every man, woman and child in the country, from members of the Royal Family to their humblest subjects, has a ration card, which will now be worth its weight in gold to the hungry. From today everyone is entitled to: twelve ounces of sugar, four ounces of bacon and ham and four ounces of butter a week. The amounts are regarded by housewives as adequate, and there has been little criticism of the scheme. Mrs Morrison, wife of the Food Minister, thinks that she will 'be able to manage beautifully'.

Sir John Anderson, Home Secretary and Minister of Home Security, speaking at Glasgow today, hinted at the lull before the storm in the air war... 'I am much more concerned lest our preparations be found after all to be not enough to meet the heavy strain they will be called upon to bear ... our civil defence organisation is in no way excessive for the task which it will be called upon to perform when the enemy delivers his attack from the air.'

Eggs were an important part of the nation's staple diet. Many were provided by friendly backyard hens for which there was more respect, and a closer relationship, than in today's TV-sanitised natural world. DEFRA and the weird health and safety brigade would certainly not have approved. Our affinity was sorely tested when it came time to consume a noisy cockerel, especially as one knew he would taste delicious. Killing the enemy was one thing, tackling your pet cockerel – that was very different!

Professional farming was very labour-intensive. Horse and cart, predominating over powered contraptions, were always a delight to view. At harvest time the reapers' effort was followed by farmhands tying the crop into sheaves, then into stooks. Impressive always was the steam traction engine that assisted in corn threshing. Hay and straw were woven into stacks, a very attractive feature of the countryside. Fires, producing large amounts of smoke, were due to stacks internally overheating. Fruit farmers placed picked plums and apples in large round baskets called skips, which contained about 28lb (2 stones) of fruit, called 'a quarter' – ie a quarter of 1 hundredweight (112lb). Most dairy farmers, whose cows were outside in summer, inside for winter, milked their cows by hand. Production was very strictly carried out and monitored. Milk was stored in traditional-shaped metal churns, delivered by horse and cart in 1-pint or ½-pint glass bottles. It could also be purchased direct from a dairy, and often from a churn on the cart. A metal jug was used to measure the quantity required. Small amounts of cream came from a gill container.

A daily essential task in a world where cows not only gave milk but also provided an amazing amount of leather, which had many uses, was shoe-polishing. It had to be done well, before setting off for work or school early and in total winter darkness wearing a hefty long coat. Anoraks and such contraptions were unheard of. Woollen scarf, thick gloves (sheepskin if one could afford them, mittens if you couldn't) and certainly a hat, all were the norm, for young and old.

Top: Bill and Len about to sow the wheat watched by Pip, the black retriever.

Left: Polly awaits her milk round. Churn aboard, also bottles and measures.

Right: Harvest home, with Prince taking Len for a ride. 'Elf and safety would now frown!

Reasons for Rationing

1: Rationing prevents waste of food We must not ask our sailors to bring unnecessary food cargoes at the risk of their lives.

2: Rationing increases our war effort Our shipping carries food and armaments in their raw and finished state, and other essential raw materials for home consumption and the export trade. To reduce our purchases of food abroad is to release ships for bringing us other imports. So we shall strengthen our war effort.

3: Rationing divides supplies equally There will be ample supplies for our 44½ million people, but we must divide them fairly, everyone being treated alike. No one must be left out.

4: Rationing prevents uncertainty Your Ration Book assures you of your fair share. Rationing means that there will be no uncertainty – and no queues.

Your ration book is your passport to easy purchasing of bacon and ham, butter and sugar.

Announcement by the Ministry of Food, Great Westminster House, London SW1

Travel to the day's hard travail would be by bicycle, bus, tram, trolleybus or train, and usually still involved a lot of walking – several miles for country dwellers. Few had private or business cars. By summer, petrol rationing reduced their use. Early departure was essential, vehicle and driver numbers having been reduced. In winter 1940 many set out before the night's 'All Clear' sounded. Thousands in large cities then passed terrible scenes, and stepped over the maze of active hosepipes lying on icy ground. For hours following big city raids the air would be packed not only with dust, but also horrendous smells and, even worse, tiny glass particles. In some ghastly instances, like the bombing of the Surrey Docks, they drifted into eyes.

During 1940 excursions a gas mask was often carried, and into late 1941 by many. Some of those rubber monstrosities remained in the pale brown cardboard boxes in which they were supplied, others nestled snugly in tall tins or shapely bags. Although there seemed no particular concern about gas attack, one usually took the thing – just in case. It was long compulsory for children to take gas masks to school.

Ample communication in wartime was essential, and so much was face-to-face or handwritten. Letter-writing, stylish and readable, using a dip-in ink pen or a fountain pen, was a national pastime. Gold-nib Conway Stewart fountain pens competed with lovely Watermans, and washable ink of many a hue supplied in fancy glass bottles. At school the class ink monitor filled each desk's china inkwell. Teachers usually marked children's work using red ink.

Pencils, available in wide array, played a great part in the war effort. Red pencils, black pencils, multi-coloured pencils, indelible pencils, hexagonal pencils, giant pencils, pencils on strings – there was no limit to this Cumberland wonder existent by the million. Important or pompous people (and children after Christmas) were ever ready to display their latest propelling pencils, sometimes gold or silver.

The telephone was regarded as an item of high technology, a business contraption that ARP men loved to use, for it gave them great insight to what the Government thought Hitler was up to. Home phones were rare, and red phone boxes were unvisited by many because correct calling, confusion over payment and when to press button A or B daunted many. Much converse was face-to-face, in person, in those very friendly times. Ballpoint pens, mobile phones, computers and such paraphernalia would have obviously had a profound effect upon the war effort.

One's images of events depended upon the extent of personal learning, observation, memory and imagination. Film for private cameras was all but unobtainable. Until viewing a Pathe cinema newsreel, or looking in one of the many daily delivered newspapers, one could only have a hazy notion of the scenes of war. One of the most disturbing early-1940 pictures showed Clacton from the air, terribly shattered after a German sea mine exploded in a Heinkel 111 that slithered along Victoria Road and slammed itself into a bungalow. Very few published pictures were in colour during wartime.

Newspaper headlines on New Year's Day 1940 differed widely. They included 'German Raider Shot Down by Coastal Command', and 'Another Nazi Attempt on Shetlands', which a pair of bombers had tried to attack. There were items still familiar including 'foot and mouth', which had hit a farm at Caldecote, Hertfordshire, where twenty-eight fat bullocks worth £3 each, prize Suffolk ewes and pigs all had to be slaughtered. There was no nationwide cull – meat was too precious to waste. The Second Sea Lord had married, a youth had stabbed a constable to protect his own mother, and the price of meat was likely to rise as we headed towards rationing. 'You must register not later than Monday 8th January' we were repeatedly warned, if you want meat. While ammunition was being stolen for dubious purposes from dumps in County Louth – for Ireland was a troubled land – 'British Tommies' were attending horse-racing at Vincennes – the first since September. Surprisingly at a time so wrapped in secrecy, the Admiralty announced that between 11 and 20 December 1939 1,454 vessels – gross tonnage 3,648,000 – had entered or cleared British ports. Three British ships (3,036 tons) had been sunk that week, and two neutrals. The German *Glucksberg* (2,680 tons), intercepted by the Royal Navy, was beached near Chipions Light, Spain. It was also reported that a German specialist had diagnosed Hitler as having throat cancer. He apparently had told Goering and Goebbels, 'I am afraid he will not live more than eighteen months.' There had been an erroneous diagnosis, and the day's news flow had, unkindly, been too optimistic.

How to Register for Meat

1 Put your name and address on the counterfoil at the bottom of the meat page of your ration book NOW

2 Write on the inside front cover of your ration book the name and address of your butcher

3 Take your ration book to your butcher and let him write his name and address on the meat counterfoil and cut it out

4 If you move to another district, take your ration book to the local Food Office in your new district

5 The numbered coupons must not be cut out yet. This will be done by your butcher when you do your shopping after meat rationing begins

6 If you registered for meat before Christmas, this registration was unauthorised. You may let it stand and it will then be effective. Or, if you wish, you may register now with another butcher by recovering the counterfoil from the butcher who holds it and taking it to the butcher you now choose.

Announcement by the Ministry of Food, Great Westminster House, London SW1

Reliance upon the ever-increasing number of BBC wireless news bulletins was an essential part of all lives. In March 1940 a second station, Forces, was introduced. Regular BBC news features included the 'Air Ministry communiqué', usually accurate and particularly so where RAF losses were concerned. News flashes were avoided; they could cause undue alarm. Much broadcasting was very sedate, with various BBC orchestras, organ recitals, talks and serious features predominating in early 1940.

What's on the wireless?

On 1 January 1940 late-afternoon broadcasting began with one of the assorted BBC orchestras followed by Children's Hour, including Mr Seth Smith, *The Zoo Man*. The BBC Men's Chorus accompanied by Ernest Lush playing the piano followed the news, there was a talk about The Royal Academy, then came *The Smiler's League*. Sir Walter G. Alcock played Salisbury Cathedral's organ before, at 7.30pm, came *Scenes from Pickwick*. *Monday Night at 8 o'clock*, a flagship programme, began with a memorable vocal signature tune:

'It's Monday night at 8 o'clock, oh can't you hear the chimes?

They're telling you to take an easy chair.

Settle by the fireside, pick up *The Radio Times*,

For *Monday Night at 8* is on the air.'

The same slot next night was filled by the greatly popular *ITMA* – 'It's that man again, Tommy Handley is here.' Mrs Mop would call upon him pleading, 'Can I do y'now sir?', and 'Funf' would speak with a German accent. All good, clean fun. Every Saturday, in the mid-evening slot, came the very popular *Garrison Theatre* starring Jack Warner. After the 9 o'clock news on the 1st came *New Year Resolutions*, Sandy MacPherson contributing on the organ. Another BBC orchestra played, and from 10.45 to 11.50 Billy Cotton's band entertained. Before the 12 o'clock news came a reading, 'O Soothest Sleep'. Hardly exhilarating New Year's entertainment!

More fascinating were spooky interventions at news time by 'Lord Haw Haw', defector William Joyce, the traitor who broadcast from Germany interrupting the BBC wavelength. He occasionally told us things our leaders did not wish us to know, generally lied profusely and presented ridiculous tales. Occasionally he revealed an amazing truth, and in late 1940 claimed that the clock on the Cambridge Catholic Church of the English Martyrs was 5 minutes slow. The crowd who checked his yarn encountered a chilling truth – he was right! Soon after, the area was bombed.

Popular wireless programmes included the 7.30am fitness call, *Up in the morning early*, with musical aerobic instructions. The Radio Doctor gave morning chats, his 'How are your bowels?' routine converting him into a figure of fun. Although many wireless sets were powered by mains electricity or batteries, the plentiful remaining accumulator type needed an acid top-up from a local garage. Lots of sets depended for signals upon outside aerials strung between tall poles or houses, and were vulnerable to lightning strike, for which china circuit-breakers were often attached to window sills.

Office, factory, school, all were run along very strict, formal lines. Sitting still and quiet was expected of many, old and young. A jacket, together with a neck-tie often nestling in a stud-attached collar shirt, was almost obligatory for men. Average pay was around £2-£4 a week, salaried staff always basking in an air of superiority. Noisy, repetitive and often dangerous factory life involved bossy overseers whom it was always unwise to disobey. Conditions improved when women were drafted in to carry out 'war work' as men of steadily increased age were called up for military service. By mid-1940 there were many once familiar faces now missing. Few women yet wore slacks, but some had overalls or dungarees, and headwear was necessary where there was machinery, or for hygienic reasons. Denim belonged to military cookhouses, nylon was not yet proving its existence, and women settled for lisle or 'fully fashioned stockings' and strong suspender belts. There was still some disapproval of women wearing make-up by such as Yardley and Coty in an age of ample, voluminous underclothing and, for some, the wearing of corsets – not the sort of image a Spitfire conjures! Seven-day, non-stop industrial activity was now the norm to support the ever-increasing war effort. Woman's place at home was being eroded, and for all time.

School was generally harsh. Dual desks sat in rows, and sometimes pupils were seated in alphabetical order. Usually there was 'no talking', plenty of blackboard-watching and copying. Organised drill or PT lessons often began with running the gauntlet, and ended with a short, simple game. One needed to learn number tables up to 12-times, and a host of other tables covering money and measures. Problem-solving and 'fractions' featured in junior school arithmetic lessons. Science often equated with nature study, and there were BBC schools broadcasts. All were taught cursive handwriting, how to lay out a letter, and endured grammar and comprehension lessons. French and Latin were grammar school topics. Woodwork was taught to nearly all boys, and domestic science was the girls' equivalent.

Winter school attire usually included the blue gabardine raincoat. When wet, en masse, hanging in a cloakroom, they produced an unforgettable smell. Contrasting vividly, many an adult cycling in rain wore a bright yellow, heavy oilskin cape and 'sou'wester', and resembled a deep-sea fisherman. Wearing a school cap was at all times obligatory for most boys. Seen without one, even far out of school hours, one risked detention after school – even on dark afternoons and Saturdays. Schools had basement shelters or air raid trench shelters. When a raid warning sounded there was a severely monitored trek to safety. Running was harshly dealt with, all understanding why. At no time, even with raiders overhead, did I see anyone old or young race irresponsibly to a shelter, although in hazardous situations it must have happened. It was always safer to take cover in order and carefully. Should one trip or fall, the consequences in public underground shelters would have been catastrophic. Once in a narrow, dimly lit slit trench school shelter lined and supported with wood, with pupils sitting facing each other, the teacher carried out an essential roll call. Older pupils soon discovered that great concern (and satisfaction, or merriment) could be achieved by not responding! Teachers then tried to count the number present in the dim electric light, or nervously departed to locate the missing child whose presence would later be revealed with the announcement, 'Please, I didn't hear you call my name.'

Gas mask checks also provided problems for teachers, especially inexperienced or less able teachers drafted into schools in ever-increasing numbers as staff were called up. Women soon teaching in boys' schools led to a wide assortment of responses, but rarely was there coarse behaviour.

Much confusion could be introduced by swapping gas masks, ensuring that they would no longer fit, or by hiding a few. Should the Head appear all would be solved within seconds. Miscreants would in many schools receive at least six hefty swipes

Headmaster to Appeal – Caned Schoolboy Allegation

Stockport Magistrates today (30 March 1940) 'unanimously convicted' Henry Robinson, of Heath Street, Stockport, Headmaster of St Thomas's Day School, for assaulting an eleven-year-old schoolboy, Alfred Shurety. It was alleged that Robinson struck Shurety with a cane eleven times after placing him over a stool. Shurety was a truant and Robinson said he tried all he knew to put the boy right without punishment, and only struck him six times. The Magistrate said they would not impose a fine, but that Robinson must pay all costs and dues.

upon the posterior using a very impressive weapon. My headmaster, an eager and dedicated exponent of corporal punishment, ceremoniously selected the most appropriate cane from the assortment in his cupboard, or so I was told. I never did anything wrong

School dinners became a widespread wartime feature when many mothers started working. They ensured that children were basically nourished and kept safe. Irrespective of the quality, dinners were child-condemned. Staple items – which extended the ration allowance – included casseroles and stews. Minced mutton had a taste I shall never forget. Yellow cabbage, sticky mashed potato (from powdered potato later in the war), parsnips, swedes, lots of carrots and turnips, all were regular fare. Milk puddings surprisingly contained not only bread but tropical rice, tapioca and semolina, occasionally brightened with a dash of jam. Baked apples were liberally drenched with lumpy custard. We survived whatever confronted us from the school cook whom Hitler, unwittingly, supplied as a love-hate figure.

Getting children home from school safely in the dark, cold winter brought much concern, although night-bombing usually started after 7.00pm. Nevertheless, German bombers, and not other interference little encountered, were by far the greater threat. Secondary school children living in the country, and travelling by train to attend schools in nearby towns, posed a special problem if a late-afternoon raid prevented them from going home. Some schools held bedding.

After school, non-parent-accompanied visits to sweet shops, and small mixed trade shops, were still a cherished highlight. Its demise in our present world is highly regrettable, for lasting friendships were often formed during that walk home. Sweets were not yet rationed, and many pre-war favourites remaining on sale in 1940 included Milky Way and Mars bars, sherbet fountains, liquorice laces and tasty Cadbury crème-filled 4d bars. Comics were available, also established popular titles, particularly for women. Specialist magazines became hard to find due to the need to import wood pulp, and new titles were few because advertisements were not carried. From early 1940 I used to visit a major newsagent by 7.00am on a Thursday to buy a copy of *Flight*, repeating the experience next day for *The Aeroplane*. Paper quality declined, both titles being scarce. 'Write your name on this list,' I was told. 'Maybe there will be a spare copy for you.' Magazines could not be viewed prior to purchase, so there was very little chance of enjoying *Men Only*. My mother told me it was only about men, a notion impressively dispelled by a lucky acquisition at school!

There was little publicly admitted interest in what we now call 'sex'. During 1940 you had it whether you wanted it or not – it just meant gender! Just before the war started I came upon what I thought to be a strange-coloured deflated toy balloon on the ground. When I went to investigate my friend, aged thirteen, spectacularly shouted, 'Don't touch it, it's got a baby inside!' I asked where it came from, but received no guidance on that. My friend Ken, who muttered something about seeing one at home, probably had little more than a very hazy idea himself. In summer 1940, after a biology lesson about 'the rabbit', my teacher braved up to the then dreaded subject, displaying great embarrassment. To our amusement she suddenly fled before completing the story and was never seen again! No sex lessons for five-year-olds in 1940, thank goodness.

Shopping in 1940 was an experience that would seem quaint in today's 'view before you buy' days. Retailers stood behind large counters defending their wares, and brought along requested items. Payment was sometimes placed in a small container that was then catapulted along a cable across the shop to a cashier, who returned receipt and change. Limited refrigeration meant that chunks of cheese, butter and meat rested on wooden boards or massive marble slabs available for unhygienic breathing upon. Required amounts were skilfully, impressively cut or patted with great flare by the shop assistant who, like the buyer, often stood on a floor clad with sawdust. In 1940 there was ever the response, 'No, can't get any. There is a war on, you know.'

Visit Laurie's Great Winter Sale!

Ladies Leatherette Raincoats, lined fleece, well cut	7/6d each
Real Marmot Fur Coat, full length. Handsome skins, value £35	£19.19
Ladies warm interlock vests with or without sleeves	1/-, 1/3d
Fleeced knickers in cream and colours	1/3d, 1/6d
Fleece lined petticoats in white and colours	2/6d, 2/11d
Women's size Winceyette nightdresses	2/6d, 3/-

(2s 6d was called 'half-a-crown')

There were still the street traders operating from horse-drawn trucks. They shouted their wares loudly enough to be heard streets away. Common, too, was the baker who delivered with the aid of a traditional tradesman's bike. Its huge basket was loaded with warm, fresh, fine-smelling bread devoid of the huge salt content ruining the 21st-century versions. Ceremoniously, and with pride, he would, by removing a cloth, unveil the result of his baking effort. Butchers also called, scissor-grinders and tramps too, the latter begging for tea to fill an aged blue and white enamelled metal tin. There was much real poverty and hardship in the land – not to mention class division.

Fortunately, nobody muttered 'health and safety'. Had anyone done so the poor soul would, at the very least, have been laughed into oblivion. The many long-term survivors from those tough times suggest that sufficient care was taken without crazy 'guidance'! Tinned food, popular and safer, was very useful in wartime, for it could easily be dispersed for long-term storage. Few homes having refrigerators, vulnerable food needed, in 1940's hot oppressive summer, to be placed in the pantry on the cold stone slab, then covered with muslin to keep flies away. In view of the risks involved in catching it at sea, it still seems surprising that fish was available quite cheaply. A bloater or kipper tea was quite usual in the later months of 1940. There was also a cottage industry called 'fruit bottling' in glass Kilner jars produced in millions. Care was needed to ensure that the rubber sealing of each jar was effective, otherwise the contents – often home-grown – would, in the term of the time, 'work'.

Butter could be made by scooping the cream top layer from milk then shaking it in a sealed container for a considerable time. The result was a miniscule amount, pale and insipid, but useful. Baked beans, spaghetti and macaroni were popular, supplemented with home-made buns. Rations could be extended by eating out, although there was a restriction on the cost of a meal. Ration allowances frequently changed, and were supplemented by a 'points' system that allowed extra items to ease storage problems due to bombing, particularly at Liverpool docks. Autumn 1940 also brought an additional sugar allowance to encourage jam-making using fruit from one's own trees or nearby farms.

At home heavy wooden furniture dominated the many small, separate rooms, each with an open coal fireplace over which hung the mantelpiece well stocked with brasses to clean. On the wall above hung, almost invariably, the big mirror. Many bedrooms had open fire facilities, fires only being lit when someone was ill, because the heavy coal in a hefty scuttle had to be taken upstairs. Houses built in the 1930s, which usually had tiled roofs in place of the hitherto usual slates, often featured pale-coloured distempered walls and whitewashed ceilings. From the latter in modern houses there often hung on chains a large glass bowl acting as an electric light shade. Glass shades normally protected the very frail gas mantles, which crumbled if handled or if a draught assailed them. Older houses usually had walls covered with patterned, often depressing wallpaper. Wooden, standard floorboards were stained or hidden under distinctively smelling linoleum, dangerously slippery if over-polished.

Should the kitchen or scullery have a stone-tiled floor, it would be frequently washed – like the doorstep – and sometimes buffed. Heavy chintz often covered any sizeable table, partially to protect it, partly to hide the hefty legs in case they still directed disturbing thoughts towards female anatomy. Victoria's and Edward's times had yet to be blown away, and when that took place it snatched not only home and the most intimate privacy from millions of lives, but the nation's soul.

Wide-scale use of paper (white, brown), card, strawboard and plywood all called for strong glue, available in a wide range. Glue was an essential item for those who enjoyed fretwork. A fine saw, possibly a custom workbench, a lot of plywood and plentiful plans, often obtained from advertisements in *Hobbies Weekly* and newspapers, were used by many young men to produce assorted household items, useful and otherwise. Bakelite, a form of plastic heading towards becoming common, once fractured, was very difficult to mend – usual adhesives were of no use. Celluloid could be mended using acetate, which one obtained from a chemist's shop. There were few plastic items as yet, but that commodity was creeping in. Components in aircraft were made of plastic, as were drinking cups, but it was heavy, bulky and not the multi-type plastic of present times. Tinplate and aluminium were in very widespread use.

Air Raid Shelter 'Casino' – 49 Men Fined

It was disclosed today (29 March 1940) at Thames Police Court that an underground room where 49 men had their names taken by the police on gaming charges had been scheduled and prepared as a public air raid shelter, and that there was an air raid warden stationed outside. Chemin de fer was being played. Three men were each fined £50 for keeping a common gaming house, and the remaining 46 were fined for frequenting.

Crime, 1940 style!

Cinemas, theatres, dance halls, staple entertainment venues and sports arenas closed at the outbreak of war. By November 1939 many had reopened, and Christmas pantomimes brought clean jokes, lots of fun, songs to sing about 'hanging the washing on the Siegfried Line' and the spreading chestnut tree. There was ample chance to be rude about Hitler, and of course suitable adaptations of 'Oh no, he isn't!' all involving controlled and respectful audience intervention. Ballroom dancing, which appealed to so many, brought much contact with Servicemen away from home, and with the usual mixed results. Plentiful cinemas, often huge with balconies and a rising theatre organ, showed roughly 3-hour-long programmes comprising a main and supporting film, newsreel and small items. A 'tanner' (6d) gave you a front seat, a 'bob'(1 shilling) a centre seat and 1s 6d one of the back seats in what one might term 'the canoodling zone'. Upstairs in the circle it often cost half-a-crown (2s 6d) or 3s 6d.. There were no 'celebrities', just great and glamorous film stars and their songs to enjoy.

Popular music emerging from film scores and suitable for ballroom dancing was the 'pop' music of the time. Vocal accompaniments were quite well performed by local and national dance bands. Some homes had walnut-cased huge radiograms (radio and gramophone combined), or a turntable gramophone, driven by electricity or clockwork, to play '78s'. 'This *is* Henry Hall speaking' preluded his broadcasts. Although invisible, he always wore evening dress when conducting his dance orchestra, which was accompanied by George Elrick. It was probably the favourite 1940 band. With my friend Ken Horn (who actually joined the Hollywood film-producing fraternity), I went in January 1940 to hear Harry Roy and his band on a Friday evening at the unheated Cambridge Festival Theatre. There were only four others in the audience. Wearing overcoats, scarves and gloves in the unheated auditorium, we sat in the bitterly cold stalls and were given the full show! Empty venues were common, not so much because of the possible aerial onslaught any day but because of the cold and misery of trudging in the blackout. The possibility of an air raid had to be accepted, and when attacks started most people seemed to accept very calmly what might occur. That did not stop parties and gatherings even when horrendous tales circulated concerning events that had happened. One later concerned a Warrington wedding. Bombs from a Heinkel He 111 attacking the swing bridge undershot, bringing terrible casualties. Another described horrific scenes when a telephone exchange in Plymouth was set on fire.

Top: Lords of the Air to encourage our air force -*still* the best!

Left: Deep Purple, two bob a sheet, by Peter de Rose with Mitchell Parish's words useful when we felt sentimental.

Right: Of course *There'll Always Be An England!* Mind you, we never thought any British government would cancel so much of the freedom all fought for, and many horrendously perished for.

What's on at 'the flicks'?

Which films and stars could one see at the pictures in 1940?

Alice Faye: *Tail Spin*

Arthur Askey: *Band Wagon*

Barbara Stanwyck: *Mad Miss Manton*

Basil Radford: *Secret Journey*

Bob Baker: *Prairie Justice*

Charles Laughton: *Jamaica Inn*

Cicely Courtneidge: *Soldiers of the King*

Claudette Colbert: *It's a Wonderful World*

Deanna Durbin: *Mad about Music*

Douglas Fairbanks Jnr and Joan Bennett: *Green Hell*

Errol Flynn: *The Sisters*

Fred Astaire and Ginger Rogers: *Follow the Fleet*

Fred MacMurray: *Husbands and Lovers*

Gary Cooper: *Beau Geste*

George Formby: *Keep Your Seat Please*

Gracie Fields: *Love, Life and Laughter*

Greta Garbo: *Ninotchka*

Jack Hulbert: *Paradise for Two*

James Dunn: *Pride of the Navy*

James Stewart: *Mr Smith Goes to Washington*

Judy Garland: *The Wizard of Oz*

Lana Turner: *Every Other Inch a Lady*

Laurence Olivier and Greer Garson: *Pride and Prejudice*

Leslie Banks: *Sons of the Sea*

Leslie Howard: *Pygmalion* and *The Scarlet Pimpernel*

Loretta Young: *Eternally Yours*

Lucille Ball: *Next Time I Marry*

Lupino Lane: *The Lambeth Walk*

Michael Redgrave: *The Stars Look Down*

Margaret Lockwood: *A Girl Must Live*

Merle Oberon: *The Lion Has Wings*

Mickey Rooney: *The Hardys Ride High*

Randolph Scott: *Coastguard*

Robert Taylor: *Lucky Night*

Shirley Temple: *The Little Princess*

Victor McLaglen: *Full Confession*

Vivien Leigh, Rex Harrison: *Storm in a Teacup*

A 1940 event that certainly deserves a mention is bathtime. Other than big houses, and those built from the mid-1930s, few had bathrooms. Coalmen, factory and farm workers, and those whose jobs made frequent bathing essential, could bath in a public bathhouse. Many braved up to it at home. That meant using a huge, sometimes shallow, often copper bath brought to a back room and filled with kettle-loads of hot water. Temperature adjustment involved cold water, although a shallow bath with ample surface area brought all too rapid cooling. Into the water went bath crystals for this primarily cleansing and non-cosmetic event, for which Lifebuoy or Sunlight soap were also used. Exposure from a modesty point of view mattered not for the very young, but by one's teens the process caused unease. Once I intruded accidentally upon a young neighbour who instinctively rose from her bath covered only in confusion. 'Walls have ears', the Government claimed. What tales they could have told!

For so many life was very hard, great numbers of inner-city dwellers living in appalling habitations, simply slums. In great swathes of London's East End, wonderful people lived in terrible conditions, and in poverty beyond belief. In late 1938 my father very deliberately took me to Bethnal Green to meet a family comprising a mother and eight children living in a miniscule, dreadful dwelling. He told me to ask them what they would be having for Christmas. They responded in unison, 'A cake.' Just a cake. Life then and into the 1940s was unbelievably hard for millions. In 1942 we returned to Bethnal Green and found a vacant space where that home once stood. Yes, it distressed me much as I pondered upon the fate of its occupants.

What shall we sing – and who's going to play the piano?

The choice was wide, some songs achieving lengthy popularity, such as:

'Somewhere over the Rainbow'

'A Nightingale Sang in Berkeley Square' (Manny Sherwin, words Oscar Hammerstein II)

'When You Look Upon a Star' (Leigh Harline, words Ned Washington)

'Whispering Grass'

'The Nearness of You' (Hoagy Carmichael, words Ned Washington)

'Blueberry Hill'

'In The Mood' (a 1939 favourite, too)

'I'll be Seeing You' (dating from 1938)

'It's a Lovely Day Tomorrow' (a 1940 composition)

'The Last Time I Saw Paris' (Jerome Kern)

Remember the leaders of the dance bands?

Billy Cotton

Carroll Gibbons

Denny Dennis

Duke Ellington

Eddie Carrol

Felix Mendelsohn (and his Hawaiian Serenaders)

Geraldo

Henry Hall

Jack Payne

Joe Loss

Lew Stone

Lou Praeger

Oscar Rabin

and the Grosvenor House dance band

'If *only* I could play like...'

Arthur Sandford (light piano music)

Charlie Kunz (very individualistic jazzy style of 'pop' piano music)

Clifford Curzon (classical piano)

Myra Hess (classical piano – her 'Jesu Joy of Man's Desiring' was widely popular)

Reginald Dixon (Blackpool's pre-war Mighty Wurlitzer man)

Sandy MacPherson (another Wurlitzer performer)

Sidney Torch (organ, like Sandy)

'...or entertain like...'

Arthur Askey and 'Stinker' Murdoch (from *Bandwagon*)

Binnie Hale, singer

Dick Bentley, comedian

Flanagan and Allen, forever 'underneath the arches'

Gert and Daisy, comedienne sisters of Jack Warner

Harry Lauder, from Glasgow, aided by a bent stick

Jack Warner, forever talking of 'my li'l gal'

Kitty McShane, whose 'Red Sails in the Sunset' announced her

Nellie Wallace, singer

Patricia Burke, a very attractive young actress and singer

Robb Wilton, master of the monologue: 'The day war broke out my missus said to me, have you put the milk bottles out...?'

Three items all with 'C'-word names held enormous importance – coal, coke and companionship. Without them in profusion the battle could never have been won. In the 1930s and '40s coal, and its derivative coke, provided most of our power, light and heat. Gas and electricity culled from coal were as essential to national survival as to the production of Hurricanes and Spitfires.

The coal that kept us warm in those long cold winters arrived by horse and cart in hundredweight (112lb/50kg) sacks, ironically the same weight as the majority of the high-explosive bombs the Germans delivered to us in 1940. Twenty hessian sacks weighed 1 ton, each hefty bag being carried on the coalman's bent back to the coal shed. In terraced houses, that often meant taking each heavy bag through the house. Coal was not rationed until long after the war.

Within industry and throughout the kingdom, where the steam-driven rail network linked remote and tiny villages with centres of life and industry, coal was King. Now so reviled, coal-fuelled power stations provided the energy without which the war would have been lost. In 1940 the enemy, realising its importance, bombed collieries, and repeatedly attacked the ships carrying coal along our East Coast, the dirty little colliers carrying vital supplies to London and the southern factories. In the 21st century, neglecting the world's vast coal reserves, and failing to devise modern techniques to extract their magic power, could yet come to be seen as a supreme act of stupidity.

Many 1940 ships bringing oil, food and commodities to the UK were also coal-dependent steamships. Tankers bringing vital oil supplies from the Middle East were obviously in great danger, manning them calling for constant courage. No oil – no fighter defence. Little realised, a need for oil was a major reason for Nazi territorial expansion.

Overriding all in 1940 was the national intention to win the war. As bad events repeatedly overtook Britain, they brought the nation together in a manner never seen at any other time. One simply had to work with others, like them or not. Usually one found far more in common than expected. Take cover in a hitherto unknown shelter during a raid and companionship was instant. Talk to that ancient old dear said to be an amazing 60 years old, and always complaining about children, and one usually discovered she wasn't such 'a bad old stick', that she had lost her dearest in 'the other lot' when he was shot down in his Sopwith Camel. 'I'll keep the door open,' she said, 'so you can pop in and cheer me up! If it's closed you can always find the key on a string – get it out through the letter box.' You talked to folk you had never met before, and when things went very wrong friendship turned to loving those you'd never liked who, with their bare hands while bombs were still falling and buildings burning, would do all they could to save any life, and extract you from catastrophe. Such comradeship pervaded the land.

Humour played a large part in achieving ultimate victory. Hitler you hated, and to the tune of 'Run, Rabbit, Run' (changed to 'Run, Adolf, Run') – making sure to include 'fat guts Goering and Goebbels too' – you sang of them with derision. With unbounded glee the entire nation loved those great lines of Robb Wilton ('The day war broke out...'), Arthur Askey ('Hallo, playmates!'), Tommy Handley ('Of course you can do me now'), and Jack Warner, with his blue pencil, rake, li'l gal, and many non-professional funny folk.. The King, the Queen and their daughters, were most revered. Although you'd probably only seen pictures of them, one felt they deeply cared. As for the Prime Minister, Mr Chamberlain with his umbrella and his Munich debacle, Flanagan and Allen demolished him with their 'Any umbrellas to fix today?' It was not good to have a weak figure, a man of ridicule, at the helm. Perhaps we were a trifle unkind, for he had won us precious time, allowing the Spitfires and Wellingtons into squadrons and the ARP to get well under way. The Royal Navy, upon which survival so much depended, had a very experienced champion always ready to express sound opinions, Mr Winston Churchill, who took command at the bleakest time, mid-May 1940. Within a few days he became the greatest political leader Britain is ever likely to know. With him in the lead we knew we'd win – possibly.

That was some of the background to 1940. Now for the action.

... Herr von Ribbentrop, you must not underrate England. She is a curious country and few foreigners can understand her mind. Do not judge by the attitude of the present administration. Once a great cause is presented to the people all kinds of unexpected actions might be taken by this very government, and by the British nation. Do not underrate England. She is very clever. If you plunge us all into another great war she will bring the whole world against you, like last time.

Winston Churchill, post-war recorded recollections

Neville Chamberlain displays Hitler's autograph at Heston in 1938.

What the papers say: 9 January 1940

Premier says, 'I will not be deflected.' Mr Neville Chamberlain, at the London Mansion House, this afternoon said that to bring the war to a successful conclusion he subordinated everything else – all thought of rest or relaxation, all partial affections and all personal feeling and consideration whatsoever. From that purpose so long as I hold my present office and until the war comes to an end I will not be deflected – nor will I shrink my inevitable responsibility .This new year, which will probably be a fateful one in the history of the world, has opened quietly, but it is the quiet of the calm before the storm.'

Evacuation : Home Secretary's warning

'I must confess that when I contemplate the probable future course of the war I should feel far more reassured if far larger numbers of people had taken advantage of the faculties which the Government offered them in September to remove their children from our crowded cities into the greater safety of the reception areas. It is a cause of great anxiety to me. A large number of the children have already been brought back to the towns.' In a recent speech Goering said, 'The German Air Force will strike at Britain with such an onslaught as has never before been known in the history of the world.'

Triumph of the convoy system: January 1940

Out of a total of 5,911 British, Allied and neutral ships convoyed up to the present, only twelve – or 6.2% – were lost by enemy action. Sinkings due to enemy action for the week 31 December to 6 January numbered: British, two (5,758 tons); Allied, nil; neutral, three (5,385 tons).

Liner's battle with submarine

The British liner *Highland Patriot* (14,172 tons) forced a German submarine to retire after a fight lasting two hours, it is reported from Rio de Janeiro. Three torpedoes are stated to have been fired by the U-boat, but they all missed. The submarine surfaced and fired shell after shell. The battle lasted two hours. The liner replied to the fires.

What the papers say: January 1940

The *Dunbar Castle* (10,000 tons), a Union Castle liner, was in an outward-bound convoy to the Cape when she was sunk by a Nazi mine off the South East coast. This was made known today. Captain H. A. Causton – 'The finest man who ever walked the deck of a ship,' as his Chief Officer described him – terribly wounded when the bridge was blown up, staggered to his cabin to secure the ship's confidential papers and died at the door. Although the ship foundered within half an hour, splitting in two as the last boat got away, only a few lives were lost. Among the forty-eight passengers was a ten-week-old baby.'

New work for women pilots

Women pilots well known in civil aviation today began their new 'ferry service' by flying planes direct from an aerodrome adjoining a factory to a Royal Air Force station. So far eight women have been selected. They form a section of the Air Transport Auxiliary. The service is being organised by British Airways.

Chapter 2

War? What war?

New Year's Day 1940 fell on a very cold, dreary Monday, washday through the kingdom. The snow, which so magically transformed Christmas morn, was still camouflaging the country. The insides of millions of bedroom windows in the multitude of unheated houses had, overnight, been decorated by Jack Frost's artistry. It was, so memorably, a cold start to a very uncertain year. While the nation's women wrestled with the heavy washing in the sink or the copper, or were facing up to a giant mangle before preparing a traditional nationwide cold midday dinner using Sunday's left-overs, others were having a more worrying time. Nine No 107 Squadron Blenheims carrying twenty-seven airmen, feeling much colder than us, set off from Wattisham at 11.05. In 'vics' of three, flying parallel tracks 16 miles apart, they searched without success for enemy shipping in reverse activity to the German Luftwaffe.

There was frequent ground activity. On 8 January French artillery pounded German villages where soldiers were billeted between 10 and 14 miles behind the entire Western Front. East of the Moselle, French infantry carried out several raids, and enemy patrols were repulsed east of the Saar.

Although the dreaded aerial assault had not developed, another expectation was fulfilled when, on 8 January, rationing (called 'fair sharing') of butter, bacon and sugar was introduced. From 11 March it also applied to meat. These blows were slightly softened when neutral sources revealed that wide-scale rationing was already in force in Germany, where even clothing was rationed.

It was an ignorant, isolated American commentator who coined the phrase 'Phoney War'. For him and his country folk, it would remain like that for years as they stayed safe in their distant ringside seats. In reality there was nothing 'phoney'. Many men had by now died, or been terribly injured in action. German bomber crews, without the courtesy of the slightest 'May I?', had been cheekily photographing us from on high with future evil intent. Without the bomber onslaught, or heavy land fighting, it was so wrongly concluded that nothing much had happened.

On New Year's Day the War Office announced that the first British soldier killed in action in this war was Corporal Thomas William Priday of Redmarley, near Ledbury, who was killed on 9 December 1939 when leading a patrol in France.

Awful situations had also overtaken those sailing off South America, Africa, in the Western Approaches and certainly the North Sea. U-boats, prowling surface warships and bombers – theirs and ours – had been busy. So, before relating the happenings of 1940, it is surely pertinent to recall events and policies that caused them, some from their 1939 introduction.

On the very first night of the war the 13,581grt Donaldson Line passenger ship *Athenia* was torpedoed at position 56°44N/14°05W (south of Rockall) by U-30, and without warning. Of those aboard 112 died and 1,300 survived. The sinking sent a shock wave throughout the land, proving that we really were at war, and distressed many who had a mere two decades ago been fighting in France or at sea.

The Prime Minister's broadcast informed us that we were already
at war and he had just ceased speaking when a strange,
prolonged wailing noise, afterwards to become familiar, broke
from the air. My wife came into the room braced by the crisis
and commented favourably upon the German promptitude and
precision, and that the quarter of an hour's notice which we had
been led to expect we should receive was now running out. We
made our way to the shelter assigned to us, armed with a bottle
of brandy and other appropriate medicinal comforts.

Winston Churchill, post-war recorded recollections

Giving ships greater protection, shipping convoys were initiated on 5 September.
Those off the East Coast, linking the Forth with the Thames, started the following
day, and on the 7th the first North America convoy left from the Channel and
Liverpool. By the 8th ten lone British merchant ships had been torpedoed and sunk,
among them the 7,242grt *Manaar* off South America and the 10,177grt oil tanker
Regent Tiger far out in the Atlantic. On the 10th the 2,796-ton *Goodwood* steamer,
mined a mile off Flamborough Head, was the first British ship sunk in the North Sea.

A hefty blow to national pride was the loss of the 22,500-ton HMS
Courageous, the aged aircraft carrier, torpedoed by U-29 on 17 September west of
Ireland. She sank within 15 minutes, and 519 of her crew died. On 30 September the
Admiral Graf Spee scored her first success when she sank, with gunfire, the 5,051grt
steamer *Clement* off Pernambuco. The crew of the 16,697-ton armed merchant
cruiser *Rawalpindi*, a converted P&O liner, had no choice but to fight to a finish
when on 23 November the German *Scharnhorst* and *Gneisenau* bombarded and sunk
their ship south-east of Iceland. Only thirty-seven of her crew were rescued.

Hardly surprising, then, that enormous delight greeted the news that off South
America the pocket battleship *Admiral Graf Spee*, which had sunk eight British
merchant ships, had been engaged and seriously damaged on 13 December by HMS
Exeter, *Ajax* and *Achilles*. She took refuge at Montevideo, Uruguay, in the neutral
River Plate, and the world and the British warships awaited the next move. It came
on 17 December when, rather than fighting to a finish, Captain Langsdorf scuttled
his impressive, beautiful and modern-looking ship bringing rejoicing throughout
Britain. A wreck buoy in the Plate now marks her war grave, while at a shore
memorial one can touch her massive anchor.

Once Poland was vanquished, Hermann Goering eagerly pressed a plan for his
beloved Luftwaffe to sink the British Home Fleet based in Scapa Flow, Orkney.
Hitler stayed his hand, nursing a belief that negotiated peace was possible. When
that notion faded, the German High Command decided that, as soon as conditions in
1940 were suitable, they would secure their supply of Swedish iron ore, obtained via
Narvik, by overrunning Norway. Although a seemingly excellent site from which to
attack the UK's assets, it was to later prove an encumbrance maintaining forces
there. Invasion of France – via Belgium, the Netherlands and Luxembourg – would

JUNKERS Ju. 88 (JUMO)

Purpose: **Long-Range**   Dimensions: **Span 59 ft. 0 in.**   Performance: **Maximum Speed 310 m.p.h.**
BOMBER.   **Length 46 ft. 6 ins.**   Cruising Speed **260 m.p.h.**

Essential aircraft recognition material, like this official 1939 item for AA gunners, was poor. Little thought was given to it in 1939, and little had been discovered about Germany's best bomber, the Junkers Ju 88.

follow. Winter months would be used to train for these ventures. In the meantime it made sense to grant Goering his wish to set about sinking Britain's Home Fleet.

By afternoon teatime on 14 October 1939 Lt Prien had penetrated Scapa Flow's defences in U-47 to torpedo the battleship HMS *Royal Oak*, causing heavy loss of life. It also caused the Admiralty to conclude that the Royal Navy did not have complete control of the North Sea, which launched the spectre of German troops landing on the East Coast. Army plans were immediately prepared to tackle the possibility. For self-protection the Home Fleet immediately moved to Forth waters off Rosyth where, two days later, it was attacked by German bombers. The destroyer HMS *Mohawk* was damaged by bomb splinters, and two cruisers, one of which was slightly damaged by a bomb that hit the ship then bounced off without exploding. On 19 October two German bombers tackled ships still at Scapa, damaging HMS *Iron Duke*, which, since 1930, had served as an accommodation vessel. One Ju 88 hit by anti-aircraft fire crashed on Hoy. The nearest fighter squadrons to Scapa were at Drem and Turnhouse, so the Fleet now transferred to the Clyde, which was unsuitable for operations in the vital and most active North Sea zone.

The debt that every civilised person owes to Air Chief Marshal Sir Hugh Dowding, C-in-C Fighter Command, can never be fully paid. His wisdom, his skill as one of the greatest military commanders of all time, were to save us – and the United States – from Nazi domination. Aloof, austere, quiet, never ready to suffer

Truly great and universally feted he should
always be, for no military commander has
shown more foresight and skill than Lord
Dowding. Here was a real celebrity who
saved us from Nazi domination. *IWM*

fools gladly and with great confidence
in his exceptionally well-thought-out
ideas, he was blessed with qualities that
did not assure him popularity among
unequals. General Pile, commander of
Army anti-aircraft forces in 1940,
worked closely with him. In his
opinion Dowding 'knew more than
anyone else about all aspects of aerial
warfare, and it would be hard to
exaggerate his influence, and that he
always wanted more – faster'. His
contribution to ultimate victory cannot
be overstated.

Dowding's principal pre-war aim was to work up his thirty-five squadrons
(twenty-two equipped with Hurricanes or Spitfires) to prevent bombing raids on the
home base, the protection of which was of overwhelming importance. Four, later
six, of his precious Hurricane squadrons were taken from his force at the outbreak of
war. They became part of the Air Component within Field Force France, and
pressure was soon put upon him to provide six more so-called 'mobile' squadrons.
That, he very wisely, most strongly and successfully resisted, fearing that even more
squadrons might, in emergency, be sucked from his home defence force. He reckoned
that fifty-two squadrons were needed to defend the UK; minus those sent to France in
September 1939, he was then left with only thirty-three.

No one ever asked him to plan for the protection of the Home Fleet at its war
station, Scapa Flow. After the first attack, barrage balloons were quickly sent there
from London, and two naval squadrons hurried to the civilian aerodrome at Hatston.

Construction of a fighter station began at Castletown, radar stations and a fighter
control system soon being initiated. Hurricane squadrons temporarily used Coastal
Command's base at Wick.

The Scapa raids were far from the first enemy sorties flown against the UK. On
6 September 1939 German aircraft opened a campaign against merchant ships –
sailing alone, or in convoy – along the East Coast from the Thames Estuary to
Shetland, activity that extended into April 1940. It was opened, and mainly carried
out, by Heinkel He 111Hs of I/KG 26, the 'Lion Geschwader', operating out of
Lübeck/Blankensee and nominally armed with thirty-six aircraft. They were
supported by examples of Germany's new and best bomber, the Ju 88. Although

based at Griefswald, Ju 88A-1s of I/KG 30 worked out of Sylt/Westerland. Backing them was an array of Bv 138s, Do 18s and He 115s, maritime aircraft operating out of Sylt/Hornum and Borkum. Coasters, colliers, fishing boats and light vessels were their usual prey. Attacking lightships was presented as a typical, evil Nazi deed, although some might consider them fair game. Light guns defended some ships, but against the Luftwaffe they stood little chance. Only the difficulty of sinking small, moving targets, and poor bomb-aiming, saved many. Ineffectiveness of bombing attacks on ships at sea seemed proven, for it was some time before a merchant ship in a convoy was bombed and sunk, and no escorting warship was even damaged. Losses were of fishing boats and very small, undefended, unescorted coasters.

The Ju 88s were recorded as first operating on 21 September, against ships sailing across Great Fisher Bank. On the 26th they attacked warships in the Firth of Forth, including HMS *Hood*. The first German aircraft to come down on land was an He 111H, which, on 28 September, crashed intact on the Lammermuir Hills south of Edinburgh. Next day saw the tenuous first attack on a coastal ship – their offensive was well under way. Nine Ju 88s of I/KG 30 attacked HMS *Southampton* and HMS *Edinburgh* in Scapa Flow on 16 and 17 October, a Ju88 was responsible for dropping bombs on Hoy, the first to explode on British territory in this war.

German coastal reconnaissance aircraft also attacked shipping, as on 7 October when destroyers at sea, HMS *Niger* and HMS *Mohawk*, were engaged by a Dornier Do 18 seaplane. On 21 October four He 115 floatplanes attacked a convoy and all were claimed to have been shot down.

Heinkel He 111s of KG 26, *The Lion Geschwader* were prominent over the North Sea 1939-1940. The He 111 could carry 2,200 lb of bombs for 1,500 miles. Top speed was 240 mph at 14,000 ft, service ceiling 26,000 ft.

DORNIER Do. 18 (JUMO 205.C)

The Luftwaffe's Dornier Do 18 small seaplane, a nuisance to British shipping.

To the fore in early fights off Scotland were RAF Auxiliaries. Here are Drem based Spitfires of No 609 (West Riding) Squadron.

The Vickers-Armstrong Wellington 1a, Britain's He 111 equivalent. With a top speed of 247 mph at 17,000 ft, it carried a 4,500 lb bomb load for 1,200 miles. Service ceiling was 18,000 ft.

Fighter protection for shipping off the East Coast was difficult to provide using short-range day-fighters. In autumn 1939 Dowding outlined his need as forty-six squadrons for home defence, four for protection of East Coast convoys, two to defend Scapa and one squadron to be kept in Northern Ireland. The Air Staff approved the formation of two long-duration Blenheim escort/fighter squadrons. Responding, Dowding suggested that it would be better to form four half-squadrons for shipping protection, and asked for an extra squadron also to be split in two. After reviewing available aircraft the Air Staff agreed to the formation of eight half-squadrons, 'cadres', which could rise to full strength when feasible. Fighter Command was further enhanced in October, by an additional ten squadrons. So by December 1939 the strength had been increased with a total of eighteen new squadrons. The number of aircraft on strength also steadily increased. Expansion had been achieved by equipping some squadrons with Fairey Battles or Blenheims, both types being converted bombers. The Battles had only one thing to commend them, their Merlin engines, which gave pilots practice for the time when sufficient Hurricanes, Spitfires or Defiants became available for conversion. By May 1940 nine of these new squadrons were flying fast fighters, and four complete Blenheim squadrons had been transferred to Coastal Command to become Trade Protection Squadrons. Two mobile squadrons were eventually sent to France. It was persistent enemy anti-shipping air activity along the eastern side of the UK that demanded attention in late 1939 and well into 1940.

After dark on 20 November 1939 He115s of Kustenfliegerstaffel 3./906 were the first to sow magnetic mines attached to parachutes from a height of 3,000ft over Harwich and at two points in the Thames Estuary. More fell on the 22nd and on the 23rd one was defused by Commander J. G. D. Ouvry on the Shoeburyness mudflats. Proof of the effectiveness of the new menace had already come, for on the 21st the destroyer HMS *Gipsy*, leaving Harwich in a destroyer flotilla, had her back broken by a mine and fifty of her crew were killed. By 7 December at least sixty-eight magnetic mines had been laid in shallow waters.

HEINKEL He. 115 (B.M.W. 132. N)

An official aircraft recognition card featuring the Heinkel He 115 floatplane minelayer. Norwegian operated examples.

Unmolested high-flying Do 17Ps of Aufklärungsgruppe 122 (Aufkl.Gr.122) were roaming high and unmolested over southern and eastern Britain, one being detected over Suffolk on 21 November. The Luftwaffe's most success so far came on 17 December when He 111s seriously damaged six small merchant vessels off the North East Coast and Scotland. Combating maritime raiders was difficult. Short-duration RAF day-fighters could patrol over ships and convoys for only a few minutes. Their pilots were untrained for necessarily uncontrolled operations at sea, and without radar warning could only respond to urgent calls for help. Standing patrols only became possible when the Blenheims were available. Short-range fighter operations were then confined to a 5-mile-wide coastal band.

Bristol Blenheim 1(f) strike fighter of No 604 (County of Warwick) Squadron at Northolt. No 99 Squadron's Wellington 1s behind were on hand for fighter affiliation training late 1939.

Blenheim 1(f) fighters wear early wartime black, white and silver under surfaces at Tangmere early 1940. *John Rawlings collection*

Do 17P-1 like 4U+DL of Aufklärungsgruppe (Reconnaissance Group) 123 carried out photo missions over the UK 1939-1940.

The Luftwaffe's anti-shipping campaign continued in 1940. On New Year's Day Ju 88s were active around the Shetlands. Reinforcement of the maritime attack force had occurred on 17 December when He 111Hs of II/KG 26 (home base Neumunster/ Schleswig-Holstein) joined the strike force.

Reconnaissance flights by Aufkl.Gr.122 on 6 and 7 January preceded considerable activity on the 9th when, between 07.30 and 12.00, He 111s of II/KG 26 prowled off the coast between Lowestoft and Aberdeen. Bombing or strafing ten British and four Danish ships, they sank the SS *Oakgreen* of 1,985 tons south-east of Cromer, and caused the Trinity House vessel SS *Reculver*, three times machine-gunned, to limp into Great Yarmouth. On 11 January Spitfires of No 66 Squadron engaged an He 111 of KG 26. It limped across the North Sea to crash-land at Skaerbaek, South Jutland, Denmark. The pilot, 'Sgt Schmidt', asked a farmer where they had landed and, when he was told, he said, 'We're lost', and told the other three crew members to set fire to the plane. Pistol shots were fired at the petrol tanks. The crew also burned papers and maps. At least fifty bullet holes could be seen in the wreck. Two days later three roaming Heinkels attempted to attack seventeen ships and three destroyers off Aldeburgh.

Unusually configured, Blohm und Voss Bv 138B reconnaissance twin-boom seaplanes operated off our shores in 1939-1940.

The authentic Gloster Gladiator N2308 which joined Fighter Flight Shetlands formed in November 1939 to protect Scapa Flow. It moved with them to Sumburgh on 4 January 1940. Remaining there until July 1940, it then left for Roborough and 247 Squadron which formed on 1 August, the only operational Gladiator squadron in the Battle of Britain. It wears mid-1940 colours.

A more unusual operation took place on 21 January when, around midnight, Ju 88s tried attacking a group of nine ships. Before concluding their night's effort, they tried without success to sink in all twenty-five ships. Although a bad weather period was setting in, on the 30th seventeen He 111s of II/KG 26 roamed around the Shetlands and in all attempted to sink thirty vessels, including two lightships. Eventually, SS *Royal Crown* (4,300 tons) heading for the USA and was sunk off Southwold. A 4,000-ton ship was attacked off Lowestoft, and a Norwegian oil tanker set on fire, neutrality being insufficient to save ships. On 3 February Ju 88s sank the minesweeper *Sphinx* in the Moray Firth, and the same day several of the twenty-four roaming Heinkels of II/KG 26 carried out their first dedicated assault on a convoy, one comprising sixteen ships, of which five were neutrals. One ship was sunk, and five damaged. At this time KG 26 held forty-eight aircraft; I/KG 26 still operated out of Lübeck/Blankensee and II/KG 26 used Schwerm. Based near Hamburg, I/KG 30 now had thirty-nine Ju 88As, which operated from Westerland. Advanced reconnaissance flights were still being provided by Aufklärungsgruppe 122, Munster-based.

February's operations were mainly off the North East Coast, and often involved flights of three aircraft dropping either 50kg or 250kg HE bombs. One Heinkel would reconnoitre, leaving the others to make bombing runs from the ship's stern before all carried out strafing. They did not have everything their own way, however. On 8 February Spitfires of No 602 (City of Glasgow) brought down He 111H 1H+EN, W Nr 6353, of 5./KG26, which crashed intact at North Berwick Law. After examination at RAE Farnborough, it was test-flown as AW177 and later joined No 1426 Enemy Aircraft Flight, Duxford.

There was rejoicing throughout the land when news was released that on 16 February the destroyer HMS *Cossack*, following a sighting by a Hudson crew of 224 Squadron, had entered Jossing Fjord, Norway. With the cry 'The Navy's here', they took from the German supply tanker *Altmark* 299 sailors captured after their vessels had been sunk by the *Graf Spee*.

Early on 16 February three Hudsons of 220 Squadron left Thornaby seeking the German fleet auxiliary *Altmark* and at 12:55 'K-King' located her. Intercepted at 14:00 by the Royal Navy, the German ship fled into Josing Fjord, Norway, seen here after trying to ram a pursuer. A search party from HMS *Cossack* went aboard and released 299 merchant seamen.

On 22/23 February another night operation was flown, by which time Blenheim fighters of 29 Squadron were flying night protection sorties over light vessels. Between 1 and 7 March enemy bombers operated spasmodically. Had they possessed sufficient range they could have attacked the 83,000-ton Cunard liner *Queen Elizabeth*, which on 2 March left the UK on her first transatlantic voyage to New York.

In March 1940 the Home Fleet returned to Scapa Flow, for fighter protection in the form of Hurricanes of 111 Squadron was now available. Two intensive attacks took place, on 8 and 16 March, on ships in Scapa Flow, Ju 88s inflicting more damage to HMS *Iron Duke*. The second raid resulted in damage to the cruiser *Norfolk* and *Iron Duke* again. Hatston was also attacked. Over the next three weeks the Luftwaffe made three more raids on Scapa, 111 Squadron successfully intercepting each of them. As a result, German bombers switched to easier targets in the Firth of Forth and persistently tackled ships at sea. During the evening of Friday 29 March two typical attacks were directed at a convoy off Northumberland. Bombing caused no damage but a German aircraft crossed the coast shortly before it crashed in the sea, the British claiming it to be their forty-ninth victim. By late March 1940 more than 400 anti-shipping sorties had been flown by the Luftwaffe for a confirmed loss of at least forty aircraft.

Hurricanes of No 111 Squadron moved north to protect Scapa Flow. This Hurricane Mk XII, ex RAF 5377 was later registered as G-AWLW for filming purposes. *P Sands*

The show must go on!

While the 16 March raid took place and the bombs rained down, Kirkwall Amateur Dramatic Society presented *Tilly of Bloomsbury* to a packed house. Outside, to quote a witness, 'Continuous red flashes from the ships' guns and shore batteries illuminated the sky like a violent sunset. The searchlights competed with the moon around which there was a huge halo.'

On 17 March a second Ju 88A Gruppe, II/KG 30, became operational at Westerland, Sylt, and on 29 March attacked shipping at sea. They were then committed, with others, to further operations directed against Scapa Flow, which Ju 88s attacked on 2 April. The reason for the resumption of attacks became obvious a few days later as large numbers of German ships sailed towards Norway. This operational phase ended with a II/KG 26 raid on Scapa delivered on 8 April.

Enemy activity between September 1939 and April 1940 had brought about the formation of two Fighter Groups, No 14 to protect the North East and Scotland, and

No 10 the South West of England. Both were important because reports suggested that long-range Fw 200 Condors were to be used for bombing raids on shipping. Radar to detect low-flying aircraft was being developed, and very high frequency radio came into use in fighters. By May 1940 Fighter Command held forty-seven squadrons, thirty-eight flying Hurricanes or Spitfires.

Throughout the winter No 264 Squadron had persevered to get the Boulton Paul Defiant turret fighter functioning. Dowding had no confidence in the aircraft, believing its concept flawed, which proved to be the case. In March 1940 a Defiant detachment at Wittering was declared operational and placed some aircraft at Bircham Newton. Technical snags not yet overcome, the Defiants were withdrawn and the squadron congregated at Martlesham Heath.

What had RAF bombers been doing while the Luftwaffe waged the anti-shipping campaign? The 1938-devised Western Plan called for a large force of bombers that, during the afternoon on the outbreak of hostilities, would cross the North Sea, turn into Germany, attack the Ruhr from the east, then head for home. Instead, with neither side wishing to start a heavy bombing campaign, the British operated a similar campaign to that of the Germans, but different in style.

When formations of Hampdens of No 5 Group and Mildenhall's Wellingtons set out on the late afternoon of 3 September 1939 they were heading for German warships at sea. None were found, and crews discovered how difficult homing was in a pitch-black world. Years elapsed before electric landing lights replaced goose-neck flares, which had to be manually lit alongside grass landing strips.

Late that first day Tiger-engined Whitley Mk IIIs of Nos 51 and 58 Squadrons* of No 4 Group, the long-range bomber group, operated from Leconfield because of runway construction at their home station, Linton-on-Ouse. They carried out Special Operations Order No 3, the first night operation of the war, involving release of propaganda leaflets. Each measuring $8^{1/2}$ by $5^{1/2}$ inches, and carried in bundles of 1,500, they were held by rubber bands that snapped after release. Each Whitley carried twelve bundles, which were dropped through the flare chute to flutter down onto Hamburg, Bremen and the Ruhr. This activity continued far into the war, and was until February 1940 the prerogative of the Whitley force. Leaflet raids were harshly compared with the brutal bombing of Poland being carried out by the Luftwaffe, but they provided useful operational night-flying experience, and intelligence material indicating strength and position of enemy searchlights and AA guns. The RAF, from the first night of the war, was displaying an ability to penetrate deeply into German territory.

Come the afternoon of 4 September 1939, Wattisham-based Blenheims of No 2 Group were opening the light day bomber campaign by joining Wellingtons having another go at German warships off Brunsbuttel. In rain and clouds they had no

---

* The Whitleys involved were 51 Sqn: K8938, K8941, K8982; 58 Sqn: K8964-R, K8969-G, K8973-K, K8990-L, K9006-E, K9009-M, K9013-W. No 58 Squadron, which operated Whitley IIIs until April 1940, was soon detached to Boscombe Down to assist Coastal Command's English Channel operations, and did not return to Linton-on-Ouse until 15 February 1940. On 1-2 October three Whitleys of 10 Squadron were the first RAF bombers to reach Berlin, which they bombarded with propaganda leaflets, proving that the city was vulnerable to air attack.

success, their 250lb general-purpose (GP) bombs bouncing off the *von Scheer*. Sinking warships by bombing was never to be easy.

On 26 September a new policy was launched that continued with little change until April 1940. Formations of bombers would carry out daylight shipping sweeps. Just how risky that could be was proven three days later when five out of a formation of eleven Hampdens were shot down by fighters near Heligoland. As a result twenty-four bombers were, instead, held at standby in case Coastal Command spotted warships at sea, and also to permit response to German attacks on our shipping. Finding ships was also far from easy.

By day, from the start of the war and into 1940, East Anglian-based 2 Group Blenheims also carried out daylight photo-reconnaissance (PR) sorties over the sea and western Germany. The importance of photo-reconnaissance had been pressed pre-war by Mr F. S. Cotton who, using a Lockheed 12a, illicitly photographed German warships. These he displayed to the Air Ministry and, as a result, on 22 March 1939 the Air Ministry Directorate of Operations initiated formation of a Photographic Development Unit. Its role would be to use 'low visibility' aircraft to photograph naval activity. The Heston Special Flight emerged and received two highly polished Blenheims. Flight Lieutenant M. Longbottom of the Flight reckoned faster, light and unarmed aircraft would be more suitable, and with Dowding's approval two Spitfires were chosen for camera fits by RAE Farnborough. On 3 October 1939 the Flight became No 2 Camouflage Unit, and at the same time the Photographic Development Unit was formed alongside and within Fighter Command. Two Spitfires, the Blenheims, the Lockheed 12a and a Hudson joined the PDU.

Both Spitfire 1s (Merlin III) carried an F24 camera, one in each wing, and were known as Type 'A'. A third modified Spitfire, Type 'B', had a 29½-gallon fuel tank in the rear fuselage.

To gain operational experience, Spitfire N3071 and both Lockheeds left for Lille/Seclin, France, under Flt Lt R. H. Niven. On 18 November 1939 Flt Lt Longbottom flew the first operational sortie using the Spitfire, unsuccessfully, for although he reached Aachen it was cloud-covered. Clear sky on the 22nd allowed very clear photography. On 21 December the Bitburg area was photographed, but the high flier was, worryingly, producing a position-give-away vapour trail. The reason for such, at this time, was not understood. That didn't daunt Longbottom who, on 29 December, secured photographs of Aachen and Cologne.

High-level flying was producing alarming medical problems including blackouts, so on 11 January 1940 the Flight returned to Heston. Work was now under way on the Type 'C' Spitfire, which carried a fuselage tank and cameras, two underwing F24s balanced by installing a 30-gallon fuel tank in the port wing. An important addition was extra oxygen supply for the pilot.

When on 1 April 1940 the PDU was declared fully operational it was holding four Spitfires, sporting quite bizarre colour schemes, a Blenheim, two Hudsons and a Harvard 1. On 1 May Flt Lt Mesurier, flying Type 'C' P9308, photographed Heligoland from 33,000 feet and from the head of a vapour trail. A new problem was caused by camera icing. That took a while to solve, but during May 1940 the Unit was active operationally.

Just how dangerous daylight operations by large bombers could be was to be forcefully shown in December 1939. On the 3rd, in good weather, twenty-four Wellingtons of Nos 38, 115 and 149 Squadrons set off to attack two cruisers reported near Heligoland. AA guns and fighters engaged them, and the bombers succeeded only in sinking a minesweeper and erroneously bombing an AA gun and ammunition store ashore, fortunately without prompting a response.

So far, so good. On 14 December, another crisp, clear day, Bomber Command tried again to sink reported warships. Hampdens found none, but the twelve Wellingtons of 99 Squadron discovered shipping, although low cloud prevented effective bombing. They encountered much AA gun fire, which brought down five aircraft and caused another to later crash. German fighters had been active, but it was believed that the bomber formation had successfully defended itself. How wrong the notion was.

On 18 December twenty-four Wellingtons drawn from Nos 9, 37 and 149 Squadrons were sent to attack warships in the Schillig Roads and off Wilhelmshaven. Two bombers returned early, the remainder having to facing Messerschmitt 109s and 110s pressing home high-beam attacks against which the bombers had no defence. For more than 80 miles they pestered the bombers, shooting down ten and causing two more to ditch later. No 37 Squadron had lost five of its six operating bombers, and four Bf 109s of JG 1 had been shot down. Non-self-sealing fuel tanks were partly responsible for losses, as well as a lack of beam defence. Operations now took place well away from enemy shores before it was decided that only Blenheims would operate by day. From 861 bomber sorties dispatched in 1939, forty-one aircraft had failed to return and ten German fighters shot down.

On 2 January 1940 two 107 Squadron 'highly polished' Blenheim IVs, with the then new 'duck-egg blue' undersurfaces, flew PR sorties, P4905 over the Sylt-Amrum area and N6190 over Wilhelmshaven, from where the navigator – using a hand-held German-built Leica camera – returned with photographs of the battleship *Tirpitz* being worked upon.

Wellington 1as of No IX (Bomber) Squadron practice flying with belly dustbin turrets extended.

On 10 January nine ship-searching Blenheims of 82 Squadron, flying with a dozen of 110 Squadron, all led by Squadron Leader Kenneth Doran DFC, were bounced from above out of the sun. Quickly the bombers descended to sea level. Flying fast at 240mph IAS, Sergeant Hanne's aircraft soon developed engine trouble, fell behind, and succumbed to the fighters, showing the vulnerability of a straggler. One Messerschmitt Bf 110 was shot down, another force-landed in Denmark. Following 2 Group's fiercest fight so far, two DFCs were awarded, seven DFMs, and Doran received a Bar to his DFC.

Early operations revealed various deficiencies. For better protection, 2 Group Blenheims began operating in boxes of six aircraft instead of twelve, one box flying lower to counter-attack from different directions. Twin guns were needed in the Blenheim's dorsal turret and most certainly self-sealing fuel tanks – or possibly the use of nitrogen to replace used fuel. Fitting a mirror in a blister on the cockpit cover side afforded the pilot a view aft. Plans were now prepared for sixty-six Blenheims to dive bomb, or attack at low level, eleven power stations in Germany should the enemy start bombing land targets in Britain.

Between 4 and 20 January 1940 RAF bombers were busy at night On the 11th/12th Hampdens of 5 Group and Wellingtons of 3 Group undertook their first operational night sorties, brought about by heavy losses in day raids before Christmas. From the Hampdens leaflets were scattered over Kiel, while Wellingtons supplied reading matter to Hamburg's residents. No 77 Squadron's Whitleys on 12th/13th, operating from Villeneuve, France, made long journeys to Prague and Vienna. On seventeen nights Whitleys carried out 'security patrols' over seaplane minelayer bases, dropping bombs to disturb watery activities. During the night of 12 January a Whitley crew accidentally dropped bombs on Westerland town, a propaganda coup for the enemy.

From 20 January to 17 February 1940 intense cold and heavy snowfalls halted RAF night operations, and prevented 2 Group Blenheim operations in daylight between 2 and 17 February. Since early autumn other Blenheims, of the Air Component in France, had undertaken photo-reconnaissance flights over Germany when the weather allowed. Fairey Battles of the Advanced Air Striking Force (AASF) flew shallow PR flights, reconnoitred Wehrmacht positions and, during several February nights, delivered early morning papers to Rhineland inhabitants.

The USSR's assault on Finland ended in February with a cease-fire coming on 13 March. Much sympathy had been aroused in Britain for the Finns, who had undergone a quite ferocious onslaught. The French and British had requested Norway and Sweden to permit them to send land forces through those countries to help Finland. This they declined to agree to, not wishing to be dragged into the fight. Ultimately, No 2 Group crews ferried twenty-four Blenheims to the Finnish Air Force.

No 2 Group operated on seventeen days in March, trebling any previous monthly effort. On the 12th they tackled German forces trying to salvage a sunken British submarine, and on the 27th fifteen Blenheims of Nos 82 and 110 Squadrons attempted to bomb four destroyers protecting a convoy off Borkum. Many ships were by then massing in German ports; on 1 April 82 Squadron lost a Blenheim trying discover the reason.

A very notable success had come to Squadron Leader M. V. Delap, 82 Squadron, on 11 March when, flying Blenheim P4852 off Borkum, he chanced upon U-boat U-31. He released four 250lb bombs from such a low height that as well as sinking the submarine their explosions seriously twisted the aircraft's airframe and made it want to fly in circles! When Delap was asked by an important personage how he sank the U-boat, he is reputed to have replied, 'Well, Sir, I dropped a bomb down the funnel.' Not all present were amused...

Hampdens, Whitleys and Wellingtons resumed leaflet drops in March, and Hampden squadrons took a turn in night patrolling over seaplane bases. Whitleys resumed deep penetration sorties, reaching Poznan on 7/8 March, then Prague and Vienna on 9/10 March, when 102 Squadron's Mk Vs N1417-B, N1420-L and N1386-P called. On 15/16 March leaflets fluttered down on Warsaw during the Whitleys' longest wartime flight so far. Participating was Flt Lt Tomlin and crew, who were briefed to land back in France. Short of fuel, they accidentally landed in Germany and, hearing locals talking, scurried back fast to their Whitley for a very prompt departure and a low-level flight to safety. During those very long night flights intense was the cold, and heavy the icing within the aircraft and on its external surfaces. A German night-fighter was first encountered in March 1940. This phase of Bomber Command activity ceased on 4 April with mine-laying by Hampdens about to take place.

Merlin-engined Whitley V (N1421) C-Charlie of No 102 Squadron seen at Driffield joined 102 on 4 January. It failed to return from raiding Fornebu on 30 April 1940. *IWM*

Whitley III K8994 with Tiger engine served with 102 Squadron from 29 September 1939 to 26 June 1940 when it moved to 10 OTU Abingdon in whose hands it is shown. *IWM*

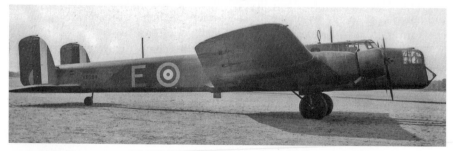

The closing weeks of 1939 had seen the introduction of Merlin-engined Whitley Vs, which replaced the Tiger-engined Mk IIIs in Nos 78 and 77 Squadrons, then No 102. Although re-equipment of Nos 51 and 58 Squadrons started in January, it was March before the last IIIs retired from No 58, and June 1940 before the last Mk III left No 51 Squadron. Last to rearm with Mk Vs, in March 1940, was No 10 Squadron. Retired Mk IIIs subsequently served at bombing and gunnery schools, and were used to train Britain's paratroops.

March 1940 also saw the introduction of the Wellington Mk 1c, of which version more than 2,500 were eventually built. Its 24-volt electrical system improved all-round capability, as did its redesigned hydraulics. These developments streamed from in-service experience. Frazer-Nash nose and tail turrets were to be supplemented with a hand-operated machine gun installed at the aft end of the side window strips. The guns replaced the 'dustbin' turret of the Mk 1a.

How the press saw it

According to one news report Macdonald was said to have 'bolted across [Driffield] like a scared rabbit when he was approached by a newspaper reporter'. Another newspaper report stated that '...aged between 40 and 50, he won the MC in the Great War, and has already won the DFC with bar and the DSO in this war. He has been over Berlin several times.' His second pilot was quoted as saying, 'We flew over the island for some time, making sure of a good run in. Anti-aircraft fire was bursting round us, and we were not steady enough, so we dropped a parachute flare. We turned and came in again, and bombed the target. We were 7 hours on the flight and returned at 3.10 am.'

The *New York Times* considered it had been 'a thorough, businesslike job of retaliation for the German attack on Scapa Flow. It is a tribute to their fighting prowess that only one from thirty or more raiding planes, according to the British, failed to return.'

Less praise came in a German High Command communiqué, which claimed that just one house had been damaged, adding, 'Most of the bombs fell in the sea. One British fighter was shot down by anti-aircraft guns. In connection with the raid British aircraft flew over Danish and Dutch territory.'

The Man from the Ministry says:

Commenting upon the raid, Captain Harold Balfour, Parliamentary Under-Secretary for Air, speaking in Margate, said, 'Our daring, successful and telling raid on Tuesday night shows that the lion has teeth as well as wings, and swift retribution came to Germany for her abortive attempts on Scapa.'

The most historic RAF bombing operation of the period took place on 19/20 March*. It was a fairly legitimate retaliation for the 16 March German bombing of Hoy, which had caused the first British civilian death as the result of an air raid in this war. For the first time an RAF bombing raid was being directed against a land target, hangars and assorted installations on Sylt/Hornum, the base for He 115 floatplane minelayers.

Spread over 7 hours, the raid, delivered from between 5,000 and 8,000 feet, started around midnight. First to intentionally bomb German territory was Sqn Ldr J. U. C. Macdonald and crew aboard Whitley V N1380 R-Robert of No 102 Squadron, Driffield. Over the target for 20 minutes, he opened the raid by dropping a parachute-illuminating flare.

The rear gunner of Whitley III K9043 of 51 Squadron, flown by Fg Off J. R. Birch, was wounded when the aircraft was intercepted by a German floatplane, then damaged by AA fire. Several others were also hit. In all, twenty-six of the thirty Whitleys operating, and fifteen out of the twenty Hampdens – the latter bombing over a 2-hour period – are listed as having bombed Sylt. In addition to an HE bombload of around 20 tons, 1,200 x 4lb incendiary bombs were dropped.

Although technical and tactical developments were obvious during the first eight months of war, the most important advance on the British side was a vast expansion and effort involving training programmes. Many new ground training schools were established, and important plans for aircrew basic training in the Dominions and colonies – in fair weather and without risk of attack – were to prove to be of immense importance throughout the war. April 1940 saw the formation of the first eight bomber operational training units (OTUs), Nos 10 to 17, where bomber crews assembled and trained as a team before proceeding to a squadron operating the same type of aircraft. In peacetime, squadrons trained their own crews. By the start of war Reserve Squadrons were in being to carry out the task, becoming the nucleus of the OTUs. Eventually, each was to hold more than fifty bombers.

That RAF heavy bombers flying in formation in daylight were unable to defend themselves from fighters was a bitter blow, for it meant that they would have to operate in darkness. That raised major operational and flying problems. Navigation aids were essential – especially now that they needed to operate in total darkness. Rapid, safe escape from bombers, together with ditching procedures, needed attention.. Homing and landing arrangements for returning night bombers required consideration. Flying in draughty, unheated aircraft at night in intense cold was unacceptable. Bomber Command, with a 6% loss rate, had discovered how difficult it would be to mount an effective strategic bombing campaign.

Phoney War? There was nothing 'phoney' about the harsh activity during the first seven months of the war. Now the action was to become really ferocious.

---

* Participants were thirty Whitleys – 10 Sqn: K9023, K9025, K9028, K9033, K9034, K9035, K9036, K9037; No 51 Sqn: K9040 (hit by flak), K9041 (bombs jettisoned, hit by flak), K9043 (hit by flak, rear gunner wounded), K9048, N1405, N1407 (missing), N1408; 77 Sqn: eight aircraft, individual identities unknown; and 102 Sqn: N1368 (aborted), N1377, N1380, N1381, N1382, N1386-P, N1415-D, N1421 – and twenty Hampdens – 44 Sqn: L4074, L4087, L4100, L4171, P1137; 50 Sqn: L4064, L4065, L4075, L4076, L4077; 61 Sqn: L4103, L4105 (missing), L4106, L4119, P1323; 144 Sqn: L4124, L4133, L4137 and four Hampdens identity uncertain. Forty-one crews claimed to have attacked the target.

A pair of Whitley Vs of 77 Squadron display their memorable nose-down flight attitude.

The Handley Page Hampden dubbed 'the flying suitcase' was very different to a Whitley but similar in design to the Messerschmitt Bf 110.

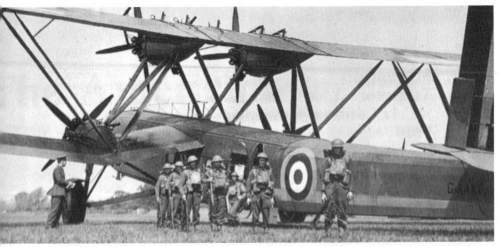

Britain was desperately short of military transport aircraft. Civilian airliners pressed into service included HP 42 G-AAXF, ex Imperial Airways seen here at Hatfield in July 1940.

Chapter 3

The fight for Norway

'Welcome to Narvik's war museum. It's always good to have British visitors. We'll never forget how in 1940 you tried to save us from German occupation.' A visit is always worthwhile, if only to see parts of a rare Dornier Do 26. A fine computerised presentation shows the German Navy sinking two aged Norwegian cruisers off the town, the occupation of Narvik and the brilliant action by Royal Navy destroyers, which sank ten German counterparts. Visit Rombaks Fjord and oil can still be seen seeping from sunken Kriegsmarine ships.

The German invasion of Norway on 9 April 1940 came as a shock to the British population, and perhaps to US President Roosevelt, awoken at 4.00am to hear the latest news of the 'Phoney War'. The British Government was not surprised. Germany obtained two-thirds of its iron ore, some of the world's best, from two Swedish ore deposits, and would surely wish to secure the supply. It was conveyed by rail to two ports, most going to the ice-free Arctic Norwegian port of Narvik. Britain also imported ore from there, and was keen to stop the supply to Germany.

When in October 1939 the USSR attacked Finland, the British Government was concerned that the Russians might later seize Sweden's ore fields, establishing also an undesirable presence in Scandinavia. Britain and France therefore asked Norway and Sweden to permit British forces to pass through their territory to Finland. Fearing that would risk war with the USSR, the request was rebuffed. A suggestion that Norwegian waters be mined, forcing German ships out to sea, was, hardly surprisingly, turned down.

Learning of Britain's request, on 12 November 1939 Hitler secretly ordered the start of preparations 'to control Norway' with the help of Mr Quisling, his Norwegian sympathiser. On 16 February 1940 the British audaciously retrieved 299 British seamen from the German ship *Altmark* hiding in Norway's Jossing Fjord. Hitler was not amused. He decided to go one better – he would now seize Norway, and on 3 March 1940 ordered the commencement of invasion planning. Occupation would secure iron ore imports and give the Germans a useful base for attacking the UK. Deep-water fjords would be ideal lurking places for warships.

On 26 March final preparations began for Operation 'Weserübung', the German seizure of Denmark and Norway, ordered to coincide with the next new moon. Two days later the British, unknowing of the German intention, decided to secretly mine Norwegian waters beginning on 8 April. One field would be sown off Narvik, the other further south, in an attempt to force German ships well away from land, thus making them more vulnerable.

Secretly, the first German invasion troopships sailed on 3 April. Warships left Wilhelmshaven Roads on the 6th and the next day a Coastal Command Hudson crew reported a large enemy convoy – two large warships, a cruiser, destroyers and merchant ships – heading north. Although its intent was uncertain, Blenheims of

107 Squadron hurried to the scene, found seventeen ships, attacked at 13.25, and achieved little. So seriously was the convoy viewed that two squadrons of Wellingtons set forth, but bad visibility prevented them from attacking. The Royal Navy would have to engage the force, which, unbeknown to the Allies, was heading north to seize Trondheim and Narvik.

Hermann Goering speaking in Berlin regarding the Western Front – to distract attention: 2 April

'It is here that the decisive blow must be struck, and for this decisive blow the Führer has mobilised all our resources. He places criminal responsibility for the war on the Allies.'

Warning by Norwegian Foreign Minister: Saturday 6 April

'Norway will at once be in the war if her free trade communications are interfered with to the advantage of one of the belligerents. We cannot think of any war which Norway might enter except one which we might be forced into in order to defend our independence and freedom,' M. Koht, Norwegian Foreign Minister, told Parliament today. The statement followed a British communication to both Norway and Sweden that one-sided neutrality must stop, and was made while Oslo newspapers were lashing Germany for her attack on the passenger ship *Mira*.

A British note to the Scandinavian countries stated that in the event of further Russian action against Finland, the Allies might feel called upon to interfere. *PA*

German offensive nearing? 6 April

Almost uninterrupted artillery action by the Germans on the Lorraine Front for the past ten days, the tightening of the Allied blockade and Field Marshal Goering's speech on Wednesday threatening a decisive blow, may herald a Nazi offensive on the Western Front.

Jour Echo de Paris

As planned, on 8 April the Navy mined the approach to Narvik. In thick mist the crew of a 204 Squadron Sunderland from Sullom Voe found the large enemy convoy (Force 1), which fired upon them. While changing heading, wrong details of the enemy course were signalled. Part of the convoy, Force 3, detached itself and made for Bergen, and, as Force 2, the cruiser *Admiral Hipper* and four destroyers headed for Trondheim. Force 4 was heading for Kristiansund, Force 6 for Egersund. That left the battleships *Scharnhorst* and *Gneisenau* with destroyers making for distant Narvik. For its part in the activity, the Luftwaffe had available some 600 combat aircraft and several hundred Ju 52 transports.

News from Berlin

Nazis tell their public: Berlin, 6 April

Britain is about to initiate a new phase of the war. In every case this new step is connected with the name of Mr Winston Churchill. Churchill's promotion to supreme minister of the armed forces proves that the Imperialist Power will make a serious attempt to widen the theatre of war.

British plan to destroy the Danube: German Government, Berlin

An elaborate plan by the British to blow up the River Danube is revealed in documents in the possession of the German Foreign Office. The plan was to blow up the banks of the Danube at certain points. It became known on 5 April that tugs accompanying a Greek vessel chartered by the British would be used. Owing to crew indiscretion it was discovered that revolvers, depth charges and high explosives were aboard, also British officers. The leader was the head of the British Secret Service in Roumania. *Berlin, 7 April*

Nazi troops mass at Baltic ports: Paris report

Following news today concerning the mining of Norwegian territorial waters came a Paris message saying that Nazi troop concentrations in German North Sea and Baltic ports had been increased. Embarkation and disembarkation exercises have been continuing at the ports for the past four months. It is regarded as impossible to determine whether landings on the coasts of Sweden, Denmark or Holland are envisaged. When dawn broke today three areas of Norwegian waters had become a death trap for Nazi ships attempting to defy Allied mastery of the sea, and run contraband into Germany.

First London-Lisbon mail plane: 7 April

A British Overseas Airways Corporation aircraft left Heston today on the first of three preliminary flights inaugurating the new London-Lisbon air service, which starts regularly at the beginning of May. The service will link up with the Pan American Airways North Atlantic route, giving a London-US schedule. With the crew of six were only four airline officials. The airliner, a Frobisher, which will make the 8-hour return flight to England on Wednesday, will bring home the service's first regular passenger, Walford Selby, British Ambassador to Portugal. *PA*

Before dawn on 9 April the assault and invasion of Norway started. He 111s of III/KG 26 attacked the naval base and guns defending the sea approach to Oslo. At the same time Denmark had also been invaded through six entry points. As German troops crossed unopposed into Denmark the first airborne forces operation began when Fallschirmjager (paratroops) landed on Aalborg airfield and Madneso fort, both captured with ease. Some of the troopships sailing through the Little Belt called at Middlefart, while others penetrated the Great Belt between Fyn and Zeeland to land forces at Nyborg and Korsor. Aboard ferries that sailed from Warnemunde, more went ashore at Gjedser and by midday had taken Copenhagen. Except in North Schleswigland, there had been very little opposition to the invasion. A German official news bulletin stated, 'The Danish authorities have promised their complete loyalty. There were no incidents. The German troops are on their way to Aalborg at the moment.' That was bad news for the Allies, because that airfield and another at Rye were within hours being used by the Luftwaffe.

Royal Norwegian Air Force aircraft at Oslo/Fornebu and Stavanger/Sola had quickly been destroyed, and airborne troops parachuted onto the landing grounds, where Ju 52s quickly arrived with more. From Fort Oscarsborg, overlooking Oslo Fjord, two torpedoes and shells from heavy guns slammed into the 665-foot-long 19,042grt cruiser *Blucher* heading Force 5 in the Drobak Narrows. She sank, taking with her many of her 1,000 crew, 900 troops of the 163rd Infantry Division, and Gestapo men hoping to deal with difficult Norwegians. Nevertheless, Oslo was in German hands by afternoon. The British believed that German forces in Norway could be cut off by naval action. Some hope! Norway was also too far away for easy RAF response, except for raids by Whitleys and Wellingtons.

Nazi General's statement – stealing a march on the British! (Berlin, Tuesday)

'An assertion that henceforward German armed forces will ensure protection against British attacks' has been made in addresses to the population of Norway and Denmark by General von Falkenhorst (commanding forces in Norway), and General Kaupisch in Denmark. Falkenhorst referred to British and French plans, 'in view of which Germany decided to steal a march on the British and to take over through her armed forces the protection of the neutrality of the kingdoms of Norway and Denmark for the duration of the war. The aim of this procedure is not to create war bases, but to prevent Scandinavia from becoming a theatre of war.

It is expected that the army, the population and the authorities will abstain from all active and passive resistance which would be completely useless and would be crushed by force. The population should perform their daily duties and take care that quiet and order is maintained.'

German notes to Norwegians and Danes: resistance would mean needless bloodshed

'Contrary to the sincere wishes of the German people and their government to live in peace and friendship with the British and French peoples, and despite lack of any sensible reason for a conflict, their rulers in London and Paris declared war on the German people. After having first tried a starvation blockade against women, children and old people, contrary to all international law, they are subjecting neutrals to their heartless blockade measures. Therefore Norway and Denmark are assured that German troops do not enter their territory in any hostile spirit, and that the German High Command has no intention of using the occupation by German forces for operations against Britain as long as it is not forced to do so. *Berlin news, 9 April*

German merchant ships in Bergen on 9 April suddenly raised the Nazi flag. They were supply ships awaiting German forces. Two German destroyers and two cruisers approached Bergen early on the 9th, supported by He 111s of III/KG 4 and I/KG 26. As the cruiser *Konigsberg* entered the approach she was damaged by gunfire. Next day, Fleet Air Arm Skuas from distant Hatston, Orkney, dive-bombed the cruiser, scoring two direct hits that sank her. She was the first major warship to be sunk in that manner during the war. Sinking such a vessel by air attack was far more difficult than had been thought. The German Navy also lost the 1929-built 6,000-ton *Karlsruhe*, the first warship to fly the Nazi flag, which was torpedoed by a submarine, HMS *Salmon*, off Kristiansund, where He 111s of III/KG 4 and I/KG 26 supported German forces as they took the town. Losses were not one-sided, for the *Admiral Hipper*, when engaged by the British 1,370-ton destroyer HMS *Gloworm*, sank the British ship. Few of the 145 aboard survived.

Two German destroyers arrived at Narvik at 05.00 on 9 April and torpedoed two aged Norwegian Navy 4,199-ton 1900-built cruisers, *Norge* and *Eidsvold*, from which only twenty of the 560 sailors aboard were rescued. A few minutes later German troops were ashore and captured the town without resistance. Around 2,000 Germans were soon engaging Norwegian forces inland.

British destroyers arrived at Narvik on the 10th. In the approaches HMS *Hunter* (1,340 tons and built in 1934) was sunk and HMS *Hardy* driven aground, but two German destroyers and several iron ore carriers were sunk. A second British naval force that reached Narvik on the 13th included the battleships HMS *Repulse* and *Warspite*. In a one-sided battle an amazing eight German destroyers were sunk.

A dozen Gladiators bought for the Norwegian Air Force and delivered in 1937-1938 could only briefly defend Oslo in 1940. The Shuttleworth Collection's hybrid Gladiator – built from parts of L8032 and N5903 – recently wore Norwegian Air Force markings.

Using heavy bombers against warships was tried on 12 April when Nos 38 and 149 Squadrons were pitted against the *Scharnhorst* and *Admiral Hipper*. The dozen Wellingtons were set upon by Bf 110s and two Ju 88C fighters, which made repeated beam attacks during a 15-minute engagement. Hampdens of Nos 44 and 50 Squadrons attempted to sink German ships at Kristiansund. Again making beam attacks, German fighters, including Ju 88Cs, shot down half of the bomber force, providing yet more evidence of the vulnerability of unescorted 'heavy' bombers during daylight operations. They would have to operate under cover of darkness.

Dutch taking no chances – strategic points guarded: 12 April

All measures have been taken to keep Holland constantly prepared in view of the international situation. All last night and again this morning special trains were rumbling through the country taking soldiers back from leave. Guards have been strengthened on strategic bridges, dykes, railways and roads. Immediate danger to Holland is now believed to be over for the moment.

Could the Germans advancing overland from southern Norway, and travelling through the area close to the Swedish border, reach their detached forces in Narvik and Trondheim? Helped by clear weather, 2 Group Blenheims operating from Lossiemouth were able to attack Stavanger/Sola airfield. At night, Whitleys and Wellingtons tried to bomb Trondheim/Vaernes. They also raided Sola in darkness on the 11th and 14th.

On 13/14 April, in an attempt to disrupt German shipping, Hampdens mined the Great and Little Belts, Elbe Estuary and Kiel Canal, places denied to British warships. Flights over heavily defended areas were made more hazardous because the 1,500lb parachute mines used had to be dropped from a mere 500 feet. By the end of

April, Hampdens – seven of which had failed to return – had sown 110 mines. More were courageously sown by Coastal Command and the Fleet Air Arm, but mining came too late to influence the campaign. Nevertheless, the Germans lost 8% of their maritime input, although only 1,000 out of the total 100,000 personnel engaged. The British failed to appreciate the extent of German naval losses, which had a serious effect on their Navy for the remainder of the war.

Aware that the Royal Navy was using Scapa Flow as a base for Norwegian operations, He 111s of I and II/KG 26 had attacked it on 8 April and did so again on the 17th. On the 10th Ju 88s of I/KG 30 unsuccessfully took Scapa's fuel storage area as their target.

Would it be possible for troops to be landed to recapture Trondheim and Narvik? It was worth a try. Allied troops would go ashore at the small ports of Andalsnes, south of Trondheim, and Namsos to the north. From both they would head inland to take Trondheim, employing a pincer movement. Another Allied force would, on 14 April, land at Harstad, an island 50 miles from the entrance to Narvik Fjord. Again, two forces would be put ashore to take Narvik.

The Namsos force was led by famed Major General Carton de Wiart VC, a veteran of the Boer War. Arriving in a Sunderland on 15 April, he was unkindly greeted by German bombs. All the landings were unopposed because German forces were well inland. A naval party and troops of the 146th British Division began going ashore on 14 April at Namsos and were followed on the 19th by the 5th French Brigade. They proceeded inland to join the 5th Norwegian Division. The Luftwaffe appeared over Namsos on the 19th and seriously damaged the small town. Although the force moved inland and joined the Norwegians, two heavy bombing raids forced the Allies to withdraw to Namsos.

Landings at Andalsnes, south of Trondheim, began on the 17th, and comprised the 1,600 men of the 148th British Brigade and the 2nd Norwegian Division. From Andalsnes their advance inland led them along an ascending valley, a route still followed by the branch railway that delights summer tourists with its aged steam-hauled trains. At Dombas Junction, where the track joins the Oslo main line, the force turned towards Lillehammer to join the Norwegian forces facing the German Army in the Oppland area. Hope was that the combined force would be sufficiently strong to advance and recapture Trondheim. Stronger than forecast, the German contingent soon forced the Norwegians to retreat. More British soldiers were then brought along to reinforce those already at the front. The RAF bombed Sola in an attempt to prevent German bombers attacking land forces, but they were unable to stop the Luftwaffe from launching a ferocious onslaught on the troops. Between 14 and 21 April some 200 difficult night-bombing sorties were flown by the RAF. Reaching Norway entailed a lengthy sea crossing, often in poor weather and usually in cloud.

On 20 April He 111s of III/KG 4, II/KG 26 and III/KG 26 with Ju 88s of II/KG 30 battered the undefended little towns of Namsos and Molde in use as entry ports, returning over the next few days to ensure their total destruction. On the 21st it was the turn of Andalsnes to be heavily bombed by Ju 88s. Without enough fighter and anti-aircraft gun protection, and now without supply bases, the Allies ashore were at grave risk. Also, it was obvious that Trondheim could not be recaptured. At best the

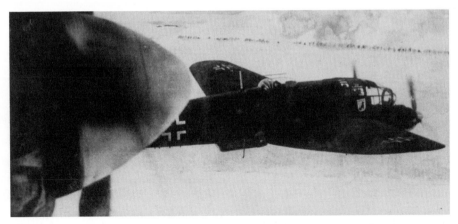

Heinkel 111s of KG 26 prominent in the Norwegian campaign.

enemy advance might be delayed. There were no airfields from which protective air cover and support could be given to the Allies. In an attempt to remedy that, the aircraft carriers HMS *Ark Royal* and *Glorious* had been recalled from the Mediterranean, and early on 23 April sailed from Scapa for Norway so that the Fleet Air Arm could provide air support.

Also aboard *Glorious* were Filton-based Gloster Gladiators of 263 Squadron commanded by Squadron Leader J. W. Donaldson, DSO. It was thought that short-field, manoeuvrable biplane fighters would be able to operate from a primitive land site, but none could be found. Instead, frozen Lake Vangsmjosa was initially chosen – until it was realised that it would be difficult to supply and was very exposed. An alternative, Lake Lesjaskog near Dombas, was substituted. With barely any supporting ground personnel and almost no support equipment, 2 feet of snow on the lake was instead unconventionally flattened by the trampling feet of 3,000 reindeer who compacted it to provide a landing strip, which was unfortunately some way from the shore. In poor weather on the afternoon of the 24th eighteen Gladiators* were flown off the aircraft carrier and guided by a Blackburn Skua to the frozen lake, set by the railway in a very exposed, wide valley.

The Gladiator pilots, hopes high, lodged in a nearby hotel. Already the ice was melting at the edge of the lake. There was severe shortage of fuel and no petrol bowser, but a horse and sledge were to hand. Rearming was difficult with so few groundcrew, getting engines to start in the cold proved difficult, and aircraft tyres froze to the ice. It took 2 hours to get ready to operate in the intense cold, so that 263 Squadron's first patrol, planned for 03.00 on the 25th, took place at 05.00, during which they bagged an He 115. German pilots soon spotted 263 Squadron's base and around 09.00 Ju 88s of KG 30 and He 111s of KG 4 began bombing the

---

* Details of the aircraft and operations of 263 Squadron during the Norwegian campaign remain patchy. The eighteen Gladiators flown off the carrier appear to have been N5504, N5579, N5585, N5589, N5628, N5632, N5633, N5634, N5635, N5639, N5647, N5680, N5700, N5714, N5894, N5898, N59805 and N5915.

Gladiators of No 263 Squadron on Lake Lesjaskog, Norway. *John Rawlings collection*

lake. Engine starts for scrambles were almost impossible and four Gladiators were soon destroyed. Even worse, bombing broke the ice covering the lake, but Flt Lt Miller managed to get off in time to destroy an He 111. A further bombing raid took place at noon and another Heinkel was shot down. Half an hour later a third raid developed and soon ten Gladiators had been destroyed. Unexpected was strafing by Ju 88C-2 heavy fighters fitted with nose guns. Belonging to Zestörerstaffel KG 30, and operating from Sola, they had previously been used as long-range escort and interceptor fighters. Now they showed their value as strike fighters.

By midday on 25 April it was almost impossible to get any Gladiators airborne, and the ice runway would be no more by evening. So, in the late afternoon Sqn Ldr Donaldson and Flt Lt Miller managed to get off to engage more enemy raiders before landing on a small area at Setnesmoen, near Andalsnes, where they were joined by four more Gladiators. Next day five Gladiators attempted to engage enemy bombers, only to find them flying too high for a fight. No 263's strength fell to three Gladiators, then to one, which was soon grounded by lack of fuel. By the end of 26 April, with all the aircraft useless, the squadron left on a ship, reaching Scapa Flow on 1 May. Their actions had been incredibly courageous, the conditions appalling

Ju 88A 4D+NH of I/KG30, first Gruppe to use the type. Active against Scapa's ships and over Norway in 1940.

Heinkel He 111 of KG 1, *The Hindenburg Geschwader.*

and the lack of equipment and support quite disgraceful. Poor treatment by shoddy politicians of our courageous armed forces is nothing new, and clearly continues as recently in the Afghanistan activity.

Having seen off the brave Gladiators, He 111s and Ju 88s called at the little town of Andalsnes to finish it off. The quay, small port facilities, railway area and the town were all decimated. As at Namsos, this was hardly the way to protect the Norwegians from the nasty British. Between 24 and 27 April the Fleet Air Arm, operating from *Glorious*, although no match for strong German forces attacking ships at sea, had done their best to protect them and the Andalsnes area, from where during the night of 1-2 May the remaining Allied troops were withdrawn. Luftwaffe attacks continued on the ships as they made for home, two destroyers being sunk. Bomber Command continued attacking Sola and Fornebu by day and night, in an attempt to reduce Luftwaffe activity. Their operations were costly on the night of 30 April/1 May when, of twenty-eight Wellingtons and Whitleys raiding Sola, five failed to return. Both British aircraft carriers were attacked by Ju 88s and He 111s as they headed home. British forces had completely left the area by 2 May, leaving the Germans in firm control of Trondheim and the inland area. By the start of May He 111s of KG 4 were soon operating from Stavanger/Sola and KG 26 from Trondheim/Vaernes.

What of the Narvik venture, 400 miles north of Trondheim, and being undertaken where snow lies between October and May? Was that area beyond enemy air intervention? There were then no airfields near Narvik, yet the essential need for troops to have air cover was in no doubt. The plan was for the British 24th Guards Brigade, French 27th Brigade, the 6th Norwegian Division and Polish forces to land on both sides of the fjord, encircle the town and take it from the east. Needing a landing ground for fighters, a Sunderland brought Wg Cdr R. L. R. Atcherley to Harstad. Seeking a landing area for RAF fighters, he concluded that one at Bardufoss could be made ready in three weeks, and that Banak was suitable as well as a strip of land at Skaanland, 25 miles from Narvik. Bardufoss was most favoured, so a large force of local people was engaged to clear away snow, prepare a runway, and add lead-offs to protective woodland. Before all was ready, a thaw set in, producing plenty of mud.

Wellington 1a L7779 of Feltwell based No 37 Squadron operated over Norway. L7779
served with No 37 from 17 April to 15 September 1940. *IWM*

More Allied troops land in Norway:
French military communiqué, 9 May

More Allied troops have been landed in Norway and operations, although slowed
by blizzards and the necessity of repairing bridges blown up by the Germans, are
proceeding. At Narvik the Nazis are withdrawing generally in the face of pressure.
They are falling back on the town of Narvik but in greater numbers on a village
east of Narvik alongside the railway. Swedish reports speak of Nazi planes
rushing fresh troops and supplies to the north and attacking Allied forces.

A headquarters component to control the operation set sail from Britain on 7
May, the Force Commander being Lt-Gen Auchinleck, later commander of the 8th
Army. On reaching his island HQ on 11 May he immediately called for many more
troops. It was the worst day to have made such a request for the German blitzkrieg
on France and the Low Countries had been launched the previous day. Even before it
began, recapture of Narvik was thus doomed, especially with expected Bomber
Command support switched elsewhere.

Nevertheless, more Gladiators, which had rearmed 263 Squadron at Hatston,
were put aboard HMS *Furious*, which sailed for Norway on 14 May. Upon reaching
the Narvik area, three Gladiators (N5677, N5693 and N5698) were flown off the
carrier and, led by a Swordfish, headed for Skaanland. Mist suddenly enveloped them
and two fighters smashed into hillsides. The survivor returned to *Furious*. Next day
the remainder of No 263 Squadron* successfully flew to Skaanland and managed
some fifty sorties that day. Further support arrived on 26 May after No 46 Squadron

---

* The identity of the Gladiators is uncertain, but those used probably included N5705, N5719A,
N5723, N5725, N5906, N5907 and N5908. At least eight were aboard HMS *Glorious* when she was
sunk, including N5681, N5695 and N5699.

historically flew Hurricanes off a carrier, HMS *Glorious*, for the first time. The surface of Skaanland being unsuitable for them, they flew instead to Bardufoss. Without a fighter control organisation, operations were greatly hampered, although the Gladiators did well.

Holding Narvik without many more troops would be impossible. Nevertheless, Allied forces landed as planned, and destroyed the port installations and rail system. They then withdrew, but not before Heinkels of KG 26 arrived in strength on 2 June. Responding RAF fighters flew seventy-five sorties with some success before it was time for them to withdraw. At least eight Gladiators and ten 'land suitable only' Hurricanes of 46 Squadron**, Squadron Leader Kenneth Cross leading, all successfully landed on HMS *Glorious*, the first Hurricanes to land on a carrier.

Unfortunately, the battleships *Scharnhorst* and *Gneisenau* – still at sea – soon found the 22,500-ton British carrier. During the afternoon of 8 June they bombarded her using their heavy guns. She did not give way easily, taking 70 minutes to go down. Her crew numbered more than 1,200 and heavy was the loss of life. From 46 Squadron only Kenneth Cross and one other member survived. It was, indeed, a terrible event. The only slight comfort came from knowing that both German battleships sustained sufficient damage during the Norwegian campaign to put them out of action until late December 1940.

The Allied Norwegian effort was a disappointment, many lives were lost, and much courage and equipment was expended to little avail. Lack of air cover had rendered all the Allied forces highly vulnerable to air attack. Coastal Command – whose crews carried out very risky lone reconnaissance flights using long-range Blenheim IV(f)s – managed to give very limited support to bombers. Between 9 April and 9/10 May Bomber Command flew a dozen daylight bombing raids involving 268 sorties, which cost seventeen aircraft and crews. In the course of their twenty raids, 2 Group Blenheims had flown 113 sorties. Seven crews did not return. During the Norwegian campaign, sixteen targets were attacked at night by heavies and thirty-six aircraft and crews failed to return from the 663 sorties flown.

Norway and Denmark had succumbed to occupation, but, fierce as the fight for Norway had been, it was outclassed by the massive, high-speed and well-delivered onslaught upon France and the Low Countries.

** Hurricane 1s lost aboard HMS *Glorious* included L1793, L1804, L1805, L1806, L1815, L1853 and L1980.

Norwegians had seen many menacing Heinkel He 111s overhead. Now it was the turn of western Europeans.

Troop deployment to Norway had featured the three-motor Ju 52. Soon the people of the Netherlands would see them arrive in hundreds.

JUNKERS Ju. 52 (B.M.W.)

Purpose: **PARACHUTE-TROOP TRANSPORT.**   Dimensions: **Span 96 ft. 0 in.**   Performance: Maximum Speed **180 m.p.h.**
Length 62 ft. 0 in.   Cruising Speed **150 m.p.h.**

An aircraft recognition card for the Ju 52.

Chapter 4

Au revoir, Paris

It certainly wasn't unexpected. November and January had brought high-alert states in Belgium, the Netherlands and France. A third invasion scare overtook the Netherlands on 8 May after American journalists reported much movement on German roads, and the Belgian Government considered that 'Holland might be invaded'. Dutch military police guarded important buildings, yet the French Government reported 'little change in the German order of battle'. So much for good intelligence – not much changes! By the close of day there were suggestions that the alarm was a German propaganda ploy.

Next day, the 9th, 600,000 troops were put at standby in the Netherlands, and Belgian forces were on high alert. Germany made no comment regarding rumours suggesting Wehrmacht groups were leaving Bremen and Dusseldorf, and in Paris there was still 'no reason for Dutch concern'. To calm nerves, the Dutch Government announced that its railways would resume normal operating on Saturday 11 May. Things didn't work out quite like that for at 03.00 on Friday 10 May German forces burst through the Dutch and Belgian frontiers. Long expected, the blitzkrieg on the Low Countries, Luxembourg and France found them surprisingly poorly prepared.

Presently a message arrived summoning me to the Palace at 6 o'clock. I was taken immediately to the King. His Majesty received me most graciously and bade me sit down. He looked at me searchingly and particularly for some moments, and then said, 'I suppose you don't know why I have sent for you.' Adopting his mood I replied, 'Sir, I simply couldn't imagine why.' He laughed and said, 'I want to ask you to form a government.' I said I would certainly do so. At last I had the authority to give direction over the whole scene. I felt as if I were walking with destiny, and that all my past life had been but a preparation for this hour and for this trial... I was sure I should not fail. Therefore, although impatient for the morning, I slept soundly and had no need for cheering dreams. Facts are better than dreams.

10 May 1940: Winston Churchill, post-war recorded recollections

General von Manstein was responsible for the German war plan. A diversion attack on Belgium and the Netherlands would be undertaken by the twenty-nine divisions of von Bock's Army Group B doing what the Allies were expecting and triggering their main response. Facing the forts of the French Maginot Line from Switzerland to Luxembourg was Group C, seventeen divisions strong. Between them were nearly all the Panzer motorised and armoured divisions under von

Runstedt. Their role was to bypass the Maginot by advancing through the Ardennes forests along narrow tracks in order to make the vital crossing of the River Meuse. Then they would race forward by as much as 50 miles a day to trap the British Expeditionary Force (BEF) in a pocket backing on the coastline. With the Panzers were many anti-aircraft guns and strong, integrated, dedicated support from Luftwaffe bombers and fighters. As soon as practicable the Luftwaffe would occupy captured airfields, since their aircraft were relatively short-ranged. As in Norway, paratroops and glider-borne soldiers went ahead of land forces, securing four key points in Belgium and capturing Dutch airfields. Ju 52 troop transports landed on a beach near the Hague to deliver more troops.

By way of contrast, the RAF's Advanced Air Striking Force (AASF) – ex-1 Group – which moved to France in September 1939, operated eight squadrons of Fairey Battle short-range bombers, and two flying Blenheims. All were intended for strategic attacks on Germany. Two Hurricane squadrons provided local defence. The Air Component supported the Army's BEF and comprised five Westland Lysander squadrons, four Blenheim reconnaissance squadrons and two Hurricane squadrons. Two more Hurricane squadrons moved to France when the blitzkrieg began.

The RAF total first line strength on 10 May 1940 amounted to 1,873 aircraft, 544 of them bombers. A total of 416 aircraft were based in France. Of the RAF's fighter squadrons, six – Nos 1 and 73 with the AASF, and Nos 85, 87, 607 and 615 in the Air Component – flew Hurricanes. Their number rose to ten when another four squadrons (Nos 3, 79, 501 and 504) joined them. Of the 261 Hurricanes said to have been sent to France, only sixty-six were listed as eventually returning to Britain.

Airmen typically warmly clad at Conde-Vraux by with a XV Squadron Fairey Battle in November 1939.

Fairey Battle K9325 of 218 Squadron which, by June 1940, had lost all their aircraft.

Battle II N2024 of No XV Squadron which returned from France to Wyton in the UK, re-armed with Blenheim IVs, then joined No 2 (Bomber) Group.

With two fighter squadrons set aside for Norway, only forty-one remained for home defence. Overall, forty-three fighter squadrons were to participate in the fight to save France. By the end of the first week of fighting, the equivalent of sixteen squadrons of Hurricanes were in position. Total loss of RAF fighters destroyed or very seriously damaged during the entire campaign was 474. Alarming for sure.

Policy called for AASF bombers based around Rheims to support the BEF when necessary by attacking troop columns, road junctions and particularly bridges – by day and night. Home-based No 2 Group, with seven squadrons of Blenheim IVs, was the rear or Second Echelon of the AASF. It held at readiness around sixty Blenheim IVs. Identifying specific targets to be dealt with in fast-changing situations proved difficult. There was also concern over vulnerability to fighter interception and concentrated AA fire, day-bomber operations resulting in 334 aircraft being lost on operations, or badly damaged during the fight for France.

Heavies of Bomber Command had a split role. They were available to raid tactical targets west of the Rhine and, only when authorised by the War Cabinet, to bomb oil plants and rail centres in the Ruhr. Two 4 Group Whitley squadrons were available to the AASF for tactical operations. During the Polish campaign, bombers provided good invasion support – but could they help to halt one? It seemed rather unlikely, but had to be attempted.

Hurricanes of No 73 Squadron, AASF, in 1939. Based at Rouvres. *Fox*

A Hurricane of No 85 Squadron serving with the Air Component, BEF, at Lille/Seclin. The squadron persisted in applying the white hexagon featured in their squadron badge on to their aircraft.

It was the expectation that Hurricanes would equip No 615 AAF Squadron before they joined the Air Component. Instead, when 615 and 607 Squadron moved to Merville, north east France, in November 1939, they retained Gladiators. Hurricanes were received shortly before the German onslaught.

Although concentration here is upon the British, the French Air Force also operated intensively. RAF conversion to 1930s modern aircraft was complete in 1939, whereas the French in May 1940 were still doing that. Their fighter squadrons used the Morane 406, similar to our Hawker Hurricane, the Bloch 152 and Dewoitine D520. The Potez 63 series was their Blenheim equivalent, but their Amiot bombers were outdated. France had ordered American-built combat aircraft, and flew Curtiss Hawk 75C-1s and a few Douglas DB-7s against the German assault. They fought hard, fought with distinction, but rapid loss of the homeland was demoralising. A few of their aircraft eventually found sanctuary in Britain, more in North Africa.

German personnel, many having seen action in Spain, Poland and Norway, possessed combat experience that the French and British lacked. Intensively trained, highly conversant with tactics, their modern weaponry integration conferred many advantages. Their tactics were cleverly conceived, and their Army and Air Force operated as a team.

Unlike the Luftwaffe's short-range tactical bombers, the RAF's core fleet of heavies, turreted for defence, possessed the range to carry them deeply into Europe. They were intended to wage a strategic bombing campaign against industry, fuel plants and communications. They were not very useful for battlefield support. Fortunately, the RAF also had a superbly organised, excellently equipped, brilliantly led fighter force, which was to become the nation's, indeed the civilised world's, saviour.

POTEZ 631 (GNOME 640 H.P.)

MORANE 406 (HISPANO 850 H.P.)

Official aircraft recognition cards depicting the main frontline aircraft of the Armée de l'Air. Illustrated are the Potez 63 reconnaissance bomber, Morane Saulnier MS 406 fighter, Bloch 152 fighter and the Breguet 691 light bomber.

BLOCH 152 (GNOME 980 H.P.)

BREGUET 691 (GNOME 640 H.P.)

Crews alongside a Breguet 270, one of the older French aircraft being replaced too late in 1940.

A Curtiss Hawk 75A which equipped eight French Air Force squadrons in May 1940 entered service late 1939.

Over 500 Ju 52 3/m transports were in Luftwaffe hands in April 1940. By August only 375 remained for they had been viewed as expendable when operationally deployed against the Netherlands. *Gerrit J Zwanenburg*

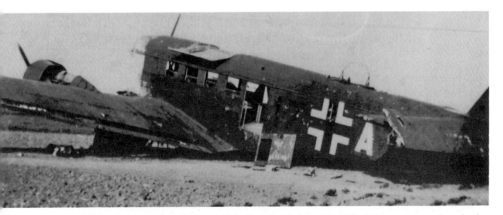

Airborne troops clearly made hasty exit from Ju 52 3/m 1Z+AU of Transportgeschwader 1. *Gerrit J Zwanenburg*

Three-engined aircraft have never been common – except for the Ju 52 3/m. Four days of operations against the Netherlands cost the Germans 220 Ju 52s. *Gerrit J Zwanenburg*

Ypenburg based Douglas 8-A3N attack bombers were employed as fighters without success. All were all destroyed. *Gerrit J Zwanenburg*

Addressing the National Defence Public Interest Committee: 8 May

Mr Anthony Eden, Britain's Dominions Minister, declared, 'The war is entering upon what all can recognise as an active phase. The people of the British Commonwealth are now braced and prepared for the stress of a harsh conflict.' He revealed that 'seventy flying schools are being established in Canada under the Empire Air Training Scheme, allowing tens of thousands to be trained every year.' The Empire war effort was 'like the opening bars of a symphony, whose theme has been announced but not elaborated... It will be a factor of immense importance in the achievement of ultimate victory... Hitler has his political roots in the Prussia of past generations, he did not invent the doctrine that might is right... We have a sober and unshakable determination to win through to victory, whatever the cost, and to take every step in our power to ensure that this time there should be a lasting peace ... three essential conditions must be realised. First, we must not underrate the enemy's strength, second we have to marshal the whole of our resources and employ them, third we have to conduct the war with all the vision, courage and resolution at our command.'

Roll up! Roll up! It's call-up time!

With certain exceptions, all male British subjects who on 9 May 1940 are within Great Britain, or subsequently enter Great Britain, and who, on 9 May 1940, have reached the age of 19 but not reached the age of 37, are liable to be called up for service.

The liability to be called up will be for 1) men born between 2 January and 9 May 1921 inclusive, and 2) men born between 10 May 1903 and 1 January 1912. The reason for including the 19s was to give power to call upon them to register on reaching the age of 20.

Government announcement, 10 May 1940

What Ribbentrop said (or, how to tell lies): statement to the press, 10 May

The Reich Government knew yesterday that Great Britain had told the Belgian and Dutch Governments that the landing of British troops on Belgian and Dutch soil was imminent. The German Army will now speak to Britain and France in the only language their rulers seem to understand, and settle them once and for all.'

As soon as German forces attacked Belgium and Holland on 10 May both appealed for Allied help. They were to put up a tough fight, but could not succeed against the powerful foe whose bombers numbered 1,758, with 417 Ju 87 dive-bombers, 1,369 Bf 109 fighters, and 367 Bf 110s. Their transport force amazingly totalled 513 aircraft.

At first light on 10 May, He 111Hs of KG 1 and He 111Ps of KG 4 caused chaos on main roads, and bombed many airfields, including nine used by the RAF. More bombs rained down on railway stations, villages and towns – as required – also upon troop concentrations. For example, central Brussels was hit, a fire at Plac Madou causing casualties. Allied help was vital, especially after the Belgian and Dutch air forces were decimated despite their courageous crews. In a 'first time', glider-borne troops had landed at Eben Emael, Belgium, where the Meuse met the Albert Canal. They destroyed the prominent fort and captured a nearby Albert Canal bridge, which, next day, the German 4th Armoured Division used as a major crossing point.

From the papers

Hitler Says 'The Hour Has Come'

Hitler has addressed this message to the German forces on the Western Front. 'The hour of the most decisive struggle for the future of the German nation has come. The German people have no hatred and no enmity towards the British and French people, but it is confronted today with the question whether it wants to live or go under. The Allies planned to advance through Belgium and Holland to attack the Ruhr while carrying out a gigantic manoeuvre of diversion in South-Eastern Europe.'

German High Command Communiqué – Hitler Takes Charge

In view of the immediately pending extension of the war by the enemy to Belgium and Dutch territory, and the threat thus involved to the Ruhr district, the German Army launched an attack at dawn on 10 May over the German western frontiers. The Führer and Supreme Commander of the Army has gone to the Western Front to take complete charge of the forces there.

British Landing in Iceland: Protection against Nazi Invasion – Foreign Office Announcement

A British Force has landed in Iceland... The Icelandic Government has been given specific guarantees that the Force is there to ensure the security of the country against German invasion. The only defence force at the disposal of the Icelandic authorities is a body of about 70 police... Its geographical configuration is such as to provide excellent shelter for submarines and facilities for refuelling them, as well as for seaplane and aeroplane bases.

---

28 operational Dutch Fokker D.XXIs were home-made fighters which gave a good account of themselves until they faced Bf109s. *Gerrit J Zwanenburg*

The Belgian Air Force suffered badly, some of their few Fairey Battles falling into enemy hands.

Enactment of Plan D (Dyle) was the main BEF response, which meant that by 11 May the British Army was lining the banks of the River Dyle, Belgium, between Wavre and Louvain. To the north were Belgian forces, reinforced after their forced withdrawal from the Albert Canal, their prime defence line. Around Namur the French 9th Army was in position.

A handful of Fokker T-VIIIW floatplanes of the Royal Netherlands Naval Air Service escaped to Britain. On 1 June 1940 No 320 Squadron formed to operate them from Pembroke Dock as inshore reconnaissance aircraft.

The Dutch Air Force operated nine Fokker T5 reconnaissance bombers from Schiphol.

The home-made Fokker fighters gave a good account of themselves but to no avail.
Gerrit J Zwanenburg

The 23 twin-boom Fokker G-1A fighters such as 312 were very effective aircraft. The orange triangle outlined in black was applied in 1940 to clearly indicate national identity as previous red-white-blue segmented marking had affinity with British roundels.

What's on the wireless this evening?

Programmes for 10 May

Home Service

5.00pm	News in Welsh
5.05pm	Talk (Welsh)
5.20pm	Children
5.30pm	Songs and a story
6.00pm	News
6.15pm	Debussy's songs
6.30pm	News in Norwegian
6.45pm	Vive la France
7.15pm	Announcements
7.30pm	Records
7.40pm	A Christian Looks at the World
8.00pm	*Red Peppers* by Noel Coward
8.30pm	The British Merchant Navy at work in war
9.00pm	Time, News
9.20pm	Once a week – a talk by Onlooker
9.35pm	Seaman Smith entertains – camp concert
10.00pm	Radio party night
10.30pm	BBC Scottish Orchestra
11.00pm	Eddie Carroll and his dance orchestra
11.30pm	Kathleen Moorhouse (cello), Frank Merrick (piano)
12.00am	Time, News
12.20-12.30am	News in Norwegian

Forces

5.00pm	Jack Simpson and his sextet
5.30pm	Sandy MacPherson (organ)
6.00pm	Foreign language bulletin
6.30pm	In Britain Now
6.50pm	Guest night
7.30pm	Fred Hartley and his sextet
8.30pm	Bram Martin and his orchestra
9.00pm	Foreign language bulletin
9.15pm	What's on tomorrow
9.20-9.35pm	George Formby
10.30-1.00am	Records

AASF Battles suffered badly in the fight, and littered the countryside. L5440 belonged to 142 Squadron.

The French 2nd Army faced the heavily forested Ardennes region, which it was thought would be very difficult for an army to pass through. How wrong that notion was. Wasted was reinforcement by the French 7th Army of the coastal region from Antwerp to the Scheldt.

Fear that bombing Germany might induce attacks on French cities caused a delay in the AASF response on 10 May. Around noon, its AOC, Air Marshal Sir Arthur S. Barratt, waited no longer to help the BEF. He gave orders for eight Fairey Battles to bomb German troops from a mere 250 feet to avoid fighter attack from below, losing three of their number for the invaders had brought with them plentiful AA weapons. At 17.05 four Battles of 12 Squadron set out to attack a road in the Luxembourg-Junglister-Echternach triangle. L5190 P was brought down and P2243 force-landed at Plennes. L4949, also shot down, was piloted by Flt Lt Bill Simpson (later BEA's PRO), who recalled so poignantly the awful burning that overcame him in the moving book *I Burnt my Hands*. Flames from the engine poured back into the cockpit, and as he tried to pull his fingers back from the control column they instead lengthened dramatically. Similar ghastly events were being encountered by many. By nightfall the small-scale response had cost thirteen Battles from a mere thirty-two sorties. That was highly alarming.

Paris Raided: 10 May 1940

Several French towns, among them Nancy, Lille, Lyons, Colmar, Pontoise (which is only 15 miles from Paris) and Luxeuil, were bombed by German aircraft today. Paris was raided and there was intense anti-aircraft fire. There were some casualties from shrapnel, but no bombs were dropped. The alarm was given in the Lyons district at 4.25am. Bombs were dropped on Bron aerodrome and one enemy plane was brought down. The 'All Clear' was given at 6.45am.

Around midday on the 10th, to aid the Dutch, six Blenheim fighters of 600 Squadron had gone to strafe Waalhaven ahead of a raid by 2 Group Blenheims. Bf 110s pounced on 600 Squadron, shooting down five aircraft. This was definitely going to be a costly campaign. After dark, thirty-six Wellingtons tried to bomb Waalhaven, which was being used intensively by Ju 52s. Whitleys, nine in number, tried attacking tactical targets west of the Rhine. Target-finding was almost impossible, raising the question of how to apply bombers defensively. Although on the first day the Luftwaffe quickly achieved air superiority, it cost them eighty-three aircraft including forty-seven bombers and twenty-five fighters, as well as skilled crews.

Watton's No 82 Squadron was outstanding in the 1940 fight. Looking just like a 1940 Blenheim IV – but a little too pristine – is Graham Warner's magnificent re-build representing R3921, resting by Duxford's tower.

German progress into Holland was critical for the Allies by 11 May, but more serious was the almost unimpeded and rapid progress by the XIXth Panzer Corps under Guderion along lanes and tracks through the Ardennes. Unrecognised as yet, it was to lead to the downfall of France.

Of nine Air Component Blenheims sent to reconnoitre in the morning, only five returned. There was sufficient information for an afternoon operation by 2 Group Blenheims of Nos 21 and 110 Squadrons, which made a low-level attack on bridges at Maastricht and over the Maas Canal. They faced an incredible AA reception. One Fairey Battle raid mounted on the advance through the Ardennes resulted in the loss of seven of the eight aircraft. On 10 May the AASF started with 135 serviceable bombers and ended with a 40% operational loss of Battles. That rose to100% of those operationally flown on the 11th. Losses again were not all one-sided, for the Luftwaffe lost twenty-two bombers, ten fighters and eight dive-bombers during this second day of intense activity.

Amsterdam 'Drome Attacked: 11 May

A savage bombing attack by massed German bombers was made on Amsterdam's airport and surrounding buildings at 6am. Many bombs were dropped and the attack lasted 25 minutes. At 6.48am bombers appeared over the city again. No sooner had the first wave of bombers appeared than the alarm was given and people went to the shelters.

A terrific explosion in the south-east of the city was caused by a German aeroplane, which was shot down and exploded.

On 12 May, while the IXth Panzer Division was at the outskirts of Rotterdam, RAF bombers again attempted, unsuccessfully, to bring down vital bridges captured by the enemy at Maastricht and over the Albert Canal. Famed Wg Cdr Basil Embry led the day's first 2 Group attack on Maastricht, the Blenheims needing to penetrate heavy flak throughout their 15-mile run in. Fighters then attacked, bringing down two bombers. Fg Off Hughie Edwards, later a VC winner, piloted one.

Nine Blenheims of No 139 Squadron, part of the Air Component, also went to Maastricht. Messerschmitt 109s brought down seven of them, almost writing off 139 Squadron. Companion 114 Squadron was all but destroyed when its base was bombed. Next to try to bring down the Albert Canal bridges were a dozen Blenheims of Wyton-based No XV Squadron. Circling Hurricanes unfortunately warned of XV's approach and, after AA fire broke the bombers' formation, Bf 109s hacked down half the Blenheim force, and only two remained serviceable after landing. Seeing eighteen of thirty-six men dying in horrendous circumstances must have been terrible to experience. By the end of the Day, ten from the two dozen 2 Group Blenheims operating had been lost, others seriously damaged. There had also been another incredibly courageous venture.

Blenheim IVs of 139 Squadron. The squadron suffered heavily due to German attacks on their base at Plivot. *IWM*

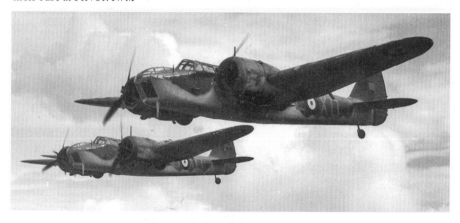

Tragic remnants of a 53 Squadron Blenheim IV at Poix.

Imperative it was that two 370-foot-long bridges over the Albert Canal were destroyed to slow the German advance. So heavily were they AA gun defended that AOC AASF called for six volunteer crews to undertake the perilous mission. From his depleted Battle squadrons he chose No 12, 'The Dirty Dozen', for what became the squadron's most memorable operation in their history.

On 13 May six Defiants left Martlesham Heath flying 264 Squadrons' first operation. Bf 109s and 110s shot down five, Pilot Officer G E Chandler's aircraft crashing behind Gedring Barracks, Breda. *via Gerrit J Zwanenburg*

Enormous courage was shown by thousands in 1940. One of the most famous operations during the fight for France was flown by 12 Squadron against two bridges over the Albert Canal. Battle III P2332 flown by Thomas was downed reasonably intact alongside the Maastricht – Tongres road, near the Vroehoven Bridge. *12 Squadron*

P2332 was intact, but not for very long because souvenir hunters soon arrived.

In response the entire squadron volunteered. Since six crews were needed, the first six on the duty roster were chosen. Fg Off N. M. Thomas was to lead three to bring down the concrete Vroenhoven bridge on the Maastricht-Tongres road, and 21-year-old Fg Off D. E. Garland would head the trio assaulting the metal Veldwezelt bridge on the Maastricht-Hasselt road.

The leaders discussed tactics, Thomas favouring a shallow dive attack, and Garland a very low-level assault. From the trio led by Thomas, one had to abort with hydraulics unserviceable. The others, Thomas in P2332 PH-F and Plt Off T. D. H. Davy in L5241 PH-G, dive-bombed the bridge from 6,000 feet, damaged it, and encountered flak that brought down Thomas. Davy's aircraft (L5241 PH-G), although damaged, landed short of fuel near base, Amifontaine, to where it was later flown.

Garland (flying P2204 PH-K) and his two companions, Plt Off I. A. McIntosh (L5439 PH-N) and Sgt Marland (L5227 PH-J), went in very low. They damaged the bridge but were all shot down near the target. While McIntosh and crew were being taken into captivity, the western end of the bridge rose skywards, probably as a result of Garland's attack.

Awards of the Victoria Cross, made sparingly, were posthumously given to Fg Off Garland and to Sgt T. Gray to mark the courage of all who participated. It was, perhaps, unfair that the third member of Garland's crew, LAC L. R. Reynolds, did not receive the award. He was one of those very courageous Leading Aircraftsmen who volunteered for aircrew duty for a small extra pittance.

The key to the entire blitzkrieg was the Schutzenregiment's advance through the Ardennes forest to cross the River Meuse. It took German forces commanded by Erwin Rommel and Heinz Guderian just 2½ days to reach the river. During late afternoon of the 12th they tried to cross the Meuse at Dinant, but as tanks of the 7th Panzer Regiment approached the bridge it was blown up. Some 7km away to the north, near Yvoir, the 31st Panzer Regiment's first vehicle was almost across this other bridge when it was blown by Belgian gunfire. When other Panzers tried to cross via a railway bridge near Houx, the Belgians beat them back. The Germans eventually found two suitable points for crossing the river using small boats. Only fifteen out of ninety-six managed to complete a crossing, but once there they quickly consolidated their position while the French commanders literally slept. Early on the 13th intensive attacks, particularly by Stukas, were made upon the French, whose force included many older men. Failure to prevent a Meuse crossing was a mighty blunder.

Unfortunately, the weather on the 13th was poor. There was only one small AASF operation, and none by 2 Group. Ju 87 Stukas, however, repeatedly aided German forces crossing the Meuse, and the 13th Panzer Group Kleist – continuously supported by Do 17s of KG 2, He 111s of KG 27 and helped by KG 3's Do 17s – broke through the French lines. This major diversion from the traditional route through Flanders prompted claims that the Germans were cheating! Discovering French reinforcements coming from the outflanked Maginot Line, German bombers attacked the rail route used.

King's Message to Three Rulers: 12 May

'The King expresses his sympathy for the brutal and wholly unwarranted German invasion, his disgust at this crime and his admiration for the gallant resistance which Belgium and Holland are putting up. I have complete faith that together our armies will again prevail, and I am confident that Belgium and Holland will remain the homes of free men.'

Heinkel He 111s of KG 54 during the afternoon of 13 May brutally destroyed the civilian heart of Rotterdam, killing some 900 inhabitants and wiping out 20,000 dwellings in one the war's most heinous deeds which virtually imposed Dutch surrender.

During the afternoon of the 13th the Luftwaffe's KG 54 delivered a devastating raid upon central Rotterdam, murdering more than 1,000 civilians, destroying 20,000 buildings and making 78,000 civilians homeless. So gruesome was the blow that early on the 14th Dutch forces laid down their arms to avoid a repetition.

In the House of Commons on Monday 13 May Churchill spoke of his formation of a new Government, and stated that all posts should be filled in a single day. 'We are in action at many other points in Norway and Holland,' he continued, 'and we have to be prepared in the Mediterranean. In the air, the battle is continuous, and many preparations have to be made here at home. I have nothing to offer but blood, toil, tears and sweat. If you ask what is our aim, I can answer in one word – it is victory'.

German communiqué: 13 May

German troops have entered the town of Liège and since this morning the swastika has been flying over the cathedral.

At 05.45 on 14 May the Germans managed to place a strong pontoon bridge across the Meuse at Sedan. It was attacked by ten Battles. All returned but, when French bombers attacked around noon, fighters shot down most of them. With the enemy now streaming across the Meuse, and a 3-mile-wide bridgehead established, the AASF mounted a mid-afternoon attack on the pontoons, incurring staggering losses. From seventy-one Battle sorties, forty failed to return, shot down mainly by Messerschmitts. Carnage around Sedan was far from complete. In the evening 2 Group Blenheims attacked, 107 Squadron losing only one of its six aircraft because Hurricanes provided protection. A dozen of No 110 Squadron followed, and this time, once the flak had forced their formation apart, Bf 109s struck. Five Blenheims fell away in flames. Last in came 21 Squadron, which lost two crews during an attack on woodland near Givons. Fg Off Sarll, a participant, later recalled that, 'Anyone who did not experience what we were called upon to perform this day, could ever visualise the tremendous courage of our people, so many of whom died.' Hardship in the 21st century surely pales to little when compared with what was experienced by so very many young people in the war years.

French forces reorganised after falling back, but their flank attacks failed and late on the 14th French troops withdrew from the Gembloux gap, bringing a parlous situation. To maintain a defensive line the BEF also needed to start withdrawal to the River Escaut. By late on the 16th Kleist's Panzers were racing into France on a 3-mile front, and faster after the BEF was hammered around Louvain.

The first two Dewoitine D.520 squadrons entered battle on 13 May and others were quickly brought into action too late.

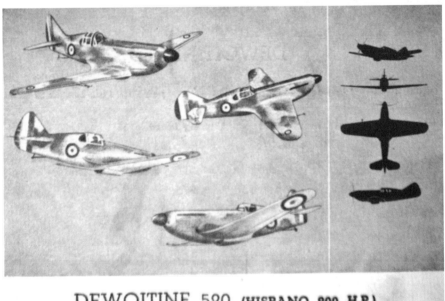

DEWOITINE 520 (HISPANO 900 H.P.)

The manoeuvrable D.520 armed with a 20mm cannon and four 7.5mm cannon had a top speed of 328 mph at 20,000ft making it more than the equal of the Hurricane.

There were ten Hurricane squadrons in France on 10 May and the French wanted far more, and additional AA guns. On the 13th thirty-two Hurricanes were dispatched to Field Force France and next day the French pleaded for ten more squadrons of Hurricanes. The British Government, although sympathetic, stalled. Air Chief Marshal Dowding reminded the politicians that since September 1939 maintaining just four fighter squadrons in France had cost the equivalent of a dozen Hurricane squadrons. However many Hurricanes were dispatched to France, he stated, it could not ensure success. Dowding was reported as privately saying that 'it's like pouring water into the sands of the desert ... we've slender hope of getting anyone back.' Publicly he said, 'The continued existence of the nation, and all its services, depends upon the Royal Navy and Fighter Command.'

You ask, what is our policy? I will say: It is to wage war, by sea, land and air, with all our might and all the strength that God can give us: to wage war against a monstrous tyranny, never surpassed in the dark, lamentable catalogue of human crime. That is our policy.

You ask, what is our aim? I can answer in one word: Victory. Victory at all costs, victory in spite of all terror; victory, however long and hard the road may be; for without victory there is no survival.

Winston Churchill, 13 May 1940

Before the War Cabinet on 15 May ACM Hugh Dowding presented his case, stressing that dispatch of more Hurricanes to France could result in a disastrous loss. Dowding said that he would rather his force faced the expected Luftwaffe response to any RAF bombing of Germany than lose any more squadrons to France.

Dowding's statement, the bombardment of Rotterdam's civilians, and the speed with which German forces were advancing into France, tipped Britain's War Cabinet into sanctioning RAF Bomber Command's launch of its coveted strategic bombing offensive. Targets east of the Rhine, in particular oil targets in the Ruhr, would suffer. Possibly – for finding them in darkness was no small task. After three nights the bombers resumed tactical employment.

Although this example took no part in the 1940 war, The Fighter Collection at Duxford holds a Curtiss Hawk 75 realistically representing a 1940 Armée de l'Air example.

Curtiss Hawk 75s acquitted themselves well in the fight, although over 30 were battle casualties. The Fighter Collection's toned-down P-36 presents, in the 2000s, a more realistic appearance than shown by many warbirds.

Despite Dowding's plea, the War Cabinet, aware of the plight of the French, decided to release Hurricanes – and irreplaceable pilots – at eight half-squadron strength, which drastically reduced Fighter Command's strength. Replacement aircraft could be built, but training pilots to operate them would take time. They were already in very short supply.

Travelling in 24 Squadron Flamingo R2764, Mr Churchill flew to Paris on the 15th.. All he heard saddened him, for he felt deeply for France. 'We just cannot desert our ally,' he said, and very late that day the Cabinet decided they must send six more Hurricane squadrons to France.

That was impracticable. There were no longer six complete Hurricane squadrons in Fighter Command, and no French airfields available to them. Instead, six Hurricane squadrons moved to advanced bases in Kent. Three would fly to France early each morning, the other three replacing them at midday.

Home air defence was mainly reliant upon the Hawker Hurricane and long established famous squadrons like No 56. One of their Hurricanes, P-Peter N2479, was North Weald based until 13 May then used by 213 Squadron until August when it was taken over by 6 OTU which trained fighter pilots.

Depletion and disruption of the Home Force against his advice deeply troubled Dowding, who told the War Cabinet of a whole Hurricane squadron in France being wiped out in 96 hours. He reminded them that his Command had only half the number of squadrons it needed. In a letter he wrote, 'I believe that, if an adequate fighter force is kept in this country, if the Fleet remains in being, and if Home Forces are organised to resist invasion, we should be able to carry on the war single-handed for some time, if not indefinitely. But if the Home Defence Force is drained away in desperate attempts to remedy the situation in France, defeat in France will involve the final, complete and irremediable defeat of this country.' His was a most accurate assessment.

Visitors to recent 'Flying Legends' shows at Duxford have been able to see a Morane Saulnier MS 406C. Although an ex-Swiss Air Force machine, it features the markings of a 1940 Armée de l'Air example. MS 406s, top speed 302mph at 16,400 ft, armed 18 of their squadrons. The MS406 carried a 20mm cannon and two 7.5mm machine guns and was being phased out of service when the blitz opened.

Meanwhile, Royal Air Force day-bomber support for France was continuing unabated despite hideous engagements producing horrendous losses. At dawn on 17 May twelve crews of Watton's 82 Squadron headed for Gembloux, now a supply centre for the Panzer advance. Even XV Squadron, which had suffered so heavily, insisted on having 'another go', and lost three of six crews attacking troops near Le Cateaux. Two of their remaining Blenheims were very badly damaged, and Fg Off Leonard Trent, another future VC recipient, piloted one that force-landed in France. Awaiting repair of P6913, he and his two companions headed for a cafe in Poix. Bad news suddenly burst upon them – Germans were approaching! Quickly, they made for the vault, filled bags with fine bottled liquid, commandeered a Citroen and hastened to their Blenheim. Despite a large hole in its wing, they flew it into darkness, concluding it would be safest to cross the coast over Norfolk. Soon lost, they roamed until airfield landing lights suddenly appeared, leading them to sanctuary at Martlesham Heath.

There was no way in which the Panzer advance into France could now be halted. Although very moved by all he heard, on 19 May Churchill decided that however strong the French cry, no more fighter squadrons must leave Britain, and the War Cabinet concurred. Indicative of the cost of the supreme effort since 10 May, 2 Group had lost 108 men killed, many had been grievously wounded, and forty-four Blenheims lost. Others were beyond repair.

Columns of German armoured fighting vehicles covered 200 miles in ten days. Abbeville was reached on the 20th, then the advance wheeled north. On 21 May the BEF and the Allies found themselves in a pocket, cut off from the main French force behind the approximate line Ghent-Tournai-Arras-St Pol and the Somme estuary. Enemy presence was so extensive that bombing could achieve little, losses would be high and targeting details were too fast outdated. By the 22nd German troops were closing on Boulogne. The Allied salient at Arras collapsed late on 23 May, and the Belgian Army was cut off from the BEF north of the Lys. The French could not close the very wide gap, and the enemy was already across the St Omer-Aire Canal. On the 26th Calais fell.

A varied assortment of French aircraft were captured at Abbeville. Included were a Potez 63-11 (right), two Mureaux reconnaissance parasol monoplanes and a Nieuport Delage fighter trainer (bottom right)

I speak to you for the first time as Prime Minister at a solemn hour in the life of our country, of our Empire, of our Allies, and, above all, of the cause of freedom... Today is Trinity Sunday. Centuries ago words were written to be a call and a spur to the faithful servants of truth and justice. 'Arm yourselves, and be ye men of valour, and be in readiness for the conflict; for it is better for us to perish in battle than to look upon the outrage of our nation and our altars. As the Will of God is in Heaven, even so let it be.'

Winston Churchill, 19 May 1940

Surrounded within a 127-mile-long perimeter, there was no land escape for the BEF. Retrieval could only be from Dunkirk's port and beach. The Germans wrongly assumed that evacuation would take place through the port of Antwerp. Unexpectedly, German High Command ordered the advance to pause on 26 May to allow support and stores to reach the advanced forces to permit further penetration into France. Lord Gort, the BEF commander, strengthened the perimeter line along the Ar, Scarpe and Yser, beyond which lay terrain unsuitable for German tracked vehicles. Goering's vaunted Luftwaffe was now ordered to destroy the BEF. It was a mighty blunder, for the German Air Force was not that capable.

The BEF could escape to England only if RAF fighters prevented the Luftwaffe from carrying out its orders. The perimeter would need to be held long enough and RAF bombers would have to pound the surrounding German forces to lessen their bombardment of Dunkirk and its beach.

Evacuation meant conveying across the English Channel, in the face of constant attack, far in excess of a quarter of a million men. Nevertheless, a chance was decided upon, and at 18.57 on 26 May, under the control of Vice-Admiral Ramsey,

Once the Dunkirk evacuation was under way RAF fighters – including Hurricanes of No 3 Squadron – provided day long protection.

Operation 'Dynamo' was launched. A large array of little ships from 9 feet to 30 feet long, and mostly civilian-manned by volunteers unaware of what was to be expected of them, was gathered to cross the English Channel. In the face of enemy attack they were to convey soldiers from Dunkirk beach to waiting ships, which would then bring them to Britain. For as long as practicable larger ships would berth by the Mole from where troops would also board. Home-based fighters would, in relays, provide dawn-to-dusk cover to prevent, as much as possible, the Luftwaffe from attacking the evacuation.

At daybreak on the 28th the Luftwaffe started in earnest to attack the assembling forces, giving Dowding an enormous challenge. Losing a complete army would mean total defeat. Fighters in No 11 Group protecting South East England were too few in number to allow very large-scale protective patrols, but denuding other parts of the country would have been foolish. German bombers were already carrying out night operations over the UK using captured airfields, and short-range German fighters were moving west to have longer over target areas.

Dowding ordered AVM Keith Park, AOC 11 Group, to mount two-squadron patrols from an eighteen-squadron force, leaving the briefest intervals between patrols. On 29 May Park increased the operating force to four-squadron strength at peak evacuation times. Blenheims attacked the encircling Germans by day, and on the 31st made a great effort to stop enemy troops from shortening the 5-mile perimeter containment line.

New Zealander Air Marshal Keith Park, commander of No 11 (Fighter Group). *(RNZAF)*

Upon Dunkirk Plage, a mere nine months before, children had played in extreme delight. Surely lovers had done what lovers do among its fringing sea grass and sand mounds, now providing trifling protection for soldiers of the BEF. That same shore – soon much blood-stained – was now the stage for a terrifying performance. To endure for days amid the dying, wounded, thirsty and helpless, while Stukas screamed, medium bombers murdered and strafing 109s took out many of the helpless, must have been as bad as life can get.

'Where's the RAF?' thousands cried when yet again an attacker performed an act of destruction. The answer was out of view, high above, where pilots of Fighter Command, mostly in Hurricanes, and at last a few in Spitfires, were trying so hard to help. That was only just effective enough to allow daylight evacuation to proceed.

Retrieving a third of a million men from under the nose of the mighty German war machine was a miraculous feat. The emotional distress involved in leaving close buddies to fate uncertain tore at the hearts of thousands. Many spent hours standing in long, snaking columns, shivering in cold water chest deep, waiting for the little ships to snatch them from death. Not until they were on home ground were they safe from a watery grave.

A precise total of 338,226 were rescued from Dunkirk, including 224,585 British the rest Belgian and French. Royal Navy ships involved numbered 222; others totalled 665. More men were rescued from Calais before that town fell on 26 May, and others – under German attack – came from Boulogne.

I had succeeded generally in keeping the Spitfire squadrons out of the Continental fighting. The reason for this was that the supply situation was so bad that they could not have maintained their existence in face of the Aircraft Casualty Rate experienced in France.

When the Dunkerque evacuation was complete I had only three Day-Fighting Squadrons which had not been engaged in Continental fighting, and twelve squadrons were in the line for the second time after having been withdrawn to rest and re-form.

I was responsible for the Air Defence of Great Britain, and I saw my resources slipping away like sand in an hour glass.

Air Chief Marshal Sir Hugh Dowding, Commander-in-Chief Fighter Command

Morale was deeply dented, many of the men on reaching England revealing nothing of their ordeals. They didn't need to: their untidy torn uniforms, often stained, revealed sufficient. Most had neither washed nor shaved for days, were very hungry, and still dazed. Nevertheless, they were not a completely broken force, and in a surprisingly short time they gathered in a new, vastly experienced and more mobile Army. My recollection from those tragic days is of a quiet sullen brooding, an eerie sensation that seemed all-engulfing. Surprisingly, the evacuation, first seen

Ships evacuating the BEF across the Channel provided tempting targets.

as a miracle, came to be seen as a victory of sorts. The disaster quietly sired a steely determination to achieve victory, impossible as that then seemed. Every adult I encountered expressed a quiet, calculated intent to avenge what had befallen across the Channel. Surrender was unthinkable.

The cost to the RAF during 'Dynamo' was high. Between 27 May and 3 June 177 RAF aircraft had been destroyed or very seriously damaged. The German loss of 240 was higher than believed at the time.

There were few 3.7in AA guns defending Dunkirk's shore.

Following the Dunkirk evacuation, No 2 Group bombed German columns thrusting into France. Evacuation also took place from southern France, and on 1 June the Orient liner *Orford*, 20,043grt, was bombed and set on fire off Toulon. In a back-stabbing act, Italy declared war on the Allies on 10 June, and ten days later occupied an area around Nice. In 1940, a time when few had travelled and many not even beyond the outskirts of their home town, Italy was a land whose joyous people were viewed with some disdain. Gondoliers, ice cream vendors, operatic singers they certainly were, but warriors? Probably not since Roman times! For the French the possibility of such an invader advancing into their land was terrible to even contemplate.

We shall go on to the end. We shall fight in France, we shall fight on the seas and oceans, we shall fight with growing confidence and growing strength in the air, we shall defend our island, whatever the cost may be. We shall fight on the beaches, we shall fight on the landing grounds, we shall fight in the fields and in the streets, we shall fight in the hills; we shall never surrender.

Winston Churchill, 4 June 1940

For the British to respond was difficult, except by opening a front in the Mediterranean theatre. That problem was solved in the North African desert. In the meantime two Wellington squadrons, Nos 99 and 149, flew to Salon from where, on 15 June, they first attempted bombing Italy, despite fears of retaliatory raids upon France. They were joined in their endeavour by Whitleys drawn from five squadrons and operating from the Channel Islands. Their crews faced, for the first time, the demanding transit or circumnavigation at night of a perilous mountainous region, and twenty-three of them were forced back by electrical storms and icing above a mere 10,000 feet. Among those flying that night was the well-known future pathfinder, Sqn Ldr Mahaddie.

Meanwhile, German forces were thrusting deep into France, pushing aside her demoralised forces. On 14 June, with much ceremony, militancy and jubilation, they entered Paris without a fight because the French did not want to see such a precious jewel damaged. Its fall was highly symbolic; Paris was the very essence of France. Those who knew her loved Paris dearly, and impressions of the fair city abounded. The Eiffel Tower, the 'Golden Arrow' hauled by a Southern Railway 'Schools' Class loco or an equally impressive baffle-plated SNCF 'Pacific', cross-Channel steamers like the *Canterbury*, flying from Croydon, Maurice Chevalier, croissants, Notre Dame, Sacré Coeur, the Champs Élysées, l'Arc de Triomphe and, of course, the Follies and the desirable mademoiselles, all combined to mean 'Paris', which in style and sentimentality was unequalled by any other city. For millions who had never been there, Paris was just as adorable. On the day she fell I know of many who were deeply distressed, just like me! Not surprisingly, there soon came a commemorative, memorable song:

'The last time saw Paris, her heart was warm and gay,
I heard the laughter of her heart in ev'ry street café;
The last time I saw Paris, her trees were dressed for spring,
And lovers walked beneath those trees and birds found songs to sing.
I dodged the same old taxi cabs that I had dodged for years,
The chorus of their squeaky horns was music to my ears.
The last time I saw Paris, her heart was warm and gay,
No matter how they change her, I'll remember her this way.'

(Words Oscar Hammerstein II, music Jerome Kern, T. B. Harms, 1940)

The plight of France fast worsened. After fighting on, the British 51st Highland Division was evacuated between 15 and 18 June among 30,000 troops taken from Cherbourg and 11,000 from Le Havre, St Malo and Brest. The largest late evacuation was of 57,000 personnel from St Nazaire. On the 17th the Cunarder *Lancastria* anchored some 3 miles off the port and, carrying possibly as many as 9,000 troops, was dive-bombed and sunk, resulting in one of the greatest losses at sea during the war. More than 2,000 died, among them personnel of 98 Squadron. A leather armchair from the ship found floating was, for very many years, a precious item in the study of the Head of the Air Historical Branch in London.

On 18-19 June the French Fleet sailed from Toulon to Casablanca and Oran. Then, on 22 June, the French signed a dreadfully humiliating surrender document, and in the same railway carriage at Compiegne where in 1918 the Allies received the German surrender. The armistice became effective on 25 June, the French Government accepting an agreement splitting France into two regions, half German controlled and the rest governed from Vichy by aged First World War hero Marshal Petain, who was now regarded as less of a hero.

Remaining Fairey Battles had flown home on 15 June, the Salon Wellingtons two days later. On many airfields in the east and the Midlands, one saw small groups of Battles mainly in deplorable state. No 1 Group needed to be completely rebuilt. In 2 Group a host of pre-war highly talented and experienced fliers had died. The hefty Lysanders, far too big for army co-operation duty, came home to patrol the coastline. Each Hurricane retrieved was now vital for our survival.

For the tough battle ahead we now had two advantages over Hitler and his 'Narzeese'. One was called Dowding, the other, our greatest leader ever, a fellow so aptly called 'Winnie'. Led by someone with a name so akin to victory, how could we possibly lose?

As early as 17 May the Luftwaffe had fighters based at Charleville, to where Ju 52s flew in supplies and fuel, for the Meuse crossings were already choked. A tank depot was also established.

Fliegergruppe II lost more aircraft on 27 May than on any other day of the campaign. German tank losses were also considerable, for seventy-three of the 2,574 in use on 10 May were eventually destroyed.

Losses during the RAF's stay and involvement in France

Aircraft that failed to return or were written off due to severe battle damage – AHB summary

		9 September 1939 to 9 May 1940	10 May to 20 June 1940
AASF	Hurricane	21	44
	Battle	8	115
	Blenheim	0	22
RAF Air Component	Hurricane	8	200
	Blenheim	21	34
	Lysander	0	3

Totals

Bomber Command	162 aircraft
Coastal Command	60 aircraft
Fighter Command	214 aircraft

		26 May 1940 to 4 June 1940 (Operation 'Dynamo')
Fighter Command	Spitfire	46
	Hurricane	52
	Defiant	8
Bomber Command	Blenheim	7
	Hampden	4
	Wellington	7
	Whitley	2
AASF	Battle	10
	Blenheim	7
	Hurricane	10
	Lysander	15
Coastal Command	Anson	5
	Beaufort	1
	Blenheim	6
	Hudson	1

Chapter 5

What's going on?

Until the night of 10 May, when twenty 50kg HEs were unloaded over the Bridge Blean rural district of Kent, the only bombs to land on Britain since the First World War fell on Orkney. Three nights later one exploded at Swanage and, on the 21st, eight at Eastleigh, Hampshire. Two fell the next night on Romney Marsh. On 22 May East Anglia received its first, which exploded near Butley church by what was later RAF Bentwaters. That night sixteen HEs also fell in the Felixstowe area. These incidents hardly constituted an organised bombing campaign.

That started on 24/25 May when Heinkel He 111s of KG 27, operating from western Germany, attacked targets in East and North East England. Five HEs fell on Catterick's landing ground, sixteen in the Holderness district, two on industrial Middlesbrough. Close to RAF West Raynham, Norfolk, a stick of eighteen 50kg HEs became the largest load yet delivered at one time. Another bomb exploded near Harleston, and two at Willow Farm, Langley, Loddon, killing a cow. Animals suffered throughout Europe just like humans.

Luftwaffe occupation of captured airfields brought an alarming and extensive problem for Fighter Command, and greatly increased the invasion threat. Luftwaffe short-range bombers were now only an hour away from London, the world's largest and most tempting target. They could outflank Britain's defences by approaching

Spitfires in traditional battle formation, altered through combat experience.

From France, the Germans took over the Channel Islands, where they requisitioned local transport as necessary. This Messerschmitt Bf 109E of JG 53 at Guernsey Airport being refuelled from petrol drums aboard Austin truck '5377' belongs to JG 53. (Bundesarchiv)

from the west, seriously interfere with shipping, and devastate vital ports on Merseyside, at Bristol and in South Wales. Fighter Command needed strengthening fast, its layout and equipment revised in responding to new threats.

An encouraging indicator towards the future reached 25 Squadron at North Weald on 30 May. It was the second prototype Westland Whirlwind fighter, L6845, brought along for assessment. Few aeroplanes have aroused the fascination afforded by this radical design. Twin-engined, tailplane carried high, teardrop canopy, the unusual

The second Westland Whirlwind prototype L6845 joined No 25 Squadron on 30 May 1940 reportedly wearing unusual red and yellow safety colouring never confirmed. On 7 July it was transferred to 263 Squadron in Scotland remaining with them until June 1941.

form was intended to be the RAF's standard cannon-armed fighter, and in June the first two production examples joined it. The trio shuttled between base and Debden. First flown on 11 October 1938, the Whirlwind encountered many technical snags and was unfortunately powered by Rolls-Royce Peregrine engines. Developing the Merlin, and trying to make the Vulture into a successful 2,000hp engine, Rolls-Royce neglected the Peregrine, production of which was halted. On 12 June 1940 No 263 Squadron reformed after its Norwegian mauling at Drem, moved to Grangemouth on 28 June, then took over Whirlwind service development from 25 Squadron.

Meanwhile small-scale night bombing continued. On 2 June, at Strumpshaw, a Norfolk civilian became the first East Anglian to be seriously injured, during a night raid on Mildenhall by He 111s. Their twenty-three 50kg HEs fell wide.

Ideal conditions late on 5 June brought the busiest night so far, enemy aircraft operating between the Orkneys and the Isle of Wight. By dawn thirty marauding bombers had generated 134 overland raid tracks, ports and airfields providing their main interest. Two bombs fell near Wick, another near Horsham St Faith, six at Driffield. By its unusually smooth engine sound, I felt certain a Ju 88 unloaded a shoal of incendiaries over New Farm, Newton, near Duxford. Morning saw a swarm of officials examining the scene. Little was known about the means of delivering the bombs, and how many had fallen. By midday the event had changed into a fine picnic for important people enjoying the pleasant countryside! More fire bombs had fallen around Gainsborough and Tilbury, ten HEs at Peterborough, another fourteen at Louth. An innovation was the dropping of parachute flares over Stoke Holy Cross near Norwich, possibly the first to drift over Britain. An overall weapon load less than expected suggested that the Heinkels were engaged in something suspicious.

The initial conclusion was that raiders established their positions through bearings on M/F (Medium Frequency) radio beacons. Physicist Professor R. V. Jones, seconded to the Air Ministry, suspected that there was more to it. Among items examined in He 111 1H+AC of KG 26, brought down on 3 April 1940, were papers referring to

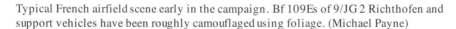

Typical French airfield scene early in the campaign. Bf 109Es of 9/JG 2 Richthofen and support vehicles have been roughly camouflaged using foliage. (Michael Payne)

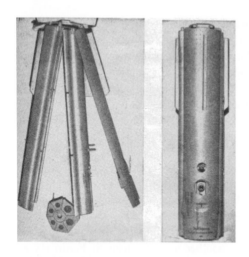

Incendiary bomb container Type BSK 36 (seen open left) was commonly used by the Luftwaffe during 1940. It carried 36 x 1kg incendiaries. An often unpainted container 3ft 7in long, it occupied the same bomb bay space as a 50kg HE bomb.

'Radio Beacon *Knickebein* from 0600 hours on 315'. Professor Jones had a hunch that German bombers flew along a short-wave beam from a beacon received by blind landing equipment in He 111s. Loads would be released just after reaching an intersection with a second beam. If so, the Luftwaffe could attack with some accuracy during darkness and bad weather – assuming the beams were correctly aligned.

On 6/7 June the Germans operated even more extensively, more than 170 tracks being plotted between Yorkshire and the South Coast. Aerodromes had certainly been targeted, for bombs fell near Beverley, Pocklington, Marham, Pulham, Upwood, Feltwell and Mildenhall. Most were still of the 50kg type, but a clutch of 250kg bombs was recorded at Bedfield, Suffolk. Next night Heinkel 111s again struck at bomber bases, including Honington, and major railway installations including Peterborough. Activity then tailed off, the lull lasting until 17 June.

Luftwaffe high explosive bombs used in 1940.

Top line left to right: commonly used SC/SD 50kg up to 45in long overall, 8in diameter. SC 250kg and SD 250kg top right. SC (*Spreng Cylindrisch*) were thinner steel cased, yellow marked weapons. SD (*Spreng Dickwandig*) type were more effective heavy splinter bombs identifiable by red markings painted usually on their tail vanes. Fuzing – complex and much varied – ranged from instant to long delay. A fall retarding *kopfring* disc sometimes encircled the nose.

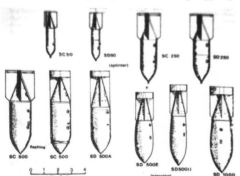

Bottom line: The left three were 500kg equivalents. The other three are armour piercing bombs the largest (right) being 1,000kg sometimes known as a PC *Panzer Cylindrisch* bomb. Armour piercing bombs wore blue striping. During the night blitz SC and SD 1,700kg, 1,800kg and 2,000kg bombs (not illustrated) were also used. A circular tail vane later became increasingly common.

The Blind Approach Training & Development Unit opened at Boscombe Down on 13 June 1940, commanded by Wg Cdr R. S. Blucke (who piloted the Heyford used for the first radar trial in February 1935). It was established with eight Ansons and three Whitleys 'to investigate signals under the code name Headache'. The first specially equipped Anson, N9945, was sent to Wyton on 19 June, followed by N9938 and L7983 the same day. The following night Flt Lt H. E. Bufton and Flt Lt Alway flew the first beam investigation sortie in N9945, to detect any active beam on a frequency to which a typical Lorenz receiver would be tuned. On the 21st Bufton and his observer Corporal Mackie, flying northerly at night from Wyton, crossed a beam near Spalding, detecting signal dots to the south and dashes to its north. They also found a second beam with dots north and dashes south. The beams, which intersected in the target area, were emitted from transmitters at Cleves and Bredstedt in Germany, and were set for an attack on Derby, home of Rolls-Royce and the Merlin engine. On the 22nd the pair flew N9945 again, and by the end of June the unit had flown for 59.15 hours. By then it was clear that German bombers relied upon beams for target-finding using adapted blind landing equipment. The task now would be to develop equipment to jam or 'bend' the beams, under the code name 'Aspirins'.

The moonlit 18/19 June had brought the largest night operation yet, bombs on Addington being the first to explode in Greater London. Sixteen He 111s of I/KG 27, twelve of II/KG 27, twelve of III/KG 27, sixteen of II/KG 4, and fifteen drawn from I and III/KG 4 operated, and 139 coastal entry tracks were recorded. The oil installation at Thameshaven was the main target for KG 4, while KG 27 was ordered to attack the LNER rail system in East Anglia along with East Anglian airfields. Some of the He 111s penetrated deeply, but most made shallow incursions. Some attacks were aimed at 3 Group Wellington bases – Marham, Honington, Mildenhall, Stradishall – and at Lincolnshire's Hampden stations. Alternatives were rail and industrial installations.

At 20 minutes to midnight a Heinkel 111, officially listed as one of KG 4 operating from Schiphol and entering from the north, made a shallow dive over Cambridge, released two bombs and, with a surge of engine power, climbed away. I shall never forget the screech of the bombs as they hurtled low overhead, one fitted with 'screamers' on its four fins. Our house shook for the first time to exploding bombs, the electric light swung merrily, the wooden window shutters vibrated for some seconds, and there was a slight detectable movement of air pressure. It happened so suddenly, so expectedly and on a beautiful, brightly moonlit June night. My mother's instant response was to make a cup of tea, which I initially thought an odd response to what was obviously happening quite near. It was the sort of response reproduced millions of times throughout the coming weeks.

Two bombs intended for Cambridge's extensive railway area had slammed, side by side, into a row of aged, small terraced houses in Vicarage Terrace. With many warnings and no activity, parents in the houses had, like many, left children asleep upstairs. In the most serious incident so far, nine civilians (three men, a woman and five children, including the Dear and Palmer children) had been killed, and ten people were injured. This was the largest number of casualties in one incident in the UK so far.

Two HE bombs which exploded on terraced houses in Vicarage Terrace, Cambridge, on 18/19 June 1940 resulted in the most serious loss of civilian life in an air raid so far. Destruction and collateral damage were quite breathtaking.

Officials investigated responses by ARP and medical teams. Damage to utilities and surrounding houses was very widespread. Were water and gas supplies rendered unsafe? If two bombs caused so much havoc, what would ten achieve? Damage was influenced by many factors – weapon case thickness, charge type, angle of approach, surface impact, proximity and confinement.

At Canvey Island/Thameshaven KG 4, trying hard to set fire to oil tanks, around 23.25 dropped forty HEs and incendiaries. By dawn incidents had occurred in at least eighteen areas as far apart as Settle, Strood, Bridlington and Chatham. In the Spilsby area, eleven out of twenty-four HEs were recorded as 'UX' (unexploded). Other bombs were reported from Rivenhall, Dunmow RD, Saffron Walden RD, Huntingdon RD and St Neots RD. One official count suggested that 127 HEs and fourteen UXHEs had been received by the time the 'All Clear' was sounded at 03.15.

An amazing feature of the night was the proven destruction of five He 111s, four of them intercepted in moonlight by fighters. Initial claims totalled eleven, of which two remained probables in additional to the confirmed. Plt Off Humphries of 29 Squadron, flying Blenheim 1(f) L1375, engaged an He 111, which, after further attention from a 74 Squadron Spitfire, crashed at Springfield Road, Chelmsford. Another 29 Squadron crew destroyed an He 111, but they did not return.

A remarkable engagement involved a Heinkel, a Spitfire, a Blenheim and searchlight crews. Four pilots of 19 Squadron, Duxford, took off soon after midnight to seek raiders. At 01.25 AA gunners at Wattisham fired at a Heinkel that, a few minutes later, dropped a salvo of bombs near Honington. Searchlights of 206 Coy illuminated it, then the German gunners tried to fire down the beams. Fg Off Petra, attracted by the activity, was soon following another He 111, 5J+AM, operating from Merville. It crossed the Norfolk coast at 16,000 feet and was repeatedly illuminated. As Petra located it, so did a Blenheim crew of 23 Squadron. Petra switched on his landing light to illuminate the bomber then opened fire. Immediately, 204 Searchlight Coy unfortunately lit the Spitfire, into which a Heinkel gunner poured enough fire to set it alight. Seriously burned, Petra baled out.

The drama was far from over, the bomber crew unloading seventeen 50kg HEs near Newmarket. Recovery being impossible, three of its crew parachuted to safety, leaving a dead colleague in the doomed Heinkel, which smashed into a field near the A11 close to the Balsham-Fulbourn road. Among the crew was an infantryman who said he had 'gone along for the experience'.

Yet another He 111 was engaged by a Blenheim of 23 Squadron, after which the fighter entered an uncontrollable spin. Its navigator baled out only to be instantly killed by a propeller. The gunner was killed in the crash and only the pilot survived. It is possible that the Heinkel was the one that ditched off Margate. There was much activity off Felixstowe, several claims resulting. One confirmed was awarded to AA gunners at Harwich. To close this remarkable night, the last He 111 to leave our shores dropped seventeen bombs around Clacton at 02.50. Two fell on marshland, an empty house in Salisbury Road received a direct hit, many fell on fields at Giles Farm, and others at Thorpe.

One bomb dropped on Vicarage Terrace had 'screamers' attached to the tail vanes, 11in long metal tubes to which a 4in nose cone was attached. The piercing scream from these organ pipes was intended to generate terror.

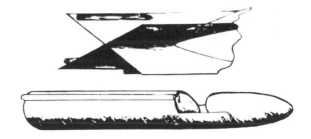

Another busy night was 21/22 June. Some eighty He 111s operated, the first bombing Parkeston Quay. Another 26 incidents followed in East Anglia, where ten HEs, the first at Ipswich, had 'organ pipe' whistling terror devices attached to their tails. In a night of 'novelties', the first 'oil bombs' fell at Melton Ross, near Brigg, Lincolnshire, and also at Rede, Suffolk. The belief was that FLAM C250 'oil bombs' might be used to set cereal crops alight. Actually, the explosive within was designed to blast a way into a building before the incendiary content ignited inflammatory liquid in the 50kg bomb case.

On most days a 'Zenit' weather-reporting sortie was flown along the East Anglian coast as far as Scotland. A flurry of such activity on 24 June preceded night operations over southern England by about sixty He 111s. Bristol received its first raid, a clothing factory at Knowle was demolished, twenty-three houses were hit, a school was set on fire and a soap factory damaged in the Old Market Street area. Five people died as a result of the listed 108 incendiaries and twenty HEs delivered. Other raiders penetrated to Liverpool, and in London there were five deaths due to shock when air raid sirens wailed.

So far mainly ineffective raids had hit widespread targets. A more concentrated three-phase operation by about seventy bombers started just before midnight on 25 June. Anti-aircraft guns shattered the sky over Bristol, Portsmouth and Southampton, gunners loosing off 141 rounds. Sharp cracks caused by shell bursts were very alarming, especially when heard for the first time. The following rain of hot shrapnel was quite disturbing, too. AA guns in use were either elderly 3-inch, hefty 4.5-inch or more usually 1934 Barrow-designed Vickers 3.7-inch types. The latter fired a 43.1-inch-long shell boosted by 2lb 5oz of TNT, and weighed 46lb 4oz when complete. Unforgettable were displays by the 90cm, 12.5 million candlepower searchlight beams. Each Regiment operated ninety-six searchlights, each light theoretically spaced 6,000 yards from another, allowing a cone of three beams to hold an aircraft then pass it to the next trio. Searchlights and crews at tented sites were common throughout much of Britain.

By the end of June, Heinkels, usually operating at around 10,000 feet – too low for their safety – had performed their 'oom-pahing' engine overture to much of Britain. Thirteen RAF airfields, sixteen industrial plants and fourteen port areas had been targeted, but little lasting damage was done. There had been twenty-two night

Many elderly 3-inch naval (emplaced) guns served as antiaircraft guns. An example photographed at Portland 26 July 1940. *IWM*

combats following searchlight illumination, and eleven German bombers had been brought down in June. There might have been more had airborne interception (AI) radar been developed faster for fighters, together with gun-laying radar for the AA forces being first tried at Liverpool. Most development surrounded ground-based early warning radar. Air raid sirens had been sounded too widely – now the alarm would wail when raiders were likely to visit a specific area.

When shall we sound the siren?

The British Isles were divided into about 130 'Warning Districts', a layout based upon the public telephone system. Raids were plotted on a map at HQ Fighter Command, and when a raid was within 20 minutes of a district the Air Raid Warning Officer telephoned a message through Trunk Exchanges in London, Liverpool or Glasgow. From these it passed to relevant districts who notified Police, Fire, hospitals, etc. This was called the 'Yellow Warning'. If a District was under threat, 5 minutes later a 'Red Warning' would cause sirens to sound. 'Green' meant 'All Clear'. At night, when essential lights remained on in places such as docks, railyards, etc, another warning, 'Purple', was used. It meant that all lights externally visible should be doused, and was often in force after the 'All Clear' sounded.

A higher price than they realised had been paid by the Luftwaffe for their night jaunts. On their second flight, Flight Lieutenant H. E. Bufton with Corporal Mackie, had discovered two radio navigation narrow beams. Professor Jones again emphasised the serious implications. Accurate night attacks would be possible on almost any place in Britain, particularly industrial centres and vital ports, many in the less well defended western half of the country.

By midsummer 1940 a German invasion seemed more a certainty than a possibility. The nation had become aware that the Royal Navy was not as invincible as was popularly thought, and that starvation by blockade was possible. Although Britain possessed ten battleships and three battle cruisers, only three of those had been built since the 1914-18 war, and only five were at one time in home waters. Ranged against our Navy was a modern, quite powerful yet already hard-hit smaller German surface fleet now supplemented by modern Italian warships. It was under the sea that the chief adversary roamed, the submarine, and that was difficult to defeat.

The War Cabinet's assessment was that effective air defence must be the No 1 priority. After reviewing the events so far, they concluded that an aerial knockout blow was probably not possible, that west coast ports could probably be kept open – just – and that with RAF intervention an invasion would prove difficult and costly. All hinged upon successful air defence of the entire country.

One invasion tactic it was thought the Germans might contemplate was night seizure by some 5,000 paratroops of seven vital fighter aerodromes in the South East. Landings would then be made upon them at dawn by troop transports and even bomber aircraft. Meanwhile, some 20,000 troops would make a beach assault. Reinforcements would arrive under strong air cover during daylight hours.

To counter that threat eight Army divisions were ordered to man coastal defences in depth. By mid-June 1940 786 field guns were in place, either by likely landing places, or inland to guard against any airborne forces landed to take coastal defence forces from the rear. The Army had not as yet been trained to cope with fast-changing situations. Across East Anglia five defence lines included a giant, deep and wide ditch – the 'Eastern Tank Trap' – dug by civilians in the evenings and soldiers at any time. All lines were established ahead of the main GHQ line. Another three in the South East provided for the defence of London. These defences in depth would prevent any breakdown in law and order. Behind them, from mid-June, were three mobile infantry divisions, centrally held. Churchill wanted 10,000 men to be available within 6 hours to reinforce any point where the enemy had landed, and groups of 20,000 ready to react as a mobile force, though, as Ironside pointed out, his troops were not trained for such activities. Tanks of the 1st Armoured Division would rush forward where needed, but it seems unlikely they would have had the necessary mobility and firepower to be of much value. The 2nd Armoured Division, with more than 150 tanks, was held in central western East Anglia to react towards the coast as necessary.

By late June more than 150,000 troops and civilians were preparing defences too often badly placed or wrongly orchestrated. East and South Coast beaches were mined during June and July 1940. Simple wire net booms were floated offshore and mines attached to scaffolding, to discourage the use of landing craft. A floating minefield sealed off The Wash, and many manned road-blocks were built on routes leading from the shore. Pleasure piers had their centre sections demolished to prevent their use as jetties. Within a host of concrete pillboxes stores of hand grenades and so-called 'sticky bombs' were established for use by the Local Defence Volunteers (LDV),

Tanks of the 5th Royal Tank Regiment, 3rd Armoured Brigade, 1st Armoured Division passing through Thursley, Sussex. *IWM*

...the Battle of France is over. I expect that the Battle of Britain is about to begin. Upon this battle depends the survival of Christian civilisation. Upon it depends our own British life, and the long continuity of our institutions and our Empire. The whole fury and might of the enemy must very soon be turned upon us. Hitler knows that he will have to break us in this island or lose the war. If we can stand up to him, all Europe may be free and the life of the world may move forward into broad, sunlit uplands. But if we fail, then the whole world – including the United States, including all that we have known and cared for – will sink into the abyss of a new dark age made more sinister, and perhaps more protracted, by the lights of perverted science. Let us therefore brace ourselves to our duties, and so bear ourselves that, if the British Empire and its Commonwealth last for a thousand years, men will still say 'This was their finest hour.'

Winston Churchill, 18 June 1940

whose task was to make life extremely unpleasant for the invaders. Had the enemy penetrated far he would have met Army reserves manning anti-tank defences and operating 167 anti-tank guns along the GHQ Line passing between natural high points from Middlesbrough to London.

With insufficient weapons, however, both the Army and the LDV would have had a hard fight. All told, the Army had operationally available fifty-two 81-pounder guns, eighty-seven 25-pounder guns, seventy-two 4.5-pounder guns and 167 anti-tank guns. Placed at its disposal were seven RAF squadrons, two operating Blenheims and the other five flying Lysanders.

Few around at the time failed to enjoy hot gossip, none of it more spine-chilling than that concerning plans to pour petrol on the sea, then set fire to it and cremate the invaders! Trials showed that releasing petrol onto the sea then igniting it was not as easy as the idea sounds, because of the action of the tide and motion of the waves. Eventually, petrol was used in land-based and relatively common defence works. Perforated pipes joined to disguised petrol tanks were laid alongside roads leading from the beaches. After turning on the flow, an LDV member was expected to hurl a lighted torch onto the petrol, more of which would flood anti-tank ditches, or flow from barrels onto the beaches themselves. Such gruesome activity was masterminded from June 1940 by the Petroleum Warfare Department.

Many critical areas remained undefended. When the military bastion of Dover came within range of German gunners at Framzelles in the Pas de Calais, it was they who largely controlled the Dover Straits. Dover's destroyers were forced to move to Portsmouth and Chatham, and British convoys had whenever possible to pass through the Straits in darkness. Few British guns had sufficient range to bombard enemy positions, such activity in any case being likely to bring unwanted retaliation. German guns and gunners had to be discouraged by the RAF – no easy task.

Harshly battered during the fight for France, the RAF, although it had lost around 1,000 aircraft, had survived more adequately equipped than the Army. Its losses were mainly of obsolete Battles and Hurricane fighters that could be replaced from reserves and ever-increasing production. German failure to destroy Britain's aircraft production sources early in the war was unquestionably a fundamental blunder.

Where did the first bombs fall?

ibs   1kg incendiary bombs
RD   Rural District
UD   Urban District (towns/cities unless otherwise stated)
Bracketed numbers are unexploded bombs additional to others

Bombs dropped

10 May		6 June		18/19 June	
Bridge Blean, Kent	20, ibs	East Kesteven RD	6 (2)	Arundel	
14 May		Newton (Cambs)	ibs	Benfleet	1
Swanage	1	Pocklington	10	Boston RD	6
21 May		Thurruck UD	ibs	Bridlington RD	6
Eastleigh (Hants)	8	Welton	6	Bury St Edmunds	4
22 May		Worlingworth (4)		Cambridge	2
Butley (Suffolk)	1	**7 June**		Chesterton RD (Cambs)	ibs
Felixstowe, in sea	5	Depwade RD	(3)	Deben RD	4
24/25 May		Swaffham	5	Docking RD	6
Middlesbrough 2		Peterborough	7	Downham RD	6
25 May		**8 June**		Dunmow RD	4
Billericay	1	Oakham RD	8	Freebridge & Lynn RD	7 (7)
Holderness RD	16	South Kesteven RD	15	Horncastle RD	1
Horsham St Faith RD	1	**9 June**		Huntingdon RD	4
Loddon RD	4	Newmarket RD	41	March	7
Walsingham	9	**10 June**		North Kesteven RD	26 (2)
2 June		Canvey Island	1 (1)	North Witchford RD	9
Blofield and Fegg RD	1	Hartismere RD	5	Rochford RD	2 (1)
4 June		**13 June**		Saffron Walden RD	2
Mildenhall RD	23	Portland	22 (23)	Sevenge	25
5/6 June		**16 June**		Southend	4 (1)
Bridlington RD	16	Isle of Wight	2	Spalding RD	3
Driffield RD	6			Spilsby RD	33 (12)
Gainsborough	15			St Neots	1 (1)
Louth RD	14			Strood RD	3
Peterborough RD	10			Witham	4
Scunthorpe					

Estimate of total weights of bombs dropped

5/6 June	158 tonnes
18/19 June	100 tonnes
19/20 June	80 tonnes

Number of bombs dropped in June 1940

1,388 high explosive of various sizes, mainly 50kg
14 oil bombs, equal to 859 metric tonnes
Incendiaries – not known

19 June
Settle   10 (3)
19/20 June
Billingham (Durham) UD 22
Caistor RD   1, ibs
Derwent RD   11
Glandford Brig   4 (2), ibs
Grimsby RD   8
Hull   1, ibs
Norton RD   1
Southampton 10
West Hartlepool   12
20 June
Cardiff   6
Cowbridge   ibs
20/21 June
South Shields   5
21/22 June
Cleethorpes   8
Erping RD   12
Grimsby   3
Romney Marsh   2
Swale RD   ibs
Tynemouth   2
22 June
Cosford RD   (1)
Forehoe & Henstead RD   2
Harwich   9
Ipswich   10
Lothingland RD   3
Smallborough UD   25 (1)
Thedwastre RD   16
Woodbridge   6
Wymondham 13
24 June
Chichester RD   30
Launditch RD   1
24/25 June
Bristol   20, ibs
Lutterworth RD   14 (1)
Melton Belvoir RD   3
Rugby   39

25 June
Battle RD   1
Colne Valley UD   7
Derby   4
Dover RD   4
Halstead RD   2
Shardlow RD   9
Wayland UD   4
25/26 June
Aldridge UD   5
Bridgewater RD   4 (1)
Edinburgh   5, ibs
Fleet   3
Hinckley   4 (1)
Midlothian, landward 29,
ibs
Newcastle-under-Lyme 12
Spalding UD   1
West Bromwich   2
26 June
Chelmsford RD   2
Cowes   2 (5)
East Lothian, landward   ibs
Fife, landward   1
Newport (Mon)   9
Perth, landward   13, ibs
Salisbury RD   4
26/27 June
Aberdeen   4
Amesbury RD   4
Hawarden   6
Stone   12
Winchester   5
Winchester RD   3 (6)
27 June
Swansea   (6)
27/28 June
Brierley Hill UD   6
East Elloe RD   8
Meriden RD   2
Newmarket   ibs
Selkirk, landward   4

28 June
Angus, landward   6
Blackwell   12
Chepstow RD   2
Hepton   10 (3)
Roxborough   ibs
Wainford RD   3 (5)
28/29 June
Poole   2
29 June
Aberdeen RD, in sea   1
Cardiff RD   6 (1)
Neath   2
Port Talbot   10
Torpoint   2
Wells next the Sea   (1)
29/30 June
West Kesteven RD   4
30 June
Chichester RD   24
Hove   2
Penarth   14 (2)

Chapter 6

When church bells ring

'They're just across the Channel, and they're looking our way! They might invade us, Dad. We've got to stop them! How can we do it?'

That was a question I never imagined I'd ask, but by the end of June a German invasion of England was looming ever more likely. Scary, most alarming!

My father, a peaceful chap, was preparing his answer – a private arsenal. The first I knew about it came when, in our large garden shed, beer bottles in profusion unexpectedly appeared. Soon they were breeding – twenty, thirty, fifty were half-hidden! Where had they come from? Dad provided a half answer when I caught him importing more.

'What are they for, Dad?'

Before he explained, he emphatically said, 'Don't you dare tell yer mother – I don't want to worry her unnecessarily.'

A count revealed ninety-eight bottles. All were empty, so someone must have known considerable 'enjoyment'. It certainly wasn't my Dad, as he wasn't much fond of beer.

'We need these, boy', he said. 'Just before they land I'm going to fill the bottles with petrol. We need some old shirts, pyjamas – flannelette would be the best. We can screw pieces and force them in the bottles. When we see them coming down the road we can set fire to the material, open the lids of their tanks or lorry doors, then drop 'em in. We can throw them at the soldiers, put them in back pockets. I'm *not* going to have any Nazis in our street.'

I was very, very worried because I felt sure that the Germans might not welcome my Dad's unfriendly attitude. I was even more alarmed when he said, 'You can help, boy. I wasn't very old when I fought the last lot. I'm not giving in this time either.'

With cans of petrol well hidden, the shed where we kept our bikes became a very hazardous bomb dump. What if Mum found out, struck a match for some reason, or if it was unfortunately attacked by the Luftwaffe with an incendiary bomb? The most disturbing aspect was that my father was so deadly serious, and although mighty scared I decided I must help him when and if the time came. Was the German Army really going to goose-step along our street saluting Adolf, passing the fish shop, viewing Mrs Mansfield's house, raiding Wortley's dairy and even daring to enter the Chief Air Raid Warden's territory? Brave Mr Churchill would think twice before doing that!

In autumn 1939 the Government had also and quite suddenly awoken to the alarming possibility that German forces might have the cheek to invade our land. In quite a leisurely fashion they began to spend a little time and money considering what to do. They didn't achieve much. Defence isn't a good vote-winner even in wartime, and the politicians were still most worried about money and re-election.

Within minutes of the May blitzkrieg they certainly panicked, and responded surprisingly well. They formed a committee. They called it the Home Defence Executive, and told its members to decide how to prepare the population for invasion as if it was to be a treat. With little certainty as to the method, they came to believe that the event would involve paratroops, some dressed as nuns. Accordingly, key points must be guarded, by troops taken from AA and searchlight sites, and quickly armed with 4,000 LMGs and 32,800 Lee-Enfield rifles. When it was pointed out that small tanks might be flown in for airborne forces, there was a suggestion that an aircraft be fitted with an anti-tank gun. Choice for the role? An ancient, slow-moving Vickers Virginia able to hover in a gale, even nudge its way backwards. Now it could be fitted with a hand-traversed, hefty 37mm cannon! Luckily, fortune did not favour the idea.

Not a scene from 'Dad's Army' but a splendid array of 'Ironsides' Quickly built four-man armoured cars' carrying a forward firing bren-gun. *IWM*

The UK had been divided into twelve theoretically autonomous regions to cope with heavy air raids. Response to an invasion would now make use of a modified form of that structure. Although infiltration by enemy agents and 'fifth columnists' was a possible threat, of more concern were widespread rumours and the spreading of false stories.

A variety of restraints controlled the number of feasible landing areas. Suitable beaches, features, knowledge of tidal flows, coastal land forms and adjacent terrain would all have to be right for success. Air support would need to take into account the operational radius of Ju 87s and fighter cover, which restricted the landing zone to the coast between Sussex and The Wash and allowed short sea crossings. As in the Low Countries, paratroops and glider-borne forces would probably be sent to

Pillboxes were built over a wide area at quite incredible speed. Complete with split trench, this one was photographed at Great Yarmouth on 1 August 1940. *IWM*

capture airfields to which transport aircraft could bring in more troops. The latter could then attack coastal defence forces from the rear, allowing more invaders to arrive by sea, possibly in shallow-draught barges of the type used on European rivers. To discourage those, coastal minefields would be laid, and beaches mined. Some 600 naval guns would increase coastal defences.

Road-blocks were quickly positioned in early July, and a multitude of strategically situated reinforced concrete pillboxes were built at an amazing rate. Across East Anglia, roughly from north-east to south-west, a deep and wide tank trap was dug by soldiers aided, after their day's work, by many civilians in an unusual version of 'dig for victory'. Signposts, place names, titles on vehicles, shop names and railway station name boards, all were removed to cause as much confusion as possible among the 1940-style illegal immigrants.

How would we know 'they' had landed? Church bells would only now be allowed to ring as a signal that the invasion had started. The code word 'Cromwell' sent to those with a need to know would announce that invaders were likely soon to be visiting.

Military call-up for the Services was drawing many to the colours. Using front-line troops as coastal guards was deemed none too sensible. The Territorial force having been mobilised, was there any other source of manpower? On 11 May the situation was discussed at the War Office and the idea mooted for the formation of a local defence force involving civilians. The outcome was a scheme allowing any man 'aged between 16 and 65 and capable of free movement' to be eligible to join an unpaid Local Defence Volunteer force. Note that it was to be an unpaid force – British Governments do not readily part with the people's money for sensible things.

So keen was the Government on the idea of a cheap army drawn from the public that it decided to go ahead with the idea, and quickly to prevent undue alarm at the extent and power of a German blitzkrieg. At 6.00pm on 14 May, Mr Anthony Eden, Secretary of State for War, made his famous call for 'every able-bodied man' to enrol at the nearest police station in his Local Defence Volunteer force.

A formation of passing aircraft had attracted me into our garden, alongside which was a passage leading onto the road. Within moments of the call an eager close neighbour passed in a mighty hurry. 'I'm off to the police station,' he said. Fifteen minutes later he arrived there and found that hundreds of 'able-bodied men' had beaten him to the 'nick', for once very eager to have their names taken! On his return we enquired just what was expected of him. He knew not. In less a week a quarter of a million men had joined him in the LDV. The disaster in France leading to the withdrawal from Dunkirk greatly boosted volunteering, and by the end of May more than one-third of a million had signed the special pledge.

What could the LDV achieve, what would their role be, and just who were they? They needed leaders, discipline and, of course, weapons. They needed meeting places and operational positioning. They certainly needed considerable training, and, being volunteers, were far more ready to form sections and companies, quickly drawing up rosters and working themselves into small units. Some – very secretly at the time – would form an underground force to engage German forces after they had attained a foothold.

Wearing civilian clothes and LDV armbands would not protect them from execution. Later, uniforms would confer some protection, but for many weeks the LDV force trained in 'civvies' and learned some weapon-handling skills using improvised items. Our neighbour, keen to acquire some hand grenades, made do instead with a scythe. We kept a sickle handy. Within a few months a load of rifles captured from the Italian Army in Libya made its way to our local Home Guards. Pity they did not have suitable ammunition.

Enormous was the task of setting up defences around the southern and eastern coasts. Long stretches were not even protected by a strand of barbed wire, and a senior office was overheard saying, 'There are so many beaches that the enemy could land on, it is hardly worth doing anything anyway. Let's do one and hope they choose that.'

Within the Army there was little understanding of the need for fast reaction to an airborne assault. Only far away in Northern Command were troops being encouraged and trained as a highly mobile reaction force. Many other commanders were planning 'static' cordon warfare involving trenches, road-blocks, strong points and pillboxes.

There were by now the inevitable rumours. Various uses for giant springs were well aired. They would be fired to ensnare aircraft and some were said to have fallen upon houses in London, enveloping them in miles of wire! Rockets of all sorts were favoured for fairy stories, like curtains of mine-carrying balloons.

Soldiers returning from France were soon telling the truth, and it was alarming because of the vast amount of war material lost. It was also clear that the Royal Navy was not as invincible as was claimed, which made starvation by blockade possible. Luckily the War Cabinet decided that the No 1 priority must be defence against air attack. Assessments based upon reliable intelligence suggested that the enemy was planning to drop 5,000 paratroops at night on seven South East fighter stations. Once seized, they could be reinforced at dawn by troops brought in aboard transports and even bombers. A force of about 20,000 troops would make a beach landing. Reinforcements would be flown in during daylight and protected by the fighters taking up station in the Pas de Calais.

German losses in France had been considerable. Their forces would need time to organise themselves. Barely realised was the heavy loss suffered by the German Navy during the Norwegian battles. Perhaps they would decide not to come, Mum suggested. What only the Germans knew was that they had lost so many Ju 52 troop transports that making the journey would have been almost impossible!

Bren gun Carriers followed by bicycling soldiers, photographed at Haven Street, on the Isle of Wight. In the carriers, men of the 6th Black Watch, 12th Brigade, 4th Division, V Corps. *IWM*

Chapter 7

Take it easy – just four days

As Britain improved its defences the Luftwaffe prepared for a part in the High Command's invasion. Before its launch, disposal of the RAF would surely be quick and easy. Hitler hoped that the British would be sensible and surrender. In case they proved awkward he enquired, on 2 July, how long the Luftwaffe needed to achieve air superiority. 'Four days,' replied the High Command, 'to remove fighter protection from southern Britain.'

Britain's Chiefs of Staff forecast a different scenario, a severe German economic crisis in 1941. They advised the Government to bear that in mind and continue the fight.

Hitler, on 16 July, decided that Britain must after all be invaded, so he issued Operations Directive No 16, which read as follows:

'As England, despite her hopeless military situation, still shows no sign of willingness to come to terms, I have decided to prepare, and if necessary to carry out, a landing operation against her.

The aim of this operation is to eliminate the English motherland as a base from which war against Germany can be continued and, if necessary, to occupy the country completely.'

The Germans, far from home, had to first prepare, forward bases in France, initially used for night raids by He 111s, one of which is being hidden under camouflage netting. (Bundesarchiv)

During the first week of August the Luftwaffe would probe British defences and attack Channel shipping. Six weeks before the invasion the Luftwaffe would launch a major offensive. Attacks on German invasion forces needed to be prevented, enemy coastal defences smashed, initial resistance broken, British Army reserves destroyed. The Germans accepted that resistance would come not only from British soldiers and the LDV, but probably most British men and women – even children. How true, with many households – like the Bowyers – building private arsenals, storing sugar rations to pour into German petrol tanks, constructing man traps, and contemplating nasty uses for boiling water.

FOOD FACTS № 1

Register now for cooking fats. On Monday 22 July cooking fats will be rationed... Butter and margarine total weekly ration 6oz – butter or all margarine or some of each. Tea is now rationed – 2oz a week. You may buy from any shop you like, no registration is necessary.

Newspapers, 15 July

Additional to those four days needed to subjugate British fighter defence south of a line from London to Gloucester, the Germans reckoned it would only take another three weeks to destroy the remainder of the RAF in Britain.

Luftflotten 2 and 3 were ordered to carry out the massacre. No 2, based in northern Germany, the Netherlands, Belgium and north-east France, was commanded by Field Marshal Kesselring, commander of Luftflotte 1 during the Polish campaign. Luftflotte 3, based in north and north-west France, was led by Field Marshal Hugo Sperrle, 1936-37 leader of the Kondor Legion in Spain. These were the Luftwaffe's most able commanders. Luftflotte 2 would operate east of the line approximately Le Havre-Solent-Oxford-Birmingham-Manchester, Luftflotte 3 to its west. Convergent raids by both Luftflotten would split the defending effort, particularly at night. Luftflotte 5, based in Denmark and Norway and commanded by General Stumpff, would operate against northern England and Scotland and mount diversion raids and widespread shipping attacks, to make the British summon defenders from the south. Between them they held about 3,500 aircraft. All straightforward and so simple.

The third week of July 1940 saw the German Air Force brought to 'full readiness' while final operations orders were worked out. Returns for 20 July from the three Luftflotten set alongside similar returns for the RAF on 22 July, as shown in the adjacent table, make for interesting comparison. About 66% of the German bombers were expected to be serviceable, 80% of the fighters. Luftflotten 2 and 3 could thus field about 800 long-range bombers, 250 dive-bombers and 820 fighters. German intelligence sources reckoned that the Metropolitan RAF held fifty operational fighter squadrons – some 900 front-line aircraft, excluding Blenheim fighters – of which about 675 would at one time be serviceable.

Looking every inch the tough Man
of the Master Race, Field Marshal
Hugo Sperrle commanded Luftflotte
3. *IWM*

The Operations Room at HQ Fighter Command. *IWM*

Comparative Strengths of Opposing Forces

Luftflotten 2 and 3	Strength	Serviceable
Long-range bombers	1,131	769
Dive-bombers	316	248
Single-engined fighters	809	656
Twin-engined fighters	246	168
Long-range reconnaissance	67	48
Short-range reconnaissance for army/invasion support	90	?

Luftflotte 5	Strength	Serviceable
Long-range bombers	129	95
Single-engined	84	?
Long-range reconnaissance	48	33
Grand totals	**2,920**	**2,076**

Total RAF	Establishment	Serviceable
Long-range bombers	320	256
Light/medium bombers	272	257
Single-engined fighters	900	606
Twin-engined fighters	160	101
Coastal/long-range/strike reconnaissance	291	156
Lysanders (Nos 22 and 61 Groups)	174	143
	2,053	**1,519**

Fighter Command's strength and resolution were much underestimated by the Germans. In early July it comprised forty-eight operational squadrons (two with Defiants and four more forming or re-equipping) – or fifty-eight, if those training, etc, were included. The six Blenheim 1(f) squadrons, and Blenheims of Tangmere's Fighter Interception Unit, now usually operated at night. Britain's AA defences were poorly regarded by the Germans, whereas searchlight defences experienced during June's training were rated effective.

Barrage balloons, reckoned by the enemy to be flown too low and vulnerable to attack and the weather, formed an important part of British defences. Pre-war planning called for 1,450 Low Zone balloons. Only 624 were operationally deployed at the outbreak of war, losses due to bad weather being higher than expected. By May 1940 there were sufficient balloons to meet pre-war plans, savings achieved by close-hauling them until required. Mobile and waterborne barrages for ship protection had been introduced, as at Harwich and in the Thames Estuary, leading to a shortfall of 600 land-based balloons.

Airfields and AA guns for protection of West Coast ports and adjacent areas were sparse, so defence relied largely upon the balloons. Dowding proposed four new western barrages, increasing the size of some existing, and placed groups of ten waterborne balloons in fourteen more estuaries to interfere with mining. The overall total would rise from 2,027 to 2,375 balloons. By the end of July the Air Staff expressed a need for 2,600, whereas balloon squadrons numbered 52 by July 1940 (listed establishment 1,865, actual strength around 1,450 balloons). Monthly production – just over 200 in September 1939 – rose to around 1,200 by September 1940.

Barrage balloons were hauled close as inclement weather approached.

To defeat dive and low level attack on cities, Low Zone Kite Balloons like those of 905 Squadron were flown in barrages. These around Buckingham Palace are close hauled. *IWM*

General arrangement — LZ Kite Balloon

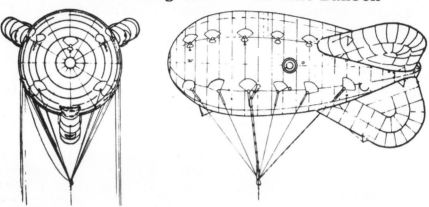

A typical Low Zone Kite Balloon used in barrages. Its length when inflated was 64.2ft, with a maximum diameter of 25.2ft and maximum overall height of 31.8ft. It was designed to lift a steel cable to between 5,000 ft and 6,500 ft. The upper section contained hydrogen which expanded displacing air as the balloon rose. The hydrogen contracted when the balloon was hauled in and the stabilizers were air-filled. Barrages were flown over main cities and vulnerable places.

The main anti-aircraft gun was the 3.7in. here in mobile form.

General Sir Frederick Pile, GOC-in-C Anti-Aircraft Command, in mid-June 1940 commanded a force of 1,204 heavy and 581 light guns, whose established strengths were 2,232 and 1,860 respectively. By late July Pile possessed half the heavies and a third of the light guns needed before France fell. In the seven gun divisions, each fifteen regiments strong, manning levels were inadequate, for the Army had siphoned off the fittest troops. Gun defences were in demand for VPs (vital points) such as aircraft factories, airfields, West Coast ports, naval bases and industrial areas. Rolls-Royce Derby was protected by twenty-two guns, Bristol Aeroplane works at Filton had eight, and HQ Fighter Command at Stanmore only four. A shortfall of Bofors guns was reduced by placing almost 4,000 Lewis guns in AA Command. The RAF believed it would need about 850 hits from one of those to ensure a kill.

'This, men, is a searchlight. It moves on caterpillar tracks. The trooper on the left controls azimuth setting, the man on the right its elevation. Now, what is it, Engineer?' 'A searchlight, SIR.' *IWM*

German assessment of British capability failed to realise the increasing effectiveness of Britain's radar warning layout. By early 1940 the coastal radar chain extended from the Firth of Forth to the Solent. It covered Scapa Flow and the Bristol area, although most of western Britain was uncovered. Remedial action during spring 1940 resulted, by mid-July, in the establishment of six CHL (Chain Home Low) and three CH (Chain Home) radar stations in South West England and South Wales. Correlating defences in that region was No 10 Fighter Group, opened on 1 June 1940. It controlled four squadrons and three Sector stations switched from 12 Group:

Pembrey, Filton (used until Colerne was available) and Middle Wallop (taken over in August 1940). Squadrons lodged on the St Eval Coastal Command station. Observer Corps cover extended over the South West and South Wales. Most of Wales, the West Midlands and the North West to the Scottish border remained under 12 Group control.

A typical Chain Home (CH) radar station of the type originally called an Air Ministry Experimental Station. Its 350-foot towers transmitted the signal (from an aerial array slung between them), and the 250-foot type received the return. *IWM*

The spartan interior of a CH radar station, with WAAF 'sparks' busy. *IWM*

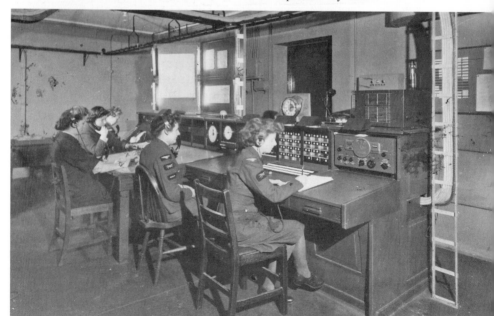

Skilled Observer Corps personnel using binoculars and a type of sextant able to swing through 360 degrees. They could identify aircraft types – which radar could not – and provided vital information on height and course of friendly as well as enemy aircraft. *IWM*

Another Group was needed to coordinate fighter and AA activity over Wales and northwards west of the Pennines. Poor land communications existed there, airfields were few, radar non-existent. A new Group – No 9 – opened on 9 August 1940, and a Filter Room at Preston on 13 August; it played little part in the summer battles. No 14 Group, to control the air defence of Scotland, began reforming on 20 July 1940. No 13 Group, opened on 24 July 1939, controlled air defence from the North East to Wick.

A valuable part was played throughout Britain by the civilian-manned Observer Corps. Keen, skilled observers and plotters elaborated upon radar information, discerned the nature of threats by discovering aircraft types employed, and often giving immediate raid warning of lone, very dangerous attackers heading for vulnerable points.

The Germans had no idea that the British had acquired Enigma code deciphering equipment. It afforded access to operational policy, planning and targeting, although the time taken to decipher the acquired signals was a problem. Incomplete information took time to evaluate. What was usually not provided were final details of tactics to be employed by raiders, a prerogative of unit commanders. Those involved with Enigma at the time seem of the opinion that it often provided information rather too late to help much in repelling raiders.

Another source of vital intelligence was the 'Y' Service (the listening service). From the start of the war it monitored German radio chatter 24 hours a day, recording and sifting it. By employing radio direction finding, hearing snippets of

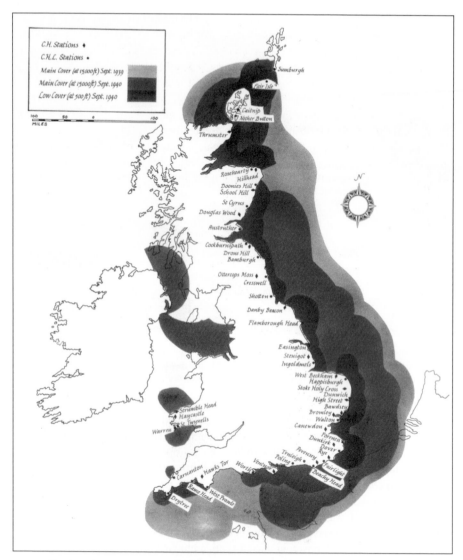

**Radar Chain, July 1940, and Radar Cover, September 1939
and September 1940**

radio talk and listening to radio homing, valuable information was acquired to set alongside other intelligence. Flights by high-flying photo reconnaissance Spitfires of the PRU resulted in excellent photographs of enemy coastal areas, particularly of invasion assemblies. Add reports from agents and embassies abroad, and the British can be seen to have been well supplied with useful material for defences.

The unravelling by Prof R. V. Jones of German 'beam riding' and radio target marking by July 1940 led to the formation under signals expert Wing Commander E. B. Addison of No 80 Wing, which in September 1940 absorbed personnel at Headquarters Fighter Command. Its task was enactment of countermeasures to *Knickebein* and its successor, *X-Gerät*. Controlled in great secrecy by the Air Ministry and a few officers at Fighter Command, it reviewed radio-jamming, produced false beams, redirected M/F transmissions to confuse crews, and handled relevant intelligence data.

'Where's Hitler?' Bow-
tie, cigar, pin-striped
suit and splendid hat –
typical of 'Winnie'.
IWM

All was of little use without servicemen and women. Although the planned Fighter Command pilot strength was 1,450, the number on 9 July 1940 – the 'official' starting date of the Battle – totalled only 1,253. Each squadron nominally held twelve aircraft, making the number available at one time about 600. Had more pilots been available that total could easily have become 700. As for the pilots, an increasing proportion lacked experience. A high percentage of those trained pre-war – more experienced and longer trained – had been lost. Replacing them was impossible. Many more should have been trained pre-war to provide a pool, but as ever that was politically impossible in peacetime when every step towards sufficient defence requirements so often meets with strong opposition. However, had there been more pilot training facilities the number of young men physically and mentally suited to becoming fighter pilots might still have proved insufficient. The Auxiliary Air Force had been reorientated into a reserve fighter force, to build a reservoir of trained pilots. Recruiting and operating its squadrons took place near large population centres where there was often a limited number of suitable young men. The problem was resolved only after establishing a sufficiently large training organisation. At Cambridge No 22 EFTS introduced a scheme whereby the most able trainees were, as a result of pressure on the Air Ministry from Arthur Marshall, then trained as instructors. That new pool greatly speeded the training of new pilots.

Instead of forming more squadrons, the establishment of many short-range day-fighter squadrons (thirty of Hurricanes and six of Spitfires) was increased by four aircraft to sixteen each, putting more aircraft available in emergencies for pilots

rested or nominally on leave. Squadron strength increased more when sixty-eight Fleet Air Arm pilots were seconded to Fighter Command – until ten had to be released for Mediterranean naval service. From June to October 1940 an average of sixty naval pilots flew in fighter squadrons and others with Coastal Command.

Squadron Leader J. R. A. Peel, the highly successful leader of 145 Squadron. *IWM*

By 10 July every coastal county of England and Wales had received unwelcome visitors. Disruption caused by air raid warnings brought official concern, but not alerting the public could prove disastrous, as at Aberdeen on 12 July, when failure to sound the sirens resulted in fifty casualties.

Two distinct new threats had evolved: 1) single or small groups of raiders who used cloud cover to make daytime key point precision attacks, which were hard to detect by radar, and 2) fighter-protected/supported relatively small raids, of which six occurred between 1 and 9 July. Seven had involved Channel convoys, particular attention being paid to shipping and port facilities at Dover, Weymouth, Portland, Plymouth and Falmouth. Protecting shipping entailed uneconomical and difficult use of resources. Attacks could range from single aircraft cloaked by fog or rain to large, escorted formations.

Intent upon conserving his forces, Dowding ordered Park to daily move squadrons forward, from Hornchurch Sector to Manston, Biggin Hill and Kenley to Hawkinge, and from Middle Wallop to Warmwell, enabling small forces to provide rapid protection of Channel convoys. When ocean-going convoys ceased passing through the English Channel there was less pressure. East Coast and Channel coastal trade convoys comprised as many as thirty ships, small colliers being very tempting targets.

Enemy activity nationwide was slowly increasing and diversifying. Early on 1 July an He 59B-2 air-sea rescue, 77-foot-wingspan, two-motor floatplane, D-ASAM of Seenotflugkommand, probably supporting KG 26, was shot down 8 miles off Sunderland by Spitfires of 72 Squadron. There was also morning activity over the Dover Straits followed by Ju 87s attacking convoy 'Jumbo' off Plymouth. Responding Hurricanes of No 145 Squadron (P3521, P2770 and N2496) shot down in the Channel a 2/KG 77 Do 17 that had prowled between Poole, Liverpool and Odiham. A spectacular afternoon fire was lit at Heddon, the Hull depot of Anglo American Oil, by a lone, Stavanger-based KG 26 He 111, which narrowly escaped the wrath of 616 Squadron. South Wales was attacked during the afternoon, and fifteen He

Hurricanes of 32 Squadron took a major part in the fighting, among them P3522 seen here. Used by 32 Squadron from 20 May 1940 and damaged in action on 23 August, it passed to 213 Squadron on 19 September and retained until 10 January 1941. *IWM*

111s of KG 55 returned after dark, half from Villacoublay, the rest from Jever and Aalborg. A Ju 88 of KG 30 bombed Wick and fourteen people died.

Action tempo heightened after a German High Command order of 2 July ordered an increase in bombing Britain. Lunchtime that day brought KG 26 to Saltburn's Skinningrove ironworks. Production was reduced there and in shipyards at Jarrow and Newcastle.

What shall we sing?
Lords of the Air

The British Empire proudly stands
As in the days of old,
Our fathers fought o'er land and sea,
Their history is told
In our new battlefield the sky,
Prepare to do or dare,
Let this be our new battlecry,
'Britannia rules the air.'
England our island home,
Land of the free,
England unconquered yet,
O'er land and sea;
Lord of the heav'ns above,
Answer our prayer,
God keep Britannia's sons
Lords of the Air
Michael North and Davy Burnaby

Using cloud and rain for protection, lone bombers from midday on 3 July raided assorted targets within the area North Foreland-Ford-Midhurst-Crystal Palace. Included was White Waltham aerodrome. Six bombs damaged seven 'Tigers' and an Anson. Late afternoon brought a score of similar incidents, mainly at coastal towns and docks. Raid M22, an He 111, sowed fifteen HEs across Ipswich. None exploded, but in a sharp onslaught on Lowestoft by a KG 77 Do 17 the town's main Co-op store caught fire. Sailors rescued delivery vans as firemen bravely rescued people sheltering in the basement.

Acting Leading Seaman Jack Hantle, awarded the Victoria Cross for his valiant manning of the guns aboard HMS *Foylebank*. *IWM*

A cheeky Do 17Z of II/KG 77, which bombed Manston, was caught by No 56 Squadron Hurricanes (P3387, P3587, P3547) and set ablaze off Burnham-on-Crouch. Another, after aiming six bombs at Kenley, was brought down by a trio of 32 Squadron Hurricanes (N2463, N2670, N2671). Three Ju 88s of 8./KG 30 were shot down off Scotland by 603 Squadron. These raids highlighted difficulties in warning coastal residents of imminent attack, and led to klaxon 'crash warnings'. Clearly, civilians would be safer inland. Rapidly gathering voluntary Civil Defence fire, rescue and first aid workers from their workplaces was seen to be difficult.

The first Stuka/fighter-escorted raids against the UK were launched on 4 July. At 08.30 Bf 110s shepherded thirty-three Ju 87s of III/StG 51 eager to treat the British to 6 minutes of classic dive-bombing. Grouped line astern, they screamed down from 15,000 feet out of the sun, aiming at Portland harbour, whose defenders welcomed them with 155 3-inch shells and 4,753 machine gun rounds. They sank the tug *Silverdial*, then slammed at least nine bombs into HMS *Foylebank*, a 5,582grt anti-aircraft ship. Aboard and displaying enormous courage, Acting Leading Seaman Jack Foreman Hantle – despite horrific wounds to his left leg – fired a 20mm pom-pom gun even after receiving further wounds. He died at his post and was posthumously awarded the Victoria Cross on 3 September 1940.

Very exposed Portland was to be attacked many times, a second raid coming mid-morning on 4 July, when two bombers killed ten people in the dockyard. Twenty miles away, KG 77 and II/Lehr 1 attacked OA178, the last deep-sea convoy to pass through the Channel. Nine large merchantmen were damaged, including *Argos Hill* of 7,178grt, *City of Melbourne* (6,630grt), *William Wilberforce* (5,004grt) and *East Wales* (4,358grt). The raiders escaped before 213 Squadron Hurricanes arrived.

A reconnaissance
photograph of
Portland Harbour.
IWM

Nine small ships off Dover had attracted two Staffeln of Do 17s protected by about thirty Bf 109s. Eight 79 Squadron Hurricanes sent from Hawkinge to intercept lost one of their number. Meantime He 111s, skilfully using cloud cover, attacked a variety of targets including Bristol's Filton works, which received four HEs before a hectic chase by three 92 Squadron Spitfires resulted in the raider's destruction at Ref U2454/Weston-super-Mare. At RAF Driffield, barrack blocks and the NAAFI were damaged by six HEs. Bombs also fell near Maidstone, Yeovilton, Ramsgate and Plymouth's Storr Point.

Early evening saw Hurricanes of 32 Squadron[1] engaging Raid 20, three Staffeln of Bf 109s, which destroyed two Hurricanes without loss. Three Spitfires of 64 Squadron (including P9450 and R6700), snooping high over the Pas de Calais, encountered Bf 109s of JG 51. They shot down Pilot Officer Milne (P9507). After dark, more than fifty bombers from KG 27, KG 51 and KG 54 operated, particularly over Kent and Eastern England.

Poor weather on 5 July continued into the following day, then provided cover for a few raiders. An He 111 circled Thorney Island, headed inland undetected from near Littlehampton, and flew to Aldershot. At 16.15 it unleashed nine HEs across Gullemonte Barracks, two cottages, Wellington Avenue and Knolly's Road, killing seven and injuring twenty-four. Meanwhile a score of Norwegian-based raiders approached Aberdeen in four groups, and more operated over the Forth Estuary. Nine other aircraft were turned away by fighter reaction. KG 55 was also operating, against Plymouth and Falmouth. At night He 111s of Schiphol's KG 4 operated over the Durham area, five bombs falling $2\frac{1}{2}$ miles from Shotton Colliery.

Fabric burnt away from the geodetic frame of 99 Squadron Wellington 1c R3170 when it was brought down near Oude Weg, Haarlem, on 6/7 July 1940 *G.J. Zwanenburg*

The Ministry Says...

What do I do when I hear guns and air raid warnings? I keep a cool head, I gather my family and gas masks, I go quietly to my shelter or refuge room. I do NOT try to have a look, I do not run about alarming people. I remember a lot of the noise is good noise, our guns firing at the enemy... Cut this out and keep it.

From the newspapers, 4 July, space presented to the nation by the Brewers' Society

Only highly trained pilots of the RAF can take up the Spitfires and Hurricanes, but you, the citizens, can provide the planes, the ships, the weapons with which the Battle of Britain can be won. Buy 2½% National War Bonds.

Newspaper advertisement

What do I do if a raid catches me in the street and I go into a public shelter? I say to myself, 'This is where I keep calm and steady. It's human to be a bit nervous, but I'm not going to show it. I don't talk loudly nor crack silly jokes because that does not help others and, much as I want to, I do not smoke because it would make the shelter stuffy.' Cut this out.

From the newspapers, space presented to the nation by the Brewers' Society

Urgent! Great events turn upon your response to this message. There are two gigantic tasks before us – to defend our island fortress and prepare the ground upon which we shall finally win victory. Every shilling you now spend on your own pleasure now means part of the nation's resource is lost, wasted. Every shilling you put into National Savings directly helps to defend our country and bring about the defeat of the enemy. There is no time to lose...

Newspaper advertisement

Maynsforth Colliery was also raided, and KG 26's target included a colliery near Dunfermline. KG 1 operated against ports in South West England. Civilian casualties in the 24-hour period ending 06.00 on 7 July included sixty-two killed.

Three Do 17P convoy-seekers were brought down early on 7 July by Hurricanes of Nos 43[2], 145[3] and 601[4] Squadrons. Bombers drawn from seven Geschwaderen caused incidents at many sites, including Ipswich, and at Eastbourne, where nine homes were demolished and sixty badly damaged. Bf 109s paraded along the South Coast, but defending gunners claimed one that crashed at Ref R7859. As No 54 Squadron's Green Section tackled an He 111 they were bounced by Bf 109s, which forced down Pilot Officer A. R. Campbell (P9398) and Flying Officer E. S. Coleman (P9399) at Barton's Hall (Ref T7865). Flying Officer D. A. P. MacMullen nursed his damaged Spitfire (P9389) into Manston. The squadron diarist recorded it as 'a most disastrous day'.

The action, hotting up, was far from ended. Over the Channel KG 1, 2 and 51 sought shipping, while KG 3 and KG 53 attacked docks. Included was a damaging attack at 17.45 on Falmouth, four bombs severely damaging the docks, stores, the Shell installation and an RAF depot. Three houses were demolished and five civilians killed. Do 17Zs of I and

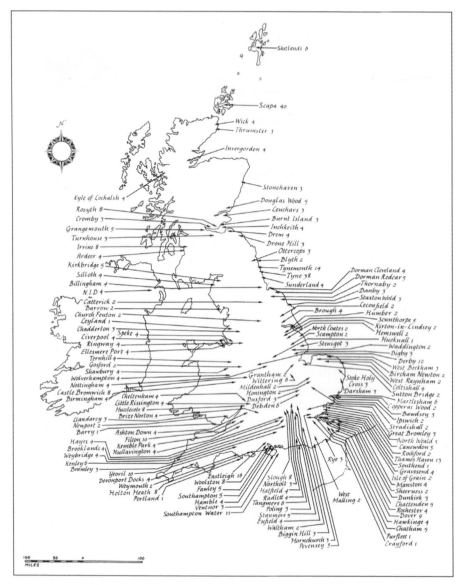

Light anti-aircraft guns as deployed on 7 July 1940

Heavy anti-aircraft guns as deployed on 7 July 1940

II/KG 2 carried out an evening strike on a CE convoy, sinking one ship and damaging three. Spitfires of 65 Squadron arrived too late, and were bounced by Bf 109s, which destroyed three. Two Bf 109s were claimed, and 64 Squadron damaged two Dorniers. Hurricanes of 79 Squadron were also engaged, and Squadron Leader J. D. C. Joslin shot down a Bf 109, which, the R maps references suggest, crashed at the wartime military reference point R726586. At night Gruppen 106 and 126 carried out sea-mining.

On 8 July eight bomber groups operated mainly against Portsmouth, Devonport, Hull and off Sunderland. Nine Do 17s trying to bomb a Channel convoy at around 14.00 were driven off. An hour later a more strongly escorted force tried. Again, 610 Squadron[5] was ordered to defend the ships. Support came from 79 Squadron, which lost two Hurricanes near Dover. Ju 88s attacking a convoy further west were driven off by 234 Squadron. Targets for around seventy night-bombers were Skinningrove ironworks and naval barracks at Devonport. Soon after dawn Norwich suffered a very sharp attack; Barnard's was hit, sixteen people being killed and seventy injured.

Shielded by cloud and rain, German aircraft reconnoitring the Thames Estuary on 9 July gathered details of an assembling large FN convoy. At 12.45 an approaching Luftwaffe strike force was radar-detected, together with a Bf 110 diversion provided by III/ZG 26. No 43 Squadron (P3796, P3464, N2621) damaged two of the latter, Squadron Leader C. G. Lott (P3464) delivering a head-on attack before serious splinter wounds forced him to ditch.

Spitfire P9496 'L Love' of 610 Squadron. It joined the squadron 2 June 1940, was shot down 26 August and crashed at Paddlesworth. Peter Else, piloting, lost an arm as he baled out, his serious burns being treated at East Grinstead by famous plastic surgeon Sir Archibold McIndoe, CBE, FRCS. That led to his membership of The Guinea Pig Club. Notwithstanding terrible injury, Peter Else later flew for many years as a flying instructor for Marshall's Flying School and 22 EFTS.

Off the South Downs, a Channel East (CE) convoy comes under air attack. *IWM*

Six 11 Group squadrons engaged the main force soon after 13.00. Included was 'A' Flight 151 Squadron from North Weald, whose Station Commander, Wing Commander Victor Beamish, was flying Hurricane P3807. Within a few minutes the six Hurricanes were facing around a hundred enemy aircraft, bombers at around 12,000 to 15,000 feet with Bf 109s giving top cover up to 20,000 feet. One Hurricane section went for the bombers as the members of 151 fought bravely for their lives. FAA pilot Midshipman O. Wightman, shot down, was rescued by a trawler. Courage caused the bomber formation to split, all but one group turning for home. The ships remained undamaged.

Around mid-afternoon a raid by seventy German aircraft developed. This time just seven Spitfires of 65 Squadron[6], Manston, reacted. With Bf 109s above, and flanked by Bf 110s and Bf 109s, the bomber formations again scattered. The Spitfires dived upon the II/JG 51 Bf 109s, Flight Sergeant N. T. Phillips destroying one. A straggling I/KG 53 He 111 – possibly from the force – was destroyed at sea by Hurricanes of 17 Squadron (P2588 Pilot Officer G. R. Bennette, P3673 Pilot Officer K. Manger, and Sergeant G. Griffiths) while guarding FN convoy 'Ancient'.

He 59 floatplanes wearing international red cross markings and civilian registrations appeared from Calais to seek German airmen in the sea. No 54 Squadron[7] halted those proceedings, forcing down He 59 D-ASUO on the Goodwin Sands. After capture, it was towed to Deal. The Germans claimed that it was involved in a mercy mission. Quite likely, but it certainly had reconnaissance content.

As the Junkers Ju 87B Stukas (A5+DH of I/StG 1 is shown here) entered a steep dive their engines emitted an horrendous scream. Their course was fairly easy for gunners to predict and, being fairly slow, they were also picked off during the climb away. *Bundesarchiv*

The Heinkel He 59 was a 77ft wing span biplane floatplane used for English Channel air-sea rescue. It operated from Calais and Cherbourg wearing Red Cross insignia.

Maintenance of German aircraft in France was carried out using makeshift equipment on primitive airfields. *Michael Payne*

Spitfires engaged the protecting Bf 109s, again of II/JG 51. In a fierce combat, Flight Lieutenant A. C. 'Al' Deere shot one down; during a head-on pass by another, the canopy of his Spitfire was brushed by its propeller. Deere force-landed near Manston after his engine stopped, his Spitfire catching fire on crashing. Pilot Officer J. W. Carton was shot down and killed near Manston, Pilot Officer A. Evershed dying in the sea.

Rounding off the day's raids, twenty-seven escorted Ju 87s of I/StG 77 made another ineffective attempt to wreck Portland. Green Section, 609 Squadron[8], destroyed a Stuka, but lost Pilot Officer Drummond-Hay in R6637. The day's fighting cost the RAF seven fighters destroyed and three pilots killed. After dark about fifty hostiles had little success when they tried to find East Anglia's bomber bases.

By deploying just handfuls of fighters Dowding had done surprisingly well to thwart large enemy forces and deceive the enemy as to Britain's fighter strength. Could that continue? The Germans thought 'not for long', believing that southern England would soon become unprotected. To quickly clear away the British nuisance in the Channel zone, II and VIII Fliegerkorps were chosen. They were under the respective command of Generals Lorzer and Richthofen, whose HQs were in the Pas de Calais and Le Havre. Lorzer, with the tough task at the Dover end, chose Johannes Fink as Channel Battle Leader. His Battle Group comprised Kampfgeschwader 2 holding about seventy-five Do 17Zs, two Stuka Gruppen with about sixty Ju 87s, and around 200 Messerschmitt 109s, which equipped JG 26 commanded by Major Adolf Galland and JG 53 led by Major Werner Molders. The other Fliegerkorps would operate between Portsmouth and Portland. Such a fine array would surely finish off the RAF in a few days!

Throughout the campaign Major Adolf Galland, here taxying his Bf 109, proved himself
an excellent leader. Telling Goering that what the Luftwaffe needed was Spitfires must
have required enormous courage, too. *Bundesarchiv*

Chapter 8

It's the Battle of Britain – official

...The Battle may be said to have started when the Germans had disposed of the French resistance.

...I have, somewhat arbitrarily, chosen the events of 10 July as the opening of the Battle. Although many attacks had previously been made on convoys, and even on land objectives such as Portland, 10 July saw the employment by the Germans of the first really big formation (seventy aircraft) intended primarily to bring our Fighter Defence to battle on a large scale.

Air Chief Marshal Sir Hugh Dowding, Commander-in-Chief Fighter Command

Around 10.00 on 10 July a Do 17P of 4(F)/121, protected by Bf 109s of JfG 51, took a look at shipping off Kent. Four Spitfires of 74 Squadron – two damaged in combat – damaged the spy and a Bf 109. No 610 Squadron[9], facing more 109s, lost Flight Lieutenant E. B. B. Smith flying P9503.

At around 13:00 radar detected an enemy force beyond Calais prompting Hurricanes of 32 Squadron[10] to protect a CW convoy off Folkestone. When twenty-seven Do 17s of I/KG 2 and forty Messerschmitts of I/JG 3 and I/ZG 26 appeared, the squadron called for assistance. The response materialised as sixteen Hurricanes of Nos 56 and 111 Squadrons, and six Spitfires of 74[11]. A fierce air battle developed over Dungeness, something never before seen. 'Treble One' Squadron's contribution opened with a head-on attack, Flying Officer T. P. K. Higgs crashing into a Do 17Z. Both fell into the sea. Flying Officer Ferris, who put a Bf 109 into the water, was immediately set upon by others. He was lucky to reach home. Another Hurricane crash-landed at Hawkinge and a fourth was damaged, together with three 74 Squadron Spitfires. The Dornier force, baulked by 'Treble One', unloaded 150 bombs wide, and sank only a small Dutch sloop. As the enemy withdrew, six of 64 Squadron's Spitfires[12] arrived on the scene at 13.40 and engaged ZG 26's Bf 110s without success.

Fighter Command analysis concluded that faster reaction time was essential, and that losses were inevitable. Co-operation among several Sectors involved was good, but additional data was needed from radar warnings for selection of the best reaction time and extent. Committing too many squadrons would leave large areas exposed, yet too few might bring disaster.

Single raiders were active over the South West throughout the day, two workers dying when two cranes were hit at Kings Dock, Swansea. A pair of Ju 88s, Rd 179H, dropped twelve delayed-action HEs on the Royal Navy oil installation at Llanreith. Luckily one bomb, resting on a tank, had its fuse incorrectly set. Another caused a leak in a 164,800-gallon container. A bomber circled for 10 minutes in cloud before aiming nine HEs at Carmarthen's Royal Ordnance factory. Nine workers were killed and fifteen injured. The raider escaped despite attention from AA guns in four areas. Cardiff docks were raided, and at 15.10 a Ju 88 faced thirty-one rounds of 3-inch shells to drop five HEs and start a small fire at Llandarcy, Neath's

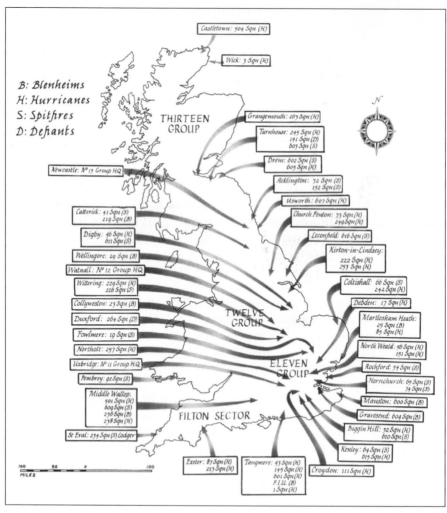

Fighter Command operational layout, 10 July 1940

National refinery. Two Ju 88s had just very successfully dive-bombed Falmouth. Scoring hits on a crane and jetty, they also sank the 6,499-ton tanker SS *Taskulsa* and set alight the SS *British Chancellor*.

At night, activity resulted in thirteen noteworthy incidents, among them bombing at Longtown, Cumbria, 8 miles north of Worthing, and at Newport, Essex, near Debden airfield. Of 170 HEs recorded, many fell wide. In all, twenty-nine people were killed and ninety-four injured during the 24 hours to dawn on 11 July. A highly alarming situation arose after mustard gas release was falsely signalled from Winchester. Although always possible, public opinion rated it unlikely on the basis that the enemy would suffer heavy retaliation. The Government, even to the end of the war, viewed it as far more likely!

'Scramble!' Pilots of 85 Squadron race to their Hurricanes. *IWM*

On 11 July the Luftwaffe made an early start, and Squadron Leader Peter Townsend, flying Hurricane P2716 VY:F of 85 Squadron, dealt with a Do 17 off Harwich. Shot down by return fire, he was soon rescued by a naval launch. Squadron Leader Douglas Bader, flying Hurricane P3048 of 242 Squadron, also shot down a Dornier, which crashed off Cromer. Another was damaged off Yarmouth by 66 Squadron. A convoy in Lyme Bay attracted a dozen Ju 87s and twenty Bf 109s of Luftflotte 3. On arrival, they met Spitfires of 609 Squadron[13] and three Hurricanes of 501 Squadron[14]. Half the Spitfires went for the Ju 87s, but German fighters picked off two (L1069 and L1095). Both pilots, Flight Lieutenant Barren and Pilot Officer Mitchell, were killed. Sergeant F. J. P. Dixon (shot down in Hurricane N2486) was drowned. Bombs from the Stukas fell wide.

No 85 Squadron's Hurricanes in traditional threes early in the fight. Markings were far from standardised, these Hurricanes having various-sized underwing roundels in varying positions on under surfaces of various blue shades. *IWM*

No 609's diarist recorded that the 'utter futility of sending small numbers of fighters to cope with intense enemy action is bitterly resented. The fact they have so often been sent off in a Section or Flight only to find themselves outnumbered is discouraging, because the British fighter then finds himself unable to do his job ... our contacts with the enemy have taken place when the numerical odds were too unreasonable.'

From cloud and poor visibility, at 08.03 a raider bombed an army camp at Melbourne, south of Derby, killing seven soldiers and wounding nine. Less effective were four bombs ironically placed on Skipsea bombing range, but midmorning HEs burst at Bridlington's town hall and railway station killing six; an ammunition truck exploded.

Improving weather in the south allowed reconnaissance aircraft to operate, and six 601 Squadron Hurricanes[15] set forth to tackle one over Lyme Bay. Instead, they soon confronted fifteen Stukas and more than thirty Bf 110s of III/ZG 76. The Hurricanes climbed then swept down out of the sun upon the intruders. Two Ju 87s were shot into the sea before their escort reacted. One merchantman was hit, and four Bf 110s were destroyed, two by 601 Squadron and one each by Nos 87 and 238[16] reinforcing squadrons.

Late afternoon brought in a dozen KG 55 He 111s escorted by Bf 110s. Approaching from Seine Bay, they met just six Hurricanes of 601 Squadron[17].

Ju 87B Stukas of II/StG 1 before a He 111.

Sergeant Woolley, shot down by AA fire, baled out wounded and left his Hurricane, P3681, to crash at Cranmore, Isle of Wight. Although they shot down one and caused two Heinkels to collide, 601 Squadron were unable to prevent a score of bombs from falling on Portsmouth at 18.00. That was the first daylight formation bombing raid on a British city. Reinforcements from Tangmere Sector arrived too late to prevent hits on a floating dock, timber yard, and a hotel. Airspeed's Hilsea factory was hit, and a gas holder, which detonated, burning itself out in 40 minutes. Ground casualties totalled seventeen killed and fifty injured.

Dowding maintained that the prevention of target bombing was the essential purpose of the fighter effort. Whereas radar stations in Kent warned of a raid up to 20 minutes away, cover elsewhere was generally less effective. Warning to plotting was taking 4 minutes, the time it took for a raid to almost cross the Straits of Dover. Scrambled fighters needed about 15 minutes to reach battle height. Controllers thus had precious little time to react, and needed excellent judgement to produce correct instructions and identify feints.

The Messerschmitt 109 was proving to be a most formidable fighter, whereas the Bf 110 was no match for a Hurricane. British fighters needed constant-speed propellers and fire-protected fuel tanks, but their incorporation meant withdrawing aircraft from the front line. The Luftwaffe possessed a well-thought-out air/sea rescue service, whereas the British relied upon small naval boats to save precious lives, both British and those of the foe.

Although briefed to bomb military and economic targets, enemy weapons often fell wide. On the night of 11/12 July precise 'legitimate' targets in Rochester and Chatham were attacked for the first time. However, instead of hitting docks and factories, a housing estate was bombed, killing thirty-six and injuring many. Ten

Messerschmitt Bf 110 of Zerstorergeschwader 2 displays its narrow rear fuselage which
reduced drag and which terminated in twin vertical tail surfaces to give better flying control.

bombs fell on marshland on the Isle of Grain from a bomber estimated to be at
24,000 feet. Another bomb exploded half a mile above ground, searchlights
illuminating a grotesque, giant smoke ring.

Media, 1940 style

12 July: 'Goering's Century with RAF Aid' – 102 planes lost on raids since 18
June. Goering has now reached his century but neither he nor his captain, Hitler,
will be happy about it.

More cloud and rain reduced activity on 12 July, and there was only one major
engagement. Off East Anglia a large FN convoy, 'Booty', attracted Raid 31, Do 17s
of II/KG 2 and He 111s of II/KG 53. As Hurricanes of 'A' Flight, 17 Squadron,
Martlesham, set out to cover the convoy, the raid was on its way. Blue Section of
85 Squadron, 'A' Flight of 19 Squadron[18] and eleven Hurricanes of 151 Squadron[19]
tackled the bombers en route. Then came No 17 Squadron's turn. They shot down
two Heinkels before turning their attention to the leading Dornier. Flown by
Hauptmann Machetzki, Staffelkapitan, it also crashed in the sea. The Dorniers in
tight formation concentrated fire upon the Hurricanes, shooting down Flying Officer
J. H. L. Allan (NZ) (P3275). Another Hurricane, P2557, flown by Sergeant L.
Jowitt of 85 Squadron, came down off Felixstowe. Extensive clouds allowed the
Luftwaffe to operate widely, bombs falling on a Hamble boat yard and shelter, and at
Aberdeen, where, at 12.55, ten bombs hit Hall, Russell & Co's ship repair yard, six
houses and a public house. No warning had been sounded and twenty-six men were
killed with seventy-nine people injured, thirty-two seriously. An He 111 of KG 26,
possibly responsible, was shot down by 603 Squadron near Aberdeen. Scotland
suffered again after dark, two tenements in Greenock being damaged.

Hurricane P3039 assigned to No 229 Squadron from 12 July to 7 October 1940 was used by 312 Squadron between May and July 1941. It later briefly served with 56 OTU.

Memories of the summer of 1940 are usually of hot days, blue skies and warm nights, yet there were many days when rain and cloud prevailed. Although 13 July was mainly overcast, it did not prevent Ju 87s of II/StG 1, protected by Bf 109s of JG 51, operating against shipping in the Portland area. Although patrolling 56 Squadron[20] claimed seven Stukas that cannot be confirmed from Luftwaffe records, two Hurricanes were lost in the action. Later, Nos 54[21] and 64[22] Squadrons fought Bf 109s over Dover, 54 Squadron's Pilot Officer Colin Gray in R6893 scoring the first of his fourteen kills. Forced to land damaged Spitfire P9795 at Hawkinge, Sergeant A. E. Binham attributed his misfortune to over-zealous AA gunners.

Cloudy conditions persisted into 14 July when Ju 87s of LG 1 escorted by JG 3 carried out the usual afternoon raid near Portland. Sixteen Hurricanes of Nos 151[23] and 615[24] Squadrons and a dozen 610 Squadron Spitfires[25] engaged them and shot down one Stuka, but Pilot Officer M. R. Mudie's Hurricane of 615 Squadron failed to return. Taking part in the engagement with 151 Squadron was Wing Commander Victor Beamish in P3871 together with the first twin-cannon-armed Hurricane (L1750 of 151 Squadron), flown by Flight Lieutenant R. L. Smith. His fire brought down a Bf 109 on the French coast, accepted as the first kill by a cannon-armed RAF fighter. On this day instructions were given to shoot down air-sea rescue He 59 biplanes, of which about thirty were in service.

Another four days of bad weather must have irritated the impatient Luftwaffe, so intent upon decimating the RAF. Overnight bombing on 14/15 July, occurring south of a line Newport-Ipswich, resulted in the main rail route to Avonmouth being cut. Thick cloud on the 15th prevented KG 2 from accurately bombing a convoy, but LG 1 placed a dozen bombs on Westland's Yeovil factory and lost a Ju 88 to 92 Squadron near Cardiff. Barry, Mount Batten and Brixham were all raided. No 603 Squadron put a KG 26 He 111 into the sea off Peterhead. Very little action took place on the 16th, but Flying Officer W. H. Moorhouse, son of Second Lieutenant W. B. Moorhouse VC, and serving with 601 Squadron, shot down a Ju 88 of II/KG 54 off the Isle of Wight.

KG 26, active over Scotland on the 17th, sent six Heinkels to wreck Ayrshire's Ardeer explosives factory. Although they destroyed its detonator house, one attacker ended its days off Fraserburgh. In the south No 92 Squadron drew blood yet again, near Bristol, where they caught a Ju 88 of 1/KG 51. A line of eleven HEs fell across the Newton Ashford marshalling yards.

The Ministry Says...

Join Britain's silent column. Sensible people who know
when not to talk. Here's something you can do, and keep
on doing. It's not spectacular. You will wear no uniform,
you'll not spend nights on lonely duty. Your only
weapon will be your conscience, your ears and your
tongue. You will be doing a duty as wide as the making
of munitions. Keep it to yourself – and make others do the same.

While the Heinkels were busy on 17 July an order was placed for a mock-up of the first British jet fighter, the Gloster F.9/40, which was to emerge in 1944 as the Meteor. On 10 April 1940 Gloster's initial twin-engined design submission had been turned down as too large. A new, smaller chosen version had a forecast top speed of 460mph at 30,000 feet, spectacular at the time. In May 1940 Gloster was ordered to cease work and concentrate on Hurricane production, but on 13 June design work was allowed to resume and during the Battle of Britain work went ahead.

It was not the only jet fighter in view. In February 1940 construction of the Gloster E.28/39 began, and on 22 April, while the fight was tough in Norway, Air Ministry officials were examining a mock-up of it. An operational version outlined in conference on 11 May was given the go-ahead as a single-engined, six-gun single-seat fighter powered by a Whittle jet engine. Its forecast top speed was at least 380mph at sea level. By 15 September 1940 the first prototype was 95% complete, although its engine was far from ready. Within a few weeks its fighter future ended and the F.9/40 took its place.

Meanwhile, more conventional aircraft were active. Early on 18 July one of them dropped three small bombs, which cratered Gooseley Lane off the Barking-East Ham bypass. Another fell close to East Ham gasworks. Possible evidence of enemy frustration came around 09.00 on the 18th. No 610 Squadron, patrolling off Dover, was furiously bounced by nine Bf 109s, which shot down Spitfire R6765-T flown by Pilot Officer Litchfield, Green Leader. Small-scale operations over southern England resulted in KG 27's commander being shot down by 145 Squadron. Near Aberdeen an He 111's gunner brought down a 603 Squadron Spitfire. KG 26 was very active at this period, and on 18 July three of its He 111s attacked Montrose aerodrome where fighter pilots trained using Miles Master Is. Another scored a hit on the Long Shed, Leith docks.

Brighter weather on July 19 resulted in a memorable day of fighting. First success came to 145 Squadron[26] at around 07.00 when a Do 17P of 4(F)/121, after

Photographs, including this of Dover, were taken pre-war from German civilian aircraft. *IWM*

Do 17Z F1+KL of KG 76 shortly after taking off and heading for England. It is easy to see why 'flying pencil' was bestowed on the rickety sounding Dornier. *Bundesarchiv*

Britain's first jet propelled aircraft, the Gloster E.28/39 Pioneer was built at Gloucester whilst the summer battles raged, and was 95% structurally complete by mid-September.

reconnoitring Surrey, was destroyed off Brighton. At 10.40 KG 26 attacked Glasgow's Rolls-Royce engine factory, the Cardonnell Royal Ordnance factory, Govan and the Scotstown area.

Park had ordered squadrons to forward bases, among them Defiant-armed and inexperienced 141 Squadron, which left West Malling for Hawkinge. In cloudless conditions and visibility of 13 miles, Raids H47 and H49 were detected at 12.15. They comprised thirty Do 17s and Ju 87s flying in three or four groups at 12,000 feet and approaching from the south-west to dive-bomb a destroyer at a two-convoy intersection in the Straits. Dover's AA guns opened fire at 12.23 as a dozen Defiants roared off from Hawkinge. To protect the harbour, AA gunners fired a 164-shell barrage, battery D1 claiming a direct hit on a Dornier. Only nine serviceable Defiants[28] took off to patrol, led by Squadron Leader W. Richardson. South of Folkestone they were suddenly bounced by some dozen Bf 109s of II/JG 2, the 'Richthofen Geschwader'. The German fighters that dived upon the Defiants then zoomed up, raking their belly blind spots. Desperately banking to allow their turret gunners to take aim, the Defiants then faced more 109s delivering head-on assaults. Within moments four Defiants – from which only Pilot Officer J. Gard'ner survived – were shot out of the sky. Flight Lieutenant I. Donald's L7009 crashed in Dover. Only the arrival of 'Treble One' Hurricanes saved the four remaining Defiants. Flight

Lieutenant M. Loudon's gunner baled out, to become the only one thus surviving, before his aircraft (L7001) crashed in Hawkinge's circuit. Pilot Officer MacDougall's mauled Defiant (L7014) was immediately declared a write-off after landing. Of his gunner who had baled out, nothing more was ever seen. Dowding never wanted Defiant turret fighters, which, in this instance, were not fielded in a manner for which they were designed – ie for attacking unescorted bomber formations.

To fill the sudden gap, No 32 Squadron[29] hastened to the scene, and attempted to drive the Ju 87s away from Dover. The situation suited the protecting 109s, which soon picked off another Hurricane. No 43 Squadron[30] in Tangmere Sector also tangled with German fighters, losing Flight Lieutenant J. Simpson, 'A' Flight Commander, in P3410, and Sergeant J. Bush, flying P3351, who died in the sea off Shoreham. Before darkness fell, Ju 87s again tried to damage Portland.

Five Fighter Command pilots died on 19 July, five were wounded and eleven aircraft were lost. In nearly every engagement, squadrons were overwhelmed. Strengthening each response could be costly, even foolhardy – but what were the alternatives? Hitler yelled 'Surrender!', and with British morale extremely high his desire was popularly greeted with derision. Although the RAF was still around after four days – in small numbers – he could be reasonably pleased with the Luftwaffe's achievements. Indeed, so certain was he of victory that he promoted Hermann Goering to Reichsmarschall.

A heavy four-gun turret but no forward firing guns made the Boulton Paul Defiant too vulnerable in combat. *Boulton Paul*

The very few aviation enthusiasts of those days craved just one sighting of a Junkers four-engined bomber. At the time an intrepid one 'discovered' from an official document that it was impossible, something echoed in the words of some born decades after. However, there remain 'old hands' who, to their dying day, maintain having seen a fighter-escorted Ju 89 or Ju 90 (and not a Stirling) south of Croydon one bright 1940 day. Liverpudlians were certainly assaulted by Focke-Wulf 200 Condors, and the most satisfied enthusiasts – if any – must have been those living between Hartlepool and Sunderland on the night of 19/20 July when searchlights illuminated a Fw 200 of I/KG 40, which was promptly forced into the sea by AA shells. Mining too close to the shore, it was one of a pair that perished at this time, the other sinking off Northern Ireland. Two prisoners taken ashore in Northumberland confirmed their exotic means of arrival.

The Ministry Says...

What do I do if I come across German or Italian broadcasts when tuning my wireless? I say to myself now this blighter wants me to listen to him. Am I going to do what he wants? I remember German lies over the air are like German troops dropping on Britain. I remember no one can trust a word the Haw Haws say, so I make them waste their time. I switch them off or tune them out...

From the newspapers, 22 July, space presented by, yes, the good old Brewers!

Remember – Careless Talk Costs Lives. Keep the enemy in the dark...

Newspaper, 22 July

Come the morn of 20 July and another two He 59s, combining humanitarianism with observation of Convoy CW7, which sailed from Southend at 07.00, were disposed of by Hurricanes. Four fighter squadrons then guarded the convoy, and not until 18.00 did fighter-protected Ju 87s of II/StG 1 try to cause trouble. No 32 Squadron[31], by diving through the top cover, sent a pair of Stukas into the water and damaged two more. No 615 Squadron[32] was also active, Flight Lieutenant L. M. Gaunce (P2966), Pilot Officer Hugo (P2963) and Flying Officer Eyre bagging a I/JG 27 Bf 109 without loss. Here was proof that, given a good start, Hurricanes could dispose of nimble Messerschmitts. Also witnessing close by was No 610 Squadron[33], which battled with the 109s near Folkestone. As for the convoy, the SS *Pulborough* was sunk, and damaged SS *Westown* had to shelter in Dover. Destroyer HMS *Brazen* was damaged and sank under tow. The final tally showed a Hurricane and a 610 Squadron Spitfire missing, the latter flown by Pilot Officer G. Keithley, who crashed at Lydden, near Canterbury. Six British fighters were still missing when darkness fell. The enemy had lost thirteen, including four Bf 109s. Encouraging, most encouraging.

Using the 'Lyssies'

Under Fighter Command control was No 22 (Army Co-operation) Group, whose squadrons were each equipped with Lysanders. Purpose-built to support the Army, their main purpose was reconnaissance. Able to land in confined spaces, they had proven large for the role and vulnerable, but by the summer of 1940 they were given two special tasks.

The entire coastline between Land's End and Duncansby Head was divided into 'beat' areas allocated to Lysander squadrons, which, at twilight and dawn, starting on 1 July, operated pairs of aircraft for patrols seeking enemy invaders.

In May 1940 they were given another task – gas spray. Fear of gas attack remained to the end of hostilities, Britain being prepared to resort to chemical warfare only in retaliation for German first use. Five Lysander squadrons (Nos 2, 4, 26, 225 and 614) and some Blenheim bomber squadrons were trained to lay gas. Each Lysander squadron was allocated forty-seven 250lb 26-gallon Smoke Curtain Installation containers, sufficient for two sorties by each of its twelve aircraft. The containers emptied in 15 seconds of spraying. From between 250 and 500 feet a dense curtain could have smothered invaders within an area 600 yards long and 60 yards wide (600 yards wide if sprayed from about 3,000 feet). Training in gas spray operations for a pilot and one senior NCO from each squadron was undertaken at RAF Halton.

Although the Lysander's main task remained Army reconnaissance, it could carry a 500lb bomb load (twelve 40lb or sixteen 20lb) on Light Series Carriers, on its spat stubs and/or beneath the fuselage, for close support. In June 1940 it was given another role, that of anti-tank. A 20mm Hispano cannon firing twelve rounds per second was fitted to each bomb stub, tested at AFDU Northolt, then by No 110 Canadian Squadron, who found it cut the aircraft's already slow speed by 12mph. Only ball ammunition was available – useless against tanks! Nevertheless, on 21 October the Air Ministry decided that 50% of squadron Lysanders should carry cannon... Early in September each Lysander squadron had its IE cut appreciably from eighteen to twelve. A new squadron, No 231, was formed from 416 Flight in Ulster, where the Government believed a landing was possible – with support from the then-dormant IRA.

At dawn and dusk every day Lysanders scoured the coastline looking for invaders. LX-T N1294 belongs to 225 Squadron, Tilshead. *IWM*

Two 20mm Hispanic cannon would have been attached to Lysanders, as here, for anti-invasion operations.

Chapter 9

Death by attrition

During the last week of July and the first two weeks of August, the Luftwaffe conducted a war of attrition prior to its main assault. Fighter Command slowly increased the strength of its responses, while holding back as much of its strength as possible. Anti-shipping operations figured prominently in enemy activity, considerable mining of the Mersey early on 21 July attracting an eighty-three-round AA barrage. Although six mines were soon exploded by sweepers, Mersey ports and also Holyhead were closed for some time.

Larger fighter reaction was evident on 21 July, relay patrols covering convoy CW7, which eventually came under attack at 14.30 by forty Do 17s 10 miles south of the Isle of Wight. It took only three Hurricanes, P3782, P3781, and N2621 of 43 Squadron, to part the bomber formation before III/JG 27 engaged them. Each side lost one fighter. Blue Section of No 238 Squadron arrived as fifteen Bf 110s surprisingly started dive-bombing the convoy, which was crawling at 7 knots south-west of St Catherine's Point. Discovery that Messerschmitt 110s (of V/LG 1) could perform as fighter-bombers provided no mean shock to the British, who soon named them 'Jaguars'. Flight Lieutenant Walsh (P3618) claimed one, and another, badly damaged by Pilot Officer B. B. Considine (P3599), crashed at its French base. The strike disorganised the convoy, sank the SS *Terlings*, left the SS *Kollskegg* burning and caused the SS *Ninaborthen* to return to Portsmouth. No 238 Squadron Hurricanes (P3823, P3462, P2947) forced down a reconnoitring Bf 110 at Goodwood, and at 15.15 Hurricanes P3599 and P3618 of the squadron destroyed over Blandford a rare Do 17M. Thunderstorms over southern England failed to discourage an evening bomber from dropping a salvo off Portland near the Dutch steamer *Stuyvesant*.

Among the incidents on cloudy 22 July was the bombing of a German PoW camp at Banff, killing six inmates and injuring eighteen. Leith docks, Torpoint, Margate and Pembroke Dock were all bombed, and at 01.35 RAF Ternhill attracted eleven HEs. In the 24 hours ending 06.00 on 23 July, 140 HE bombs were reckoned to have fallen on Britain. During the night Tangmere's Fighter Interception Unit scored the first kill with the aid of AI radar.

Mid-afternoon on 23 July brought two of those ever-memorable lone Dornier penetrations. One was to Pulham, where bombs dropped from 700 feet exploded in the old airship shed, causing an eerie moaning and sighing that engulfed the giant cavern. The other, Raid UB56H, came in west of Shoreham. Skilfully using cloud cover, the crew slipped into the circuit at the Vickers-Armstrong Weybridge works at 15.19 while two Wellingtons were being air tested and lots of Tiger Moths were flying from nearby schools. Cunningly, the Dornier crew courted the other fliers at 4,000 feet, then put their bomber's undercarriage down and lined up – for a bombing run. Fighters had sought the raider in vain and now, as soon as it was recognised, Bofors gunners loosed off fifty-one rounds of AEB and the four 3.7-inch guns another five, many shells bursting prematurely, such was the hasty response. An initial salvo of six bombs fell along the landing ground's edge, a second six at St George's Hill and another five at the Wandsworth Gas Co premises in North Road, Walton. Vickers and Brooklands certainly had a lucky escape. Again, this event showed how much damage could be caused by just one raider.

Heinkel 111s resumed mining the Mersey early on 24 July. Searchlight crews illuminated one that fired on their sites at New Brighton. That, or another Heinkel, was again illuminated and held lit for 3 minutes. Coastguards at Hoylake and Formby Point independently claimed that it crashed in the sea as a result of dazzle. Could it have been the Fw 200 of I/KG 40 repeatedly reported as having crashed in the Irish Sea off Belfast?

Long-range Focke-Wulf Fw 200 Condors of KG 40 mined off the west and east coasts, this example reputedly being Fw 200C-1 F8+EH, which crashed off Hartlepool.

The damaging potential of sneak raids was later demonstrated on 24 July, by a low-flying He 111 whose HEs and incendiaries were hurled onto Glasgow's Hillington Industrial Estate. They damaged a printing works and sugar and oil cake factories and injured eighteen people. Soon after, Welsh-based 92 Squadron Spitfires (K9998, N3167, N3297) engaged a Ju 88 of KG 51 over Porthcawl. Pilot Officer R. P. Beamont of 87 Squadron later poured in more shots, ensuring its demise near Lynton.

Late morning brought what 54 Squadron dubbed 'The Battle of the Thames Estuary'. Some eighteen Do 17s escorted by JG 52 attempting to bomb a convoy, caused a ship to run for shallow water and provided the squadron[34] with its 'biggest fight since Dunkirk'. So furious and confused was the fight over Margate that No 54 claimed sixteen 109s, whereas Luftwaffe records suggest that two, possibly three fell, a more likely score. Pilot Officer Allen (R6812) engaged one near Margate, before his engine stopped. He managed to restart it and tried to reach Manston, but instead his aircraft spun in, crashing on an electricity substation in Omer Road, Cliftonville. Sergeant G. R. Collett (N3192) chased a Bf 109 too far, ran out of fuel and crashed at Sizewell, Suffolk. As for the Messerschmitts, one came down in Dane Valley Road and another in Byron Avenue, Margate; the pilot became a prize for local AFS men. Nos 65[35] and 610 Squadrons had been vectored to Dover to engage the Bf 109s as the latter were getting short of fuel and vulnerable. Unfortunately the advantage vanished when a fresh formation of Bf 109s arrived to deal with just such a situation. Fighter Command lost a pilot and two aircraft in the engagement, the Germans five Bf 109s of JG 26 and JG 52.

Bofors guns were very useful against low-level minelayers. This example was sited by the River Mersey. *IWM*

With a clear blue sky, 25 July was ideal for large-scale formation operations. The first major attack came in at 10.40, and Ju 87s of III/StG 1 tried again to damage Portland. No 152 Squadron later bagged a Do 17M west of Eastfleet, as well as one of the Ju 87s west of Portland Bill.

Bf 109s and several bombers approaching Dover around noon provided a temptation British fighters could well have ignored. Instead, 65 Squadron went into action. Flight Sergeant Franklin, by manoeuvring extremely low in N3164, caused a Bf 109 chasing him to plunge into the sea. No 32 Squadron's Hurricanes[36] joined 615 Squadron[37] in another fight, which resulted in limited success. Pilot Officer V. G. Daw of 32 Squadron, mixing with six 109s, received leg wounds, and was forced to land a badly damaged P3677. A few bombs fell harmlessly in Dover harbour and four more behind the cliffs at Swingate. Sheep were cruelly machine-gunned.

Convoy CW8 comprising small ships carrying coal, cement and general cargo sailed at 07.00 from Southend. By 14.30 it was off Dover while many British fighters were rearming. Ju 87s steeply dive-bombed the convoy, sinking three small ships and damaging two. Defence had rested entirely with AA gunners, Dover Site D1 claiming a Ju 87 before frantic calls brought along Spitfires of 54 Squadron[38], then 65 Squadron, upon which a hoard of Bf 109s immediately pounced. Two Spitfires were destroyed including R6707 flown by 54 Squadron's 'B' Flight commander, Flight Lieutenant B. H. Way, who was killed. Little wonder No 54 called this 'Black Thursday'.

A trio of No 65 Squadron's Spitfires taking-off from Hornchurch. YT-N is R6712 which was used 10 July to 25 October and YT-M is R6714 used 10 July to 16 October when it was written off during an operational flight.

Hurricanes of 17 Squadron return from patrol on 25 July. *IWM*

When eight Spitfires of 64 Squadron[39] arrived they faced another onslaught, this time by thirty Ju 88s of III/KG 4 being escorted by more than fifty Bf 109s. Three more 64 Squadron Spitfires (N3230, R6700, L1035) reinforced their companions, as well as twelve Hurricanes of 111 Squadron. Although they engaged the bombers, they could not prevent the sinking of two more ships. Sub Lieutenant Dawson Paul RN, flying L1035, after earlier claiming a 109, was shot down. The convoy had now lost SS *Corhaven*, *Henry Moon*, *Leo*, *Polgrange* and *Porslade*. Five ships were damaged.

It was at 16.21 that Spitfires of 54 Squadron patrolling off Dover sent an alarming message, for they had spotted E-boats leaving Boulogne. Two destroyers, HMS *Boreas* and *Brilliant*, together with two MTBs, hastened out of Dover and soon two E-boats were foundering off Calais. In a fierce response, Ju 87s dive-bombed the destroyers, which were further pestered by gunfire from the French coast. *Boreas* was hit and called for smoke and tugs. More Ju 87s screamed down upon her as she and the other destroyer slowly headed for Dover, whose No 4 LAA gunsite claimed a Stuka. More Spitfires of 54 and 64 Squadrons attempted to protect the warships, together with Hurricanes of 56 Squadron, even though they were challenged by more than 100 enemy aircraft. Just as the destroyers came under further attack, 610 Squadron's Spitfires arrived to bag a couple of JG 52's Bf 109s and damage several more without loss. While the remnants of CW8 later ploughed on into an uncertain night, Flying Officer Haynes of 600 Squadron tried in vain to deal with a rescue He 59 brightly lit off Foulness by searchlights. In the early hours of the 26th E-boats fired on the convoy before it was ordered to anchor in St Helen's Roads.

Balloons for Dover

Few targets provided such understandable fascination for Messerschmitt pilots as Dover's balloons. The question of a Dover barrage was first raised on 15 May 1940 when Dover was the main port for crossings to Calais. Balloons, it was argued, would prevent dive-bombing. Eight sites were suggested, manned by 956 Squadron. The Air Ministry was strongly against the idea, arguing that it would interfere with RAF operations, and the notion lapsed.

The intensity of raids on Dover in July 1940 led to a revival of schemes for a Dover Low Zone Balloon Barrage. On high-level authorisation the go-ahead was given on 30 July, suggestions being for balloons to be waterborne, possibly flown from six barges withdrawn from the Thames Yantlet Barrage.

Events moved with astonishing speed. A new squadron, No 992, was formed in 30 Group at 23 Marine Parade, Dover, by midnight on 30 July, by which time seventeen sites had been chosen. Next day Fighter Command escorted to Dover three drifters, two power barges and their balloons from Southend – the balloons withdrawn from Sheerness-based 952 Squadron. By midday sixteen land sites were in use and eight waterborne balloons floated above their moorings.

The Dover balloons seriously handicapped the area's anti-aircraft gunners, who were initially ordered to fuse their shells to burst above 3,000 feet.

The successful dive-bombing of HMS *Codrington* in Dover on 27 July, which had contributed towards the Navy's decision to move its destroyers to Portsmouth or Sheerness, had worried the Navy, whose MTBs, with less firepower than E-boats, would not have been able to prevent landings on the South Coast before destroyers arrived. The Navy, therefore, was eager to have the destroyers back in Dover and hoped that balloon cover would permit that. During the recent major raid Stukas and Bf 109s had successfully dived through the AA fire.

The first attack upon Dover's balloons developed at 14.30 on 30 July during an aerial battle over Folkestone involving nine Bf 109s at 15,000 feet. One Bf 109 then dived using light cloud cover to attack, with the balloons at 4,500 feet. First to fall in flames was one on a cliff edge site, and by keeping close to the balloons the pilot shot down a second.

To discourage such pursuits orders were then given to fly each balloon independently and just above the base of any thick cloud, at 8,000 feet if there was no cloud and just above 4,500 feet if fewer than four aircraft were attacking, because that made balloons harder to destroy. AA gunners therefore had to be careful not to score a balloon! On 5 August the entire barrage was reorganised as 961 Squadron with twenty-four balloons, eight of them waterborne.

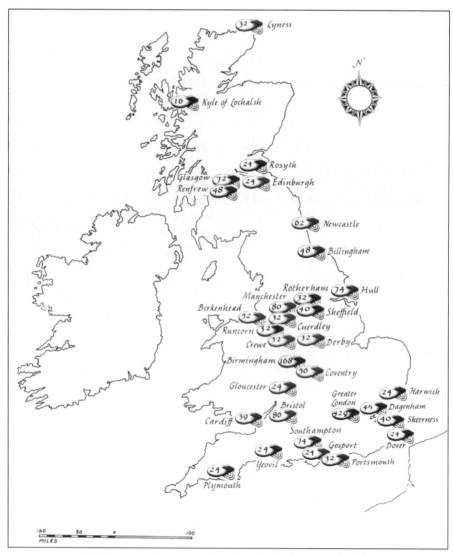

Barrage balloons as deployed in August 1940

Tough fighting over the Straits had been supported by the usual activity around Portland. There No 1 Squadron[40] entered the campaign, after temporarily replacing 43 Squadron at Tangmere. Their patrolling Hurricanes met Bf 109s of III/JG 27, destroying one that fell to Pilot Officer G. E. Goodman.

The daylight fighting had cost six Spitfires – three each from 54 and 64 Squadrons – and four pilots killed, in the most hectic day's fighting in the campaign so far. Prominent among the fifteen RAF fighter squadrons operating had been No 54, and it was time for the squadron to rest. It moved to Catterick next day from where 41 Squadron came to replace it. During July twelve 54 Squadron

In less than a year the strict style of RAF flying dress had changed to suit individual tastes and, one suspects, comfort! In the centre stands Squadron Leader D. O. Finlay, who flew with both 41 and 54 Squadrons. *IWM*

Spitfires had been shot down, five pilots killed and three wounded. An astonishing 504 sorties and more than 800 operational hours had been flown by its handful of pilots during three weeks of bitter fighting – no mean achievement by what might reasonably be called the first of The Few.

Rain and low cloud gave some respite on 26 July although No 238 Squadron[41] managed a fight with JG 27, Sergeant R. Little (P3702) having part of a boot shot away and two bullets lodged in his parachute. Off Portland Flight Lieutenant S. C. Walch (P3618) destroyed a Bf 109.

The day featured a noteworthy event. First flown on 20 July 1939, the Bristol Beaufighter twin-engined cannon-armed fighter was cleared for squadron service on 26 July 1940, initially with No 25 Squadron, North Weald. In May 1940 Lord Beaverbrook chose six aircraft types to have production priority, and the Beaufighter was one. Two were delivered in June 1940, five in July. By the end of the year 110 examples were in RAF hands.

Night activity, quite widespread, included ten HEs falling on the Fraserburgh Consolidated Pneumatic Tool Co. At Chigwell houses suffered, and also at Staple Hill, Bristol, in Dagenham and on Canvey Island. Bombs intended for the ICI plant at Winnington, Cheshire, fell instead, without exploding, among houses at Northwich. Off Flatholme, Wales, a sand ship was blown up (possibly by mines), eight crewmen being lost. Night raiders were mostly dropping salvoes of from two to four bombs and multiples of thirty-six incendiaries.

Fine weather returned to the south on 27 July, the Germans taking advantage of it to dispatch about thirty Stukas of I/StG 77 escorted by JG 27 to deal with a convoy off Swanage. The Stukas were peeling off into the attack when Hurricanes (P3462, P3823, P2947) of 238 Squadron arrived, and Flying Officer Davis (P3462) picked off one. By the time the second wave arrived, three Hurricanes together with Spitfires of 609 Squadron[42] were protecting the ships. Thundery weather crossing southern England calmed the contest until late afternoon, then the second of two attacks on Dover damaged barracks and the marine station, and, more spectacularly, resulted in four direct hits on the destroyer HMS *Codrington*, causing its boilers to explode. That, and the discovery that emplacements for heavy-calibre long-range guns were being built near Calais, forced the Admiralty to move the destroyer flotilla from Dover to the Nore. Dowding received that news with relief, for it would diminish the harbour's importance. The Air Ministry, though, stressed its continuing usefulness, in consequence of which the number of fighter squadrons in the South East was increased to twenty-eight and more use was made of Hawkinge and Manston, which became forward bases.

Codrington (1,540 tons) was not the only destroyer lost that day. HMS *Wren* (1,120 tons) was bombed and sunk off Aldeburgh by He 111s of KG 53, and another destroyer was damaged. At 18.46 Hurricanes of 615 Squadron (P2801, P3161, P3111, P3158, P2587, P3162) downed an air-sea rescue He 59 off the Foreland.

Not all patrols and scrambles resulted in combat; sections of No 145 Squadron patrolling all day made just one contact. Spitfires, however, were in action against Bf 109s 20 miles south of the Needles, and Blue Section of 145 Squadron joined them. Three 109s latched onto Flight Lieutenant A. D. Boyd and P3221. Try as he might, he was unable to shake them off until at sea level he reached the French coast. He was lucky to escape, and at the end of his 2-hour flight had only 5 gallons of fuel left after landing.

Whenever any warship was lost it was bad for national morale. Sustained protection of shipping from air attack demanded repeated sorties for each pilot each day, and could easily have brought exhaustion to both them and the groundcrews. Dowding, realising how serious that would be, ordered that each pilot be given 8 hours rest a day, and one day off per week. That assumed that sufficient pilots remained on hand to fight.

A night attack on Belfast highlighted the inadequacy of night defences and the vulnerability of the west. A score of bombers had operated over Ireland and Anglesey, while others over the South East dropped sixty HEs and an oil bomb on Gillingham, as well as bombs on Maidstone and near Sevenoaks.

German conclusions that British pilots were exhausted might have seemed confirmed when, during fine weather on 28 July, a large morning gathering over the Channel failed to attract response. Fighter Command – conserving its strength for an enemy formation that advanced on Dover at around 14.00 – had placed eight squadrons at forward airfields. A dozen Spitfires of 74 Squadron[43] led by the famous South African 'Sailor' Malan, thus known because of his merchant navy days, waded among thirty-six Bf 109s of I/JG 51 over Dover. Hawkinge's Hurricane

Spitfire LZ-U at Gravesend and flown by Sqn Ldr R H A Leigh, No 66's Squadron Commander.
A S Thomas collection

Delivered on 11 June 1940, Hurricane P3059 'N Nuts' joined 501 Squadron 9 July 1940.
Shot down near Canterbury on 18 August, it had flown only 49.20 hours. It is pictured
taking-off from Gravesend.

squadrons went for the bombers. Such clear division of effort, probably overdue,
meant that squadrons would, whenever possible, no longer split at the battle site.
Maybe the enemy detected this tactical change, for his bombers readily turned about,
leaving their escort battling with RAF fighters.

FOOD FACTS № 2

...cut out extras, cut out waste, don't eat more than you need.

TEA TIPS: You can save that extra one for the pot if you get the best out of your tea, so remember: i) As soon as the water is boiling really fast you should be ready with a well-warmed teapot. The teapot should come to the kettle, not the kettle to the pot. You should give the tea enough time to brew, and stir it just before pouring...

Don't make the mistake of using lettuce just as a salad. Lettuce cooked in a little water makes a delicious vegetable. You can enjoy the outside leaves even...

You can hear unusual tips on the wireless at 8.15 every morning.

Bake any stale bread in slices and use as toast or serve as rusks with soup or stews...

Cut a medium-sized marrow in two and scoop out the seeds. Fill with stuffing made of two heaped tablespoonfuls of breadcrumbs, two of minced bacon or cold meat, one of chopped suet, one small onion grated and a sprinkling of mixed herbs. Add pepper and salt ... if preferred the bacon or meat may be omitted ... more suet should then be included.

A sharp fight ensued, 41[44], 74, 257[45] and 111 Squadrons combating I and II/JG 51 being led by Major Werner Molders. He had to force-land his Bf 109 in France after it was badly damaged by Squadron Leader 'Sailor' Malan. No 74 Squadron did extremely well, Malan (N3091), Pilot Officer Freeborn (R6706) and Flight Lieutenant Kelly (K9878) each destroying a Bf 109. Another three were damaged, for the loss of two Spitfires and Pilot Officer J. H. R. Young.

He 59 seaplanes arrived to snatch German survivors from the sea, only to encounter No 111 Squadron, which destroyed one and seriously damaged another. Darkness cloaked more sinister floatplanes, He 115s, which accompanied He 111s and Ju 88s to extensively mine British waters. Bombers operating on a greater scale than recently attacked Newcastle. A dozen HEs fell in a line parallel to, and a mile from, the Tyne. Barry, Port Talbot, Colchester, Salford, Newcastle-under-Lyme, Seaford, Staplehurst, Ashford and Edenbridge were all bombed. Two HEs that failed to explode had the cheek to fall near the beautiful Cotswold Slaughters. Midlothian, Cheshire and the Otmoor bombing range also attracted the enemy.

When morning mist lifted on Monday 29 July, it revealed Britain splendidly and brilliantly sunlit, conditions advantageous to the foe. After feints on the previous day, controllers very cautiously committed aircraft to engagements until radar detected a large enemy force bypassing two convoys and obviously heading for Dover. It needed interception so Spitfires of 41 Squadron[46] were scrambled from Manston at 07.25 to engage the enemy on his northern flank. Ten Hurricanes of 501 Squadron raced in from the sunward side, and when they met the Luftwaffe they realised that they were facing one of the largest raids yet. Four formations of eighty-plus had assembled near Cap Gris Nez and now revealed themselves as Bf 109s escorting two waves of Stukas soon screeching down from 12,000 to 1,000 feet to dive-bomb Dover Harbour. There

Spitfires of No 41 Squadron. EB-K, X4178, joined the squadron on 25 September and crashed in the English Channel 15 October.

they sank the previously damaged *Gronland* (1,264grt) and started a fire aboard a submarine depot ship. No 41 Squadron engaged the Stukas as Bf 109s bore down upon the Spitfires. The squadron, forced to split and engaging both enemy aircraft, lost one aircraft in combat and four more in crash-landings for the destruction of one Messerschmitt. Nos 64[47] and 56[48] Squadrons had been vectored to help, the latter's Hurricanes engaging the 109s. No 501 Squadron[49] penetrated to the Stukas, and shot down two into the sea. Incendiaries and HEs that had fallen on the Royal Navy oil depot broke a supply pipe from which spilt fuel gushed, then blazed upon the water. Dover's AA guns merrily added to the confusion by claiming 501's Ju 87s!

What's on at the pictures in July?

Susannah of the Mountain (Shirley Temple)

Hardy and Son (Mickey Rooney and Lewis Stone)

Hollywood Cavalcade (in Technicolor – Alice Faye and Don Ameche)

The Great Victor Herbert (Allan Jones and Mary Martin – yes, JR's Mum!)

The Saint Strikes Back (George Sanders)

The Gates of Alcatraz (Walter Connolly and Oslo Stevens)

Drums Along the Mohawk (Claudette Colbert and Henry Fonda)

At the Regal all next week: Sam Goldwyn presents *Raffles* with David Niven and Olivia de Havilland.

29 July: For six days only (no Sunday opening) – *Melody of Youth*; two prices only – 6d and 1/-.

Soon after midday attention switched to Channel convoys, one of which, off Dungeness at 13.10, was subjected to a low-level onslaught by Ju 88s of II/KG 76, whose lead aircraft clouted a ship's balloon cable. Another was claimed by AA gunners. No 610 Squadron's Spitfires[50] arrived too late to participate, the raiders having approached below the radar screen.

Convoy 'Agent' off Orfordness, Essex, came under attack at 17.15 by a mixture of thirty-three escort fighter Bf 110s, mainly of ZG 26, and eight fighter-bomber Bf 110s of St Omer-based Erpr 210. They were engaged by 151 Squadron. From 45 miles off Felixstowe a snooping Do 17 of KG 2 had earlier been chased as far as the Belgian coast by Fg Off Woods-Scawen of 85 Squadron, and three pilots of 85 Squadron claimed an He 111 approaching 'Agent'. A few minutes later another of KG 53 was destroyed off Lowestoft by three pilots of 66 Squadron.

Meanwhile, off Portland, bombers had achieved a notable success by sinking the small destroyer HMS *Delight*. Among limited raids the following night were nine on North East England. At Hull, five shops and a public house were damaged, while near Bury St Edmunds soon after midnight a Ju 88 crashed due to circumstances never established.

Penetrating cloud and drizzle on 30 July, at 06.04 a Dornier 17 released fifteen HEs across Norwich, causing considerable damage, killing ten and injuring sixteen residents. Additional to other cloud-cover attacks over the east, south, Scotland and the Orkneys, Erpr 210 repeated its anti-shipping foray off Suffolk and lost a Bf 110C off Harwich, shot down by 85 Squadron. Unusual was an early evening bombing raid on Esher's balloon sites, during which an ARP post was hit. Night operations – including plentiful mining of Liverpool Bay, partly by Fw 200s – were mainly directed at Wales, Barry Docks in particular. On Monmouth thirteen HEs fell, and Heysham, Lancashire, was another target.

Hazy conditions on 31 July generated single aircraft operations – soon after dawn – until Bf 109s of JG 2 began shooting down Dover's balloons. Spitfires of 74 Squadron, arriving to stop the game, found that some of the Messerschmitts had a height advantage, rapidly exploited to bring down the Spitfires of Sergeant Eley (P9398) and Pilot Officer Gunn (P9379), for the loss of one of their number, which crashed in France.

Many raiders operated widely after dark south of a line from Newcastle to Liverpool, and some fifty mined off the East Coast. A procession of bombers crossed the Beachy Head-Shoreham area to the Thames region, then released their loads upon Croydon, Romford, Gravesend, Ipswich and Martlesham Heath.

British records compiled at the end of July suggested that 1,921 HE bombs, an unknown quantity of incendiaries, 162 oil bombs and nineteen mines of uncertain types had fallen on the United Kingdom during a month that had seen varying amounts of enemy activity on every day and night. The Luftwaffe was only playing the overture.

Luftwaffe Losses during operations by operational units, 1-31 July 1940

Captured Luftwaffe Quartermaster General's ledgers listing losses and accidents to the end of 1943 form the basis for official statistics of losses, together with further material from unreleased documents. The listing here and later is based upon the Quartermaster General's documents.

July	1			2			3			4			5		
Type	a	b	c	a	b	c	a	b	c	a	b	c	a	b	c
Do 17M	–	–	–	–	–	–	–	–	–	–	–	–	–	–	–
Do 17P	–	–	–	–	–	–	–	–	–	–	–	–	–	–	–
Do 17Z	6	1	1	1	1	1	1	–	–	–	–	–	–	–	–
Do 18	–	–	–	–	–	–	–	–	–	–	–	–	–	–	–
Do 215	2	–	–	1	–	–	–	–	–	–	–	–	–	–	–
Fw 200	–	–	–	–	–	–	–	–	–	–	–	–	–	–	–
He 59	1	–	–	–	–	–	–	–	–	–	–	–	–	–	–
He 111D	–	–	–	–	–	–	–	–	–	–	–	–	–	–	–
He 111H	–	1	–	–	–	–	–	–	–	–	–	–	1	–	–
He 111P	–	–	–	–	–	–	–	–	–	1	–	–	–	–	–
He 115	–	–	–	–	–	–	–	–	–	–	–	–	–	–	–
Ju 87B	–	–	–	–	–	–	–	–	1	–	–	–	–	–	–
Ju 88A	1	–	1	–	1	–	3	–	–	–	–	–	–	1	–
Ju 88C	–	–	–	–	–	–	–	–	–	–	–	–	–	1	–
Me/Bf 109	–	–	–	–	1	–	–	1	–	–	–	2	–	–	–
Me/Bf 110	–	–	–	–	–	–	–	–	–	–	–	–	–	–	–
Totals	10	2	2	2	3	0	4	1	1	1	0	2	1	2	0

July	6			7			8			9			10		
Type	a	b	c	a	b	c	a	b	c	a	b	c	a	b	c
Do 17M	–	–	–	–	–	–	–	–	–	–	–	–	–	–	–
Do 17P	–	1	–	2	1	1	–	–	–	–	–	–	–	–	1
Do 17Z	–	1	–	–	–	1	–	–	–	–	–	–	3	–	1
Do 18	–	–	–	–	–	–	–	–	–	–	–	–	–	–	–
Do 215	–	–	–	–	–	–	–	–	–	–	–	2	1	–	–
Fw 200	–	–	–	–	–	–	–	–	–	–	–	–	–	–	–
He 59	–	–	–	–	–	–	–	–	–	1	–	–	–	–	–
He 111D	–	–	–	–	–	–	–	–	–	–	–	–	–	–	–
He 111H	–	–	–	–	–	–	2	–	–	1	–	–	1	–	–
He 111P	–	–	–	–	–	–	–	–	–	–	–	–	–	–	–
He 115	–	–	–	–	–	–	–	–	–	–	–	–	–	–	–
Ju 87B	–	–	–	–	–	–	–	1	–	1	–	–	–	–	–
Ju 88A	–	–	–	2	–	–	1	–	–	–	1	–	–	–	–
Ju 88C	–	–	–	–	–	–	–	–	–	–	–	–	–	–	–
Me/Bf 109	–	2	–	–	1	2	4	1	1	2	–	–	2	–	–
Me/Bf 110	1	–	–	–	–	–	–	–	–	4	1	1	1	–	–
Totals	1	4	0	4	2	4	7	2	1	9	1	3	8	1	2

a = failed to return from operational flight/shot down, b = destroyed as a result of battle damage and written off, uneconomic to repair, etc, c = seriously damaged, and needing contractor's attention

July	11			12			13			14			15		
Type	a	b	c	a	b	c	a	b	c	a	b	c	a	b	c
Do 17M	–	–	–	–	–	–	–	–	–	–	–	–	–	–	–
Do 17P	2	–	–	–	–	–	–	–	–	–	–	–	–	–	–
Do 17Z	–	–	2	2	–	–	–	–	–	–	–	–	–	–	–
Do 18	–	–	–	–	–	–	–	–	–	–	–	–	1	–	–
Do 215	–	–	–	–	–	–	–	–	–	–	–	–	–	–	–
Fw 200	–	–	–	–	–	–	1	–	–	–	–	–	–	–	–
He 59	1	–	–	–	–	–	–	–	–	–	–	–	–	–	–
He 111D	–	–	–	–	–	–	–	–	–	–	–	–	–	–	–
He 111H	4	–	2	4	–	1	–	–	–	–	–	–	1	–	1
He 111P	1	–	–	–	–	–	–	–	–	–	–	–	–	–	–
He 115	–	–	–	–	–	–	1	–	–	–	–	–	–	–	–
Ju 87B	2	1	–	–	–	–	–	–	1	1	–	–	–	–	–
Ju 88A	2	1	–	–	1	–	2	–	–	–	1	–	1	1	–
Ju 88C	–	1	–	–	–	–	–	–	–	–	–	–	–	–	–
Me/Bf 109	–	–	1	–	–	–	2	–	2	1	–	–	–	–	–
Me/Bf 110	–	4	–	–	–	–	–	–	3	–	–	–	–	–	–
Totals	15	3	5	7	1	1	6	0	6	2	1	0	3	1	1

July	16			17			18			19			20		
Type	a	b	c	a	b	c	a	b	c	a	b	c	a	b	c
Do 17M	–	–	–	–	–	–	1	–	–	–	–	–	–	1	–
Do 17P	–	–	–	–	–	–	–	–	–	1	–	–	1	–	–
Do 17Z	1	–	–	–	–	1	–	–	–	–	–	–	–	–	1
Do 18	–	–	–	–	–	–	–	–	–	–	–	–	–	–	–
Do 215	–	–	–	–	–	–	–	–	–	–	–	–	–	–	–
Fw 200	–	–	–	–	–	–	–	–	–	–	–	–	2	–	–
He 59	–	–	–	–	–	–	–	–	–	–	–	–	2	–	–
He 111D	–	–	–	–	–	–	–	–	–	–	–	–	–	–	–
He 111H	–	–	–	1	–	–	–	–	–	–	–	–	–	–	–
He 111P	–	–	–	–	–	1	–	–	–	1	–	–	–	1	–
He 115	–	–	–	–	–	1	–	–	–	–	–	–	–	–	–
Ju 87B	–	–	–	–	–	–	–	–	–	–	–	–	2	–	–
Ju 88A	1	–	–	1	1	–	2	–	1	–	–	–	1	–	–
Ju 88C	–	–	–	–	–	–	–	–	–	–	–	–	–	–	–
Me/Bf 109	–	1	–	–	–	–	–	–	–	1	–	–	–	5	–
Me/Bf 110	–	–	–	–	–	–	–	–	–	–	–	–	–	–	–
TOTALS	2	1	0	2	1	2	4	0	1	4	0	0	11	4	1

a = failed to return from operational flight/shot down, b = destroyed as a result of battle damage and written off, uneconomic to repair, etc, c = seriously damaged, and needing contractor's attention

July	21			22			23			24			25		
Type	a	b	c	a	b	c	a	b	c	a	b	c	a	b	c
Do 17M	1	–	–	–	–	–	–	–	–	–	–	–	1	–	–
Do 17P	1	–	–	1	–	–	1	–	–	–	–	–	–	–	–
Do 17Z	–	–	–	–	–	–	1	–	–	–	–	–	–	1	–
Do 18	1	1	–	–	–	–	–	–	–	–	–	.–	–	2	–
Do 215	–	–	–	–	–	–	–	–	–	–	–	–	–	–	–
Fw 200	–	–	–	–	–	–	–	–	–	–	–	–	–	–	–
He 59	–	–	–	–	–	–	–	–	–	–	–	–	–	1	–
He 111D	–	–	–	–	–	–	–	–	–	–	–	–	–	–	–
He 111H	–	–	–	–	–	–	–	–	–	–	–	–	–	–	–
He 111P	–	–	–	–	–	–	–	–	–	–	–	1	–	–	–
He 115	–	–	–	–	–	–	–	–	–	–	–	–	–	–	–
Ju 87B	–	1	–	–	–	–	–	–	–	–	–	–	1	–	–
Ju 88A	–	1	–	–	1	1	1	1	–	1	1	–	1	–	–
Ju 88C	–	–	–	–	–	–	–	–	–	–	–	–	–	–	–
Me/Bf 109	2	–	1	–	–	–	–	–	–	6	–	–	–	5	–
Me/Bf 110	1	–	1	–	–	–	–	–	–	–	–	–	2	–	1
TOTALS	6	2	3	1	1	1	3	2	0	8	3	1	7	9	1

July	26			27			28			29			30		
Type	a	b	c	a	b	c	a	b	c	a	b	c	a	b	c
Do 17M	–	–	–	–	–	–	–	–	–	–	–	–	–	–	–
Do 17P	–	–	–	–	–	–	–	–	–	–	–	–	–	–	–
Do 17Z	1	–	–	–	–	–	–	1	–	–	–	1	–	–	1
Do 18	–	–	–	–	–	–	–	–	–	–	–	–	–	–	–
Do 215	–	–	–	–	–	–	–	–	–	–	–	–	–	–	–
Fw 200	–	–	–	–	–	–	–	–	–	–	–	–	–	–	–
He 59	–	–	–	1	–	1	–	–	–	–	–	–	–	–	–
He 111D	–	–	–	–	–	–	–	–	–	–	–	–	–	–	–
He 111H	–	–	–	–	–	–	–	–	–	2	1	–	1	–	–
He 111P	–	–	–	–	–	–	–	–	–	1	–	–	1	2	1
He 115	–	–	–	–	–	–	–	–	–	–	–	–	–	–	–
Ju 87B	–	–	–	1	–	–	–	–	–	4	–	–	–	–	–
Ju 88A	–	–	–	1	–	–	1	2	–	3	1	2	–	–	–
Ju 88C	–	–	–	–	–	–	–	–	–	–	–	–	–	–	–
Me/Bf 109	1	–	1	–	–	–	3	–	3	–	–	–	–	–	1
Me/Bf 110	–	–	–	–	–	–	–	1	–	–	–	–	1	–	–
Totals	2	0	1	4	0	1	4	4	3	10	2	3	3	2	2

a = failed to return from operational flight/shot down, b = destroyed as a result of battle damage and written off, uneconomic to repair, etc, c = seriously damaged, and needing contractor's attention

July		31		Grand totals		
Type	a	b	c	a	b	c
Do 17M	–	–	–	3	1	0
Do 17P	–	–	–	9	2	2
Do 17Z	–	–	1	15	5	9
Do 18	–	–	–	2	3	0
Do 215	–	1	–	4	1	2
Fw 200	–	–	–	3	0	0
He 59	–	–	–	6	1	1
He 111D	–	–	–	1	0	0
He 111H	–	–	–	22	5	4
He 111P	–	–	–	5	3	3
He 115	–	–	–	2	–	–
Ju 87B	–	–	–	10	4	3
Ju 88A	–	1	1	26	15	6
Ju 88C	–	–	–	–	2	–
Me/Bf 109	–	1	1	29	14	15
Me/Bf 110	–	–	1	14	2	7
Totals	0	3	4	151	58	52

a = failed to return from operational flight/shot down, b = destroyed as a result of battle damage and written off, uneconomic to repair, etc, c = seriously damaged, and needing contractor's attention

Many Battles were available in 1940, some like L5136 serving at bombing and gunnery schools. Between 1 July and 15 October 1940, 227 Battles saw squadron service and 9 were lost during operations. 124 battles were shipped to Canada, 37 to Australia and 21 to South Africa for use in the Empire Training Scheme. *(Fairey)*

Eleven Hurricanes were shipped to Malta in June 1940 and 17 more in July including P2627, to prevent Italian attacks. P2627 later served with 273 Squadron. *(Hawker)*

RAF bomber, coastal and fighter aircraft losses, 1–31 July 1940

General note relating to loss tabulations:

British and German losses in the accompanying tables are grouped within three basic entries - a shot down, b written off due to battle damage, and c suffered major damage but repairable. All the entries relate to loss or damage sustained during operational flying. Tabulations such as these can only give a general picture of the results of combat flying. Some damaged aircraft were quickly returned to front-line service while others, even with little damage, were not repaired until many weeks, even months, had passed. Others, particularly on the British side, were removed for repair by civilian contractors, which led to their return to RAF squadrons and units via Aircraft Storage Units (MUs) where sometimes they tarried long and underwent modification programmes. Generally, if the fuselage of an RAF aircraft survived an accident sufficiently well for it to be repairable, the identity number (its 'serial') was retained – even if other major components needed replacing. Thus, the mainplanes of a written-off aircraft could well be wedded to a repairable fuselage of another. The Luftwaffe assessed the damage of its aircraft on what seems a rather imperfect percentage basis. An aircraft with 40% or more damage required considerable attention, that rated at 60% and over being very badly damaged. Just how complete the German records were can only be surmised, although without recording a loss a unit would not have received its replacement. Certainly the German records became ever more detailed as the fighting developed. Indeed, earlier omissions are often included at much later dates. British individual aircraft record cards (Form 78s) were generally amended some time after the events they record, in some instances at the end of the relating calendar month. Their brief entries cover wide possibilities, as, for example, when the category of damage was amended and not always recorded on the card. Fates and dates, too, for a variety of reasons, may differ from those listed. The subject of losses is indeed a highly complex one.

July	1			2			3			4			5		
Type	a	b	c	a	b	c	a	b	c	a	b	c	a	b	c
Blenheim F	–	1	–	–	–	–	–	–	–	–	–	–	–	1	–
Defiant	–	–	–	–	–	–	–	–	–	–	–	–	–	–	–
Hurricane	–	–	1	–	–	–	1	1	2	–	–	1	–	1	–
Spitfire	–	1	–	–	–	–	–	1	–	–	–	–	1	1	1
Blenheim B	–	–	–	1	–	–	–	–	–	1	–	–	2	–	–
Hampden	–	–	–	1	–	–	–	–	–	–	–	–	–	–	–
Wellington	–	–	–	–	–	–	–	–	–	–	–	–	1	–	–
Whitley	1	–	–	–	–	–	–	–	–	–	–	–	–	–	–
Coastal Cmd	–	–	–	2	–	–	–	–	–	2	–	–	–	–	–
Totals	1	2	1	4	–	–	1	2	2	3	–	1	4	3	1

a = failed to return from operational flight/shot down, b = destroyed as a result of battle damage and written off, uneconomic to repair, etc, c = seriously damaged, and needing contractor's attention

July	6			7			8			9			10		
Type	a	b	c	a	b	c	a	b	c	a	b	c	a	b	c
Blenheim F	–	–	–	–	–	1	1	–	–	–	–	–	–	–	–
Defiant	–	–	–	–	–	–	–	–	2	–	–	–	–	–	–
Hurricane	–	1	–	1	–	1	3	–	–	2	1	–	1	–	1
Spitfire	–	1	–	5	1	–	2	1	–	2	1	–	–	–	3
Blenheim B	1	–	–	2	–	–	–	–	–	–	1	–	–	–	1
Hampden	–	–	–	–	–	–	2	–	1	–	–	–	–	–	–
Wellington	1	–	–	–	–	–	–	–	–	–	–	–	–	–	–
Whitley	1	–	–	–	–	–	1	–	–	1	–	–	–	–	–
Coastal Cmd	2	–	–	–	–	–	1	–	–	1	–	–	1	–	–
Totals	5	2	–	8	1	2	10	1	3	6	3	–	2	–	5

July	11			12			13			14			15		
Type	a	b	c	a	b	c	a	b	c	a	b	c	a	b	c
Blenheim F	–	–	–	–	–	–	–	–	1	–	–	–	–	–	–
Defiant	–	–	–	–	–	–	–	–	–	–	–	–	–	–	–
Hurricane	4	1	–	2	5	3	2	2	1	1	–	1	1	2	2
Spitfire	2	–	–	–	1	–	–	1	1	–	–	–	–	–	–
Blenheim B	–	–	–	–	–	–	–	–	–	–	–	–	–	–	–
Hampden	–	–	–	–	–	–	–	–	–	–	–	–	–	–	–
Wellington	1	–	–	–	–	–	–	–	–	1	–	–	–	–	–
Whitley	1	–	–	–	–	–	–	–	–	1	–	1	–	–	–
Coastal Cmd	1	–	–	1	–	–	1	–	–	3	–	–	1	–	–
Totals	9	1	–	3	6	3	3	3	3	6	–	2	2	2	2

July	16			17			18			19			20		
Type	a	b	c	a	b	c	a	b	c	a	b	c	a	b	c
Blenheim F	–	–	–	–	–	–	2	–	–	–	–	–	1	–	–
Defiant	–	–	–	–	–	–	–	–	–	5	1	1	–	–	–
Hurricane	–	–	–	–	–	–	–	–	1	4	–	1	4	1	–
Spitfire	–	–	–	–	2	–	3	1	3	–	–	–	1	1	–
Blenheim B	–	–	–	–	–	–	2	–	1	–	–	–	1	–	–
Hampden	–	–	–	–	–	–	–	–	–	1	–	–	4	1	–
Wellington	–	–	–	–	–	–	–	–	1	1	–	–	1	1	–
Whitley	–	–	–	–	–	–	–	–	–	1	–	–	–	–	–
Coastal Cmd	–	–	–	–	–	–	4	–	–	–	–	–	–	–	–
Totals	–	–	–	–	2	–	11	1	6	12	1	2	12	4	–

a = failed to return from operational flight/shot down, b = destroyed as a result of battle damage and written off, uneconomic to repair, etc, c = seriously damaged, and needing contractor's attention

July	21			22			23			24			25		
Type	a	b	c	a	b	c	a	b	c	a	b	c	a	b	c
Blenheim F	–	–	–	–	–	1	–	–	–	–	–	–	–	–	–
Defiant	–	–	–	–	–	–	–	–	–	–	–	–	–	–	–
Hurricane	1	–	–	–	2	–	–	3	–	–	2	–	1	–	1
Spitfire	1	–	–	–	–	3	–	1	–	1	2	–	6	2	1
Blenheim B	–	–	–	–	–	–	1	–	–	1	–	–	1	–	1
Hampden	1	1	–	–	–	–	1	–	–	–	–	–	2	–	–
Wellington	2	–	1	–	–	–	–	–	–	–	–	–	2	1	–
Whitley	1	–	–	1	–	–	–	–	–	–	–	–	–	–	–
Coastal Cmd	–	–	–	–	–	–	2	–	–	–	–	–	2	–	–
Totals	6	1	1	1	2	4	4	4	–	2	4	–	14	3	3

July	26			27			28			29			30		
Type	a	b	c	a	b	c	a	b	c	a	b	c	a	b	c
Blenheim F	–	–	–	–	–	1	–	–	–	–	–	–	–	1	–
Defiant	–	–	–	–	–	–	–	–	–	–	–	–	–	–	–
Hurricane	2	1	–	–	1	1	1	1	–	1	1	2	–	–	–
Spitfire	–	1	2	1	1	–	2	1	1	1	1	5	–	–	–
Blenheim B	–	–	2	–	–	–	–	–	1	1	–	–	1	–	–
Hampden	2	–	–	–	–	–	1	–	–	–	1	–	–	–	–
Wellington	–	–	2	–	–	–	–	–	–	–	–	1	–	–	–
Whitley	1	–	–	–	–	–	–	–	–	–	–	–	–	–	–
Coastal Cmd	2	–	–	–	–	–	–	–	–	–	–	–	–	–	–
Totals	7	2	6	1	2	2	4	2	2	3	3	8	1	1	–

July	31			Grand totals, July		
Type	a	b	c			
Blenheim F	–	–	–	1	3	4
Defiant	–	–	–	5	1	3
Hurricane	–	2	–	33	29	19
Spitfire	2	1	1	32	28	20
Blenheim B	2	–	–	17	1	6
Hampden	1	2	–	17	5	1
Wellington	–	–	–	10	2	5
Whitley	–	–	–	10	0	1
Coastal Cmd	3	–	–	29	0	0
Totals	8	5	1	154	69	59

a = failed to return from operational flight/shot down, b = destroyed as a result of battle damage and written off, uneconomic to repair, etc, c = seriously damaged, and needing contractor's attention

Chapter 10

No, you can't go to the seaside this year

Invasion seemed more likely every day – we all realised that, but it still induced questioning and unease rather that fear. Nothing like it had happened for almost a thousand years, so – could it really happen now? August Bank Holiday – then held on the first Monday of the month – fell on the 5th. It was definitely a 'stay at home' event. Leaving one's home at this most uncertain time was most unwise. I clearly remember Dad and I spending the holiday pottering around the plot of land he used as a garden. On arriving home we checked, as usual, our arsenal. Would we soon be using them? I never quite visualised what that event would be like. Popping a 'Molotov cocktail' into a tank – surely that would be quite difficult. A very sobering sight had recently manifested itself on nearby Midsummer Common, Cambridge, which was now festooned with poles and trip wires to make it impossible for Ju 52s or gliders to land. What a thought – Ju 52s full of Nazis slipping over our rooftop. Very creepy!

Overhead on most days flew lonesome or grouped Hurricanes and Spitfires keeping us reasonably safe. Locally based Blenheims and Wellingtons helped raise morale with their 'hitting back', albeit on a small scale. Whatever may now be said, in 1940 it was good to know that the Germans were also being bombed. Much has been made in post-war times of the inaccuracy of RAF night-bombing before 1942, and it is undoubtedly true. Only when they were relying upon radio beams did the Germans do any better – except when employing lone aircraft using cloud cover for many very effective raids.

Since the mid-1930s East Anglians had become used to seeing ever-increasing numbers of aircraft and aerodromes. Although it was 2 and 3 Group bomber territory, a very wide assortment of aircraft types made use of our sky. Almost daily there would be the sighting of an impressed pre-war civil light aircraft. Cambridge aerodrome throughout the war, as nowadays, attracted an amazing assortment of aircraft types. In 1940 Whitleys of all marks were passing through the civilian repair organisation, together with hosts of Airspeed Oxford trainers. Hawker Hart variants came too, including a Hector of 614 Squadron with undersurfaces unusually wearing a green-tinted version of 'Sky'. Of the August 1940 visitors, pride of place must go to a Handley Page Heyford (nearly yellow overall), which arrived on the 26th while Debden was being bombed. Of course, had I glimpsed the lone RAF Ford Tri-motor that once trundled by the west side of Cambridge…

The long summer school holiday provided an excellent opportunity for a cautious look around and to enjoy the assortment of anti-invasion Lysanders locally based. Road blocks dammed some roads but there many places to visit, pillboxes to see, bomb craters to descend into, aerodromes to very cautiously, carefully gaze upon. One of most fascinating moments for me came with the discovery at RAF Bottisham of an unguarded Tiger Moth 'No 26' of 22 EFTS carrying under its fuselage 20lb light bombs. No fence, no barbed wire, just open grass. By dusk I'd added a replica to my model air force.

During summer eves, as one exchanged the latest alarming rumours and enjoyed Official material courageously 'confiscated' during the day, etc, a local Gladiator would brilliantly perform aerobatics during a flight test following local overhaul, usually in the hands of Mr (later Sir) Arthur Marshall. He told me years later that he 'acquired' some ammunition in case he had the chance to...

By 9 o'clock the sky was frequently overclouding from the south, not naturally but with what were called 'smoke trails'. In our more sophisticated times we would call them vapour trails or contrails. The 1940s equivalents were remnants of those etched in the sky during big battles, which slowly merged as they slipped across more northern skies.

There was something else from this period that cannot go unmentioned: the enormously overcoming and demanding, authoritative voice of Mr Winston Churchill. To make sure of hearing this grandest of all champions, everyone seemed to be indoors in good time, which left every street silent. To have heard live, usually at 9.00pm, one of his electrifying speeches was to have garnered a great experience. National addresses by today's political lightweights are so rightly scorned; in 1940 the entire nation eagerly enthused to every moment of Churchill's magnificent oratory. Unforgettable, so unforgettable, those ominously silent moments during summer eves punctuated boldly by the brilliance of his soul-drenching language, which so skilfully he delivered. How greatly lifted was the spirit when, as a party piece, he all but spat the word 'Narzies'. 'If we fail' – well no, we were not going to fail, we wouldn't dare. If we did, we might have to face Winston to explain ourselves! 'We will never surrender,' he said, and he meant it, and so we daren't, either. Time to make sure our weapons of mini-destruction were ready, just in case we needed them during the night. I think I'd rather have faced a tank than Winnie!

It was business as usual in the early hours of August's opening day when a handful of minelayers opened the momentous month. Responding to intelligence information, Fighter Command mounted early patrols off the East Coast. Ships off Yorkshire were interesting the Luftwaffe, but before Nos 607 and 616 Squadrons could reach them, the German aircraft left the battleground.

A very unusual event occurred 10 miles south of Hastings when No 145 Squadron destroyed a Henschel Hs 126 army co-operation machine of 4(H)/31. It was shot down by Pilot Officer E. C. J. Wakeham (P3163) aided by Sub-Lieutenant I. H. Kestin (P3155), the latter tragically killed by return fire. Later, an He 111 of I/KG 4 managed a highly effective sneak raid, temporarily closing the Norwich Boulton & Paul factory, damaging Thorpe station's goods facility, setting fire to a timber yard and causing forty-three casualties. Around 18.50 Ju 88s of 9./KG 4, attempting to attack convoy 'Pilot' off Norfolk, were discovered by a trio of 242 Squadron Hurricanes and one bomber was shot down.

A highlight of the following night was, without doubt, the first arrival of a large supply of what are now high-value curious yellow and green leaflets then freely distributed to residents of Backwell, Clevedon, Axbridge, Brecon, Taly Uyn, Southampton, Marchwood and Epping. Carrying Hitler's 'Last Appeal to Reason', the 1940 version of junk mail was eagerly sought and greeted with delight and derision. Sold for 6d each in Bristol, the leaflets aided the national effort to 'help the Red Cross help our boys'. Others copies performed well in a less glamorous but most useful manner. The British Government, in pompous British style, applauded

What the papers had to say

2 August: 'First Leaflet Raid on Britain Last Night... They have a streamer heading "The Last Appeal to Reason by Adolf Hitler". The printing is good, the paper of fair quality.' (Does one detect some disappointment with Britain's blockade?)

2 August: From an Air Ministry announcement and a Swedish diplomat, about two German towns bombed by the RAF: 'Hamburg is said to be in ruins. Within a gigantic circle we've inflicted irreparable damage on such places as Duisburg, Dusseldorf, Essen ... and Wesel.' (Does one now detect optimism?)

in an Official 'Secret' report 'the quality of paper and print'! Wartime charity sales – to which the leaflets found their way – were nothing new. At one such sale, two chickens 'murdered' by a German cannon shell at Fleet End raised £16 for the Red Cross. This macabre approach to tragedy was essential, especially as 'incidents' such as one the night before involving a parachuted mine that exploded near Taunton and produced a 60-foot crater 18 feet deep, which would have to be filled. Neither a Social Security Office nor social supporter would have been of much help, let alone the Health and Safety souls. One sensibly sorted oneself out. If you survived, then you might have a tale to tell that could grow in wonder by the minute!

Coastal shipping again bore the brunt of enemy fascination throughout 2 August. It was undertaken in the belief that it was both damaging to Britain and part of an attempt to mount an increasing blockade. Off Harwich, fighter-bombers of Erpr 210 sank with a direct hit HM Trawler *Cape Finisterre*. Off Scotland gunners aboard the SS *Highlander* in a convoy managed to bring down one of ten attacking KG 26 He 111s. Their most unusual catch was much of the Heinkel, which fell on their deck and became a conspicuous trophy as they sailed into Leith. A second He 111 had also been brought down. The following night the Luftwaffe left noisy calling cards on RAF property at Halton, Catterick, Farnborough and Rochford. An impertinent, ineffective attempt was also made to break the Forth Bridge.

Dull weather on 3 August much reduced the German Channel effort. Nuisance sorties included one by a Ju 88, which flew so low by Wembury Cliff searchlight site that gunners there fired down upon it. Scotland, Tyneside, Humber, Harwich, Crewe – all had night raids, and sea-mining continued. Cornfield fires in Essex aroused an erroneous suspicion that the Luftwaffe really was using oil bombs to burn ripening grain after the manner of the RAF's use of phosphorus-impregnated strips dropped upon Germany – 'razzling' as it was called. The latest analysis suggested that about 5,800 HE bombs had in total so far fallen on Britain. About 4% were of 250kg, the others 50kg variants.

Cloudy weather throughout 4 August brought respite to both sides. The following night saw bombs fall around Mildenhall, Ely, Newark and near Debden. By contrast Monday the 5th, August Bank Holiday, would have been ideal in peacetime. It was hot, hazy, ideal for lazing and bathing, but not on a barbed wire and mined South Coast beach in 1940. In any case, coastal fringes were largely inaccessible, and

FOOD FACTS Nº 3

Save sugar – stew apples with chopped figs. It's a new way, a nice way, and you'll need less sugar.

Use the remains of today's rice pudding to thicken tomorrow's soup…

Plums are in season. Make less use of tinned fruit, which should be kept for winter.

If everyone in Great Britain wasted 1/2oz of bread daily we'd be wasting 250,000 tons of wheat a year. Thirty ships would be required to carry that amount. (*I wonder how much we presently waste each day*)

Do you throw away scraps of food rather than bother to make them up? Do you have odd snacks during the day? Do you eat just a little more than you need at mealtimes? In peacetime these indulgences don't matter.

Newspaper, 6 August

many who resided there were moving, or were moved elsewhere for their own safety. Proof of that was provided by six Spitfires of 64 Squadron[51] skirmishing with JG 54's Bf 109s. Two Spitfires were shot down and a 109 made it across the Channel only to crash in France. Pilots of JG 54 might have reported a convoy, for a few escorted Ju 88s were later engaged off Dover by 151 Squadron[52], and a Bf 109 was shot down.

Tuesday 6 August, cloudy and breezy, saw activity limited to Channel forays and a handful of inland sorties. Off East Anglia three 85 Squadron Hurricanes[53] led by the highly successful Sergeant Geoffrey Allard provided at 06.15 a watery grave for a Do 17 of 7./KG 3. Improved weather on 7 August brought more anti-shipping sorties and a convoy attack off Cromer. A successful raid was made by Blenheims on Haamstede airfield just as Bf 109s of JG 54 were taking off to intercept. Two taxying Bf 109s were destroyed, five badly damaged and three pilots were killed in an episode similar to, but more successful than, that which overtook Spitfires at Hornchurch.

Early on the 8th two misplaced mines exploded near Stannington Sanatorium, near Plessy Viaduct and 4 miles south or Morpeth. They brought down the boiler house roof and generally blasted the hospital. A supposedly magnetic mine fell late that day on Lower Marsh Farm, Fairlight, by which time Salford's residents had received free reading matter, courtesy of the Führer.

Showery and bright, 8 August witnessed the heaviest daylight assault so far. Included were three major raids on the Channel convoy CW9 codenamed 'Peewit', comprising twenty ships and a nine-ship naval escort. Sailing from the Thames late on the 7th, the hope was to avoid trouble in the Dover Straits by passing through in darkness. New German Freya radar detected it, E-boats roared out at dawn and two coasters (*Holme Force* and *Fife Coast*) were sunk and others damaged. Off Portland the sister CE Channel convoy was proceeding easterly when, at 06.39, two of its balloons were shot down, for the enemy was aware of the positions of both convoys. With bomber forces almost in place for the long-awaited big blow, German commanders must have decided to practise their skills.

At 08.30 Ju 87s escorted by JG 27 and LG 1 sallied forth from the direction of Cherbourg. Now British radar did the detecting, enabling five 11 Group squadrons and one from 10 Group to tackle the attackers. Between 08.49 and 09.43 two assaults each of a hundred-plus raiders attacked the convoy 15 miles west of the Isle of Wight, and sank SS *Conquerdale* (1,597 tons) and 1,042 ton SS *Empire Crusader*. In the thick of the fight were Squadron Leader J. R. A. Peel's Hurricanes of 145 Squadron[54]. By the end of the engagement RAF fighters had destroyed two Ju 87s. Solent guns fired twenty-seven rounds during the encounter and claimed another two raiders.

...It is difficult to fix the exact date on which the 'Battle of Britain' can be said to have begun. Operations of various kinds merged into one another almost insensibly, and there are grounds for choosing the date of 8 August, on which was made the first attack in force against land objectives in this country, as the beginning of the Battle.

...The essence of their strategy was so to weaken our Fighter Defences that their Air Arm should be able to give adequate support in an attempted invasion of the British Isles.

...Long after the policy of 'crashing through' with heavy bomber formations had been abandoned owing to shattering losses incurred, the battle went on. Large fighter formations were sent over, a proportion of the fighters being adapted to carry bombs, in order that the attacks might not be ignorable. This last phase was perhaps the most difficult to deal with tactically.

Air Chief Marshal Sir Hugh Dowding, Commander-in-Chief Fighter Command

Just east of the Isle of Wight at about 12.45 came the second assault on CW8. It was delivered by sixty Ju 87s of three Stuka Geschwaderen – Nos 2, 3 and 77. Supporting them as they set forth from Caen were Bf 110s of V/LG 1 protected by around thirty Bf 109s of JG 27. The advance of the balbo was spotted by Ventnor Radar. Patrolling nearby were Hurricanes drawn from Nos 43[55], 145[56], 238[57] and 257[58] Squadrons and Spitfires of 609[59] Squadron – more than fifty fighters.

No 257 Squadron, led by Flight Lieutenant N. M. Hall, opened the contest off St Catherine's Point. A participant in many early actions, J. R. A. Peel's 145 Squadron was also soon busy. They dived between flanking Bf 109s and picked off a couple of Ju 87s. In all, three Stukas were shot down and four damaged, the enemy also losing a Bf 110 of V/LG 1 and three Bf 109s, with three more 110s and a 109 damaged. Cost to the RAF? Three pilots and their Hurricanes. The British fighters, drawn off into battle, were therefore unable to prevent a very successful raid upon the ships after their balloon cover had partly been disposed of. The Stukas dive-bombed and soon four ships were sunk, with seven variously damaged. Then the convoy scattered. After the engagement, No 238 Squadron's commander, Squadron Leader H. A. Fenton, recently returned to command after being wounded, returned in P3827 to search for his two lost men. In doing so he tackled an He 59, was brought down by its return fire and was lucky to have been rescued by a trawler.

By late afternoon the remains of the convoy was off St Catherine's Point protected by 10 Group squadrons. The Luftwaffe decided to have another go at 'Peewit'. By 16.00 eighty-two Stukas protected by sixty-eight Bf 109s and 110s were heading for Weymouth Bay. Radar spotted their approach and two squadrons of Hurricanes raced to be south. Spotting the enemy approaching, Peel took his squadron behind them, No 43 joined in and they attacked the Ju 87s from out of the sun before the escort had spotted them. Meanwhile the Bf 110s were shooting down the remaining barrage balloons. Peel's Hurricanes[60] at 16,000 feet confronted many Bf 109s stepped up to 20,000 feet. This time advantageously placed up-sun, the Hurricanes swooped upon the Stukas, undetected by the enemy fighters. Flight Lieutenant R. Dutton, Flight Commander of 145 Squadron, destroyed two Stukas before limping home with engine trouble and Squadron Leader Peel (P3164) claimed two Messerschmitt 109s. No 43 Squadron[61], which operated three times during the day, also did well, possibly shooting down II/JG 27's Gruppenkommandeur, Werner Andres.

The Bofors performed well against Ju 87s – these belonged to 9./StG 2, and T6+AT in the foreground is carrying two bombs beneath each outer mainplane. *Bundesarchiv*

By dusk, competing contemporary analysts were crediting the RAF with twenty-four German bombers and thirty-six fighters destroyed, while the Luftwaffe was settling for forty-nine RAF fighters. Likely true scores are thirty-one German aircraft shot down, and nineteen RAF fighters. An exceptionally high score – ten destroyed, one damaged – seems to have been achieved by 145 Squadron, but its claim of twenty-one remains unsubstantiated. Three rounds of bitter fighting had taken five pilots from the squadron. Seven merchant ships had been sunk, and six naval ships damaged. Only four ships finally reached Swanage. Those aboard strongly questioned why coastal voyagers should risk their lives conveying goods able to travel quite safely on land. Reality was that by attracting enemy effort from more worthwhile targets ashore they played, at a terrible price, a useful part in the battle.

What the papers had to say

8 August: 'Latest score – today's successes bring total ... to 275 since 18 June, 349 since war was declared.'

By 9 August the fine weather had deteriorated. Clouds shielded lone operators, including a 'Zenit' crew from Schiphol who flew to Mildenhall and London. The meteorological reconnaissance flights were vital, for the opening next day of the main attack, Adlerangriff – 'Eagle Attack' as scheduled.

Night-bombers were nevertheless still active, KG 26 visiting Wearmouth where it dropped fourteen bombs on shipbuilding and railway facilities, injuring seventy-three people. Saltburn's Skinningrove was attacked once more, and Sunderland's shipyards came under attack before 79 Squadron disposed of an offender. At both Shorts and Pobjoy's Rochester works, bombs narrowly missed their targets. At 16.50 balloons at Dover were set on fire by JG 51's Bf 109s, before 64 Squadron and the local gunners drove the shooting party away.

On 9/10 August the Luftwaffe roamed between Wiltshire and Wallasey, called on Harwich, Yeovil and Liverpool, delivered nineteen bombs to Warkworth in Northumberland, and donated biased literature to Oxford's dons. In what was one of the deepest, concentrated night-bombing operations so far, Birmingham, Lichfield and Sutton Coldfield were visited. By dawn on the 10th 190 HEs had fallen in 24 hours, killing seven and injuring 100 people.

Mighty as the Luftwaffe conceived itself to be, it could not arrange the weather to its liking. 'Adlertag' – 'Eagle Day' – was blown away by squalls and thundery conditions on 10 August. So, Channel tantalisation continued, and Bf 110 pilots of elite fighter-bomber Erpr 210 attempted a surprise evening strike on Norwich. A lone, undetected Do 17 put eleven HEs close to RAF West Malling, despite 501 Squadron's attempts to stop it. Activity through the following night brought serious damage to Llandore GWR viaduct near Swansea, and a direct hit on a shelter, killing four.

Maintaining the amassed force at high efficiency waiting to 'go' was difficult. Not surprisingly, 11 August saw a spate of '*Zenit*' flights. Reporting fine weather, they also told of clouds looming. With increased operational tempo feasible, at 07.00 Bf 109s began 3 hours of tempting feints off Dover, with Erpr 210's Bf 109s and 110s attacking its balloons and aiming sixty HEs at the harbour area. Little damage resulted. After threatening a Channel convoy, the Luftwaffe again picked on Dover. They met a mixture of AA gunfire and fighters from Nos. 32[62], 64[63] and 74[64] Squadrons, which disposed of two 109s. The Dover activity was, however, a diversion.

While it took place, radar stations detected a large formation heading for the Weymouth area. Fighter Command ordered off thirty-eight Hurricanes of Nos 87[65], 145[66], 213, 238[67] and 601[68] Squadrons, together with Spitfires of Nos 152 and of 609[69] Squadrons, which were soon challenging more than 150 raiders – Ju 88s of I and II/KG 54 and He 111s of KG 27 – escorted by Bf 109s of III/JG 2 and Bf 110s of I and II/ZG 2. Novel was a smokescreen laid west from the Needles behind which the raiders approached before splitting into two formations to simultaneously approach the target, from both east and west. As they ran in at 10.30 two destroyers hurriedly put to sea to engage them. Some raiders came in very low to attack Portland's Vrne and Citadel oil tanks, while a furious engagement ensued high above. Neither high-level nor dive-bombing could be prevented, seventy HEs raining upon the naval hospital, two oil tanks, including a 40,000-gallon underground variant, the floating dock, a signal box and the barracks at Portland. In Weymouth 120 private houses, a brewery, public utilities and ships in the bay were bombed. In protecting the installations, gunners fired 162 large rounds and more than 27,000 rounds of small arms fire

As the large force withdrew, Dover's balloons yet again received attention from Bf 109s maintaining the pressure. From Lille and Antwerp bombers then mounted shipping raids between Dover and Lowestoft until bad weather forced abandonment of daylight operations.

An unusual strike to set alight waterborne He 59s off France had been carried out by two 604 Squadron Blenheims (L6728, Pilot Officer E. D. Crew, and L6774, Squadron Leader M. F. Anderson) escorted by three 152 Squadron Spitfires. Some 30 miles off Cherbourg they found a seaplane with two rescue launches being protected by Bf 109s, which the Spitfires attended to while the He 59 was destroyed. Another He 59, also of the Calais Detachment, Seenotzentrale Cherbourg, had been ordered to the same area. It was shot down by Flt Lt Edward Smith of 610 Squadron, which lost two pilots during the engagement.

Convoy 'Booty' was sailing between Clacton and Harwich when, at 11.50, Bf 110 fighter-bombers of Erpr 210, accompanied by eight Do 17s of 9./KG 2 and all escorted by twenty Bf 110s of ZG 26, attacked the ships. Foreness radar had located the force allowing eleven Spitfires of 74 Squadron to set upon the attackers as they approached the convoy. Six waiting Hurricanes of 17 Squadron shot down a Bf 110, and the Spitfires destroyed three more.

Taking advantage of the RAF fighters' need to refuel, forty-five Do 17s of KG 2 and a group of Ju 87s escorted by Bf 109s attacked a convoy in the Thames Estuary. Luckily, Malan's 74 Squadron, as well as Nos 111 and 54, were on hand to greet them, ruining their action, but the fighters only damaged the enemy aircraft. Menacing storm clouds ended the day's activity. Such had been the desperate need that most of 74 Squadron's pilots had flown four sorties before lunch and experienced action three times.

In moonlight on 11/12 August, thirty-three HEs were distributed over Cardiff and Bristol's residential areas of Sneyd Park, Knowle and Shirehampton. Searchlight Site 53725 held in its beam He 111H-3 1G+AC of Stab II/KG 27, which enabled a Hurricane to cause its demise near Wimborne, thereby bringing 10 Group its first night success. Merseyside, Yorkshire and Devon were also raided, while the Bristol Channel and Plymouth Sound were mined. Off Pendennis Point a mine exploded on impact with the sea, and another damaged Boveisand Lodge.

Claims and losses on the 11th revealed both sides incurring similar misfortunes. Fighter Command lost thirty-two aircraft, the enemy thirty-eight, of which thirteen were Bf 109s, including six of JG 2. Another ten were Bf 110s, two of them belonging to Erpr 210, lost during anti-shipping operations off East Anglia. In the continuing saga of losses and claims some were from the start certainties, among them a Ju 88 that arrived intact near St George's Church, Blacknore, west of which another plunged into the sea, joining a third that smashed itself in West Bay. From an He 111 off Chesil Beach five prisoners were taken, after two burning aircraft found watery graves west of Wyke Regis. An He 111 crashing near Searchlight 53531 yielded another four prisoners. A Hurricane in flames came down at 54172, another force-landing at U.6715.

With better weather on the horizon, the Luftwaffe command decided that 12 August must witness the opening of the four-day grand slam. Although destruction of fighter airfields and radar stations would be the paramount task, pressure on shipping and harbours would be maintained. No more probing – this was the real thing at last. Large-scale escorted raids inland to wipe out the RAF fighter force, the rest, and then – INVASION!

About 200 Bf 109s in strength launched the activity on the glorious 12th by flying over the Channel and Kent, and probing towards Dover, eleven sweeps being recorded. Four RAF Squadrons responded, fierce fighting developing over Dungeness between 610 Squadron Spitfires[70] and nine Bf 109s of II/JG 52. As 610 went into action another twelve Bf 109s swept down upon them and Flight Lieutenant E. B. B. Smith (H-K9818) received face and neck burns from two cannon shells in his cockpit; he baled out and was rescued from the sea. Flight Lieutenant Gardiner (N3124-N) was wounded, and his aircraft was badly damaged. Two Bf 109s were destroyed, and nine were claimed damaged. together with four more Spitfires lost, this was an expensive quarrel.

Many a Bf 109E 'Emil' only just made it to France, this one by the narrowest of margins. *Bundesarchiv*

Around 09.00 a high-flying Dornier surveyed the Channel coast for a final assessment prior to the most alarming attack yet. Bf 110 fighter-bombers of legendary Erpr 210, making skilled use of the 2,000-foot cloud base, flew unobserved along the Channel shedding elements each of which released HEs and oil bombs on the vital South Coast radar stations. Here was something new, very alarmingly and exceedingly damaging to the defence layout.

Anti-aircraft gunners by Dover's CH station had just stood down for gun-cleaning when Raid 59H swept in almost silently. In line astern and from out of the sun, the Bf 110s bombed from 600 feet. Before the Bofors guns could respond, twelve HEs surrounded the station, the nearest 5-foot-wide shallow craters being a mere 60 yards from a radar pylon. Three bombs lay unexploded among five demolished huts. Although the RDF/radar equipment was undamaged, one person was killed and twenty-five injured.

Next to be attacked was Rye's CH station, bombed at 09.40. Ten HEs fell, one exploding 20 feet from a pylon. At Poling and Pevensey the events were similar, with electricity cables to the latter station being cut. Shortly after the attack on Dover radar, Bf 109 fighter-bombers delivered a follow-up strike during which a blazing balloon fell by the base of an RDF mast. Adding variety to the assault, five 8.2-inch shells hurled across the Channel exploded near Dover gasworks at 10.15.

More shells were fired at Deal and Folkestone. Although not seriously damaged by bombing, the CH stations – apart from Rye – had been put out of action, fortunately for only around 6 hours. Radar stations were not all that easy to destroy because their tall pylons prohibited very low attacks.

Elsewhere, the Luftwaffe was more successful. Mid-morning saw about eighty Ju 88s of I, II and III/KG 51, some 120 Bf 110s of ZG 2 and ZG 76, and twenty-five Bf 109s of JG 53, organising themselves into a huge formation over France. They then headed for Brighton before turning towards the Isle of Wight. The Commanders of 11 and 10 Groups, Park and Brand, realising that a major threat was developing, ordered up forty-eight Hurricanes and ten Spitfires from Tangmere, Middle Wallop, Warmwell and Exeter to patrol, and fifty-eight fighters to engage more than 200 of the enemy off the Isle of Wight. The Bf 110s established a huge battle circle and tried to draw off and distract the British fighters, while the Ju 88s formed into two attack groups. Now the reasons for another early-morning Do 215 W2 weather sortie across the area at 22,000 feet became clear.

Twenty minutes ahead of this main force, fighter-bombers had dealt with the Portsmouth balloon barrage, bombed two balloon sites, and killed eight men. At 12.10 there now came from out of the sun about fifty Ju 88s to deliver at least fifty-seven HEs from varying altitudes during a classic, level, formation attack on Portsmouth, the first upon a British city. A direct hit was scored on a 200-person shelter in St George's Square, and other bombs exploded behind White's furniture store in Penroy Street. The harbour pier was demolished, its station set ablaze. Brickwood's Brewery was hit and the pontoon dock holed, but the main dockyard escaped damage and most bombs fell on old Portsmouth. Serious fires broke out and casualties totalled ninety-six, seventeen of them fatal. Gosport was also bombed by Ju 88s causing another thirty-nine casualties, fifteen fatal. From sixteen heavy gun

A huge fire at Portsmouth Harbour station, bombed on 12 August. *Courtesy of The News, Portsmouth*

and eight Bofors sites, a tremendous barrage of 624 and 409 rounds respectively was hurled at the raiders, which attacked at between 8,000 and 12,000 feet. AA gunners in the area claimed two Ju 88s, and as the bombers retired 213 Squadron picked off the leading aircraft flown by the Geschwaderkommodore.

While the 88s ran into Portsmouth, Bf 109s and 110s circled the Isle of Wight. They were providing top cover for a group of about fifteen Ju 88s, which turned towards the island, broke formation and made steep dive-bombing attacks on the CH radar station above Ventnor. They dropped seventy-two HEs and ten delayed-action bombs on the site, demolishing nearly every building. Bofors gun defence was lost and, most disastrous of all, vital aerials between the 350-foot towers were brought down. Civilian buildings suffered in Ventnor and Bonchurch. Spitfires of 152 and 609 Squadrons arrived too late to prevent the bombing.

Loss of Ventnor radar was exceedingly serious, for it watched over the approaches to Portsmouth and Southampton. The outcome of the raid was not entirely one-sided for, by sparingly employing the Hurricanes against the bombers, and making a break by top-cover German fighters barely worth while for fear of British attacks from above, our fighters picked off eight Ju 88s. Park, by carefully positioning 615 Squadron[71], had a dozen Hurricanes ready to prevent the Bf 109s sweeping in to save the bombers. No 609 Squadron[72], concentrating upon the escorting fighters, claimed seven of them.

Already the enemy was building on what he felt sure was earlier stunning success, the action returning to Kent. At 12.45 Bf 110s of Erpr 210, taking advantage of the damaged radar chain, raced low across Manston aerodrome, bombing

A Bf 110 fighter-bomber of Erpr. 210 being prepared for operations.

and strafing this vital forward base. Following came eighteen Do 17s of KG 2 flying at 14,000 feet to deliver the second carpet bombing of the day. Try as they did, No 54 Squadron[73], back in the fray, could not prevent the raid. Among bursting bombs, 65 Squadron tried to get airborne. One of the few pilots to succeed was the famous Supermarine test pilot Geoffrey Quill, on secondment to the squadron. Eight Hurricanes of 56 Squadron also tackled the raiders, but only as they were retiring. As for Manston, 141 of the 242 HEs dropped fell on RAF property, causing twelve casualties. They destroyed its workshops, damaged two hangars, destroyed a 600 Squadron Blenheim, a Proctor, Magister and Puss Moth, and cratered the landing ground. Although the station was soon operational again, No 600 Squadron was forced to switch night-operating to Hornchurch, the parent station. Ramsgate had received seventeen of the stray bombs.

While Manston was being attacked, two groups of Ju 87s tackling convoys managed to hit two small vessels. That action showed that the Germans were unaware that Foreness CHL radar was fully functioning, and that their approach was observed. Six Spitfires of 65 Squadron, sent to ward them off, arrived too late to prevent the dive-bombing, but were embroiled with escorting Bf 109s. Just as the Spitfires landed at Manston for rearming, a second Ju 87 formation arrived over a convoy off Deal. A dozen Hurricanes of 501 and three of 151 Squadron confronted them, preventing effective bombing albeit at the cost of two pilots and four aircraft.

There was little time for rest, pressure on the RAF being maintained by recourse to large-scale Channel sweeps by Bf 109s between 14.00 and 15.00. Those preceded the next major onslaught of the day, which caused serious damage to airfields. Fortunately, Kent's radar stations were fully operational again, whereas the Germans believed that they had been wiped out. Two large forces delivered heavy attacks at 17.30, upon the unimportant satellite fighter station at Lympne and on Hawkinge. At the former, 170 bombs were reckoned to have fallen on the airfield, seventy on surrounding fields and the Bekesbourne-Patrixbourne area. During the second bombing run, Ju 88s of II/KG 76, following the canal from Dymchurch to approach, demolished two hangars, station workshops and four fighters. Casualties totalled five killed and seven seriously wounded. Despite the severity of the Lympne attack the station was operating next day. Aerodromes would be very hard to put out of action, and extremely difficult to destroy.

At 17.28 Ju 88s of KG 76 arrived over Folkestone and 2 minutes later attacked Hawkinge, dive-bombing and carpet-bombing from 18,000 feet. Enemy aircraft arrived from out of the sun at between 3,000 and 5,000 feet, the raid damaging some buildings and putting the landing ground out of use. Much official interest surrounded one giant crater on the aerodrome. Two level attackers were hit by anti-aircraft fire. One, at 17.42, had its tail unit seriously damaged. It was said to have come down in the sea off Dover.

While these heavy raids took place, fighter-bombers were once more slipping in, this time to deal with the radar station at Dunkirk, west of Canterbury. They were first spotted, about half a dozen of them, circling the target at about 12,000 feet and in line astern. Then they dived, each releasing a bomb from about 2,500 feet. The attack very much interested observers, who recorded that the bombs came from Bf 109s, and were 'carried below the cockpit'. For propaganda reasons they dismissed the idea, attributing it to a shortage of bombers. In reality the Luftwaffe was pioneering the use of fast fighters as bombers, an extremely important development.

Widespread night operations followed, including a sharp raid on Cardiff, whose guns had earlier engaged an He 111 spying at 27,000 feet. Bekesbourne was among many other places bombed, as well as Stratford-upon-Avon, Birmingham, Bircham Newton, Newport, Hereford, Ipswich, Plymouth, Felixstowe, Westbury-on-Severn and Eastchurch. Free reading matter this time was given to the people of Worksop.

By the end of the day the Germans were claiming seventy-one RAF aircraft shot down. In reality the RAF, in mounting 196 patrols and flying 798 sorties, lost twenty-two fighters. German casualties arising from about 1,200 sorties totalled thirty-one aircraft in the toughest day's fighting yet.

Patrols and sorties flown by Fighter Command
10 July-12 August 1940

Surviving statistics list slight variations in totals, probably due to the inclusion or otherwise of dusk, dawn and night patrols. The listing includes all Fighter Command interception sorties, patrols, escorts, etc.

Date: 24-hour period ending at 06.00 on the given date	Fighter Command		
	Patrols	Sorties	
	Day	Day	Night
July			
10	200	609	32
11	151	479	47
12	207	670	30
13	143	449	24
14	163	593	19
15	154	470	–
16	128	313	7
17	70	253	13
18	166	549	34
19	175	701	34
20	191	611	44
21	120	571	25
22	208	611	26
23	182	470	25
24	?	561	?
25	191	641	?
26	144	584	28
27	141	487	35
28	220	794	29
29	185	724	35
30	205	688	?
31	130	395	21
August			
1	?	659	61
2	147	477	24
3	144	411	26
4	?	261	4
5	99	402	26
6	?	416	?
7	?	393	?
8	152	621	33
9	142	409	14
10	116	336	11
11	165	679	62
12	196	732	?

RAF losses during operations 1-12 August 1940

a = failed to return/shot down, b = written off as a battle casualty, c = seriously damaged

August	1			2			3			4			5		
Type	a	b	c	a	b	c	a	b	c	a	b	c	a	b	c
Blenheim F	–	–	–	–	–	1	–	–	–	–	–	–	–	–	2
Defiant	–	–	–	–	–	–	–	–	–	–	1	1	–	–	–
Hurricane	1	–	2	–	–	1	–	–	–	–	–	1	–	–	–
Spitfire	–	1	–	–	2	–	–	–	–	–	1	–	2	–	–
Battle	1	–	–	–	–	–	–	–	–	–	–	–	–	–	–
Blenheim B	1	–	–	2	–	–	–	1	–	–	–	–	–	–	–
Hampden	2	–	–	–	–	–	1	1	–	1	–	–	–	–	–
Wellington	–	–	–	–	1	–	–	1	–	–	–	–	–	–	–
Whitley	–	–	–	–	–	–	–	–	–	1	–	1	–	–	–
Coastal Cmd	3	–	–	2	–	–	–	–	–	4	–	–	1	–	–
Totals	8	1	2	4	3	2	1	3	–	6	2	2	3	–	2

August	6			7			8			9			10		
Type	a	b	c	a	b	c	a	b	c	a	b	c	a	b	c
Blenheim F	–	1	–	–	–	–	1	–	–	–	1	–	–	–	–
Defiant	–	–	–	–	–	–	–	–	–	–	–	–	–	–	–
Hurricane	–	2	–	–	2	1	11	–	2	–	1	1	–	–	–
Spitfire	–	2	–	–	2	–	3	2	2	–	–	2	–	–	1
Battle	–	–	–	–	–	–	–	–	–	–	–	–	–	–	–
Blenheim B	–	–	–	–	–	–	1	–	–	–	–	–	2	–	–
Hampden	1	–	–	1	1	–	1	–	–	–	1	–	1	–	–
Wellington	–	–	–	–	–	–	–	–	–	–	–	1	–	–	–
Whitley	–	–	1	–	–	–	–	–	–	–	–	–	–	–	–
Coastal Cmd	2	–	–	3	–	–	2	–	–	1	–	–	–	–	–
Totals	3	5	1	4	5	1	19	2	4	1	3	4	3	–	1

August	11			12			Grand totals		
Type	a	b	c	a	b	c	a	b	c
Blenheim F	–	–	–	–	–	–	1	2	3
Defiant	–	–	–	–	–	–	–	1	1
Hurricane	23	2	4	12	–	2	47	7	14
Spitfire	5	–	2	5	3	5	15	12	12
Blenheim B	1	–	–	–	–	–	7	0	0
Hampden	1	–	–	–	–	–	9	3	0
Wellington	–	1	–	–	–	–	0	4	1
Whitley	–	–	–	–	–	–	1	0	2
Coastal Cmd	3	–	–	–	–	–	21	0	0
Totals	33	3	6	17	3	7	101	29	33

Where did bombs first fall? 1 July-12 August 1940

ibs   1kg incendiary bombs
RD   Rural District
UD   Urban District (towns/cities unless otherwise stated)
Bracketed numbers are unexploded bombs additional to others

Bombs dropped

1 July
Barry	20
Caerphilly	5 (3)
Gosport	1 (1)
Wick	2

2/3 July
Frome RD	5
Ledbury	6
Newcastle-upon-Tyne	3

3 July
Bognor	4
Catown	3
Deal	1
Hailsham	4 (1)
Hambledon RD	3 (1)
Lowestoft, in sea	16
Newhaven	12
Pen-y-Bont RD	13
Seaford	4

3/4 July
Tendring RD	2, ibs

4 July
Pontypool	6 (1)
Sodbury RD	2

4/5 July
West Ashford RD	2

5 July
Lowestoft	14
Ramsgate	9 (1)

5/6 July
Folkestone	1 (2)

6 July
Plymouth	5
Farnham	3

6/7 July
Dover	10

7 July
Falmouth	4
Shoreham	1
Ventnor, in sea	2

8/9 July
Inverness, landward	6
Moray, landward	20

9 July
Abercarn	14
Gower	17 (3)
Llanelly	5
Lleynrd RD	4
	Norwich
Tadcaster RD	6

10 July
Aberdare	11
Berwick, landward	8
Brecknock RD	1
Carmarthen	10
Crickhowell RD	10
Cwmaman	1
Hadleigh	1 (1)
Looe	12 (2)
Llanelly RD	13
Pembroke	4
Pontarllawerd RD	1

11 July
Argyllshire	5
Ely RD	9
Great Yarmouth	7
Portsmouth	20 (2)

11/12 July
Tavistock RD	10 (1), ibs

12 July
Ryde	2

12/13 July
Banff, landward	3
Bdwast Machen UD	2
Dumbarton, landward	8
Greenock	9
Tiverton RD	1
Wadebridge	4

13 July
Lanark, landward	1
Magor & St Mallons RD	9
	(2)
Mountain Ash	3
Pontypridd	3, ibs
Renfrew	18 (1)

14/15 July
Amesbury RD	9
Brixham	6

15 July
Narbeth RD	4 (8)

16 July
Fraserburgh	4
Peterhead	7

17 July
Auchtermuchty	11 (1)
Custon RD	6
Montrose	16

18 July
Braintree	1

18/19 July
Chatham	2

19 July
Edinburgh	7 (1)
Glasgow	8
Horsham RD	4

20 July
Dumfries, landward	3
Stirling	2 mines

20/21 July
Sunderland	1

22 July
Banff	5 (1)
Maldon RD	6

22/23 July
Cleethorpes	ibs
Drayton RD	11
Hocktonprice UD	? 4
Newtown and Llandeilo RD	7

ibs   1kg incendiary bombs
RD   Rural District
UD   Urban District (towns/cities unless otherwise stated)
Bracketed numbers are unexploded bombs additional to others

Bombs dropped

23 July		29 July		4 August	
Llwchwr	? 2	Belper	ibs	Cwnbrau	4, ibs
Neyland	2	Crewe	3	**7 August**	
Worthing	3 (1)	Dorking RD	3	Exeter	5
24 July		Neath	ibs	**8 August**	
Renfrew	11, ibs	Salford	6	Truro	5 (1)
Samford RD	17	**30 July**		**8/9 August**	
Waltham and Weybridge	17	Merthyr Tydfil	11	Birmingham	4
26 July		**30/31 July**		**9 August**	
Brentwood	5	Clun RD	7	Birkenhead	6
26/26 July		Colne RD	2	**10 August**	
Faversham	2	Denbighshire RD	18 (2)	Abergavenny	7
Sheppey	3	Devizes RD	6	Malling RD	15 (11)
27/28 July		Leominster RD	3	Rochester	10
Penllyn RD	2 (1)	Ross and Whitchurch RD	1	Wallasey	11
Sevenoaks RD	12 (2)	Welshpool	5	**11 August**	
Truro RD	4	**31 July**		York	2 (1)
Wenlock	2	Monmouth	5	**11/12 August**	
West Penwith	4	Monmouth RD	8	Wilton	6
28 July		Morecambe and	11	**12 August**	
Kidwelly	3	Heysham		Broadstairs	11
Runcorn	2	**1 August**		Eastly RD	30 (8)
28/29 July		Ellesmere Port	1		
Lydd	5	Hornchurch UD	9 (1)		
Maidstone RD	1	**2 August**			
Wellington RD	14	Dundee	24		
West Lancashire RD	8	**3 August**			
Wrexham RD	1	Frimley	8		

Incidents involving eight or more high explosive bombs
1 July-12 August

ibs   1kg incendiary bombs
RD   Rural District
UD   Urban District (towns/cities unless otherwise stated)
Bracketed numbers are unexploded bombs additional to others

Bombs dropped

1 July		**19 July**		**6 August**	
Holderness RD	12	Narbeth	10 (1)	Swansea	10
3 July		Plymouth	21	**6/7 August**	
Battle RD	26	**19/20 July**		Midlothian	12, ibs
Swale RD	14	Dumbarton, landward	9	**7 August**	
6/7 July		Lanark, landward	8	Poole	8
Aldershot	6	**20/21 July**		**8 August**	
8/9 July		Orkney	11	Midlothian	14
Billingham UD	8	**21/22 July**		Truro	12
9 July		Derby	10	**8/9 August**	
Benfleet	24	**22 July**		Meir and Tisbury RD	9
Sodbury RD	6 (8)	Banff, landward	9 (1)	**9 August**	
10 July		Pembroke	20	Rochford RD	6 (3)
Neath	4 (12)	Shardlow RD	8	Sunderland	10 (5)
10/11 July		**22/23 July**		**9/10 August**	
Bridlington	8	Swale RD	26 (2)	Bournemouth	12
Spilsby RD	9	**23 July**		Salisbury and	23
12 July		Cardiff RD	2 (8)	Wilton RD	
Aberdeen	16	Pembroke	15	South Shields	1 mine
Aberdeenshire	23 (1)	**26/27 July**		**10 August**	
Cardiff	12	Aberdeenshire	9	Swansea	26 (4)
12/13 July		**27 July**		**10/11 August**	
West Hartlepool	24	Canvey Island	17 (1)	Weymouth	(14)
13/14 July		**28/29 July**		**11/12 August**	
East Lothian, landward	8	Aberdeenshire	24	Bristol	50
14/15 July		Berwick, landward	27	Plymouth	2 mines
Dover RD	12, ibs	Calne	11 (1)	**12 August**	
15 July		Newcastle	27	Cardiff RD	28 (1)
Cowbridge	4 (6)	**1 August**		Folkestone	150 (1), ibs
Hove	8	Pembroke	9 (1)	Gosport	40 (1)
16 July		**2 August**		Havant	6, 1 OB
Orkney	18 (3)	Bridge Blean RD	200 (4),	Portsmouth	18 (1), 1 OB
18 July		ibs		Ramsgate	17
Neath	9	Swansea	10 (3)	Ventnor	30 (6)
18/19 July		**3 August**		Isle of Wight RDs	24 (4)
Lanark, landward	8	Swansea	10	**12/13 August**	
				Plymouth	12 (3)

A Dornier Do 17Z of KG 2 joining another setting off for England from Le Culot, their Belgian base.

Famous Spitfire Mk II P7350, surely top star of the Battle of Britain Memorial Flight, participated in the Battle from September. It joined the RAF in mid August 1940 and within days was with No 611 Squadron transferring to No 266 on 6 September before joining No 603 Squadron on 17 October 1940. It later operated with Nos 64 and 616 Squadrons.

Chapter 11

Deutschland Uber Alles

'Destroy the enemy air force as soon as possible,' impatient Adolf had decreed, suggesting 5 August as a suitable day to carry out the foul deed while leaving the final choice to Goering and his companions.

To destroy Fighter Command, its operational layout needed to be understood. The early warning radar network, positioning of squadrons, purpose of dispersal and forward aerodromes – the part that each played in UK defence should have been thoroughly investigated in order to deliver a knock-out blow. Most of all, the skill and determination of the opposition should have been assessed. Instead, the Germans were less well informed on all aspects than many schoolboys. July they had wasted instead of using the time to cripple Britain's aircraft factories and aircraft storage units.

Without knocking out radar stations and keeping to a properly conceived battle plan, the great assault was about to be frittered away, hurled against irrelevant objects whose destruction could have little bearing on the outcome of the battle.

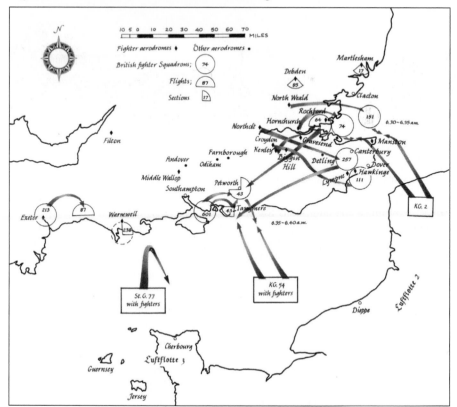

13 August Morning Action

FOOD FACTS № 4

Never waste anything, never eat more than enough. You'll be fitter, you'll save money. Every time you cook you can help or hinder Hitler. Always scrape paper in which margarine or butter is wrapped.

Newspaper, 12 August

Group Captain 'Sailor' Malan, who earlier flew with 74 Squadron. *IWM*

Even the weather provided them with time to stop and think. Dull, cloudy conditions over southern England and northern France on 13 August delayed the 'final' blow until the afternoon. So poor was the overall direction of the operation that postponement orders failed to reach all units, and in murky weather 'Adlertag' was mistakenly launched.

First success came to the RAF when a reconnoitring Do 17P was brought down at 06.20 off Kent by Squadron Leader A. G. Malan, in K9953, partnered by Flying Officer J. C. Mungo Park (R6084), soon after the first signs of daylight activity were detected. As early as 05.30 radar stations identified two forces, about sixty aircraft, assembling slowly over France. No 11 Group ordered two squadrons, No 64[74] from Hornchurch and No 111 from Croydon, to protect damaged Hawkinge and Manston, the assumption being that the enemy would hit them again to ensure their demise.

Hurricanes from North Weald took station over a Thames convoy, while others watched over Tangmere. As the two enemy formations advanced, another of about a hundred was detected off Dieppe. Then about forty more aircraft were discovered off Cherbourg before a smaller group was found by radar near the Channel Islands.

Hurricanes of North Weald's 56 Squadron. US-P in the foreground is possibly R4093, shot down on 13 August. US-G (R2689) and T (V6628?) are airborne. *IWM*

In France, as in England, the harvest was being gathered while bombers such as this He 111 A1 +L? of KG 53 taxied by. *Bundesarchiv*

To oppose these large formations, a section of Hurricanes from Northolt flew to the Canterbury area while others, from Tangmere, barred the way between Arundel and Petworth. From Middle Wallop more fighters hurried to protect Warmwell before Hurricanes of Nos 43[75] and 601[76] Squadrons scrambled from Tangmere to guard 11 Group's western flank. Additional fighters from Kenley protected the Thames Estuary, and No 10 Group squadrons the Exeter area. About 120 fighters dispersed mainly over Kent – particularly in sections, and not squadrons – were deployed to face maybe 300 attackers.

The Shuttleworth Collection's Gladiator, masquerading as N2308 of 247 Squadron formed on 1 August 1940, wears the squadron identity letters HP B carried by the real N2308 at Roborough, Plymouth, during August 1940. The under surfaces had been black and white, but the aircraft wore Sky by then.

Escort for about eighty Dornier 17Zs of I, II and III/KG 2 had been cancelled due to dense clouds around 5,000 feet, but the bomber crews pressed on, swung left shortly before 07.00, then split into groups. They headed towards Coastal Command's aerodrome at Eastchurch and Sheerness dockyard. Above thick cloud the larger formation headed for Eastchurch and, near Whitstable, was engaged by 74 Squadron[77]. Off the North Foreland, Hurricanes of 151 Squadron tackled the others and L1750, the first cannon-armed Hurricane and the RAF's first cannon-armed fighter (flown by Flight Lieutenant R. Smith), scored a certain success.

'Treble One' went into action near Herne Bay, the combined effort forcing KG 2 to jettison their load. The other element dropped about a hundred bombs on Eastchurch, hitting hangars, airmen's quarters and the Officers' Mess. Ammunition and equipment stores burned, and the Operations Block and a Spitfire of 266 Squadron – on the station to support Coastal Command Fairey Battles – were destroyed and several Blenheims damaged. Two Bofors guns fired twenty-five rounds, sixteen men were killed and forty-eight injured. Eastchurch was fully operational again by evening. Five Do 17s had been shot down.

Another morning operation was carried out by two groups of Ju 88s of KG 54, which, in poor weather, attempted to bomb Farnborough and Odiham, more irrelevant choices. Hurricanes of 43[78], 257 and 601[79] Squadrons vectored from Canterbury, together with 64 Squadron's Spitfire[80] greeted them, forcing the Ju 88s to abandon their operation.

Next, it was the turn of thirty Bf 110s of I/ZG 2, which headed in from Cherbourg. By noon, and without the Ju 88s they were expecting to escort, the Messerschmitts discovered Hurricanes of 87, 213 and 238 Squadrons closing in as they approached Portland. Five Bf 110s were claimed, though Luftwaffe records show the loss of only one.

Afternoon brought better weather, allowing the first really hefty blow to be launched at 16.00. 'Adlerangriff' was at last under way, a bit late and with a massive attack spread along a 40-mile front. Around forty Ju 88s of KG 54 and I, II, III/LG 1 of Luftflotte 2 headed for Southampton and Middle Wallop while to their west were about thirty Ju 87s of II/StG 2 followed by fifty more Stukas of StG 77 closely escorted by JG 27 – formidable indeed, and entering the 10 Group area. Forward support by Bf 109s of JG 53 came in between the Isle of Wight and Lyme Bay. Low on fuel, they were easily chased away by 152 Squadron, which also engaged the dive-bombers.

Already scrambled, 10 Group's squadrons supported by 43 and 257 Squadrons could not prevent LG 1's Ju 88s from reaching Southampton. At least twenty-three bombs fell at 16.23, on the International Cold Storage Company's premises and dock warehouses, killing five and injuring twenty-five workers. Later, a delayed-action bomb exploded at Empress Dock.

KG 54, heading for Portland, faced Nos 152, 213, 238[81] and 601[82] Squadrons, the latter destroying three escorting Bf 110s. As the first Stukas of II/StG 2 arrived, so did No 609 Squadron[83]. Unfortunately for the dive-bombers, their escort, being short of fuel, headed home allowing the Spitfires to dive out of the sun to slaughter six of them. Other Ju 87s, seeking Warmwell and failing to locate it, released their bombs over a wide area. Another KG 54 attack intended for Middle Wallop strayed. A few bombs fell near the Wallops, and others on Andover aerodrome mistaken for the target.

In the afternoon Ju 87s and Bf 110s turned their attention to Rochford aerodrome, only to find thick cloud. That caused the abandonment of their operation. No 56 Squadron[84], operating for the day from Rochford, intercepted its would-be attackers over Kent, forcing them to unload, through cloud, in the Canterbury area. Accompanying Bf 109s of JG 26 skilfully drew off No 65 Squadron[85], which opened the way for another forty Ju 87s of LG 1 to devastate Detling. They destroyed its hangars, operations block, cratered its tarmac, severely dealt with twenty-two aircraft and killed sixty-seven, including the Station Commander, Group Captain E. David. Yet again, and within hours, Detling became functional.

Small-scale shipping attacks had continued throughout the day, after which He 111s of KGr 100 attempted a night precision attack on Castle Bromwich's Spitfire factory. A purple warning was received at 22.54 and 10 minutes later five He 111s were running in from the south. Sirens wailed at 23.18 just before AA guns went into action. On to the 60-acre site nineteen 50kg bombs were dropped, some falling on roads. Others exploded in F and Q Blocks, and six on D Block, damaging machinery. At 00.02 the 'All Clear' sounded, then more bombs fell. A second warning was quickly sounded. In all eight workers were killed, forty-one seriously wounded and 100 had minor injuries. During the night another sixteen HEs fell on farmland near Wolverhampton and a dozen at Bacton, Herefordshire.

By dawn on 14 August, the Luftwaffe, which in 24 hours had lost forty-six aircraft (thirty-nine directly to the defenders), had flown 1,485 sorties (about two-thirds by fighters). They had attacked three non-Fighter Command aerodromes and damaged Southampton, Castle Bromwich and a number of other places. As a result 100 casualties were recorded. Fighter Command, in mounting 727 fighter sorties, lost thirteen aircraft and seven pilots.

The German effort during 14 August amounted to almost 500 sorties. Proceedings started with a high-speed, low-level attack on Manston. 'A' Flight of 56 Squadron, flying a precautionary patrol above cloud over the aerodrome, was oblivious to a dozen audacious Bf 110s of Erpr Gr 210 racing in very low to bomb and strafe the station. Although only four bombs hit the aerodrome, one caused the end of a hangar to be blown onto the station's Puss Moth. Two more exploded inside a hangar on the east side containing two 600 Squadron Blenheims. The fourth produced an impressive crater 12 feet deep and 30 feet across. Two oil bombs fell on a nearby village. Ground defences brought down two Bf 110s on the edge of the landing ground, and three out of the four crew were killed. The survivor revealed that the formation had set forth from Denain, refuelled at St Omer and that each aircraft carried two 250kg bombs. As escort they had seven Bf 109s. No 32 Squadron[86] had come speeding upon the scene from Biggin Hill and No 615[87] from Kenley, but they had arrived too late to prevent the bombing.

The main Stuka force, above cloud and with visibility poor, arrived at 12.20 then split into two forces, one to attack Hawkinge and the other Dover. Defenders drove off the Hawkinge raid, then three of the Ju 87s – protected by a Gruppe of Bf 109s – attacked the Gate Light Vessel, dropping ten HEs and sinking the ship. Two of its crew were killed, one injured. The remainder of the crew were strafed as they struggled in the water. Such bestial acts of extreme cruelty are part of war, but it does well to remember that they were not as commonplace as wartime propagandists led the populace to believe.

Meanwhile Hurricanes of 615 Squadron engaged Bf 109s of III/JG 2, which claimed two of the defenders. One fell to Adolf Galland. In answer, the squadron claimed three Bf 109s, one almost certainly falling to Pilot Officer Lofts (P3161). Pilot Officer E. B. Rogers (L1983) belly-landed at Hawkinge, the squadron's forward base. Meanwhile, the main bomber force had headed inland to Ashford, spasmodically bombing and being attacked during its withdrawal by the Biggin Hill squadron.

Hurricane R4194 used by No 615 (County of Surrey) Squadron from 15 August to 7 December 1940.

Mid-afternoon saw Raid H5, Do 17s, heading towards Pevensey. Upon being engaged at 16.15, they jettisoned their loads in the Fairlight area. The enemy did not, however, give up that easily. At 17.37 Raid H44 (reputedly a lone Do 17) ran up on Pevensey RDF station at 7,000 feet and placed four HEs in the compound without causing much damage. Apparently hit by AA fire, the raider descended and was fired upon by the crew of searchlight 51733. The pilot baled out before the aircraft crashed, and was taken to Hayward's Heath police station.

Between 15.30 and 21.00 small groups of unescorted bombers operated over a 100-mile front, aerodromes and rail centres being their targets. Radar stations accurately identified the strength of each raid, which allowed small, accurate responses. Six raiders were destroyed during eleven engagements. On the outskirts of Swindon twenty HEs fell. Of eight RAF stations attacked, only three reported much damage. Andover's W/T station was hit, Kemble too, and at Hullavington there were thirteen casualties. At Middle Wallop 609 Squadron's hangar received a direct hit, and adjacent offices were destroyed at 17.00 by three He 111Ps of KG 55. Three airmen, Corporal R. W. Smith and Leading Aircraftmen H. Thorley and K. Wilson, were killed attempting to close a giant hangar door, which crashed down upon them. Swift vengeance was wrought by Sergeant Feary (L1065)[88], who raced away and claimed the lead He 111P G1+AA carrying senior personnel. Other Heinkel 111s dropped fourteen large bombs on Portland, damaging roads, and KG 27 produced slight damage at Colerne ASU. A trio of bombers reached Sealand and three staff pilots of No 7 OTU Hawarden set off in hot pursuit. Their Spitfires downed Heinkel 111 1G + FS near Chester. At least seventeen German aircraft fell variously to the defences during 14 August. Fighter Command lost eight fighters.

Late on the 14th fifteen He 111s of KGr 100 from Vannes in Brittany bombed the Short & Harland factory at Belfast, where thirty Short Stirlings were in various states of completion. The sharp onslaught damaged the final assembly shop, completely wrecked four bombers and splintered many others. It was but a foretaste of what would happen next day at Rochester, considerably impairing the RAF's embryo new long-range bomber force. Despite the raid, a Belfast-built Stirling was first flown on 18 October 1940.

The Luftwaffe had certainly underestimated the strength, ability and clever leadership of Fighter Command. The successes the Germans claimed were prodigious – 40,000 tons of merchant shipping sunk, 300 British fighters destroyed, more than thirty aerodromes and major factories wiped out – and all in three days. There is little doubt that many in the enemy camp did believe these claims, but those in the fight must have realised that the opposition remained strong, was skilfully mounted, and that their own losses were higher than predicted. Goering was quick to apportion blame, citing as foolish the small-scale raids on the 14th carried out by specially chosen crews. He condemned the choice of targets, too many having no bearing on Fighter Command's ability to survive. He reckoned that the RAF was particularly singling out Ju 87s for interception, and ordered that each Stuka now be protected by three Bf 109s. He also expressed concern about Bf 110 wastage. Poor liaison between senior officers and units was apparent, to which the British could have added 'Your bombing accuracy is lousy!' Luckily, the enemy seems not to have realised that.

Crews of Stuka-equipped IV Gruppe, Lehrgeschwader 1, await the battle call.

Thursday 15 August began with the usual reconnaissance sorties, a Do 17 of Aufkl.Gr 3(F)/31 being picked off south of Ventnor by Spitfires, and Medway guns fired at a Ju 88. Clouds over the north and west were breaking by mid-morning, and as a general improvement set in, fighter squadrons dispersed to forward bases. Aircraft serviceability had improved during the enforced pause and now the aircraft stood at readiness. The British knew, through enigma and 'Y' Service intercepts, of intended widespread operations, with aerodromes the primary targets.

Activity began with fighter sweeps over the Channel between 09.00 and 11.00. They prompted 11 Group to mount precautionary patrols over two Thames convoys. An inkling of big trouble came at 10.45 when a large force – Ju 87s of IV/LG 1 and II/StG 1 escorted by Bf 109s – began assembling over the Pas de Calais. Four 11 Group squadrons were ordered to patrol Manston-Dungeness, and at 11.25 forty strongly escorted Ju 87s crossed the coast on their way to bomb Lympne and Hawkinge. Twenty-four of the Stukas abruptly turned towards Folkestone, British fighters engaging them and claiming their leader. Some bombs fell on Folkestone town, others damaging a hangar and barrack block at Hawkinge. Lympne was bombed at 11.36 by the other Ju 87s, which were engaged from out of the sun by fighters who claimed two Stukas. The three squadrons involved were unable to prevent StG 1 from putting Lympne out of use for two days.

Just after midday a totally new feature of the campaign began to unfold. Northern radar stations detected unidentified aircraft approaching from far to the east of the Firth of Forth. Their progress was extremely slow, and they were eventually identified as He 115 floatplanes of Kfl Gr 506 flying a feint towards Montrose. The number of raiders increased to well over thirty, so No 13 Group was ordered to respond to the first large-scale day raid on its territory. By 12.35 Spitfires of 41 Squadron[89], now stationed again at Catterick, were heading to meet what turned out to

Heinkel He 115 floatplanes similar to this flew a feint towards Scotland on 15 August.

be a second enemy force off the Farne Islands. Hurricanes of 605 Squadron[90] had meanwhile left Drem in order to protect Tyneside, No 79 Squadron and 607 Squadron, Usworth, also being scrambled. A formidable force manned by rested, combat-experienced pilots was eager to show its prowess. The Luftwaffe's belief that the north was poorly defended, that all our fighters were in the south, was about to be disproved. As many as seventy-two He 111s of Stavanger's KG 26 are believed to have set forth, although only sixty-five are thought to have completed the North Sea crossing. Bomber bases – Driffield and Linton-on-Ouse – were their designated targets; Newcastle-upon-Tyne, Sunderland and Middlesbrough were secondaries. Above the Heinkels was an escort of about thirty-five Bf 110s of I/ZG 76.

A serious navigation error was leading the bombers well north of their prescribed track, and that gave the defenders ample time for positioning. When the Heinkels were 30 miles out to sea from the Farne Islands, 41 Squadron, amazed at the number of bombers, pounced upon them. The He 111s were packed in threes at 18,000 feet, while the escort was 1,000 feet above and in two groups. No 41 Squadron, 3,000 feet higher and up-sun, bore down upon the raiders, taking them by surprise. Some jettisoned their loads, others ran for cloud cover, and the 110s quickly adopted their usual strange defensive circle, leaving the bombers to their fate. The Spitfire pilots claimed eleven enemy aircraft destroyed – Luftwaffe records suggest two 110s and an He 111 – but the truth could well rest between these figures.

Confusion certainly gripped the German force. Part of it headed for Tyneside only to meet 79 Squadron while leaving the remainder heading south. After engaging the Bf 110s, No 79 tackled the Heinkels approaching Newcastle or Usworth. Tyne guns greeted them, as well as 605 Squadron, which claimed four He 111s. Most bombs fell in the sea. The other force, engaged by 41 and 607

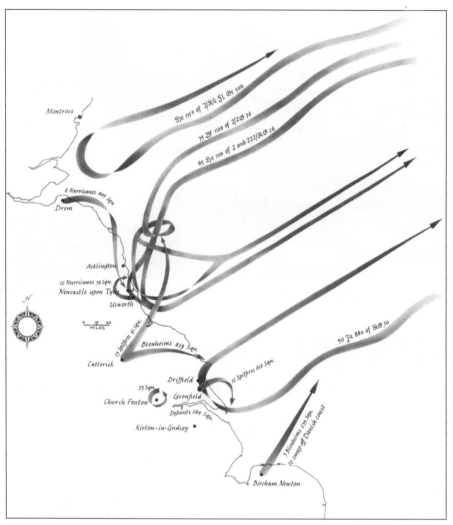

15 August 1940. Attacks on North-East England by Luftlotte 5

Squadrons as well as Teesside guns, unloaded mainly near Seaham Harbour. Seven remaining Bf 110s had been shot down and the rest fled. As for the Heinkels, eight of which are known to have been shot down, they made for home in groups, one of which unfortunately met Coastal Command Blenheim IV fighters of 235 Squadron[91] whose Pilot Officer Jackson-Smith destroyed yet another Heinkel. Debriefing reports examined years later showed that, on return, the crews stated that results of their 'attacks on Linton-on-Ouse and another airfield to the north were not observed'! In reality, ten bombs fell on South Shields, twenty-seven at Cleadon and seven houses

Scramble! A pilot of 64 Squadron races to his Spitfire on 15 August 1940. *IWM*

were destroyed in Seaham Harbour. At Dawdon twelve houses were damaged, and fifteen at Easington, where fifteen people were injured. Sunderland, where twenty-four houses were damaged, bore the brunt of the bombing. The Germans claimed to have shot down at least twenty British fighters – in truth, none were lost. Assuming they knew, that truth would surely have been too hard to bear.

It was not yet all over. Radar stations detected another threat developing from Denmark towards Spurn Head, which resolved itself as about fifty Ju 88s of KG 30. With them was a sprinkling of Ju 88C long-range fighters to ward off opposition. This threat was a matter for 12 Group, and at 13.00 Air Vice-Marshal T. Leigh-Mallory ordered Leconfield's 616 Squadron (twelve Spitfires) to patrol over Hornsea and 264 Squadron's Defiants to guard a Humber convoy. No 73 Squadron scrambled from Church Fenton to protect its base and a second convoy. Blenheim Ifs of 219 Squadron were 13 Group's contribution.

No 616 Squadron soared into action, forcing the Ju 88s to hurry into cloud, then six Hurricanes of 73 Squadron fell upon them as they crossed the coast. Although mauled, the Ju 88 force courageously pressed on to Driffield where, at 13.20, they seriously damaged a dozen Whitleys, four hangars and three blocks of buildings. Onto fields around rained forty-six 250kg bombs. More bombs were unloaded onto Bridlington and, perchance, an ammunition truck 6 miles away at Burton Agnes was hit.

My wife said, 'If you meet Churchill, grab hold of him – hard.' In truth, this is a confident crew of KG 30's Ju 88 A W Nr 4021 alongside another, 4D+LS. *Bundesarchiv*

Now it was the turn of 219 Squadron's Blenheims[92] to pester the 88s for up to 100 miles out to sea. When KG 30 reached home it was short of eight aircraft. Sergeant Dube flying Blenheim L8698 had been injured by return fire, as well as his air gunner, Sergeant Bannister. The latter, although not a pilot, skilfully nursed his new charge to Driffield where he had to execute a wheels-up landing – no mean achievement. Both mentioned were awarded DFMs for their efforts. Apart from that, Fighter Command lost neither aircraft nor crews, whereas General Stumpff had sacrificed an eighth of his bomber force and a fifth of his long-range fighter force. Implications for the Luftwaffe were serious. Unescorted bomber raids in daylight over the half of Britain where much of its industry was sited were clearly out of the question. They were never repeated. Small-scale daylight cloud-cover precision attacks were effectively mounted, but Goering and his team wanted large-scale spectaculars.

Around 14.00 on the 15th a complex operation that became Raid 20 was launched by Dorniers of KG 3 in league with Bf 109s of JG 51, JG 52 and JG 54. Ahead went sixty Bf 109s of JG 26 to provide forward support. Erpr 210 was also very much on the move, and detected only moments before its Bf 110s raced in low across Martlesham Heath at 15.10 to give it 'the Manston treatment'. Official and private reports differ in their accounts of this raid. Some, including Martlesham's anti-aircraft gunners and two very keen local aviation enthusiasts, emphatically believe that it was nine Ju 87s and not Bf 109 fighter-bombers in two vics, one of four, the other of five, which dived from about 5,000 to 2,000 feet to drop eight 250kg HEs. It is just possible that some of them had been ordered to attack Bawdsey radar, for some reports tell of them aiming for a 'radio station' east of Martlesham aerodrome. As for the Bf 110s, at least six, and possibly nine, bombed and strafed Martlesham Heath, dropping at least one oil bomb in their assault. Above, at 15,000 to 20,000 feet and awaiting an RAF response, flew the Bf 109 top cover. Three Hurricanes of 17 Squadron[93] took off just in time to evade the bombs, whereas a visiting Battle of 12 Squadron was blown apart and the nearby watch office was wrecked. Two hangars suffered badly, as well as Station Workshops and the Officers' Mess. The Hurricanes of No 17 Squadron, quickly reinforced by nine Hurricanes of No 1 Squadron[94], chased after the top cover, which picked off three British fighters.

While that 'smart raid' progressed, twenty-four Hurricanes of 111 and 151[95] Squadrons and Spitfires of 64 Squadron[96] were over Kent tangling with a Bf 109 forward sweep. Four other squadrons were positioned between Manston and Hawkinge to disrupt any approaching bomber force. The huge protective force of Bf 109s made their task tough, a freelancing JG 26 claiming to destroy at least eight British fighters. KG 3 led by Chamier-Glisczinski pressed on and divided over Faversham. Gruppen I and II/KG 3 in two waves approached from the south-east out of range of Chatham's guns and between 15.35 and 15.43 aimed more than 100 HEs at the Short and Pobjoy Rochester factories. A later count found ninety-four bomb craters. There were also UXHEs. Eight bombs had exploded in Shorts main factory, where a fire took 2 hours to control. One large bomb burst in the wing shop at Pobjoy's, putting a third of the factory out of use. As a result of the raid, six Stirlings were destroyed and their production at Rochester was all but eliminated. Gunners at a dozen sites fired 235 rounds at the Dorniers. One of the 3.7in guns of the 159th Bty, 53 Regt, at Site S.11 scored a direct hit on a Do 17Z of 6./KG 3, the remains of which fell in the sea off Garrison Point, Sheerness. A second Do 17Z came down near Sevenoaks.

Maintaining the pressure, about eighty bombers and many fighters challenged 10 Group, which, between 17.00 and 17.20, scrambled the largest number of fighters it had yet fielded. Three squadrons made for Swanage, there to engage about forty Ju 87s of I/StG 1 and II/StG 2 protected by Bf 109s of JG 27 and JG 53, and BF 110s of V/LG 2. All were yet again heading for tortured Portland. Nos 87[97] and 213 Squadrons tackled the bombers and the 110s, leaving fourteen Spitfires of 234[98] Squadron to engage first the Bf 110s then the Bf 109s, which, overwhelming their interceptors, shot down four. The Stukas were forced to jettison their loads before heading home, cheated of attacking their targets.

Patrolling off the Isle of Wight, 43 Squadron[99] was vectored towards sixty Ju 88s of LG 1 escorted by about forty Bf 110s of ZG 2. They battled with raiders heading towards Southampton. Successively, five Hurricane squadrons, including Nos 601[100] and 249[101], fought them, not to mention the Solent and Southampton gunners, who also joined in. That did not prevent the Ju 88s from reaching Middle Wallop fighter station, where two hangars were hit, an aircraft was destroyed and

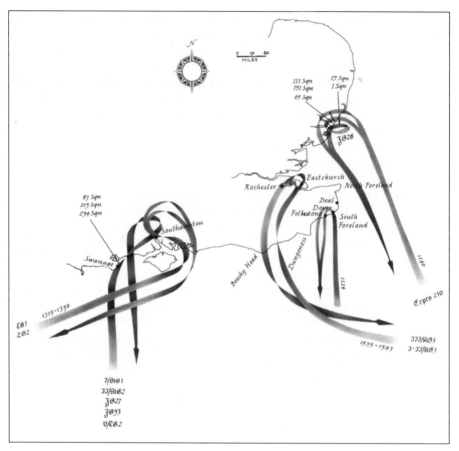

15-August 1940 – Attacks on South East England

five were damaged. At Worthy Down little damage was done, and seven of the fifteen would-be destroyers soon lay shattered. Only three crews even claimed to have reached their target. A few bombed Odiham, and five bombers fell to 601 Squadron alone. The entire operation cost Luftflotte 3 eight bombers, four dive-bombers and thirteen Bf 110s. Fighter Command lost sixteen aircraft.

Just after 6 o'clock Park faced one of his most difficult moments so far. Dorniers of KG 1 and KG 2 escorted by Bf 109s of I/LG 1 were approaching, while many of his pilots – recently landed – had already flown two or three tiring operations during the day. No 501 Squadron had been airborne for 45 minutes, and had twice been in action, but Park retained it in position. He called upon four more squadrons to assist, reinforcing those with a further four and a half. Maybe he had been advised of, or was assuming, an attack on inland aerodromes. The raiders were

A Spitfire of 609 Squadron in one of Middle Wallop's revetments during August.

intercepted at the coast by three squadrons, 501 included, which spoiled their operation so much that those bound for Biggin Hill unloaded upon West Malling, and intended Redhill entirely escaped. At 18.50 anti-aircraft gunners of Site S25 claimed a direct hit with a 3-inch shell on the aircraft leading the West Malling raid and recorded that their prize fell at Burrough Green (Ref R050760).

There remained just one spectacular event to unfold before darkness fell – the bombing of Croydon. 'Croydon'. Everyone in those times knew of Croydon, home of Imperial Airways, starting point for Amy Johnson and many more record-breakers. Few had ever flown from it due to the expense, but most would recognise Croydon Airport's distinctive terminal and well-known tower from many a cinema newsreel.

Concurrent with the last big raid of the day, Erpr 210 was racing in at high speed to ruin Kenley. Maybe a navigation error or mistaken identity allowed that station to escape. For reason uncertain, the Bf 110s instead blitzed Croydon moments after nine Hurricanes of 'Treble One' had taken off in time to escape the bombing that wrecked hangars and ammunition stores – for Croydon was now a fighter base – damaged Rollason's aircraft repair section, killed sixty-eight people (only six Service personnel) and injured 192. No civilian warning had wailed in time. The Bf 110s and shepherding Bf 109s climbed away, with 111[102] Squadron and some of 32 Squadron chasing after them. Squadron Leader J. Thompson of 111 Squadron dispatched a Bf 110 to its doom over Rotherfield in a spectacular, fiery victory. His victim was Swiss-born Hauptmann Walter Rubensdorffer, leader of Erpr 210. Six Bf 110s were shot down in the skirmish, depriving the Luftwaffe of brave warriors.

Barely had those remaining departed our shores when an unusual newsflash on the wireless announced that the Germans had just dive-bombed Croydon. Initially the raid was attributed to Stukas, encouraging an image of merciless, screaming Nazi butchers. It was some time before bomb-carrying Me 110s were blamed. Somehow, hitting Croydon seemed a highly immoral, completely unacceptable act that aroused cultivated anger. Mind you, its use as a fighter station was quietly overlooked! The Ministry of Information was undoubtedly orchestrating a skilful public relations exercise.

By late evening it was being suggested 'on the news' that during 15 August the Luftwaffe had flown more than 2,000 sorties. Against that, Fighter Command had dispatched 974 sorties during an exceptional day of aerial conflict. Wild claims suggested that more than 150 German aircraft had been destroyed for a loss of twenty-nine fighters. Around a score of other aircraft were wrecked by bombing. The Luftwaffe reckoned it lost sixty-nine aircraft. What remains certain is that, after a tragic day of bitter conflict between two of the world's most cultured nations, neither side was a clear winner. Both had lost very brave men – but Fighter Command, and its aerodromes, were still very much a going concern.

In the 24 hours ended 06.00 on 16 August it was reckoned that 867 HEs and 1,566 incendiaries had fallen on Britain, killing seventy-nine civilians, seriously injuring 196 and variously injuring another 175.

Across the Channel the German Air Staff had also been doing their sums, concluding, hopefully, that Fighter Command's losses since the start of July left it with about only 300 aircraft.

German fighter pilots form a reception committee for one of their number, safely back. *Bundesarchiv*

The stored reserve of Hurricanes and Spitfires had certainly fallen by 16 August, current output and loss rates meaning that the necessary reserve could be maintained for only two months. If loss rates rose, if factories were destroyed... Each squadron currently held an average of nineteen pilots – barely enough to replace casualties and allow essential rest. To equate with listed establishments, nearly 350 more pilots were needed, but only about eighty would complete operational training during the next week, and there was no let up in the fight.

Spitfires and Hurricanes in Aircraft Storage Units

	Number outstanding 18.00	Dispatched since 18.00 yesterday	In hand during the day	Ready for dispatch	Likely to be ready by noon next day	Additional but still deficient in equipment
Spitfires						
31.7.40	3	1	79 + 17 Mk II	22	33 + 9 Mk 11	2
12.8.40	3	3	105 + 34 Mk II	22	33 + 9 Mk II	6
15.8.40	2	10	98 + 34 Mk II	22	20 + 2 Mk II	7
24.8.40	–	6	51 + 31 Mk II	19	21 + 11 Mk II	–
Hurricanes						
31.7.40	12	2	140 + 15 for Middle East*	45	133	11
13.8.40	4	24	152 + 3 for Middle East	45	136	21
24.8.40	–	11	88 + 3 Mk II**	56	18 + 5 Mk II	–

* between 1 July and 30 September 84 Hurricanes were shipped to the Middle East
** first Hurricane Mk II received by ASUs

The morning haze lifted late on 16 August, delaying fighter-escorted Dornier raids. Around noon a two-pronged operation by KG 2 came in over Dover and soon faced Spitfires of Nos 64[103], 65[104] and 266[105] Squadrons, and Hurricanes of 32[106] and 111[107] Squadrons – more than fifty RAF fighters all told. Head-on attacks by Hurricanes forced opened the bomber force but brought disaster to Flight Lieutenant H. Ferris (R4193) of 111 Squadron, who careered into a Do 17. The combined wreckage fell at Marden, Kent. Undaunted, the Dorniers pressed on and at 12.25, from a high-level pass, aimed eighty bombs on West Malling, sixty-six of them exploding in surrounding farmland. Four No 266 Squadron Spitfires were shot down in an associated bitter struggle with II/JG 26 over Deal.

Next it was the turn of II/KG 2, which swung in over the North Foreland where a dozen anti-aircraft gun sites greeted the twenty-four Dornier 17s. They were prevented from attacking Hornchurch by fighters over the Thames Estuary. While Spitfires of 54 Squadron tangled with accompanying fuel-short Bf 109s, the Dorniers instead dropped seven bombs upon Tilbury. They then crossed the river to Northfleet's Pepper Hill and Hazels districts and delivered extensive punishment. Included was a gruesome incident at Bowaters Paper Mill where ten bombs started a fire and casualties amounted to twenty-five workers killed and thirty-two injured.

The most damaging intrusion evolved east of the Isle of Wight at around 12.30. It comprised Ju 87s of StG 2 supported by Bf 109s of JG 2, and Ju 88s of KG 54 shepherded by Bf 110s of III/ZG 76. Eight defending fighter squadrons were airborne as the approaching force split into four groups. The Stukas almost immediately bearing down upon Tangmere were challenged by Hurricanes of Nos 1[108], 43[109] and 601[110] Squadrons, while No 602[111] Squadron's Spitfires tackled their escort. They were unable to prevent Tangmere's mutilation by twenty accurately aimed bombs, which disposed of its hangars, Station Workshops, sick quarters and the Officers' Mess. The Blenheim-equipped Fighter Interception Unit developing AI radar and operational techniques was mauled. Five Hurricanes blazed in hangar fires, and fifteen Tangmere aircraft were, in total, smashed. Six civilians and twelve Service personnel were killed, and forty-one injured. One bomb exploded in a slit trench, causing terrible scenes. In the midst of the raid Pilot Officer W. Fiske had to force-land his Hurricane P3358, which was then strafed and burned. Next day Fiske became the first volunteer American pilot to die in the Battle. Losses were not one-sided, for No 43 Squadron alone claimed seventeen Ju 87s – Luftwaffe records show that nine were lost.

Shortly afterwards more Ju 87s hurled twenty-two bombs onto Ventnor Radar. No 152 Squadron engaged their escorting Bf 109s while No 213 Squadron tried unsuccessfully to prevent more Stukas from attacking Lee-on-Solent, where three hangars were hit and naval aircraft were left burning.

Gosport was the target for KG 54, which distributed fifty-three bombs onto the town and Gosport/Fort Grange aerodrome. There a hangar was left blazing, seven personnel were killed and fifteen injured. Three Hurricanes of 249 Squadron[112] from the Ringwood area, sent to deal with escorting Bf 110s, instead became embroiled with the rescuing Bf 109s. Flight Lieutenant J. B. Nicolson, his Hurricane P3576 hit, courageously continued fighting. The aircraft was burning furiously by the time he baled out. Both he and Pilot Officer M. A. King (P3616), also forced to parachute to safety, were, in error, subjected to ground fire. King died, and Nicolson, further injured, was awarded the first Victoria Cross given to a Fighter Command pilot.

Late afternoon saw He 111s of KG 27 escorted by Bf 110s crossing the coast near Brighton and heading for Brooklands. They were met by Nos 1[113], 64[114] and 615[115] Squadrons, which thwarted the bombers' intent. HEs and incendiaries fell on Wimbledon station and a factory, killing eighteen and injuring fifty-seven. Other bombs dropped on Merton, Mitcham and shops in Esher. Ten minutes later more burst on the railway near Basingstoke. At Eastbourne eighteen HEs had earlier killed three and injured one person. Defending fighters, in trying hard to prevent all this, destroyed four He 111s and two Bf 110s. One He 111 was brought down at Steyning by Pilot Officer K. T. Lofts (P3111), and Pilot Officer C. R. Young (L2075), also of 615 Squadron, destroyed another off Bognor. Squadron Leader Macdonnell (P9554) of 64 Squadron helped destroy a third, and Pilot Officer Simpson shared another before his Spitfire L1068 was damaged by cannon fire.

Simultaneously, Raid B headed along the Thames Estuary bound for Biggin Hill. It was driven off track by Nos. 32[116], 501[117] and 610[118] Squadrons. No 56 Squadron, scrambled at 16.50, engaged a third formation comprising twenty-seven Do 17s near Eastchurch. They claimed two Dorniers and two Bf 109s for the loss of a Hurricane burnt out at Whitstable.

Controlling the Battle

Vital to Fighter Command's success was its fighter control system, whose layout was basically this:

1. All aircraft plots obtained by radar stations, Observer Corps and searchlight detachments were notified to the Filter Room at HQ Fighter Command.

2. These were analysed, identified and plotted on the HQ Operations table.

3. Relevant Fighter Group HQ were notified of approaching raids.

4. Group Commander decided which Sector should meet the enemy, and the number of aircraft it should deploy.

5. Sector Commander detailed squadron(s) to intercept and the means by which they should operate.

6. Sector Commander maintained control of his fighters by R/T (Radio Telephony) and D/F (Direction Finding).

R/T signals were transmitted automatically for 15 seconds each minute by selected fighters and picked up by two or three D/F stations and passed by direct telephone link to Sector HQ where a mechanical plotting device gave an almost instant plot of the fighters' position. Where no D/F station was available, pilots had to be given speed and direction orders – acceptable if the wind at various altitudes was accurately known.

During 1940 IFF (Identification Friend and Foe) was slowly introduced. It modified the 'echo' received by a radar station from a friendly aircraft, greatly easing the problem of identity.

Simple voice instructions and terms:

'Scramble' = take off

'Orbit' = circle

'Vector 180' = fly on course 180°

'Pancake' = land

'Angels 21' = fly at 21,000 feet (sometimes a secret addition could mean, say, add 3,000 – so that 'Angels 21' meant fly at 24,000 feet)

'Released' = not to be called upon for action

'Available' = to be ready to operate in 20 minutes

'Readiness' = ready to operate in 5 minutes

'Stand-by' = available for take-off in 2 minutes' time

Around 18.00 single aircraft began attacking inland airfields, their attempts stunningly effective. Four bombs at Harwell set fire to petrol bowsers, one of which was courageously driven away to open ground. Three Wellingtons were destroyed and two men were killed. Ten bombs at RAF Farnborough destroyed wooden structures. The highlight involved Brize Norton. At 18.05 two hitherto unnoticed, wheels-down Ju 88s cheekily joined the circuit then suddenly switched to attack mode. Within moments they started furious fires that gutted two hangars and consumed no fewer than forty-six fully fuelled wooden Airspeed Oxford trainers of

No 2 Service Flying Training School. Six more were badly damaged, as well as eleven Hurricanes at adjacent 6 MU, an ASU that was surely their intended and most important target. A gigantic pall of black smoke billowed over Oxfordshire from one of the most damaging attacks ever delivered on a British military airfield. Meanwhile, Bf 109s strafed Manston. With longer duration, the 109s would have posed a great threat. How easily, cheaply, more safely, a handful of intruders could achieve far more than a clumsy fleet of big boys. Shades of future Mosquito raids!

As soon as it was dark, KG 27 set out to attack South Wales. Central Cardiff was hit by fifteen HEs (and five UX), and KG 4, operating from Schiphol, interfered with active aerodromes in East Anglia. Late on 16 August Birmingham was attacked for the third time, about sixty HEs being distributed over Castle Bromwich, Erdington, Small Heath and the Singer Motors works. In the 24 hours ending 06.00 on the 17th, ground casualties in Britain totalled eighty-eight killed and 192 injured. In the same period the Luftwaffe's 1,700 sorties cost it forty-five aircraft, and the RAF lost twenty-five fighters. Since 11 August seventy-eight RAF fighter pilots had died and twenty-seven had been seriously wounded. More than half were very experienced.

Replacing aircraft was so much easier than replacing pilots. Dowding requested the Air Staff to agree to releasing pilots from Merlin-engined Fairey Battle bomber squadrons despite their anti-E-boat and invasion attack roles. Losing ninety-four fighter pilots killed and sixty-five wounded since 8 August was acutely alarming – especially since Fighter Command had entered the Battle far below pilot establishment. The Air Staff, accepting Dowding's proposal, then invited a total of twenty Battle pilots to volunteer for transfer, and thirty-three from 22 Group whose Lysander army co-operation

NCO pilots of 610 Squadron wearing 'Mae Wests' on a hot summer day at Hawkinge.
IWM

squadrons (already administered by Fighter Command) also had a major anti-invasion role. By that route fifty-three fighter pilots – additional to about eighty less experienced and still expected from fighter OTUs – would soon become available.

Another source of pilots were those waiting to avenge misappropriation of their homelands. These were the experienced Czech and Polish pilots who had reached England often most courageously. The Air Ministry had sanctioned formation of one Czech and three Polish squadrons at half strength – on the understanding that they trained more of their pilots. Although the first squadron, No 302 (Polish), was formed on 13 July, none could become operational for some time. Shortage of aircraft and operational stations for them also retarded their progress.

A day of drastically reduced activity, 17 August saw single aircraft seeking coastal shipping. Around 17.00 a photo-reconnaissance aircraft lingered ominously and high over London before another one, reckoned to be at 35,000 feet at least, and possibly even higher, surveyed the Thames and its Estuary. Was a raid on London likely to follow? Early in the evening Fg Off R. E. P. Brooker of 56 Squadron, flying Hurricane P3513 on an air test, was vectored to Do 17Z-3 of 8./KG 2, which he shot down near Claydon, Suffolk. It crashed near Stonelodge Lane, Gippeswyk Park, Ipswich, the crew of four having baled out. Two landed on the rooftops of houses in Harland Street and Waterside, Ipswich, where they were soon facing a hostile crowd, including housewives brandishing carving knives. Luckily for the illegal immigrants, a policeman was soon on the scene.

Fighting for freedom meant, for the Poles and Czechs, a long difficult trek, language problems, and adjustment to strange food and ways. At Duxford Czech pilots formed No 310 (Czech) Squadron, and one of its Hurricanes, NN-D P3143, forms a backdrop. It joined 310 on 24 July and was destroyed on 16 October in a crash near Ely. *IWM*

During night attacks that commenced around midnight, homes were destroyed in Aberavon. Bombs also fell south-west of Coventry, and a dozen on Liverpool. By the end of October 893 HE bombs would have fallen there, nearly 150 on Birkenhead and seventy or so on Wallasey. Liverpool County Borough was assessed by the time of its last raid, on 10/11 January 1942, as having received 2,345 HEs, 117 parachute mines and fifty oil bombs, which gives some idea of its ultimate punishment and provides a guide against which to measure the August attacks.

Birmingham's fourth raid took place on 17/18 August, some 500-600 incendiaries and twenty-two HEs aimed at Castle Bromwich Spitfire works falling wide on open country, and seventeen on Hodge Hill Common near Sutton Coldfield. Birmingham was ultimately listed as receiving 4,429 HEs, eighty-six oil bombs and fifty mines. In the 24 hours ending 06.00 on 18 August twenty-three civilians had died in Britain and eighty had been seriously injured. Incendiaries dropped totalled around 1,000. By way of comparison, during the 1943-1944 RAF night raids on Germany as many as 900,000 incendiaries were dropped in one attack.

During the night Pilot Officer R. A. Rhodes and Sergeant Gregory had notched up a notable night success. Operating a Mersey Blue Line patrol from Ternhill in Blenheim 1 fighter L6741 of 29 Squadron, they were vectored onto a raider discovered 15 miles south-west of Chester. After locating it by aid of lights exposed in its rear position, they followed it over Hucknall, Newark and Lincoln, then caught it out to sea. Rhodes fired from 400 yards, then his gunner opened up towards the starboard beam. The Heinkel He 111 of II/KG 53 slowly spiralled down and eventually ditched 10 miles west of Cromer Knoll Light Vessel. Killed in the encounter was II/KG 53's Gruppenkommandeur.

Daylight on 18 August saw the Luftwaffe, which had already taken six days trying to finish off Fighter Command, make a massive effort to complete the task.. Action began when six high spies roamed over South East England. Included was a Bf 110 of LG 2, shot down from 31,000 feet over Manston. Around midday an enormous force 350-strong was assembling, Nos 10 and 11 Groups' squadrons being called to readiness. Three waves of raiders that crossed the coast between North Foreland and Dungeness were eager to reach targets south and south-east of London. First up to challenge them was veteran 56[119] Squadron and 54 Squadron[120] scrambled at 12.40 from its Manston advanced base. Another seventy fighters from nine other squadrons soon joined them, but to achieve success larger forces were needed in view of the strength of the invaders. One raid unleashed thirty-three bombs on Deal, while the others pressed on.

A complex hi-lo raid, heavily fighter-protected, was now injected into the action, its aiming points the vitally important Fighter Sector Stations at Biggin Hill and Kenley. Two diversionary bomber formations flying at 15,000 feet bombed West Malling, the first at 12.52 and the second at 13.20. Local AA gunners challenged the attackers before defending fighters arrived, and claimed hits on two aircraft, from one of which two men baled out. Fifty HEs fell on West Malling; two direct hits on hangars were scored and three Lysanders were wrecked. While that deception was performed, the two main, specialised attacks were launched.

At the same time as Kenley was raided, nine Do 17Zs of 9./KG 76 raced extremely low over Kent, confusing ground observers. They reached their objective at

Mid-August saw sharp, low-level and effective attacks on Sector aerodromes. This famous shot taken on 18 August from a Do 17 of 9./KG 76 during a raid on Kenley shows Spitfire SH-G of 64 Squadron in a protective earthy revetment doubling as an air raid shelter. Extensive hard taxiways are in evidence. *Bundesarchiv*

13.30. It was Biggin Hill, which they crossed at low level, strafing as they delivered short- and long-delay mixed bombs. Such activity demanded faster aircraft than the Do 17, Nos 32[121], 12 and 111 Squadrons catching two Dorniers, including that of the leader. A further two crashed in the Channel, and three force-landed in France.

Running in very low over Newhaven came nine Do 17Zs of KG 76 to attack Kenley aerodrome at 13.22 from as low as 50 to 100 feet. The three leading bomber crews machine-gunned the station's anti-aircraft defences before dropping their bombs on the north-east side of the camp. Meanwhile, their colleagues dealt with the hangars and sick quarters. Five minutes later came another force flying at 10,000 feet, arriving by way of Dungeness. Their bombs scored hits on the Station Armoury and Station Sick Quarters. They variously damaged eight aircraft (including six of 615 Squadron's Hurricanes) and dropped many delayed-action bombs. No 111 Squadron tackled the low-flyers, two of which were brought down by Parachute and Cable rocket defences (see the accompanying feature). About 100 bombs were dropped; twelve personnel died, and twenty were injured. No 615 Squadron[122], in responding as quickly as possible to the raid, was set upon by the rear-support Bf 109s. As a result Flight Lieutenant Gaunce (P2966) was forced to bale out near Sevenoaks and Pilot Officer Hugo (R4221) was wounded and crash-landed; Pilot Officer Looker's Hurricane (L1592) caught fire, and was landed at Croydon, Flight Lieutenant Sanders (P3111) was shot down near Kenley, and Sergeant Walley (P2768), who crashed at Morden, Kent, was killed.

Parachute and Cable

By February 1940 arrangements were complete for the installation of a novel rocket defence system for the aerodromes at Manston and Wattisham, and Great Bromley radar station. The weapon consisted of a standard Schermuly rocket carrying a 37-inch-diameter parachute in a small metal container. The bottom of a second metal container also contained a parachute, the two being connected by 480 feet of 1-ton cable. Propelled to 600 feet (later 1,000 feet), the rocket was fired from a tube set in the ground, or at radar stations from a 23-foot-square platform carrying rocket tubes mounted in batches of fours, and sited on the top of a high tower.

The tubes at aerodromes were arranged in groups of twenty-five, each 60 feet from the next, and in three rows set 20 feet apart. Each bank of rockets could be fired independently. The fire controller was given the best possible view of aircraft approaching the airfield.

The intention was that batteries of the small rockets would be positioned at both French and British airfields to prohibit the types of low-level attack experienced by the Poles. Then, on 30 April, all the units built were suddenly ordered to Norway – and lost.

Training to use 'PAC' began at Exeter on 6 May 1940. On 25 May it was decided to initially install the system at eight aircraft and engine factories, then at airfields in this order: Manston, Hornchurch, North Weald, Biggin Hill, Kenley, Tangmere, Debden. Installation, by No 1 PAC Rocket Unit, was to be completed by 5 June.

On 21 June the scheme was extended to twenty-seven airfields, thirteen of them bomber airfields and all manned by personnel from PAC Pool Uxbridge. Concern about rockets possibly landing on dispersed aircraft was brushed aside by the supporters, who stated that 'when they come down they only weigh 15lb'. By 15 July installation was complete at twenty-six sites (eight of them factories) and another twenty-two sites were chosen. Biggin Hill had four sets, North Weald four – roughly in each corner of the aerodrome – and Northolt six sets. Hawkinge's five sets, installed on 14 June, were controlled from the Station Commander's house.

The first suitable low attack for engagement was reckoned to have been against Manston on 17 August, although the aircraft might have been out of range. The firing staff were officially rated 'not proficient', for they took shelter instead of opening fire. 'Unreliable people', claimed the higher echelons! On 20 August twelve Bf 109s shot up Manston in two waves, diving in from 5,000 to 400 feet. Since they approached over buildings, PAC engagement was not practicable.

By then some success had been achieved. On 18 August nine Do 17Zs ran in at 500 feet to attack Kenley, the Observer Corps stating that near Hartfield these aircraft had laid a smoke screen for cover. As the Dorniers approached Kenley, 914844 AC2 Roberts of 1 PACU Post B Line quickly checked the circuitry of his equipment and found three units ready. He saw a twin-engined aircraft 50 feet above a hangar release its bombs, then the bombers flew in a straight line in a vic across the airfield machine-gunning ground defences and gathering height, three of them heading directly for his line of rockets. When the leading aircraft was within range he released his first line of nine rockets and watched the aircraft fly directly into a mass of cables and release a bomb, which exploded beneath it. By then the other two were within range of No 2 line, so he pressed the firing button. Both this and Line 3 were out of use, their circuits having been concussed by the bombing. He looked up and, about 100 yards away, saw smoke rising above trees from a crashed aircraft, which he and Wing Commander England inspected. The wrecked Dornier had cable caught around one of its mainplanes. By then the station had been dive-bombed, against which PAC was of little use because the attackers pulled out quite high. PAC Mk II with a 1,500-foot range was later developed to help cope with that. Two other units of the Kenley barrages had been fired inefficiently due to miscalculation of the speed of the aircraft.

Lord Beaverbrook thought the weapons very effective as factory defences. More than fifty were fired when North Weald was under threat on 30 August, and by mid-September they were installed at seventy-two sites. In October, the Navy asked for its aerodromes to have them and by the end of that month Castletown, Skaebrae and Skitten in Scotland had them. They were a feature of very many operational airfields until well into the war. Phase-out started from bomber stations in July 1942, by which time ample light machine guns were available.

Mainwaring's men?

Among many claims as to who shot down enemy aircraft was one by the Home Guard. The Captain involved, who had served in France in the First World War, said, 'I gave the order for rapid fire and my second in command directed the distance and the height of the firing. We saw the machine stagger and lose height. Although some of my men were of the younger generation they all behaved splendidly. Their discipline was beyond praise.'

Such was Kenley's state that 615 Squadron's remaining aircraft had to divert to Croydon. Conditions there were also extremely bad. Bombing had caused a serious fire; there was devastation in Purley Way and also at the Rollason works. Widespread damage was caused in Coulsdon, and a gasometer was left burning at Sevenoaks together with a dozen goods wagons at Paddock Wood station. No 64 Squadron[123], which laid many claims, managed later to land at Kenley on a narrow flag-marked track. Fires there were still raging 6 hours after the raid. Phone lines were down, which disrupted 11 Group activity at both vital Sector Stations – and the day was still young.

Just after the Dorniers cleared Biggin Hill, three tiered groups of Ju 88s of KG 76 heading easterly at 12,000, 15,000 and 18,000 feet cratered the station's landing ground. Of 150 HEs released, only sixty hit the aerodrome. The remainder disturbed the grass of the nearby golf course. Small anti-personnel bombs dropped upon gun sites killed two men alongside a Bofors gun. Two of the Ju 88s were shot down, one by Flight Lieutenant Stanford Tuck, who was forced by return fire to bale out of his 92 Squadron Spitfire (N3040).

Oberleutnant Lamberty's Do 17Z-2 F1+DT, leading 9/KG 76, was shot down near Biggin Hill on Sunday 18 August. Few raiders landed as intact as this. *IWM*

The second afternoon phase opened when six raids approached the Isle of Wight from the east shortly after 14.00. About seventy Ju 87s of StG 77 accompanied by twenty-four Ju 88s of KG 54 arrived to deliver four sharp strikes. At Poling CH radar station, forty-four HEs from screeching Stukas brought down two pylons and disabled the installation for a week. Another forty-three bombs exploded outside its perimeter. Ford naval air station was dive-bombed and two hangars were mutilated. Raiders destroyed a third of the quarters, killed fourteen and started a huge petroleum fire. The third attack was directed upon Gosport, where follow-up Ju 88s caused further damage. Thorney Island was raided at 14.30 by a handful of Ju 87s, which managed to score hits on a hangar and start a fire.

German fighters were still providing area top cover when 43 Squadron[124] latched on to the Poling Stukas and attacked them in both dive and recovery phases. For the Stukas much worse followed, for after they had regrouped the dive-bombers were furiously engaged by Nos 152, 601[125] and 602[126] Squadrons, leaving 234 Squadron[127] challenging the top cover. The Stuka formation was devastated, no fewer than sixteen Ju 87s being shot down. Two others crash-landed, and another four were badly damaged. Surprisingly, even eight of the escorting Bf 109s were brought down, and all for the loss of four Spitfires and two Hurricanes.

During fourteen main raids within two weeks, thirty-nine Ju 87s had been destroyed in action. Now, one Stuka Geschwader had lost another sixteen aircraft . Clearly, Fighter Command had cut short the Stuka's reign, and whose role was now performed by the fast fighter-bomber. A milestone had been passed, but few yet recognised it. Proof of the newcomer's value came at 15.30 when a dozen Bf 109s, performing as strike fighters, strafed Manston destroying two Spitfires, killing one man and injuring fifteen. They could so easily have also bombed the aerodrome.

Another new development followed 2 hours later when eight raids crossed in mainly over the Essex coast using the Blackwater and Thames estuaries for entry. The Luftwaffe was extending its theatre of operations. That brought Nos 54[128] and 151[129] Squadrons into action, and they prevented much of the bombing of North Weald and Hornchurch. Some bombers veered away before the target and at 17.45 jettisoned 150 HEs on Shoebury. Another sixty-nine bombs exploded near Strood, seventy-seven in the countryside beyond. These raids by the Medway caused numerous casualties, for no sirens had sounded.

Outside the Market Inn, Salisbury, a rare Do 17P,5D+JL of Aufkl.Gr 3(F)/31 shot down on 27 August by 238 Squadron Hurricanes near Tavistock, Devon

About seventy German bombers operated after darkness fell, forty over South Wales. Sealand was bombed, and a considerable number of delayed-action HEs fell in Birmingham and Wolverhampton. Another, at Hook, Hampshire, exploded, killing five members of a bomb disposal squad dealing with it.

Grim as all the incidents involving civilians were, they were eclipsed by the main event, the defeat of the Stuka during what turned out to be one of the toughest days of the Battle for both sides. Although the Luftwaffe had lost sixty-nine aircraft, the RAF loss of sixty-eight fighters was a most alarming disaster.

Goering was enraged when told that his fighters had been proven incapable of defending the Stukas, which would now have to be held back for their designated invasion tasks. He must have been quite cross when presented with details of the previous week's losses, for on three days they exceeded fifty aircraft. Luftflotte 5's bombers operating beyond Bf 109 range in daytime were shown to be so vulnerable that he ordered them to switch to night raids on Glasgow, and make only cloud-cover daytime precision attacks. Despite the poor combat showing of the Bf 110, it retained Goering's confidence, although he hedged his bets by ordering that Bf 109 fighters must now protect the 110 fighters! Even more restricting was his order that

Prime Luftwaffe fighter, the Bf 109E had a performance superior to the Hurricane's but not quite equal to the Spitfire.

Bf 109s must stay close to bombers, and shield them instead of breaking away to fight the enemy. That had profound consequences, particularly as the Luftwaffe's prime task remained the destruction of Fighter Command. Did Adolf phone Hermann to enquire about the 'all over in four days' idea?

Cloudy conditions on 19 August limited operations. Yet again, one small-scale attack achieved success out of all proportion to the effort. Two Ju 88s of KG 51 at 15.15 scored hits with eight bombs on the Llanreith oil farm, Pembroke, instantly causing a huge conflagration that blazed for many days. Another III/KG 51 Ju 88 struck at Bibury grass airfield, killing an airman and damaging two Spitfires of newly arrived 92 Squadron. Flight Lieutenant T. S. Wade, later Hawker's Chief Test Pilot, and Pilot Officer J. A. Paterson quickly climbed aboard Spitfires R6703 and P9368. They gave chase, eventually disposing of the cheeky raider in the Solent. In a crash-landing, Wade had to get away fast from his exploding aircraft. East Anglia was also subjected to a host of afternoon intrusions directed mainly at aerodromes. Some twenty-three bombs fell on residential property at Chelmsford, killing two and injuring five. Other incidents occurred at Dover Castle, Shoeburyness, Canterbury and Deal Royal Marine Infirmary. No 19 Squadron's cannon-armed Spitfires R6882, R6897 and R6911 destroyed a 7./KG 2 Do 17Z off Essex, but scores reflected a quieter day – three raiders destroyed, four RAF fighters lost.

After dusk, He 111s of KG 27, carrying out Goering's recent instruction, aimed a few bombs towards Liverpool and Birkenhead. KGr 100 dropped forty-three HEs in an attempted beam-guided precision attack on Derby, after which three He 111s crashed on return due to fuel shortages. In a low-level strike on Driffield, a hangar was damaged as well as two Whitleys. Bombing also took place at Hull, Leicester, Nottingham and Sheffield, with twenty-three dying and seventy-four being injured by dawn.

Attempts were made on 20 August to stoke the Llanreith fire, and Erpr 210 interfered with a convoy off Aldeburgh before striking sharply at Southwold's coastal defences. Early afternoon brought in twenty-seven Do 17s of KG 3 escorted by Bf 109s of I/JG 51, which flew via Dover and Canterbury to the Thames Estuary. In the process they faced six squadrons – forty fighters. No 615 Squadron[130] claimed two bombers and a Bf 109, which were again heading for Coastal Command's Eastchurch anti-invasion station. No 65 Squadron[131] claimed another and, in engaging the escort, destroyed two Bf 109s. Smaller-scale activities included a convoy attack off Dunwich. A Do 17 was shot down off Southwold by 257 Squadron. The Ju 88 of KG 30 brought down near Withernsea provided the eager members of 302 (Polish) Squadron – declared operational only the previous day – with their first victory. Convoy CE9 was shelled by Cap Gris Nez guns, the ships being among those that carried each week around 40,000 tons of coal to South Coast ports. Sailors on the ships of CE11 formally enquired of the Ministry of Shipping as to why coal could not travel overland. On the 20th/21st, among the sixty raids plotted was a repeat attack directed at Rolls-Royce Derby. Casualties for the 24 hours ending 06.00 on the 21st were forty-six civilians killed and 108 injured.

The great air battle which had been in progress over this island for the last few weeks has recently attained a high intensity. It is too soon to attempt to assign limits either to its scale or to its duration... It is quite plain that Herr Hitler could not admit defeat in his air attack on Great Britain without sustaining most serious injury... The gratitude of every home in our island, in our Empire, and indeed throughout the world, except in the abodes of the guilty, goes out to the British airmen who, undaunted by odds, unwearied in their constant challenge and mortal danger, are turning the tide of the world war by their prowess and by their devotion. Never in the field of human conflict was so much owed by so many to so few. All our hearts go out to the fighter pilots, whose brilliant action we see with our own eyes day after day... I hope – indeed I pray – that we shall not be found unworthy of our victory if after toil and tribulation it is granted to us.

Winston Churchill, 20 August 1940

Widespread operations mainly by individual or small formations of bombers continued on 21 August. One of three KG 3 Dorniers visiting Norfolk had the distinction of being destroyed at Burnham Market by 611 Squadron using its new Spitfire IIs (P7290, P7303, P7304). Another three of the squadron's Spitfires (P7314, P7292, P7305) destroyed two more raiders off Mablethorpe. Airfields came under attack, plentiful damage at Bircham Newton affecting both buildings and aircraft. There were twenty-two casualties. No 242 Squadron downed a Do 17 near Harlesdon soon after midday, and 56 Squadron another near Ipswich. In Southwold three houses were wrecked, and seven at Leicester where five died and thirteen were injured during the city's first bombing episode. Trains were strafed at Umberleigh and Guildford, civilian property was hit in Canterbury and Hastings, three trawlers were damaged at Falmouth, and balloons shot down at Southampton, where a dredger was also sunk. Bombing at St Eval damaged six 236 Squadron Blenheims.

Convoy CE9 had left Plymouth on the 20th, embarked kite protection at Southampton, and was running the Dover Straits by 09.30 on the 21st when shelling commenced. At around 10.55 high-level bombing was added. Between 11.20 and 12.07 every salvo of four to six shells straddled the convoy. By that time 134 rounds had been hurled at the ships, the worst problem being 5 feet of water accumulated aboard the SS *Eddystone*. Soon after, sixteen bombers tried in vain to sink the ships, which drove them away with intense AA fire. Low-level attack was prevented by kite flying, but eventually those were close-hauled due to afternoon rain squalls. The cost to the Luftwaffe of the day's activity was thirteen aircraft; to the RAF, four fighters.

Southern and eastern airfield targets on 22 August generated about 120 sorties. 'B' Flight of 54 Squadron[132], ordered to bring down an aircraft that was range-spotting for guns shelling trawlers in the Dover Straits, arrived simultaneously with thirty Bf 110s and twenty Bf 109s of Erpr 210. Driving them off resulted in one of each destroyed, and a Spitfire lost. Erpr 210's Bf 110s mounted an evening strike upon Manston, 616 Squadron dealing with accompanying Bf 109s while other intruders were sweeping in Kent's skies. Some thirty shells from Cap Gris Nez guns damaged houses and a church at Dover. Off Scotland, Ju 88s of KG 30 bombarded a convoy, and in the South West St Eval endured more fire bombs. Night-bombing included the dropping of thirty-three HEs at Bristol, while Filton's aero engine No 4 works attracted ten HEs, five oil bombs and 200 incendiaries. Bombs were also dropped on nearby Patchway and Almondsbury. Other targets included Aberdeen, Swindon (fourteen HEs), Harrow, Pontefract, a convoy off Kinnaird's Head, Bradford, Middlesbrough and Liverpool. At all there was minimal damage. A notable event occurred at 03.10 when a 250kg HE, exploding in a boiler house, demolished Edmonton's Alcazar Cinema. Another three bombs fell at Willesden Green, Middlesex, one hitting a large house. These incidents again raised concern that London was about to be heavily bombed.

Poor weather continued to restrict daytime operations, whereas night activity continued apace. Manston received another thirty bombs at 01.25 on the 23rd, and three Ju 88s attacked Thorney Island. Other incidents involved the Scillies, where fifteen HEs fell on and around the radio station. At Colchester there were forty casualties, and Cromer, Harwich, Maidstone, Portsmouth and Tangmere were all bombed. Darkness on the 23/24th concealed He 111s bombing Cardiff, Pembroke Dock and Birmingham's Fort Dunlop factory, the latter attracting specialists of KGr 100. In improved weather, HEs and fire bombs fell widely over Wiltshire, Somerset, Dorset, Devon and, more precisely, at Westbury, Shepton Mallet, Camerton, Yeovil, Crewkerne, Wareham and near Exeter.

From the papers:

23 August: 'For the first time since the war started Londoners were aroused from their beds by the crashing of AA guns, wailing of sirens and distant thud of bombs. Gunfire was described as tremendous and heard miles from the scene of the attack. Three areas on the outskirts are reported to have had bombs.'

For almost a week activity had been restricted by inclement weather, but a large anticyclone was now creeping in from the Atlantic. Not surprisingly, dawn on 24 August saw the Luftwaffe resume operations in strength. By evening, perhaps more by carelessness than certain intent, it had delivered two brutal attacks.

Early morning saw RAF fighter squadrons move forward, one to Manston, another to Hawkinge, and parts of two more to Martlesham Heath and Tangmere. Intelligence reports suggested that the day ahead would involve extensive and heavy attacks.

Fighter feints between 06.00 and 08.00 were followed by forty bombers and sixty fighters intent upon wrecking Dover. Although Hurricanes were concentrating upon destroying the bombers, leaving the fighters to the nimble Spitfires, penetrating the bombers' tight escort was more difficult. Only two squadrons managed it, No 85[133] managing to become well placed when Dover's AA guns opened fire. That probably caused the bombers to unload onto the town's residential areas before their rear support unsuccessfully interrupted British fighters returning to forward stations. Pressure upon Dover was resumed at 09.55 when long-range guns put three shells into the town and two more fell nearby.

With only three Defiants flying on guard while its other fighters refuelled, the murder of Manston began, heralded by thirty Ju 88s in three vics. Three minutes later twenty-five He 111s arrived for a follow-up attack from 4,000 feet, a dozen watchful Bf 109s patrolling almost four miles above them. Intense anti-aircraft fire greeted this second wave, together with clouds of chalk dust and smoke. That brought welcome protection to what little was left of the station. Heinkel crews, unable to aim through the chaos, continued on track, unleashed their loads on tiny Ramsgate airport and the town. They wrecked seventy-eight houses, made 300 uninhabitable and seriously damaged another 700. Fierce flames engulfed the gasworks and its sulphur plant; ARP workers and other civilians were machine-gunned; a military HQ, the fish market and customs house, all were wrecked. Another sixty bombs fell on Broadstairs. Two serious and thirty minor fires raged at Ramsgate, where seventeen UXBs needed attention. Casualties – fewer than expected – totalled twenty killed outright in the relatively heaviest daylight bombing of a populated region (apart from London) during the Battle. Official assessment of the total load jettisoned at sea was at one time quoted as 500 HEs. Later that was reduced, although a considerable number of bombs fell in the sea.

Manston's Defiants had scrambled and escaped the bombing only just in time. Dowding, despite his lack of confidence in the turret fighter, had No 264 Defiant Squadron moved to Hornchurch on 22 August in case massed bomber raids on London – expected at any time – allowed deployment of the aircraft in their intended tactical gunnery formation role. The squadron advanced to Manston and soon faced tasks for which it was never intended. Before 264 could even assemble in battle formation, three Defiants were shot down; Squadron Leader P. A. Hunter, their leader, flying N1535, was last seen heading out across the Channel chasing a Ju 88. The sad remnants of the squadron were ordered back to Hornchurch.

Throughout the morning Luftwaffe fighters patrolled over the Channel, trying to confuse British radar and disguise various ventures. Until late afternoon, only minor threats were apparent, but the activity caused scrambles and bringing varying

Before engagement Defiant rear fuselage combing had to be lowered to allow gun traversing as visible on this 264 Squadron example. *Boulton Paul*

fuel states to the formations on patrol. Between 13.00 and 14.00 about thirty enemy aircraft were active between North Foreland and Deal. Manston, between 13.11 and 13.30, was yet again dive-bombed, and the station's ordeal still wasn't over. At 14.47 twenty Bf 109s/110s returned to strafe and bomb it. They wrecked a hangar, airmen's quarters and cut remaining phone links. A freakish event was the hurling of a searchlight onto a wrecked hangar roof, where it busily swayed.

The principal afternoon activity commenced at 15.20 when four large raids crossed Kent. Two were bound for Hornchurch and North Weald. One of the others bombed Manston yet again, the station being hit because its fighters were too low on fuel to prevent it. Manston had now to be all but evacuated due to the presence of so many UXBs. It did not reopen until 26 August.

As Hornchurch came under attack by He 111s and Ju 88s, No 264 Squadron[134] was again in the throes of scrambling. Heinkel 111s of Raid H8 flying in formation at 15,000 feet aimed their bombs at the aerodrome, which in total was hit only by six. Predicted AA fire proved accurate, the fourth salvo from battery N11 scoring at 15.41 a direct hit on an He 111, knocking out its port engine. As it curled away to the north-west a fighter finished it off and it crashed at North Ockenden. Battery N20 seriously damaged the wing of another He 111. Most of the salvoes fell around Dagenham and Upminster not long after at 16.00, and in the Rainham area about 10 minutes later. Many single bombs fell very wide. After banking left, the enemy formation progressed along the Thames Estuary to the unwelcomed accompaniment of riverside gunfire. The cost of the raid to III/KG 53 was five He 111s.

North Weald was bombed at the same time as Hornchurch. About fifteen He 111s entering from the east at 12,500 feet followed the main road to the aerodrome. Spirited action by 111 and 151 Squadrons prevented other raiders from reaching their objective, 111 Squadron making head-on attacks to break the formation then leave the rest to 151 Squadron[135]. Covering Bf 109s, with fuel shortage looming and too

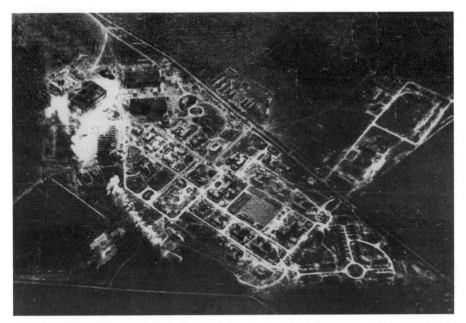

Middle Wallop being bombed on 24 August.

high to intervene, left bomber protection to supporting Bf 110s, which, for once, guarded their charge well against the fifty RAF fighters then active. Although there were many casualties at North Weald, restricted damage was caused to the radio station and huts, a nearby woodland fire producing a deceiving huge pall of smoke after 300 incendiaries ignited.

The extent of the afternoon raids was such that nearly all of 11 Group's serviceable aircraft operated, intelligence sources having indicated that London was about to be bombed. Warned of that potential development, Keith Park at around 16.00 asked 12 Group's Commander, Leigh-Mallory, to provide cover for the 11 Group stations north of London. No 12 Group responded by attempting to marshal a large group of fighters over Duxford for the defence of London, but it took too long to assemble. Without ample practice the scheme seemed impracticable. Six 19 Squadron cannon-armed Spitfires[136], ordered to North Weald, arrived in time to see smoke rising from there and around Hornchurch. Before gun stoppages occurred (caused by spent cartridges jamming in breeches because the cannon had to lie on their sides in the thin wings), the Spitfires claimed three Bf 110s. All told, five bombers were destroyed and four fighters. Fighter Command lost eight aircraft and three pilots.

While the London area was under threat, Ventnor Radar, barely working again, detected many raiders approaching from Cherbourg and the Channel Islands at between 13,000 and 18,000 feet. They turned out to be about fifty Ju 88s of LG 1 escorted by Bf 110s of Luftflotte 3 mounting one of its last major day raids prior to unit rearrangement for the coming invasion.

Unaware of the withdrawal of the 87s, some fighters scrambled by Middle Wallop and Tangmere to patrol to the east and west of the Isle of Wight flew low to dispose of the expected Stukas. That allowed the Ju 88s to deliver a devastating 4-minute deluge on Portsmouth soon after 16.00. Around 100 HEs (reckoned to be eighty 250kg and twenty 50kg) caused widespread damage, killing 118 civilians, injuring 230 and slightly wounding 191. Three Anderson shelters received direct hits and all their occupants died. Naval casualties at Victoria Barracks totalled another fifty. A direct hit on a cinema, the Princes Theatre, produced an awful incident in which eight out of thirty-five people in the balcony died, while another eighty-four in the building – many children – were grievously injured. Three workmen repairing a fractured water main were killed when a UXB exploded. A 250kg bomb on a shelter killed twenty occupants, and another twenty-five sheltering in a trench were killed when a bomb exploded within it. Bombing of houses claimed another thirty-one killed and ninety-eight badly injured, for there were many direct hits on domestic property. Another eight were killed in shops, five more in the open, with twenty-one injured. As a result of this, the heaviest and sharpest daylight raid on a city so far, 700 were made homeless and a fuel oil store burned for 36 hours. Two naval ships were damaged and rail links cut. The Battle of Britain was certainly no glamorous event and, as it moved towards its climax, worse came almost daily.

North Weald's Station Commander in August 1940 was Wing Commander Victor Beamish (right), seen here with Squadron Leader E. M. Donaldson, Commanding Officer of No 151 Squadron. *IWM*

This Ju 88 was the first victim of 17 Squadron to fall on British soil.

The Princes Theatre, Lake Road, Portsmouth, was the scene of a major incident on 24 August. *Courtesy of The News, Portsmouth*

The eleven Solent anti-aircraft batteries fired intensively between 16.19 and 17.30, loosing off 384 heavy rounds. Site 1 destroyed a Ju 88, which fell at Q079188. Five enemy aircraft were claimed between 16.20 and 16.50, and two RAF fighters were shot down. In a diversionary raid on Warmwell, a hangar roof was damaged, the station sick quarters were burned out, and a Battle and a Wellington ravaged, but luckily there were no casualties.

Enemy activity around Portsmouth led to a serious example of mistaken identity. At 16.15 over Thorney Island three Blenheim IVs[137] – not unlike Ju 88s at first glance – were set upon by Hurricanes of the freshly arrived No 1 Squadron, Royal Canadian Air Force. Despite firing off the colours of the day, Blenheim T1804-E was shot down off Wittering. Six Hurricanes then attacked a second Blenheim, getting hits in its mainplanes and starboard engine, despite its crew repeatedly firing the colours of the day. It was forced to crash-land. The other Blenheim was also damaged. Soon after that tragic event a further eight heavy shells were ineffectively fired towards Dover and Hawkinge, then came the day's final major incursion by more than 100 fighters over Kent. By dusk thirty-two enemy aircraft had been destroyed, and twenty-three RAF fighters.

All through the day expectation rose concerning an imminent attack upon London. When darkness came it was soon apparent that the developing activity was on a greater scale than ever before. More than 150 bombers were counted, and they made more than 350 intrusions, losing two of their number, He 111 GI+TC of KG 55 shot down by Flight Lieutenant J. G. Sanders of 615 Squadron (V7314) and another that succumbed to Swansea AA.

What made night activity special was the long-expected, extensive bombing of Greater London, and the first bombing of the City of London. While the latter might have been in error, intelligence sources knew of a planned attack on the capital and it had provoked the extensive reception given to the afternoon's raiders. Peripheral targets also listed for attack included Hawker's Kingston works and Short's at Rochester. Over Thameshaven oil installations the aim was poor. It is untrue that London was not widely and intentionally bombed before September 1940. Hitler thought that raids on London would lower morale during the run-up to the September invasion.

The night of the 24/25th was troubling for the defenders because they had not previously experienced heavy round-the-clock raids. In Bethnal Green alone nine were killed, fifty-eight injured and 100 made homeless. Early on 25 August bombs fell in Millwall, Tottenham, Highbury, Islington, Leyton, Enfield, Stepney, Canonbury, Wood Green, Hampton and Kingston as well as Banstead, Watford, Feltham, Maldon, Coulsdon and Feltham. Nos 3, 4 and 11 Warehouses, West India Dock, were soon blazing. Other incendiaries on the old Canary Wharf, West India Dock, burned themselves out on the roof, and three on the SS *Boka* did no damage. The worst incident occurred at Bethnal Green where, at 00.16, the LNER Hackney viaduct north of Cambridge Heath was hit. Only by a stroke of luck did a derailed train not fall into the crater on the crown of the 35-foot-span bridge. A second bomb, on a kerbstone in Wadeson Street, blasted two houses, injuring five occupants. Twenty minutes later three bombs set Stepney's Dundee Wharf ablaze, as well as a house in Phoebe Street. In Garford Street a single-storey factory was burned out, and next the Imperial Tobacco factory. Carter Paterson's works in Goswell Road also suffered slight fire damage.

Most portentous of all was that first bombing of the City, brought about by a high-flying Heinkel 111 of KG 53, which released four bombs. The first fell in Fore Street, the second at St Giles in Cripplegate, the third in Castle Street and a fourth on the Aldersgate Street/Manchester Avenue junction. A large fire gutted a four-storey wooden-floored building in Fore Street, spread to London Wall and started another blaze among straw and wax. The St Giles bomb exploded at the base of a stone turret, while the Aldersgate bomb dealt a blow to a five-storey building.

South of a line from Northumberland to Lancashire, raiders were rampaging, facing little opposition. The Luftwaffe roamed in particular over Kent, Sussex, Surrey, Reading, Oxford, Devon, Gloucestershire, Cardiff (where the main railway line was hit and a train bombed), Liverpool, Sheffield, Bradford, Hull (where eight 250kg HEs fell), Middlesbrough, near Tadcaster, Hedomb, Withernsea (12), Hartlepool, South Shields, the Midlands, East Anglia and Surrey. Birmingham received spasmodic attacks over a 4-hour period, with bombs falling at Fort Dunlop and close to the Castle Bromwich Nuffield factory. Incendiary droppers led the attack, a second wave dropping 50kg HEs. One bomb exploded by the railway bridge in Chester Road, causing two gaping holes in the structure. Some twenty-two HEs and incendiaries fell on fields by Penns Lane, and residential property suffered in Yardley. Six HEs fell on Plymouth docks, a fire was started at ICI's Billingham works, UXBs nestled into Swan Hunter at Newcastle, and at Coventry a theatre was hit. More serious was a fire at Rootes No 2 Ryton engine factory. At RAF St Athan the hospital received a direct hit, likewise the Sergeants Mess at Driffield, from where the Whitley squadrons were

Oberleutenant Priller (centre) Staffelkäpitan of 6./JG 51 with his pilots at Wissant and his Ace of Hearts Bf 109 in the background. Possibly taken on 24 August when Fritz Beeck (hands behind his back) was shot down by Flying Officer Wicks of 56 Squadron. *Michael Payne*

two days later evacuated for safety. Aerodromes at Acklington, Catterick and White Waltham were also raided and coastal waters extensively mined. In the 24 hours ending 06.00 on the 25th 102 civilians had died and 335 had been injured in operations carried out by thirteen Kampfgeschwaderen. London reported seventy-six bombing incidents, eleven of them needing attention from a dozen or more fire pumps.

Perhaps unsurprisingly, the morning of 25 August was unnaturally quiet. Apart from feints and Channel patrols, no large raids appeared until about 16.00. Then a strong force headed for Weymouth. Nos. 10 and 11 Groups faced it with all available aircraft, between Tangmere and Exeter, Nos 87[138] and 609[139] Squadrons defending Portland and 17 Squadron protecting Warmwell. Before they could engage them, Ju 88s of II/KG 51 and II/KG 54, protected by many Bf 110s, split into three groups to attack Portland, Weymouth and Warmwell. No 87 Squadron took on the Portland bombers, leaving the Bf 110s to 609 Squadron. The latter rapidly came under attack by Bf 109s of JG 53. Although Warmwell's attackers were assaulted, 17 Squadron[140] found the bombers impossible to reach through the dense fighter screen. So, Warmwell succumbed. As that group withdrew they were short of a Ju 88, fighters from Nos 92, 152, 213 and 602 Squadrons having reinforced No 17. In the fight the RAF lost twelve fighters and had eight pilot casualties.

The only other sizeable raid of the day developed over Kent at around 18.00. Six 11 Group squadrons were in action, 32 Squadron[141] operating from Hawkinge and to engage a dozen Do 17s until Bf 109s drove them off and destroyed a Hurricane. By then, more squadrons were airborne and the enemy had gone home. The day's scoreboard showed fourteen RAF fighters lost, and twenty German aircraft.

After dark there was night bombing, and it was not all carried out by the Luftwaffe.

No 85 Squadron fought in France and throughout most of the 1940 summer. Delivered on 12 April 1940, P3408 with 85 from 30 May until 10 October 1940 joined 306 (Polish) Squadron in December, served with 257 Squadron from April to June 1941 then subsequently 55 OTU, 9 SFTS, 247 Squadron, 56 OTU and Scottish-based Nos 1 and 2 Tactical Exercise Units. It was struck off charge on 17 July 1944. *IWM*

RAF losses during operations, 13-25 August 1940

a = failed to return/shot down, b = written off as a battle casualty, c = seriously damaged

August	13			14			15			16			17		
Type	a	b	c	a	b	c	a	b	c	a	b	c	a	b	c
Blenheim F	–	–	–	–	3	–	–	–	–	–	6	1	–	–	–
Defiant	–	–	–	–	–	–	–	–	–	–	–	–	–	–	–
Hurricane	12	–	4	3	–	4	–	–	–	7	4	2	–	–	–
Spitfire	1	1	1	1	–	–	–	–	–	11	2	–	–	–	–
Blenheim B	13	–	–	–	–	–	2	–	–	2	–	–	–	–	–
Hampden	4	–	–	1	–	–	1	–	–	–	–	–	–	–	–
Wellington	–	–	–	–	–	–	–	–	–	3	–	–	1	–	–
Whitley	1	–	–	2	–	–	1	–	–	1	–	–	3	–	–
Coastal Cmd	10	–	–	1	–	–	1	–	–	3	–	–	1	–	–
Totals	41	1	5	8	3	4	5	–	–	27	12	3	5	–	–

August	18			19			20			21			22		
Type	a	b	c	a	b	c	a	b	c	a	b	c	a	b	c
Blenheim F	–	–	–	–	–	–	–	–	1	–	–	–	–	2	–
Defiant	–	–	–	–	–	–	–	–	–	–	–	–	–	–	–
Hurricane	26	10	4	–	–	–	–	1	–	1	–	–	–	–	1
Spitfire	4	1	–	3	1	–	1	–	–	–	–	–	4	–	–
Blenheim B	–	–	–	1	–	–	2	–	–	–	–	–	–	–	–
Hampden	–	–	–	1	–	–	–	–	–	1	–	–	–	–	–
Wellington	–	–	–	3	–	–	–	–	–	–	–	–	–	–	–
Whitley	–	–	–	1	–	–	–	–	–	–	–	–	–	–	–
Coastal Cmd	8	–	–	1	–	–	2	–	–	3	–	–	2	–	–
Totals	38	11	4	10	1	–	5	1	1	5	–	–	6	2	1

August	23			24			25			Total loss during period		
Type	a	b	c	a	b	c	a	b	c	a	b	c
Blenheim F	–	–	–	–	–	–	–	2	–	0	13	2
Defiant	–	–	–	4	1	1	–	–	–	4	1	1
Hurricane	–	1	1	–	2	2	7	–	–	56	18	18
Spitfire	1	–	–	6	–	1	7	1	2	39	6	4
Blenheim B	–	–	–	–	–	–	–	–	–	20	0	0
Hampden	–	–	–	2	–	–	–	1	–	10	1	0
Wellington	1	–	–	–	–	–	–	–	–	8	0	0
Whitley	–	–	–	1	–	–	–	1	–	10	1	0
Coastal Cmd	2	–	–	4	–	–	–	–	–	38	0	0
Totals	4	1	1	17	3	4	14	5	2	185	40	25

Luftwaffe losses during operations 1-12 August 1940

a = shot down, b = crashed after action, c = seriously damaged

August	1 a	1 b	1 c	2 a	2 b	2 c	3 a	3 b	3 c	4 a	4 b	4 c	5 a	5 b	5 c
Type	a	b	c	a	b	c	a	b	c	a	b	c	a	b	c
Do 17Z	–	1	–	–	–	–	–	–	–	–	–	–	–	–	–
He 59	–	1	–	–	–	–	–	–	–	–	–	–	–	–	–
He 111H	–	–	1	2	–	–	–	–	–	–	–	–	–	–	–
He 111P	–	–	–	–	–	–	1	–	–	–	–	–	–	–	–
He 115	–	2	–	–	–	–	1	–	–	–	–	–	–	–	–
Hs 126	1	–	–	–	–	–	–	–	–	–	–	–	–	–	–
Ju 87B	–	–	–	–	–	–	–	–	–	–	–	–	–	–	–
Ju 88A	2	2	–	–	1	–	–	–	–	–	–	–	–	–	–
Bf109	–	1	1	–	–	–	–	–	–	1	–	1	1	–	–
Bf110	–	–	–	–	–	–	–	–	–	–	–	–	–	–	–
Totals	3	7	2	2	1	1	2	0	0	1	0	1	1	0	0

August	6 a	6 b	6 c	7 a	7 b	7 c	8 a	8 b	8 c	9 a	9 b	9 c	10 a	10 b	10 c
Type	a	b	c	a	b	c	a	b	c	a	b	c	a	b	c
Do 17Z	1	–	–	–	–	–	–	–	–	–	–	–	–	–	–
He 59	–	–	–	–	–	–	1	–	–	–	–	–	–	–	–
He 111H	–	–	–	–	–	–	1	–	–	2	–	–	–	–	–
He 111P	–	–	–	–	–	–	–	–	–	–	–	–	–	–	–
He 115	–	–	–	–	–	–	–	–	–	–	–	–	–	–	–
Hs 126	–	–	–	–	–	–	–	–	–	–	–	–	–	–	–
Ju 87B	–	–	–	–	–	–	8	–	3	–	–	–	–	–	–
Ju 88A	–	–	–	2	–	–	–	–	–	1	1	–	–	–	–
Bf109	–	–	–	–	–	–	10	–	1	–	–	–	–	–	–
Bf110	–	–	–	–	2	–	1	–	3	–	–	–	–	–	–
Totals	1	0	0	2	2	0	21	0	7	3	1	0	0	0	0

August	11 a	11 b	11 c	12 a	12 b	12 c	Grand totals a	b	c
Type	a	b	c	a	b	c	a	b	c
Do 17Z	3	–	–	–	–	–	4	1	0
He 59	–	–	–	–	–	–	2	1	0
He 111H	1	–	1	–	1	–	6	1	2
He 111P	–	–	–	–	–	–	1	0	0
He 115	–	–	–	–	–	–	1	2	0
Hs 126	–	–	–	–	–	–	1	0	0
Ju 87B	1	1	–	–	–	–	9	1	3
Ju 88A	5	–	–	10	–	1	20	4	1
Bf 109	10	2	1	11	1	1	33	4	5
Bf 110	10	–	1	5	1	–	16	3	4
Totals	30	3	3	26	3	1	90	17	15

Luftwaffe losses during operations 13-25 August 1940

a = shot down, b = crashed during course of sortie, c = seriously damaged

August	13 a	b	c	14 a	b	c	15 a	b	c	16 a	b	c	17 a	b	c
Type	a	b	c	a	b	c	a	b	c	a	b	c	a	b	c
Do 17P	1	–	–	–	–	–	1	–	–	–	–	–	–	–	–
Do 17Z	5	–	1	–	–	–	2	–	1	4	1	–	–	–	–
He 59	–	–	–	–	–	–	1	–	–	–	–	–	–	–	–
He 111H	–	1	–	–	–	2	13	2	1	1	–	–	–	–	–
He 111P	1	–	–	7	2	–	–	–	–	4	–	1	–	–	–
He 115	–	–	–	–	–	–	1	–	–	–	–	–	–	–	–
Ju 87B	–	–	1	4	–	–	2	–	–	9	–	–	–	–	–
Ju 87R	5	1	–	–	–	–	5	–	–	–	–	–	–	–	–
Ju 88A	6	1	4	2	–	–	12	–	–	1	–	2	–	–	–
Ju 88C	–	–	–	–	–	–	5	–	1	–	–	–	1	–	–
Bf 109	5	1	4	6	–	–	6	2	–	11	5	3	–	–	–
Bf 110	8	1	6	2	–	–	25	2	1	7	–	1	–	–	–
Totals	31	5	16	19	0	0	73	6	4	37	6	7	1	0	0

August	18 a	b	c	19 a	b	c	20 a	b	c	21 a	b	c	22 a	b	c
Type	a	b	c	a	b	c	a	b	c	a	b	c	a	b	c
Do 17P	–	–	–	–	–	–	–	–	–	–	–	–	–	–	–
Do 17Z	5	1	4	1	–	–	2	–	–	6	–	–	–	–	–
He 59	–	–	–	–	–	–	–	–	–	–	–	–	–	–	–
He 111H	4	1	–	–	1	2	–	–	–	1	–	–	–	–	–
He 111P	1	2	1	1	–	–	–	–	–	–	–	–	–	–	–
He 115	–	–	–	–	–	–	–	–	–	–	–	–	–	–	–
Ju 87B	14	2	2	–	–	–	–	–	–	–	–	–	–	–	–
Ju 87R	–	–	–	–	–	–	–	–	–	–	–	–	–	–	–
Ju 88A	2	–	1	1	–	1	1	–	–	6	–	–	2	1	–
Ju 88C	–	–	–	–	–	–	–	–	–	–	–	–	–	–	–
Bf 109	15	1	3	–	–	–	1	–	1	–	–	–	–	–	–
Bf 110	12	1	1	–	–	–	1	–	–	–	–	–	–	–	–
Totals	53	8	12	4	1	3	5	0	1	13	0	0	2	1	0

August	23 a	b	c	24 a	b	c	25 a	b	c	Grand totals a	b	c
Type	a	b	c	a	b	c	a	b	c	a	b	c
Do 17P	–	–	–	–	–	–	–	–	–	2	0	0
Do 17Z	1	–	1	–	–	–	1	–	–	27	2	7
He 59	–	–	–	–	–	–	–	–	–	1	0	0
He 111H	1	–	–	5	–	–	–	1	–	25	6	5
He 111P	–	–	–	–	–	–	–	1	–	14	5	2
He 115	–	–	–	–	–	–	–	–	–	1	0	0
Ju 87B	–	–	–	–	–	–	–	–	–	29	2	3
Ju 87R	–	–	–	–	–	–	–	–	–	10	1	0
Ju 88A	1	–	–	5	2	1	–	1	–	39	5	9
Ju 88C	–	–	–	–	–	–	–	–	–	6	0	1
Bf 109	–	–	–	12	7	–	7	–	3	63	16	14
Bf 110	–	–	–	2	–	–	7	2	1	64	6	10
Totals	3	0	1	24	9	1	15	5	4	281	43	51

Sufficient pilots and other aircrew were vital to survival in 1940, and most pilots were initially trained on Tiger Moths. The latter served as light transports, N9305 depicted seeing service in 1940 with PRU at Heston. Later it was used by PRU at Benson followed by service with 544 Squadron.

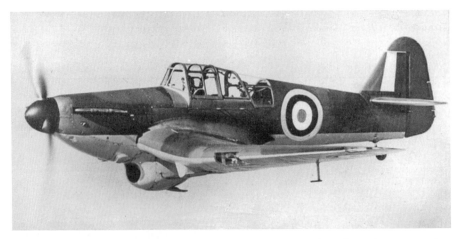

Fighter pilots in 1940 undertook advanced flying training on Miles Master 1s, many at the Montrose FTS and OTUs. N7547 shown here was similarly employed by the Fleet Air Arm in 1940. A few were modified to carry wing guns with others being fitted with bomb racks.

Chapter 12

How dare you bomb London?

'RAF aircraft continued their attacks on military objectives in Germany last night. Targets in North-West Germany and the Ruhr were bombed, as well as armament factories in the Berlin area.' With those last two words appearing like an afterthought, the Air Ministry communiqué of 26 August gave the nation an excellent tonic, even if the bombs had very much missed their targets. Reply to the bombing of London it may primarily have been, but its significance became transcendent. 'Berlin. Good!' It undoubtedly encouraged Hitler's desire for heavy attacks on central London in addition to its vital dockland. In doing so the Germans made a fundamental error, for it meant relaxing the war on RAF fighter stations. Bomber Command, none too keen on raiding distant Berlin and believing there were more worthwhile targets closer at hand, had bowed to political power.

It was 17.00 on 25 August when the Operations Order detailing targets to be dealt with in Berlin reached bomber stations. Few in the crews attending the briefings could have much relished what would be a long and uneasy night ride. Berlin was packed with worthwhile industrial targets, but reaching them, let alone finding them, entailed a round trip of more than 1,300 miles – about 10 hours flying. Most of the time that would be spent over hostile territory and, on this first occasion, be during a very cloudy night. Yet bombing Berlin would bring delight to the suffering British civilians who knew little or nothing of the traumas Bomber Command crews experienced.

Accurate weather forecasting was essential for night operations, but conditions at distant targets were conjectural for as yet there were no deep reconnaissance flights. Target photographs, if they existed, were ancient. Lacking navigation aids and target-marking items, bombing accuracy depended upon good weather, perfect timing, excellent map-reading and radio fixes all supported with visual and astro navigation and good luck. After bombing and passing through searchlight and flak areas, probably for a second time, came the tricky task of homing. Often came the worry of a low fuel state on a breezy night in the rain, and having to land on a poorly lit aerodrome with the ever-increasing possibility of German intruder activity.

Whitley and Wellington crews were told on the 25th, 'Your main target is the Siemens & Halske factory in Siemenstadt, producing 85% of the electrical equipment used by the German forces.' Hampden crews were briefed to demolish Berlin's Klingenberg power station, output 200,000kW. Other objectives for destruction were the Henschel aircraft factory, the Bucker training aircraft factory at Rangsdorf, Templehof aerodrome, used by the Nazi mighty, and Tegel's gasworks. At dawn next morning all remained unscathed, but Berliners had some cause for concern because they had experienced something they were told would never happen.

Finding those targets even in moonlight, and with guidance from Berlin's lakes, would have been difficult. Arriving around midnight, the crews instead discovered 9/10 cloud down to 2,000 feet lit below by searchlights. That certainly ruined aiming. Heavy flak – luckily inaccurate – also had to be faced, together with trios of balloons in and above the clouds. Such discouragements to night-touring of Germany were nothing new, and were spasmodically encountered en route. For those on the ground the masculine coarse cry of German air raid sirens showed that the RAF was still around. Neutral correspondents reported the raid, adding that bombs had been dropped. Almost all fell in open country.

Bomber Command's ultimate intelligence analysis suggested that only one Wellington and two Whitleys had dropped their loads – a total of twenty-five 500lb GPs and 400 4lb incendiaries – anywhere near Siemens. Two Wellington and six Whitley crews claimed to have bombed their designated factory areas, and fourteen Hampden crews reckoned to have put thirty-six 500lb and thirty-two 250lb GPs around Klingenberg. Another Hampden attacked the Henschel works, one the Bucker factory, three Templehof, one Tegel, and seven others vaguely bombed Berlin. Perhaps the reality was too hard to accept.

Elsewhere, five out of eight Wellingtons dispatched as instructed dropped their bombs around Hamm, Schwerte and Cologne marshalling yards, while Whitleys attacked Bremen docks and the Oranienburg Heinkel works. Seven out of twelve Blenheims tried to disrupt nightlife on aerodromes at St Inglevert, Ploescat, Lisieux, Le Tréport and searchlight campers at Hardelot. A returning Hampden of 83 Squadron ditched off Grimsby, its crew spending 7 hours in their dinghy prior to rescue. Two other Hampden crews ditched due to fuel shortage, and three Hampdens failed to return.

On 28/29 August Wellingtons and Hampdens carried out a second raid on Berlin and were given the same targets, as was the case on 31 August/1 September. Although little material damage was caused, the psychological effect was worth the effort.

By revealing news of any RAF raids, neutrals angered the Nazis. 'Unprovoked', 'indiscriminate', 'attacks on women and children' chorused the enemy. 'Unprovoked'? And how many of these civilian women readily encouraged their regime when it was doing well, eagerly working within its war machine? Complex, cynical attitudes to such activities may be controversial, but for the British, heavily under attack, the bombing of Germany was a morale-booster when it was most needed, and an adjunct to the Battle of Britain. 'To ignore Bomber Command's contribution is like having a Christmas dinner without the pudding,' a senior officer once commented. For Hitler, every bomb on German soil was galling. Although the Berlin raids certainly angered him, they did not by themselves provoke the impending heavy bombing of London. Those were intended to generate chaos immediately prior to an invasion.

Bomber Command was dropping mainly 250lb and 500lb general-purpose high-explosive bombs, and 4lb incendiaries delivered via Small Bomb Containers (SBCs), which shed their contents indiscriminately. That was the only practicable means of delivery. Unlike the German 1kg basic cylindrical incendiary, the British used a slender bomb of hexagonal section, shaped thus to induce its lodgement on buildings, and particularly in guttering. The 25lb incendiary bomb, sometimes used, relied upon weight for penetration.

On 1/2 July, from Hampden L4070 of 83 Squadron flown by a tough, very handsome Flying Officer G. P. Gibson, later of 'dambuster' fame, had fallen the first RAF large weapon, a 2,000lb SAP (Semi-Armour Piercing) bomb dropped on Kiel. Although the four-man Hampden gave the impression of being the poor relation of the Whitley and Wellington, it was unsuitable for much development, its weapons bay readily accommodated large sea mines and the lengthy 2,000-pounder. Under each wing a 250lb GP was at this period sometimes carried. Hampdens outnumbered other medium bomber types in the summer of 1940.

On 18/19 July three Wellingtons of 15 OTU dropped leaflets over the French coast, and on 25/26 July a few Hampdens of 16 OTU operated similarly. The use of crews in training showed a level of desperation emphasised when, on 28 July, the Air Council decided that operations must take precedence over training. Bomber Command ordered on 8 August that each OTU must undertake up to eight operational sorties a week.

In a class of their own were the Blenheim IVs of supremely courageous 2 Group. During June 1940 each Blenheim station was ordered to make twenty-four aircraft available once in three days to carry out cloud-covered attacks on oil targets and marshalling yards in Germany, intended to encourage the enemy to retain fighters for daylight home defence. Other Groups bombed these and aircraft production resources at night.

On 19 June Blenheims began daylight formation raids on airfields in France, supplemented by moon period night raids. As fear of invasion mounted, Bomber Command's Blenheims assisted Coastal Command in observing activity in Channel ports. On 21 June the cloud-cover raiding commenced, Blenheims proceeding only when at least 7/10 cloud-cover offered protection. Although 90% of all such attempts had to be abandoned in July, very courageous deep penetration sorties were flown. That month saw ports and shipping elevated into No 1 priority targets. Until Channel ports were filling with invasion craft, airfields and factories were particularly raided. Listing was soon extended to include oil installations, railway centres, canals and power stations. From early June discussion had concerned employment of Bomber Command in the event of an enemy invasion force sailing. About 120 Ansons, Audaxes and Blenheims from training units would have immediately joined 2 Group forces, Bomber Command concentrating upon sinking ships at sea and vessels directly participating in the landings. Troops ashore would be dealt with by other forces. On 30 June a decision was made to keep, from the following night and thereafter nightly, a minimum of three bombers per squadron bombed up with 250lb/500lb GP HE bombs in case the enemy launched a surprise invasion force. The move was timely, for on 9 July the first few ships intended for invasion use reached the Channel ports. Their destruction received high priority. Blenheim crews were then told to reconnoitre and attack 'Rhine barges', feasible invasion transports, in canals leading to Zwolle, and to strike at coastal shipping.

Fear of seaborne landing parties making raids mounted from Norway caused Nos 21 and 57 Blenheim squadrons to daily fly sea searches from Lossiemouth. On 9 July, when twelve Blenheims attempted to bomb Stavanger/Sola airfield, flak broke the formation apart and Bf 109s swept in, destroying half the force. Next day No 107 Squadron, ordered to destroy grounded aircraft near Amiens, barely escaped destruction. Heavy losses, common in 2 Group, prompted more night employment for its

Total numbers of aircraft available on bomber squadrons at 18.00 on given dates

	0	200	400	600	800	1,000	
1.7.40							348
12.7.40							461
22.7.40							484
12.8.40							447
21.8.40							458
30.8.40							514
7.9.40							509
15.9.40							586
18.9.40							585
29.9.40							583

Blenheims, and on 17/18 July Squadron Leader Webster of XV Squadron made the first dedicated night intruder attack on any airfield mounted as such by the RAF when he attacked Caen/Carpiquet. Several night raids on airfields were exceptionally effective.

Although more than 400 aerodromes had by August been listed for attack, the Air Staff showed little inclination to concentrate on the task, mainly because insufficient fragmentation bombs were available. Standard GP weapons, they argued, were often wasted on such ventures. Fighter strikes against aircraft massed on French aerodromes would undoubtedly have been effective, but Dowding had none to spare for such hazardous operations. On all except three nights in July and August 1940 Bomber Command's Main Force operated, fielding 100 or more bombers only twice in a period when the nightly average was sixty. On 25/26 July 122 medium bombers – fifty-seven Wellingtons, twenty-four Whitleys and forty-one Hampdens – operated, and typically, for they did not concentrate their effort. Well over 100 crews claimed to have completed effective sorties. July 13/14 was the second busiest night.

Bombers were often guarded by the Army in 1940 for there was no RAF Regiment which would now carry out the task. Hampden PL-L shown at Hemswell belonged to No 144 Squadron.

Hampden P1333 of 49 Squadron is being loaded at Scampton with 500lb GPs. Joining the squadron in May 1940, the aircraft flew eleven sorties between 1 July and 16 August, when it was missing from a raid on Merseburg. There are no hard dispersals yet – the aircraft is standing on perimeter grass. *IWM*

Particularly long flights were mostly undertaken by the Whitleys, and included raids on Augsburg (27/28 August), attacks on Berlin and six on Italy. About 30% of the crews dispatched on night raids did not complete their primary tasks, but many of those attempted to find and bomb secondary or alternative targets.

By August bomber crews were undertaking a task made necessary by Italy's entry into the war. This was the ferrying of Wellingtons to Malta from where they proceeded to the Suez Canal Zone. Such was the distance that long-range tanks needed to be fitted in the Wellington fuselage. Flights often started out from Newmarket Heath, whose grass runway over the horse-racing course was almost certainly the longest in Europe. The Devil's Ditch, an embankment bordering the western side of the heath, was a topographical feature all had to cross with care. Ferry flights lasted between 9 and 10 hours, part of the time being spent over enemy territory and all of it a difficult task for which crews were specially trained.

Hampdens additionally undertook two more specialised tasks. In April 1940, it will be recalled, they commenced mining enemy shipping lanes. Drops were often made from between 400 and about 800 feet – dangerous activity, for a glassy sea always seems deceptively distant, and mines were laid where enemy shipping and flakships were present. Each Hampden carried one sea mine and often a few 250lb GP bombs to deal with annoying defenders or coastal aerodromes. Both were prime objects of interest to the 'Special Reconnaissance' Hampden force, which supported the minelayers and sought enemy minelayers at their bases.

The most spectacular night raids were executed on 12/13 August. Five Hampden crews drawn from Scampton's 49 and 83 Squadrons attacked the Ladbergen aqueduct on the Dortmund Ems Canal, which called for very accurate low flying and the use of special M bombs. Two of the first four Hampdens to attack were shot down, the others seriously damaged. Then came Flight Lieutenant R. A. B. Learoyd, flying hazardously in fifth place. He dived through searchlight beams and flak to score a very near miss, nursed P4403 home, and circled base until daylight before landing. His courage, and that of all who bravely operated that night, was marked by his being awarded the Victoria Cross. The raid blocked the notorious canal for ten days, delaying the progress of barges sailing from inland waterways to the Channel ports. It was claimed to have forced back the projected invasion date by several days.

One of Bomber Command's heaviest one-raid losses was then but hours away. A dozen Blenheims of 82 Squadron, led by Wing Commander E. C. Lart, set off from Watton in brilliant weather for Aalborg airfield in Denmark. Nearing the enemy coast a pilot broke radio silence. Claiming his fuel state low, he signalled that he was turning back. That radio call denied the raid an element of surprise, and alerted gunners and fighters of 6./JG 77. All held their fire until the Blenheims were near Aalborg. Then they massacred the lot.

Flight Lieutenant Roderick Learoyd, awarded the Victoria Cross for his gallantry when he made a low-level attack on the Dortmund-Ems Canal on 12 August. *IWM*

Blenheim IV R3600 of Wattisham's 110 Squadron was certainly a survivor, serving the squadron from 26 May 1940 until it failed to return on 6 May, 1941. It is being loaded with a Small Bomb Container (SBC) and 250lb General Purpose (GP) HE bombs.

The most publicised Wellington squadron was No 149. Mildenhall, their 1940 base, was regarded by the Luftwaffe as Britain's most important bomber station. P9273 N-Nuts, nearest, joined the squadron in March and was ditched on 9/10 October while returning from an operational sortie.

Chapter 13

Approaching the climax

Although it had no immediate effect upon the campaign, the bombing of Berlin certainly annoyed the enemy. Throughout the last week of August, with increasing intensity, the Luftwaffe made deeper daylight penetrations, frequently using the Thames as an approach route. No 11 Group therefore mainly operated from its inland stations, and heavy raids had, in any case, rendered Manston and Hawkinge barely tenable.

Night raids continued unabated, 25/26 August seeing factories on Croydon's Whaddon Estate hit, railway shops and the Dorman Long steel works at Stockton-on Tees bombed, and three Cottesmore Hampdens damaged. At Birmingham the Electric Furnace Co, British Timken and the Birdlee Works at Erdington were hit.

Early reconnaissance flights over the region between Harwich and Land's End on 26 August preceded three major operations. Arranged in five formations totalling about fifty bombers and eighty fighters, they flew over Kent, the first assault commencing at 11.37. There was some strafing of east Kent targets. Responding from 11 Group were forty Hurricanes and thirty Spitfires protecting their bases. A battle ensued between Canterbury and Maidstone. He 111s bombed Folkestone, damaging the railway and a laundry, killing two and injuring twenty-two people. Seven No 616 Squadron Spitfires, arriving too late to prevent it, ran into a host of Bf 109s. Another five Spitfires joined in, but could do little when faced by so many German fighters. The Yorkshire squadron, which lost seven aircraft, had two pilots killed and four injured.

Warned of an intended attack on Hornchurch, 264 Squadron[142] hastened to engage KG 3's Do 17s over Herne Bay. Defiants, assuming their specified battle formation for bomber interception, were no match for Bf 109s, which soon destroyed three. No 264

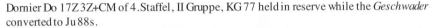

Dornier Do 17Z 3Z+CM of 4.Staffel, II Gruppe, KG 77 held in reserve while the *Geschwader* converted to Ju 88s.

Squadron claimed six Do 17s and a fighter. The fierce struggle soon reduced the Bf 109s' fuel states, forcing them to head for home, and making it unwise for the unprotected Dorniers to proceed. The bomber crews jettisoned their loads mainly upon Swale Rural District. As the defenders were landing, more Bf 109s arrived seeking easy kills and Dover's balloons.

A number of lone 'pirates' penetrated deeply during the day, one placing four HEs on Harwell, killing six and injuring ten, and damaging buildings and two Wellingtons. Whitleys, which later landed at Harwell to refuel for a long flight to Fiat Torino, may have been their main target.

Shortly after 13.00 the day's second major operation, composed of eight parts, developed. After assembling near Lille, its two bomber formations – seventy-eight Do 17s of II/KG 2 and III/KG 3 – picked up escorting Bf 110s of ZG 26 and ZG 76 and Bf 109s. Intelligence sources had discovered their targets to be Debden, North Weald and Hornchurch, so it was not surprising to the well-informed when, over the mouth of the River Crouch, half the bombers turned west. Seven 11 Group squadrons scrambled just in case a London raid developed, thwarting the attack by engaging escorting 109s, which were soon short of fuel. Again, bombs fell widely over Kent, including thirty-two on Broadstairs and more on Manston.

Other Dorniers (believed now to number thirty-nine), escorted by long-range tanked Bf 110s, continued to the River Blackwater estuary, then turned towards Debden. Although Colchester's AA guns caused several Dorniers to turn away, two 11 Group squadrons unable to break through to the bombers included No 1 Squadron. RCAF, operational since 17 August and now participating in their its combat. In reckoning to have destroyed six Dorniers near Braintree, the Canadians were being over-optimistic. Their true successes were probably two Bf 110s and a Do 17. A second Dornier, which fell at Whepstead, Suffolk, may have been theirs,

Much had been expected, by both sides, from the Messerschmitt Bf 110 long-range fighter. Instead, it proved a disappointment. *Bundesarchiv*

although the situation was soon so confusing that certainty was not possible. The Canadians very usefully drove the Bf 110s away from the bombers and harried them.

Debden, an 11 Group station and the most northerly yet raided in daylight, was close to the 12 Group boundary, so Park urgently asked Leigh-Mallory for assistance. It arrived too late to protect Debden from being bombed at 15.20. Its protection rested in the hands of the local Bofors gunners; Site M3 scored a direct hit on a Do 17, 160 bombs rained over the area, and a score of Bf 110s raced low across the aerodrome before No 310 (Czech) Squadron[143], scrambled from 12 Group's Duxford, tackled the retreating raiders near Little Hallenbury. Many bombs were been jettisoned over a wide area. The entire operation by this time was chaotic, with some Czechs fighting lone battles. Sergeant Pilot Prchal, who chased a Dornier out to sea, had the wing nearly blown off his Hurricane by cannon fire from a Bf 109 before he baled out near Upminster. Squadron Leader G. D. M. Blackwood, their leader, was shot down, and Pilot Officer Bergman baled out near Southminster and landed a few yards from his blazing Hurricane.

Some idea of the day's events can be gleaned from the intelligence summary prepared late on 26 August at HQ Fighter Command, and reproduced here.

Debden suffered considerable damage. There were hits on a hangar, the NAAFI and the MT Section, and one Hurricane was burned out. At 15.40 an estimated 250

The British made considerable use of the Swedish 40mm Bofors gun. Fast-firing and mobile, it was ideal for defence of KPs and VPs (Key and Vulnerable Points). *IWM*

Fighter Command intelligence summary, 26 August

No of aircraft	Squadron	Time up/down	Combat area	Losses	Claims
12	615	14.45-15.45	Thames Estuary	3 FTR	Four Bf 109s damaged
12	85	14.45-15.56	Thames Estuary	1 FTR	Three Do 17s, one probable Bf 109
11	1 RCAF	14.45-17.00	Essex-Eastchurch	1 FTR	Two Do 17s destroyed, two Do 17s damaged
9	111	15.00-15.50	off Clacton	1 FTR	One Do 17 destroyed, one Bf 109 destroyed
12	56	15.02-?	Colchester	–	Two Bf 110s and one probable
12	310	15.30-?	E of North Weald	3 FTR	One Do 17, one Bf 110

enemy aircraft were operating between Bury St Edmunds and Dungeness. In a costly afternoon No 1 RCAF Squadron had lost its leader, Squadron Leader N. E. McNab.

The third large-scale operation of the day, which materialised in the late afternoon, was directed against Portsmouth and Southampton. The final large-scale day raid mounted by Luftflotte 3, it comprised about fifty He 111s of I and II/KG 55 escorted by Bf 109s and 110s. Of eight fighter squadrons ordered to engage, Nos 43[144], 602[145] and 234[146] Squadrons prevented the bombing of Southampton and brought down four He 111s and four Bf 109s. Four fighters were lost and three pilots were wounded. Bombs released at 16.00, partly through cloud, fell on the outskirts of Portsmouth, in Langstone Harbour, demolished Fort Cumberland and started a small fire at Hilsea gasworks. They fell well short of the dockyard target. Later, an escorted rescue He 59 was shot down south of the Isle of Wight.

Life jackets on, briefcase and maps ready, an He 111 crew awaits the action call. *IWM*

By the end of the day Fighter Command had lost thirty-one aircraft and sixteen pilots – heavy losses indeed, although the enemy fared worse by losing forty-one aircraft, nineteen of them bombers.

Indicative of the future, KG 55 was switched to night raids, the extent of which was considerable on 26/27 August. About 200 German aircraft were operating mainly singly. Bombed in Greater London were Tottenham, Wood Green, Wormwood Scrubs and Southgate, with major damage at the latter. Also hit were Dartford, Tilbury, Bournemouth, Coventry (for the first time), Middlesbrough, Newcastle, RAF North Coates (one of six airfields attacked) and the Plymouth area, where more than fifty HEs fell and damaged Millbay Dock. Birmingham suffered the most when, between 21.25 and 03.00, a score of He 111s attacked industrial targets, including the Castle Bromwich Spitfire factory. It was little damaged, but not so Small Heath goods and timber yard, where a large fire was started. Bordesley Junction GWR station was badly damaged, and fierce fires gutted George Jones foundry in Lionel Street. Other incidents involved Dunlop, Humber, Daimler and Smith's Stamping Works. More than sixty fires were started, an oil bomb causing the consummation of the 100-year-old City Market Hall. The weapon penetrated the floor and burst in the basement, a designated shelter for 600 people, but fortunately unoccupied. Although firemen reached the scene within 3 minutes, they were unable to put out the ferocious fire. Low cloud had handicapped both searchlights and gunners. In the 24 hours to dawn on the 27th thirty-seven civilians had been killed, and 102 injured.

On 27 August early drizzle and low cloud over southern England were soon replaced by clear, warm weather. Six reconnaissance flights overflew the Portsmouth-Southampton areas, small formations operated over Kent, and single aircraft with little success attacked airfields, among them Edzell, Montrose, Gravesend, Cranfield, Biggin Hill, Cottesmore, Kirton-in-Lindsey and Catfoss, as well as HQ RAF Fighter Command, Bentley Priory. Two squadrons that had borne much of the fighting, Nos 32 and 65, were about to be withdrawn for rest.

He 111 9K+FP of KG 51 'Edelweiss' photographed from another He 111.

When such changes were made they often involved the use of air transport for groundcrews. Suitable aircraft being in very short supply, the RAF made use of a handful of converted pre-war Handley Page Harrow bombers operated from mid-placed Doncaster by 271 Squadron. They were supported by a few Bristol Bombays and several impressed HP 42 airliners. The Harrows, busy most days shifting men and materials, played a very useful part in the Battle without, apparently, ever being set upon by enemy fighters. Harrows were not the only aged pre-war bombers still flying; it was at this time that the remaining Heyfords serving as trainers were retired.

Fighter squadron movements 1 July-31 October 1940

Throughout the campaign RAF fighter squadrons were moved for tactical reasons or to rest them from front-line action. These movements occurred as follows:

Squadron	Base on/from 1 July 1940	Movement/date
1	Tangmere	Northolt 1 August, Wittering 9 September
3	Wick	Castletown 2 September, Turnhouse 14 September, Dyce 9 October, Castletown 12 October
19	Fowlmere	Duxford 3 July, Fowlmere 24 July, Duxford 30 October
25	Martlesham	North Weald 1 September, Debden 8 October
29	Digby	Wellingore 8 July
32	Biggin Hill	Acklington 28 August
41	Catterick	Hornchurch 26 July, Catterick 8 August, Hornchurch 3 September
43	Tangmere	(Northolt detached 23 July-1 August, Usworth 8 September
46	Digby	Stapleford Tawney 1 September
54	Rochford	Hornchurch 24 July, Catterick 28 July, Hornchurch 8 August, Catterick 3 September
56	North Weald	Boscombe Down 1 September
64	Kenley	Leconfield 19 August, Biggin Hill 13 October, Coltishall 15 October
65	Hornchurch	Turnhouse 28 August
66	Coltishall	Kenley 3 September, Gravesend 11 September, West Malling 30 October
72	Acklington	Biggin Hill 31 August, Croydon 1 September, Biggin Hill 14 September, Coltishall 13 October, Matlask 30 October
73	Church Fenton	Castle Camps 5 September
74	Hornchurch	Wittering 14 August, Kirton-in-Lindsey 21 August, Coltishall 9 September, Biggin Hill 15 October
79	Hawkinge	Acklington 11 July via Sealand, Biggin Hill 27 August, Pembrey 8 September
85	Debden	Croydon 19 August, Castle Camps 3 September, Church Fenton 5 September, Kirton-in-Lindsey 23 October
87	Church Fenton	Exeter 5 July
92	Pembrey	Biggin Hill 8 September
111	Croydon	Debden 19 August, Croydon 3 September, Drem 8 September, Dyce 12 October
141	Turnhouse	West Malling 12 July, Prestwick 21 July, Turnhouse 30 August, (Biggin Hill detached 13 September-22 October), Drem 15 October

Squadron	Base on/from 1 July 1940	Movement/date
145	Tangmere	Westhampnett 31 July, Drem 14 August, Dyce 31 August, Tangmere 9 October
151	North Weald	Stapleford Tawney 29 August, Digby 1 September
152	Acklington	Warmwell 12 July
213	Exeter	Tangmere 7 September
219	Catterick	Redhill 12 October
222	Kirton-in-Lindsey	Hornchurch 29 August
234	St Eval	Middle Wallop 13 August, St Eval 11 September
236	Middle Wallop	Using Thorney Island as advanced base, where squadron consolidated 4 July on leaving Fighter Command
238	Middle Wallop	St Eval 14 August, Middle Wallop 10 September, Chilbolton 30 September
242	Coltishall	Duxford 26 October
245	Turnhouse	Aldergrove 20 July
247	Roborough	– not formed until 1 August
249	Leconfield	Church Fenton 8 July, Boscombe Down 14 August, North Weald 1 September
253	Kirton-in-Lindsey	Turnhouse 21 July, Prestwick 23 August, Kenley 29 August
257	Hendon	Northolt 4 July, Debden 15 August, Martlesham 5 September, North Weald 8 October
263	Grangemouth	Drem 2 September for work up on Whirlwind
264	Duxford	Kirton-in-Lindsey 23 July, Hornchurch 22 August, Rochford 27 August, Kirton-in-Lindsey 28 August, Rochford 29 October
266	Wittering	Tangmere 9 August, Eastchurch 12 August, Hornchurch 14 August, Wittering 21 August
302	Leconfield	(formed 13 July), Northolt 11 October
303	Northolt	(formed 2 August), Leconfield 11 October
306	Church Fenton	(formed 28 August, became operational 8 September)
307	Kirton-in-Lindsey	(formed 5 September)
310	Duxford	(formed 10 July, operational 18 August)
501	Croydon	Middle Wallop 4 July, Gravesend 25 July, Kenley 10 September
504	Castletown	Catterick 1 September, Hendon 5 September, Exeter 26 September
600	Manston	Hornchurch 22 August, Redhill 12 September, Catterick 12 October
601	Tangmere	Debden 19 August, Tangmere 2 September, Exeter 7 September
602	Drem	Westhampnett 13 August
603	Turnhouse	Hornchurch 27 August
604	Manston	Gravesend 3 July, Middle Wallop 26 July
605	Drem	Croydon 7 September
607	Usworth	Tangmere 1 September, Turnhouse 10 October
609	Northolt	Middle Wallop 5 July
610	Gravesend	Biggin Hill 2 July, Acklington 13 September
611	Digby	
615	Kenley	Prestwick 29 August, Northolt 10 October
616	Leconfield	Kenley 19 August, Coltishall 3 September, Kirton-in-Lindsey 9 September

Across the Channel, the switch of Luftflotte 3 to mainly night operations released fighters to support Luftflotte 2, but Dowding still resisted the temptation to bring more squadrons into 11 Group for fear that it would permit attacks in other Group areas. Instead, he rotated six squadrons. From 24 August about a third of 11 Group squadrons were manned by inexperienced pilots, many recently trained at OTUs. That may have accounted for increased losses and fewer successes, although additional enemy fighters were now operating over the South East. Dowding's only alternative would have been to keep experienced pilots in 11 Group until exhaustion overcame them.

Large bomber formations splitting to attack several targets were presenting difficult tasks for the defenders, precise positions of enemy groups, once scattered and beyond radar search, being hard to locate however much the Observer Corps tried. Fighter squadron leaders were therefore told to give their positions upon entering combat so that reinforcement could readily be sent. As soon as it was realised that Luftflotte 3 had halted large-scale day raids, and passed their fighters to Luftflotte 2, both Nos 10 and 12 Groups could be used to reinforce No 11 Group. Nos 10 and 12 Groups were also gradually switched to night fighting.

...this loyal and public spirited body of men [the Observer Corps] had maintained their watch with admirable efficiency since the beginning of the war ... at this time they constituted the sole means of tracking enemy raids once they had crossed the coastline. The country was divided into about 130 'Warning Districts' the boundaries of which were determined by the layout of the public telephone system.

Air Chief Marshal Sir Hugh Dowding
Commander-in-Chief Fighter Command

Birmingham was again bombed on the 27/28th. Although a water main to the Castle Bromwich Spitfire factory was shattered, bombs intended for the works burst mainly in Gravelly Hill which, like Sutton Coldfield and the Pype Hayes area, bore almost every attack on the factory, which was only once seriously damaged during the seventy-seven raids on Birmingham. Parachute marker flares released over the works persistently and quickly drifted, leading to claims of indiscriminate bombing. Fires were started at BSA Tools, Montgomery Street, around which area forty-six HEs fell.

In the early hours of 28 August Gillingham, Kent, received its third attack within a few hours when it was dive-bombed – a very frightening experience at night – and again probably in error for another Medway target. Hundreds of incendiaries were released, twenty houses were damaged, sixteen fires caused and sixteen people killed in a sombre prelude to another day's tough fighting.

Reconnaissance flights, including three along the south-east coast at dawn, preceded a large build-up of forces over France. He 111s and Do 17s escorted by Bf 109s of I and III/JG 51 proceeded north near Sandwich. Ahead had gone forward support fighter sweeps met by squadrons of Hurricanes including Nos 501[147] and

Impressive formation of HE 111s reputedly heading for London and engagement by fighters. *IWM*

615[148], together with a dozen 264 Squadron Defiants[149]. They were unable to prevent the Dorniers of I/KG 3 from reaching Eastchurch, and He 111s of II and III/KG 53 from raiding Rochford. Enemy fighters engaged the Defiants trying to deal with the He 111s, No 264 Squadron destroying a Heinkel. The leader's gunner damaged another before his Defiant (L7021) was shot down. Two more Defiants (L7026 and N1574) were also destroyed, N1569 force-landed, and out of eight that returned to Hornchurch five were damaged. Some fifteen Heinkels broke through to Rochford – despite the ferocity of its AA defences cratering its turf with 15 tons of bombs. The eighteen Dorniers, by dropping forty-four HEs from 15,000 feet, seriously damaged Eastchurch, where two Battles were destroyed and another pair damaged. Eight RAF fighters and six pilots were lost, and five enemy aircraft destroyed.

Rochford was attacked again at 12.40 by Raid 13H, which headed in from the south-east and left after damaging some buildings. Carried out by twenty-seven Do 17s of II and III/KG 3 attacking from 18,000 feet, it was delivered just too late to prevent 264 Squadron[150] yet again managing to get away just before bombs began bursting on its flying field. Spitfires of 54 Squadron[151] positioned at 30,000 feet dived upon the escort, Flight Lieutenant Deere claiming a Bf 109, Flight Lieutenant George Gribble another at the end of an eleven-aircraft line, and Squadron Leader Leathart a Dornier. In a quite astonishing chase of a Bf 109, Gribble (R6899) and Norwell (R6898) ended the fight so low that Gribble's shooting killed a cow. After landing he discovered pieces of a tree lodged in his Spitfire. Al Deere (R6832) was less fortunate – he had to bale out. As the raiders approached Rochford, Hurricanes of No 1 Squadron[152] downed a Do 17 of 6/KG 3 on the aerodrome, its crew becoming PoWs.

Afternoon fighting exposed a disturbing feature, the success of a Bf 109 and 110 seven-formation excursion over Kent. Fighters from seven squadrons responded in case bombers were included, and it led to a wasting high-level battle observed by Mr Churchill, who was viewing coastal defences at Dover. At between 25,000 and 30,000 feet over the Canterbury-Dungeness-Margate area, a fierce battle developed exclusively between fighters, with eleven Hurricanes of Squadron Leader Peter Townsend's 85 Squadron[153] opening the fight for the defence. Attacking twenty Bf 109s out of the sun over Dungeness, Flying Officer Woods-Scawen (P3150) shot down one. Another fell in the sea two-thirds of a mile off Folkestone to the great satisfaction of Mr Churchill. Eight Bf 109s of JG 51 and JG 53 are thought to have been variously destroyed during this phase, one of I/JG 53 crashing on land at a site visited by the Prime Minister. Nos 56[154] and 151 Squadrons each lost two Hurricanes, and 54 Squadron[155] Spitfire X4053, flown by Squadron Leader Donald Finlay, who baled out and was injured. By the end of the day sixteen British fighters had been lost, the same as the number of Bf 109s believed lost by five Geschwaderen. Dowding expressed his feelings very strongly over precious fighters being committed to pointless fighter-versus-fighter engagements, issuing clear orders that such activity must not be repeated.

Night operations spearheaded by beam-riding He 111s of KGr 100 were certainly increasing. On the 28/29th the first major attack upon one target was mounted, 150 crews being briefed to bomb Merseyside. Although pathfinders led the main force in from Selsey to Liverpool and Sealand, and houses were destroyed and fires started in

---

FOOD FACTS Nº 5

Are you collecting these useful advertisements?

Coffee for breakfast – there are ample supplies. The rules for making it are quite simple. Allow two heaped teaspoons of coffee for each cup. Be sure the kettle is boiling fast. Take the jug to the kettle. Pour, stir, cover, allow to stand for two minutes, give another stir and leave for two more minutes before pouring.

We've got through to the final, we're good at finals, but we're going to train you for finals. We're going to discipline ourselves in our kitchens so we can field a team unbeatable.

Lord Woolton, Minister of Food

Pulp plums for winter – and curb your liking for fresh bread. Don't keep it in a closely sealed tin. If you use a biscuit tin, punch a few holes in the lid. Brown bread is best wrapped in muslin and kept on a shelf. Try mustard and cress, watercress or even young nasturtium leaves instead of jam at tea time. It makes a change.

Newspapers

Liverpool, the bombing went so badly astray that the recipients were convinced that, despite intelligence indications, the Midlands and the London area were instead the main targets! London, under Red Alert for 7 hours, the longest yet, reported incidents in many suburbs, at Enfield where a gas main was ruptured, at Cricklewood and at Lambeth. Bombing was also recorded at Birmingham, Bournemouth, Derby, Manchester and Sheffield. At Avonmouth the Shell Mex installations and the National Smelting Co works were hit, and in Coventry thirteen houses and shops were damaged and eleven fires started. At Altrincham a 50,000-gallon oil tank at the Anglo-American oil depot caught fire, incendiaries being suspected. Despite the extent of enemy activities, patrolling night-fighters caught only one glimpse of the foe.

Concentration on night raids may well have reduced the daylight effort on 29 August, for it was mid-afternoon, in clear conditions and using Do 17s and He 111s as bait, before a small Channel sweep was flown between Beachy Head and Hastings, while high overhead Bf 109s and Bf 110s waited to pounce. No 85 Squadron[156] patrolling Hawkinge nibbled at them, claiming two Bf 109s for the loss of two Hurricanes. Sergeant Walker's was hit by cannon fire, which deprived him of throttle and rudder control and forced him down at Hawkhurst. Sergeant Ellis, his Hurricane hit in the engine, cockpit and soon blazing, crashed a hundred yards offshore 12 miles west of Battle after he had baled out. By then Nos 603[157] and 610[158] Squadrons were on hand, 610 sweeping into action over Mayfield carrying a cautionary warning from Command. A Bf 110 was destroyed and several Dorniers damaged, but Sergeant Manton was shot down. Pevensey guns claimed a Bf 109. About 170 tempting enemy aircraft are thought to have swept inland towards Biggin Hill during the afternoon, which earlier included a small attack on Warmwell and at 15.58 one on Tresco Radio, Scilly Isles.

Around 18.00 a twenty-aircraft provocation flight to the Rochester area ended with Hurricanes of 501 Squadron battling over Hawkinge with Bf 109s and losing two of their number. Other Bf 109s, some of which strafed gun sites at Dover, tangled with Nos 85[159], 603[160] and 610[161] Squadrons. During a day that had seen only two bombing raids aimed at the Kent coast, seven Bf 109s had been shot down and nine RAF fighters lost.

At dusk, single-bomber sorties struck at Debden, Duxford and other East Anglian aerodromes before the Luftwaffe arrived in strength, about 200 raiders heading for Merseyside, which was the target for four-fifths of the force. From a cloudless sky they released incendiaries intended for warehouses packed with food, but of an intended 130 tons of HE they managed to deliver only 50 tons to Merseyside. The Rootes factory and Speke industrial estate were hit, but most affected were domestic properties and public utilities in Birkenhead, Blundell Sands, Seaforth, Wallasey, Bootle and Hightown. Bombs also fell on very many other parts of the country, including Swinton, Manchester, the Midlands, Cheshire, Kent (including the Canterbury area), Gloucestershire, Minehead, near Launceston, Chalfont St George, Fenny Stratford, Great Missenden, South Wales, Carlisle, the Tees and Tyne region and Scotland. Little wonder the British were, once more, doubting that Merseyside really was the target, particularly since many raiders had concentrated over Portsmouth! There was no doubt by dawn that night-bombing was steadily increasing, for ten of the twelve Civil Defence Regions reported bombing incidents.

Photographed on 25 July wearing unusual markings, Hurricane P2923 VY-R joined 85 Squadron on 11 June 1940, and was last seen – being flown by Flying Officer R. H. A. Lee on 18 August – engaging Bf 109s 30 miles out from Foulness. It was credited with 110hr 20min flying. *IWM*

Doubts concerning that might have been entertained on 30 August when a period of hot, excellent weather arrived and morning cloud at 7,000 feet over Kent put the Observer Corps at a disadvantage. With invasion preparations well under way across the Channel, the Battle was undoubtedly proceeding towards a climax. By nightfall the greatest number of sorties in one day had been flown in the biggest enemy effort since the middle of August. It resulted in thirty-six enemy aircraft being destroyed, and twenty-six RAF fighters being lost.

Leading the assault, 100-plus aircraft arrived in the Deal-Dungeness area at 07.06, Do 17s escorted by Bf 110s of ZG 76 and heading for a convoy sailing from the Thames to Methil. Then at 10.30 the first part of phase one of a three-part operation revealed itself as three Gruppen of Bf 109s coming in over the Kent coast to pave the way for forty He 111s, thirty Do 17s and another ninety fighters. No 151 Squadron[162] engaged the Heinkels, claiming three for the loss of two Hurricanes before 85[163] Squadron made head-on attacks that widely split the bomber formation. Two escorting Bf 110s were then shot down, and another Hurricane lost.

Scattered groups of bombers produced another confusing and dangerous situation, prompting Park to order part of 253 Squadron (new to the campaign and patrolling over Maidstone) to guard Kenley, whose fighters were scrambled. At about this time a small, hitherto undetected, formation of Ju 88s over Biggin Hill at 18,000 feet unloaded their wares, most of which luckily fell wide. They were able to bomb mainly because Biggin's guard sent to patrol over Maidstone believed their base to be in 12 Group's care. Upon retiring, the three formations, each of nine Ju 88s with thirty fighters providing top cover, were met by No 253 Squadron[164] vectored from Kenley, which had not come under the expected attack. 'B' Flight set about the bombers and soon had the help of 43 Squadron near Brighton. Other newcomers soon in action were Spitfires of 222 Squadron[165] whose 'B' Flight north-west of Dover contacted 109s. Destruction of six enemy aircraft during the operation cost Fighter Command ten aircraft and five pilots.

A surprising security lapse is evident on 85 Squadron Hurricanes carrying the squadron's white hexagonal motif beneath the cockpit canopy. VY-U is V6611, with the squadron from 2 September to 21 November, and VY-Q P3854, with 85 from 18 September to 25 November 1940. *IWM*

'If you speak to me any more like that I shall lock you up. You must account for your movements, and why you are trespassing. Your name and address, sir, if you please.' Left to right: a Home Guard, an ARP man, a serious civilian, a German airman *mit* Iron Cross – and PC 217. *IWM*

Pressure was building, and before the squadrons completed their turn-rounds Kesselring dispatched small groups of bombers protected by many fighters, which crossed the Kent coast from 13.00 at around 15,000 feet and at 20-minute intervals. They were largely unplotted because power supplies to radar stations had been cut during morning raids. For more than 2 hours the enemy roamed over South East England. Five fighter squadrons responded, among them 222 Squadron, which was to operate three times during the day, having eight of its Spitfires put out of use, losing five, having a pilot killed and two injured. Twelve of 222 Squadron's Spitfires on patrol at 16,000 feet over Lympne sighted fifteen escorted He 111s near Canterbury. As the Spitfires attacked they were set upon by the Messerschmitts. They claimed a Bf 110 damaged, but Pilot Officer Asheton was forced to land on the obstructed Bekesbourne airfield, Sergeant Baxter had to put down at Eastchurch, and Pilot Officer Carpenter baled out of P9378 near Rochford.

Early in the afternoon another 'new' squadron strode boldly into the main arena. Since the start of the Battle 12 Group's Coltishall-based 242 Squadron, led by Squadron Leader Douglas Bader, had been flying convoy patrols off the East Anglian coast and had seen little fighting. Around midday of 30 August 242 Squadron was ordered to Duxford, from where fourteen Hurricanes[166] set off to police the North Weald area. Led by Bader (P3061), they tackled Raid X33, a diamond formation of KG I's He 111s, which had already braved fifty-four rounds of heavy AA fire, and shot down two. Before returning to Coltishall that evening, 242 operated on two occasions.

By 16.00 a huge group of enemy aircraft, probably more than 300, had crossed the Kent coast, some heading for distant inland targets. Thirteen squadrons were scrambled to deal with them. Over Kent and the Thames Estuary they proceeded during the ensuing 2 hours, a mighty array drawn from 19 Gruppen and which divided into smaller groups that headed for Hawker's at Slough, the Hurricane and Spitfire repair centres at Oxford, for Luton and towards three vital airfields – North Weald, Kenley and Biggin Hill. One small formation, intercepted by only one squadron, managed to put Detling out of use for 15 hours. The biggest, potentially most damaging operation so far had to be ferociously dealt with by using as many fighters as possible.

The first bombing incident occurred at Lambeth. Soon after, a group of fewer than ten Ju 88s made low and fast for Sheppey, suddenly veered south, then delivered a devastating 15-ton blow on Biggin Hill, smashing a hangar, the workshops, armoury, barrack blocks, MT Section and WAAF quarters, killing thirty-nine and injuring twenty-six. Too late, six Hurricanes of the recently arrived 79 Squadron chased after the 88s claiming two of them. By then other raids were well inland. That directed at Oxford was forced back over Surrey.

It was around 16.10 that twenty He 111s of II/KG 1 escorted by Bf 110s flew across Southend, then North Weald, bound for Luton's industrial area. Despite spirited efforts by Hurricanes of 1, 56, 242 and 501 Squadrons – Nos 1 and 56 each destroying a Heinkel – the raiders reached Luton, where at 16.40 they carried out 5 minutes of bombing during which 207 HEs fell, many on the Vauxhall Motors factory. No air raid warning had sounded, and horrific scenes followed the sudden destruction of the factory's main internal stairway. Casualties totalled fifty-nine killed and 141 injured. More than sixty bombs fell very wide of the target, eighteen of them in Whipsnade Zoo.

Biggin Hill is under attack from high-flying Ju 88s, despite the attempt to camouflage its surface with painted hedgerows. Bombs are bursting, mainly among buildings. *Bundesarchiv*

During daylight 1,054 sorties were flown by the twenty-two fighter squadrons involved. In some cases they had been in action as many as four times, a rate not long sustainable. Nine Hurricanes and eleven Spitfires had been destroyed, while the enemy had lost eight bombers and fourteen fighters.

Throughout the hours of darkness Fighter Command licked its wounds while the Luftwaffe was preparing to worsen them – and soon – with an even larger effort. This most crucial week was seeing heavy onslaughts on Sector Stations vital to the defence of London, which had to be destroyed before an invasion was feasible. Losses over the period proved about equal, Fighter Command losing 161 aircraft between 31 August and 6 September and the Luftwaffe 189, of which 154 were shot down. The brunt of the battle was to be borne by a score of 11 Group squadrons and

Castle Camps, Debden's spartan satellite, complete with painted hedgerows, was photographed on 31 August by a passing Dornier. *via P. H. T. Green*

400 pilots, for Dowding still refused to reduce the strength of 10 and 12 Groups. That made it imperative that Park's squadrons avoided wasted effort. Although larger formations of fighters – attractive in principle – would waste precious moments assembling, on 2 September Park ordered squadrons to commence operating in pairs, and when practicable to formate on other couples. Like Dowding, he stressed the advisability, indeed practicability, of this only when targets were well inland. With Manston lost and Biggin Hill and Kenley seriously damaged, the need to protect the other main fighter stations was now paramount.

I must disclaim any exact accuracy in the estimates of enemy losses. All that I can say is that the utmost care was taken to arrive at the closest possible approximation. Special intelligence officers examined pilots individually after their combats, and the figures claimed are those recorded as 'certain'.

Air Chief Marshal Sir Hugh Dowding
Commander-in-Chief Fighter Command

At 08.05 on Saturday 31 August the first of the day's four major onslaughts began to cross the Kent coast. Within the four-wave array flying at between 15,000 and 20,000 feet were formations soon swinging over the Thames Estuary. Park ordered ten squadrons to intercept. One raid, heading north, crossed over Essex, there dividing. On its western flank were protective long-range-tanked Bf 110s, which Hurricanes of 257 Squadron[167] led by Flight Lieutenant Beresford (P3705) tackled soon after they had crossed the coast south of Clacton, then formed a defensive circle. Pilot Officer Henderson claimed two before his aircraft was shot down in flames. He was plucked from the water by the Navy, together with a German airman. Pilot Officer Gundry (P3704) chased a Bf 110 as far as Deal but then faced a huge enemy force, so decided to turn back. Pilot Officer Moffat was shot down and killed.

Near Colchester it was the turn of 56 Squadron[168] to engage. They lost a pilot killed and four Hurricanes while attempting in vain to hold back the invaders. At 08.40 Colchester was bombed, the Davey Paxman works being hit. At Hythe the water main was broken causing flooding. Bombs also fell at Maldon.

Nineteen Dorniers of KG 2 headed for Debden, the main target bombed at 09.00. Nine Hurricanes of No 1 Squadron[169] now tackled the Bf 110 escort near Chelmsford, claiming one for the loss of two aircraft. No 111 Squadron, also in the battle, destroyed a Dornier and a Bf 110, but lost yet another Hurricane – V7375, flown by Sergeant H. J. Merchant.

'They're still all behind us, Fritz. We've come all this way and the Duxford gunners are firing at us. What a welcome, what gratitude. Better swerve a bit!'

The bombing of Debden caused eighteen casualties including eight military, and the 350 50kg bombs and 546 BSKs damaged fourteen Hurricanes on the airfield. The station's fire-fighting equipment was wiped out and damage was caused to hangars and shelters. Bombs also fell at Bishops Stortford, Haverhill (incendiaries), Saffron Walden, Woodham Walter and Burnham. As the raiders turned for home, fourteen Do 17Zs of KG 2, carrying 252 50kg HEs and 420 BSKs, were heading for 12 Group's Duxford, whose AA defences very effectively forced the raid off track to the north. Soon after 08.30 they jettisoned most of their 252 HE load in one enormous salvo of about 245 HEs, 215 of which exploded almost simultaneously in a narrow line across open country between a watercress farm at Fowlmere and Shepreth village. At least three dozen incendiaries intended for use as markers burned in cornfields. The exploding HEs formed the largest number of bombs simultaneously dropped on the UK, causing a mini earthquake-like shudder for miles around. Indeed, the 9-inch-thick concrete walls of our Cambridge shelter shuddered. Cannon-armed Spitfires of 19 Squadron[170], scrambled at the last minute from Fowlmere, were vectored on to the bombers, which swung and passed north of Duxford before turning right for home. The Spitfires had little success in preventing their exit, but they were credited with two Bf 110s shot down as the escort rejoined their charge. Several bomb hang-ups were released as the Dorniers departed from the arena. The official survey listed HEs as falling between 08.20 and 08.50 at Balsham, Fowlmere, Great Shelford, Harston, Harlston, Hildersham, Meldreth, Shepreth, Stapleford and West Wickham.

Imperial War Duxford's realistic exhibit in Duxford Sector Operations Room as at 08:30 31 August 1940.

While that engagement took place, other Dorniers again battered Eastchurch, while Bf 109s and 110s strafed other airfields, Detling included. Strange the persistent attention afforded Eastchurch, although its Battle squadrons had an anti-invasion role, which possibly the enemy overrated. More purposeful was the activity over Kent by rear-support and diversionary Bf 109s, some of which at 08.45 shot down no fewer than twenty-three of Dover's balloons. At 09.40 a high-flying Dornier inspected damage at Debden and Duxford then left the UK via Bircham Newton, by which time a second major intrusion over Kent and the Thames Estuary was being prepared.

Shortly after noon another major operation unfolded. Raiders approaching along two corridors over Dungeness and heading for Croydon or Biggin Hill were opposed by thirteen RAF squadrons. The former aerodrome came under attack at 12.55, Do 17s completely destroying the Rollason aircraft works and placing bombs along one edge and upon a hangar as a dozen Hurricanes of 85 Squadron[171] took off to deal with them. Waterman's dyeworks was damaged at Purley Way, where three were killed and sixty injured. Launching its attack over Tunbridge, 85 Squadron was soon in the sights of Bf 109s, which shot down Squadron Leader Townsend's VY-Q P3166 and Pilot Officer P. A. Worrall's Hurricane V6581, in exchange for which 85 Squadron claimed two Bf 109s and a 110.

Close by, two Staffeln of He 111s were running in at 12,000 feet to deal Biggin Hill another mighty blow. They blasted its two remaining hangars, messes and quarters, and set fire to the operations block. Most of the station's aircraft had now to be withdrawn to adjacent Sectors. No 253 Squadron[172] managed to decisively punish a Heinkel, while another casualty was well-known 253's Squadron Leader Tom Gleave (P3115), who, wounded, was shot down by a Bf 109.

There was more blasting to come, from a portion of the II/KG 3 Dornier force that broke through to Hornchurch. Spitfires of 54 Squadron were taking off just as the bombs fell. Flight Lieutenant Deere (R6895) and Sergeant J. Davis (X4235) had amazing escapes, their aircraft being written off, and Pilot Officer E. F. Edsall's Spitfire (X4236) fared little better. AA gunners claimed one of the three Do 17s shot down (which are generally credited to 151 Squadron[173] and 310 Czech Squadron[174]), and which at 13.25 fell near Canewdon. Reconnaissance aircraft again sought evidence of success and a spying Do 17 was claimed 20 miles off Bawdsey.

Afternoon attacks by fighter-bombers of Erpr 210, directed at radar stations in Kent and Sussex, were insufficiently effective to prevent them operating. Later, the same unit and a few hand-picked Ju 88 crews carried out small-scale attacks on Hornchurch, and at 18.38 on Biggin Hill.

Between 17.30 and 19.15 more than 300 enemy aircraft, attempting six raids on airfields in Kent and near London, found that they were opposed by twenty squadrons. In ferocious fighting around Hornchurch, Spitfires of 54[175] and 603[176] Squadrons claimed two Bf 109s for three of their number. Medway gunners, too, made claims before, to round off their daylight adventures, four Bf 109s pestering Dover's balloons disposed of another fifteen. Defending gunners insisted that they destroyed three attackers!

 During air attacks only non-essential personnel took cover; aircraft crews and the staff of the Operations Room remained at their posts. At Kenley and Biggin Hill direct hits were sustained on shelter trenches, at the latter place by a bomb of 500 kilogrammes or more. The trench and its forty occupants were annihilated. The trenches in use were lined with concrete and covered with earth. They had to be within a short distance of the hangars and offices. Wooden hangars were generally set on fire by a bombing attack, and everything in them destroyed. Steel, brick and concrete hangars, on the other hand, stood up well against attack, though, of course, acres of glass were broken. Hangars were generally empty, or near so. Damage to aerodrome surfaces was not a major difficulty.

The main safeguard for aircraft against air attack was dispersal. Experiments on Salisbury Plain in summer 1938 had shown that dispersal alone, without any form of splinter-proof protection, afforded a reasonable safeguard against the forms of attack practised by our own Bomber Command. Thirty unserviceable fighters were dispersed in a ring of about 1,000 yards diameter and Bomber Command attacked them for a week. The result was three were destroyed, one damaged beyond repair, eleven seriously damaged. I therefore asked that small splinter-proof pens for single aircraft should be provided at all fighter aerodromes. This was not approved, but I was offered pens for groups of three. I think they were too big, they had a large open face to the front and a concrete area the size of two tennis courts, which made an ideal surface for the bursting of direct action bombs. Eventually, splinter-proof partitions were made inside the pens, and till then some aircraft were parked in the open. As for aircraft damaged in battle, any returning to its base was capable of another 15 minutes straight flight to a Repair Depot. Two were improvised about 30 miles west of London.

Air Chief Marshal Sir Hugh Dowding, Commander-in-Chief Fighter Command

By the end of the day, twenty-five Hurricanes and nine Spitfires had been written off, whereas German losses amounted to nine bombers and twenty-nine fighters. That did not prevent 160 night-bombers from heading mainly for Merseyside. Up to 03.00 raids on the UK streamed across the South Coast to the Midlands and Leeds. Some crossed central London on course to attempt night-bombing of Hornchurch, Debden, Biggin Hill and, incredibly, Eastchurch!

Merseyside had now been subjected, theoretically, to more heavy bombing than any other British target. Over four nights 70% of the crews involved claimed to have bombed the area, each nightly dropping an average of 114 tons of HE and 257 BSK 36 incendiary containers. This quartet of raids was almost certainly Luftflotte 3's biggest effort so far, and included naval crews of KGr 606 and Fw 200 Condors of KG 40. The first and third attacks were the most effective. On 29/30 August 137 crews of the 176 dispatched to Merseyside claimed to have bombed their targets with 130 tons of HE and 313 incendiary containers; however, most of the 180 aircraft dispatched on the second raid bombed elsewhere. The 112 sent on the 30th/31st

Ill-prepared briefings for many German bombing raids were often open-air events, in much contrast to the highly sophisticated briefings of RAF crews prior to bombing operations. *IWM*

dropped 40 tons, which missed the docks and hit mainly houses and suburbs. On the fourth night Liverpool was badly hit, although there was bombing creep. In the commercial area fires were started. Birkenhead was bombed yet again, but few bombs found the dock areas. For a loss of seven aircraft, 1% of the whole force, these Liverpool raids were a moderately successful investment.

While invasion preparations advanced, there was no let-up in day raids. To counter them Fighter Command's main strength on 1 September comprised thirty-seven squadrons of Hurricanes armed with 703 aircraft, and nineteen Spitfire squadrons with 349 effective aircraft.

September opened with a very heavily fighter-screened operation, Goering's flyers violating Kent over a 5-mile-wide front mid-morning before splitting into two groups, then into another two. That gave the defenders four huge forces to grapple with, each plentifully wrapped within fighter protection. Despite the increasingly urgent need to destroy Sector Stations, the Luftwaffe was still crazily fascinated by Detling and Eastchurch and, more sensibly, Biggin Hill. Some success was achieved at Tilbury, raided at 11.05 by a diversionary force. Riverside station was damaged, as well as dock buildings, workshops and the Harland & Wolff area. Five workers were killed and twenty-eight injured.

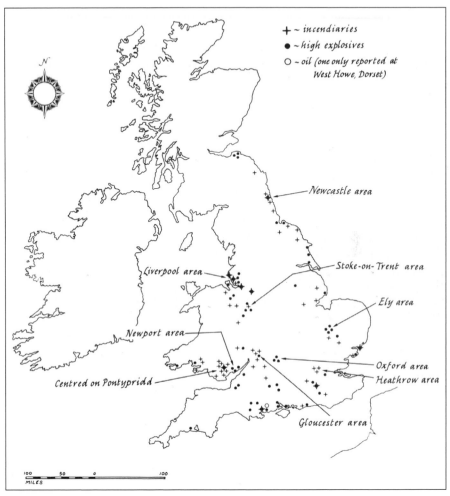

+ ~ incendiaries
● ~ high explosives
O ~ oil (one only reported at West Howe, Dorset)

N

Newcastle area

Liverpool area

Stoke-on-Trent area

Ely area

Newport area

Oxford area

Centred on Pontypridd

Heathrow area

Gloucester area

100   50   0   100
MILES

Night Bombing
29 August 1940 – 30 August 1940
18.00hrs-06.00hrs 119 incidents

Around 13.45 a similar operation against aerodromes was repeated, but it was the third that became one of the most notorious raids of the Battle of Britain. Prior to that, large groups of fighters attempted yet again to distract the British into wasteful combat. Failing to do so, they contented themselves by bombing and mainly strafing Hawkinge and Lympne aerodromes.

Meanwhile a clutch of very low-flying Dorniers penetrated to Biggin Hill and delivered the third and most damaging bombing of the day. One crew scored a direct hit with a 250kg HE on the Sector Operations Room. Its reinforced concrete ceiling collapsed into the building where two WAAF's remained at their posts. Such devotion to duty won for Sergeant Helen Turner and Corporal Elspeth Henderson a Military Medal. A new, temporary, operations room was established in a village shop at night while more than 100 bombers operated mainly individually over much of the country.

The first of four major daylight operations on 2 September was carried out by Dorniers of KG 3 heavily escorted by many Bf 109s, which approached Kent at 07.00. Although Park scrambled five squadrons, few contacted the enemy, for close protection of Sector Stations had been prescribed. The Dornier formations parted near Maidstone and headed for Rochford, North Weald, Biggin Hill and also Gravesend, where eleven bombs fell around the airfield at 08.00. Around the same time, forty-eight bombs caused considerable damage to houses at Rochester, and 20 minutes later Chatham received ten HEs. At the initial division point No 72 Squadron[177] busily dealt with Dorniers and Bf 110s at around 13,000 feet as another nine Do 17s, contour-hugging, again struck Biggin Hill. No 603 Squadron, patrolling over Hornchurch, was vectored to withdrawing Bf 109s, and Pilot Officer Richard Hillary (X4277) felled one. He later became famous as the author of the book *The Last Enemy*.

Around noon, with about 250 enemy aircraft approaching, Park decided this time to order his squadrons forward. While resultant scores were not high, and the tactic diminished the military effectiveness of the operation, it resulted in the bombing of Maidstone, where many houses suffered and fifteen casualties resulted. More raids in similar strength followed, taxing the defenders to the extreme. At 16.40 Maidstone endured a second onslaught.

Soon after 17.00 a tremendous battle resulted when about ninety RAF fighters took on 160 Bf 109s. By then seven aerodromes had been bombed – including, yes, Eastchurch – where this time the bomb dump exploded. Detling, Kenley, Biggin Hill and Hornchurch were hit, as well as Brooklands, where the Hawker and Vickers-Armstrong factories were sited. At night, four civilians died during incidents at Bristol/Knowle.

Guns and lights of London's Inner Artillery Zone

	Ready for action on		
	31.8.40	**30.9.40**	**31.10.40**
4.5in	48	48	60
3.7in static	32	32	40
3.7in mobile	14	113	127
3in	34	6	6
40mm Bofors	36	55	47
Vickers Twin Mk.8	3	5	9
Vickers .5in Single	–	1	1
Vickers .5in Twin	–	1	1
Searchlights	240	265	265

The war was now a year old. There had been some terrible disasters and for many deep grief, even from the start when the *Athenia* was torpedoed on day one. But there had been moments of euphoria for the British when the *Graf Spee* was sunk, and the *Altmark* was boarded in a Norwegian fjord. Every hour now seemed packed with tremendous excitement. One was certainly aware of the momentous, traumatic days through which all were passing. There was increasing uncertainty of what terrors were ahead as an invasion loomed ever more close. There were wonderful tales relating to secret weapons – death beams, wire coils and springs ensnaring raiders or wrapping around chimney pots. Wild talk was of gigantic German bombs, terrible oil bombs and booby traps falling from the skies. Don't eat any sweets you may find in bags that were being dropped by German airmen, some said, because they were poisoned. Yet none of theses terrors did anything to dent our high morale. 'Careless talk costs lives' we were for ever being told, yet it was quite easy to build a reasonably accurate picture of what was going and the units involved. By autumn 1940 Cambridge residents were even whispering (privately) about a terrible thing called an 'atom bomb'. Once an atom was broken, its was claimed, a chain reaction would follow and we might all be doomed! It's amazing that German spies parachuted into this country seem to have discovered so little.

Air Marshal Trafford Leigh-Mallory, whose 'Big Wing' idea won some official favour to the detriment, said some, of the generally better concepts of Dowding and Park. *IWM*

The largest bombing attack on 3 September, made by fifty Do 17s (preceded by many fighters) was the first to thread its way westerly along the Thames Estuary. Fear that London was their target caused Park, by 09.40, to have sixteen squadrons (122 fighters) over Kent and Essex. Suddenly, on reaching Southend, the Dorniers swung westerly, then carpet-bombed North Weald before the fighters could stop them. Most bombs fell on the aerodrome, killing four men, gutting two hangars, hitting the operations block and damaging many other buildings. Three Blenheim crews of 25 Squadron scrambled, intent upon fighting the Dorniers, but this unusual injection proved disastrous when surprised Hurricane pilots erroneously attacked them. Sergeant Powell, gunner in Pilot Officer Hogg's aircraft, crawled to the nose, only to find his pilot slumped dead over the controls. He then baled out, leaving L1512 to crash near Greenstead Green, Essex. Squadron Leader Loxton landed safely, but Pilot Officer Cassidy had to force-land his damaged Blenheim L1409 at Hatfield Heath. As the enemy was making for home, cannon Spitfires of 19 Squadron[178] troubled the Bf 110s only to encounter the usual gun stoppages. Hurricanes of Nos 1, 17[179], 46[180], 257[181] and 310[182] Squadrons, soon on hand, forced the Bf 110 escort into combat. Despite the extent of the damage, North Weald remained operational.

For persevering, No 19 – the first Spitfire squadron, and the first Spitfire squadron to use cannon-equipped examples – received a reward the next day, replacement in the form of eight-gun Spitfires. Time-expired 'heaps', they were kindly donated by No 7 OTU! Fate was also unkind to 25 Squadron, for when Pilot

Spitfire P9386 of 19 Squadron, Fowlmere. Duxford, home of the RAFs first Spitfires was mainly a Hurricane Battle of Britain station, with 19 Squadron positioned at the Fowlmere satellite from where the cannon-armed Spitfires frequented Duxford. P9386 with No 19 from 3 to 26 September came from 7 OTU as a cannon-Spitfire replacement and next served 152 Squadron from 23 March 1941. Used by Nos 52 and 58 OTUs, it crashed in East Lothian on 5 May 1944. *John Rawlings collection*

Officer Rofe made a night patrol and engaged three raiders, heavy AA guns fired upon his Blenheim, twice putting it into dangerous spins. But all was not failure – Pilot Officer Herrick in another Blenheim shot down two night raiders.

Their main target again was Merseyside, to reach which He 111s of Luftflotte 3 overflew Dorset, performing their distinctive signature tunes. For a night-fighter to catch one was a rare event, even when searchlights illuminated it. Mounting an interception without radar remained difficult until 2 September when the Bristol Beaufighter entered squadron service.

The first Beaufighters to serve RAF units were R2066, delivered to Tangmere Special Flight on 12 August 1940, and R2055, which joined AFDU Northolt the next day. On 2 September R2073 reached 604 Squadron and R2072, the first squadron aircraft to operate, came on the strength of 29 Squadron at Wellingore. R2057 went next day to 25 Squadron, North Weald, the squadron originally chosen to nurse the aircraft into service. Nos 23 and 600 Squadrons each received a Beaufighter on 8 September. The first operational patrol was flown over Hoylake by Squadron Leader S. C. Widows on 17/18 September.

Trials with early production Beaufighters revealed top speeds of between 312 and 325mph at 15,000 feet – and German bombers now were persistently operating higher than that. Early Beaufighters carried only four cannon. While they did not yet have AI radar, their capacious fuselages had ample room for the quite bulky equipment.

The Short Brothers Rochester factory under attack in September 1940. *Bundesarchiv*

Bristol Beaufighter 1f R2069 initially served with 25 Squadron at North Weald. It was used between 8 September 1940 and 24 August 1941. Note its day camouflage. The designation Mk 1f was allotted to distinguish it from the Coastal Command version, Mk 1c.

Purely by chance, a new version of the Hurricane, the eight-gun Mk IIa, also entered squadron service on 2 September and with No 111, the premier Hurricane squadron. A dozen had reached ASUs in the last week of August, and ten were on hand when, on 3 September, and from Croydon, they first and briefly operated. With a Merlin XX engine the Mk II's top speed was around 335mph at 21,000 feet, but only when the full supercharger was engaged. Mid-September saw these Mk IIs withdrawn for modifications, reissue coming in October and to No 421 Flight for special observation duties.

More immediately successful was the Spitfire Mk II (Merlin XII), first flown from Castle Bromwich in June 1940. The first to use it was No 611 Squadron at Digby, and a few days later No 266 at Wittering began rearming with Mk IIs, whose ceiling and rate of climb showed improvements over the Mk I. Placing the Mk II in 12 Group allowed last-minute snags to be cleared before 611 Squadron flew within the 12 Group Wing. Not many fighters were in the pristine condition of these Mk IIs. After two months of fighting, many Spitfires and Hurricanes were very obviously battle weary, oil-stained, much patched, colours variable like the roundels and fin stripes, and usually in need of very considerable attention. Aircraft suffering from serious battle damage beyond a unit's capacity to repair it were placed in the hands of the Civilian Repair Organisation. Hurricanes and Spitfires were taken to Morris Motors at Oxford and de Havilland at Witney for rebuilding and modification, Rolls-Royce helping too – mainly with engines. After test flying, the aircraft were passed to MUs for final modifications and checks before being placed in ASUs, mainly at Little Rissington and Brize Norton.

The entry into the Battle of new, superior fighters was very encouraging to the defenders. Incredible as it now seems, the Luftwaffe never made a planned determined attempt to destroy Britain's aircraft and engine factories and storage depots. By this stage of the fight they clearly appreciated their folly. So, on 4 September, after further morning raids on irrelevant airfields, heavily protected Do 17s and He 111s headed for targets in Kent, including Short's Rochester aerodrome. A small group of low-flying, bomb-carrying Bf 110s of ZG 76 crossed the coast at Littlehampton, then made for the Brooklands Hurricane factory. Hurricanes of 253 Squadron[183] patrolling near Guildford, and using Observer Corps information, swooped upon the 110s, destroying six. Confusion overtook the remainder at their target as they hurled their bombs into the Vickers Wellington factory, killing eighty-eight and causing more than 700 casualties as a result of heavy machinery, materials and glass being hurled around factory shops. The intention was that Bf 110s and 109s of Erpr 210, after attacking Poling CH station, would provide withdrawal cover for ZG 76. Instead, RAF fighters dealt effectively with the escort, picking off its Gruppenkommandeur and forcing ZG 76 to find its own way home.

There were two main raids on the South East on 5 September, the first between 10.15 and 10.45 being directed at targets in the suburbs of south-east London. In a second and more serious phase, between 15.15 and 16.30 Detling aerodrome was bombed and five oil tanks at Thameshaven set on fire. That came to serve as a useful beacon, despite the efforts of 43 and 303 Squadrons to prevent the bombing. During the engagement Flight Lieutenant A. Rabagliati of 46 Squadron took a four-

Hornchurch Spitfires at the start of September 1940. ZD-D of 222 Squadron is X4278.
XT-M X4272 joined 603 Squadron on 31 August and was shot down on 4 September.

cannon Hurricane, V7360, into action for the first time. Operating alongside 249
Squadron, No 46[184] encountered Bf 109s over the Thames Estuary, one being blown
apart by cannon fire. The day's engagements cost Fighter Command twenty-three
aircraft written off and the Luftwaffe lost three bombers and sixteen Bf 109s.

At night the Luftwaffe roamed almost with impunity over a wide area, many
single aircraft overflying London's IAZ (Inner Artillery Zone). The only
encouragement for the defenders rested in the first night patrol by an AI-equipped
FIU Beaufighter. That was of little consequence to the people of Greenwich, where
fires were started at the Green & Silley Weir buildings. Shops and buildings in
Clifton, Bristol, were hit and four people killed, while at Liverpool bombs found
the docks, Dunlop's Walton works, domestic buildings and shops in Bootle, Lime
Street station and Rainhill Mental Hospital. At Prescot, St Helens, four died, and
others in incidents at Birkenhead, Wallasey and Wigan.

In the last few days, five forward airfields and six 11 Group Sector Stations had
been damaged. Another week of such activity and London would be laid bare for
destruction. There were still surprises though, one occurring at 18.00 on 6 September
when a few Ju 87s – two of which were claimed by Wing Commander Victor Beamish
– helped stoke the beacon fires at Shell Mex, Thameshaven. There were two main
operations that day, the first coming between 09.00 and 10.00 when No 303 Polish
Squadron[185], tackling Ju 88s and Do 17s over Kent, together with 249 Squadron[186], was
set upon by Bf 109s, which quickly disposed of five Hurricanes. Such heavy losses
meant replacement by completely new, inexperienced squadrons whose losses would
certainly rapidly mount. The alternative was to briefly rest the remainder of a fractured
squadron before posting its more experienced fliers into squadrons in the thick of a fight
that still showed no sign of abatement that day and cost the RAF twenty-three fighters.
The Luftwaffe lost thirty-three aircraft, eight of them bombers. Main rail lines at Oxted
and Caterham had been slightly damaged, as well as Hawker at Brooklands and
Pobjoy's Rochester works. While the intensity of attacks might have eased, relentless
pressure over many weeks had produced battle weariness throughout 11 Group. Only a
respite could cure it, and that seemed most unlikely.

Bf 110 U8+CL, Nr 2146 of IIZG 26, ended its days at 09.30 on Cannons Hill golf course, Coulsdon, Surrey, on 6 September 1940. U8+FL is in the distance, and the tail of an Fw 58 is visible. Both 110s belonged to 3. Staffel, I Gruppe based at Yvrech/Conteville. *Bundesarchiv*

Double Summer Time – surely a splendid idea – meant that it was barely dark when at 20.43 bombs fell on West Ham. Others following damaged houses, railway lines and the Victoria Docks and caused fifty-five casualties. More bombing overtook Woolwich, Southwark and London's south-east suburbs, where more than seventy casualties were caused before the night's bombing petered out. Nevertheless, there was not the slightest indication that London was on the threshold of what had so long been dreaded. Probably nobody realised that what was most feared would provide a miraculous turning point in the war.

RAF losses during operations 26 August-31 August 1940

a = failed to return/shot down, b = written off as a battle casualty, c = seriously damaged

Aug/Sept	26			27			28			29			30		
Type	a	b	c	a	b	c	a	b	c	a	b	c	a	b	c
Blenheim F	–	–	–	–	–	–	–	–	–	–	–	–	–	–	–
Defiant	3	–	–	–	–	–	4	–	1	–	–	–	–	–	–
Hurricane	14	–	1	–	1	–	6	–	1	6	–	–	10	–	1
Spitfire	7	2	3	1	–	–	7	–	–	3	–	–	10	4	2
Blenheim B	–	–	–	–	–	–	–	–	–	–	–	–	2	–	–
Hampden	2	–	–	–	1	–	1	–	–	1	–	–	1	–	–
Wellington	–	–	–	1	–	–	–	–	–	–	–	–	1	1	–
Whitley	1	–	–	–	–	–	–	–	–	–	–	–	1	–	–
Coastal Cmd	–	–	–	2	–	–	3	–	–	1	–	–	–	–	–
Totals	27	2	4	4	2	–	21	–	2	10	–	–	25	5	3

Aug/Sept	31			Totals		
Type	a	b	c	a	b	c
Blenheim F	–	–	–	1	0	0
Defiant	–	–	–	7	0	1
Hurricane	24	1	–	60	2	3
Spitfire	6	3	2	34	9	7
Blenheim B	3	–	–	5	0	0
Hampden	1	–	–	6	1	0
Wellington	–	–	–	2	1	0
Whitley	–	–	–	2	0	0
Coastal Cmd	2	–	–	8	0	0
Totals	36	4	2	125	13	11

Luftwaffe losses during operations 26 August-31 August 1940

a = shot down, b = crashed during sortie, c = seriously damaged

August	26			27			28			29			30		
Type	a	b	c	a	b	c	a	b	c	a	b	c	a	b	c
Do 17P	1	–	–	1	–	–	–	–	–	–	–	–	1	–	–
Do 17Z	4	7	3	–	1	–	2	2	–	2	2	–	–	1	–
Do 215	–	–	–	–	–	–	–	–	–	–	–	–	1	–	–
He 59	1	–	–	–	–	–	2	–	–	–	–	–	–	–	–
He 111H	–	1	–	1	–	–	–	5	2	1	1	1	11	–	–
He 111P	4	1	–	–	–	–	–	1	–	–	1	–	–	1	–
He 115	–	–	–	–	–	–	–	–	–	–	–	2	–	–	–
Ju 88	1	2	–	1	1	–	–	2	–	–	1	–	–	–	–
Bf 109	15	1	–	–	–	1	15	–	–	7	2	–	13	1	1
Bf 110	3	1	–	–	–	–	–	–	–	–	–	–	4	–	–
Totals	29	13	3	3	2	1	19	10	2	10	7	3	30	3	1

August	31			Grand total August		
Type	a	b	c	a	b	c
Do 17P	1	–	–	5	0	0
Do 17Z	4	2	1	48	7	7
Do 215	–	–	–	1	0	0
He 59	–	–	–	5	1	0
He 111H	–	–	–	35	11	4
He 111P	–	–	–	20	4	2
He 115	–	–	–	1	0	2
Ju 88	–	1	1	49	9	13
Bf 109	19	2	–	139	16	15
Bf 110	8	1	2	95	6	18
Totals	32	6	4	398	54	61

**Luftwaffe units, aircraft types, identity letters and bases –
Luftwaffe, 7 September 1940**

Luftflotte 2

BOMBERS

KG 1	He 111	V4	Stab/Rosieres-en-Santerre, I/Montdidier, Clairmont, II/Montdidier, Nijmegen
	Ju 88		III/Rosieres-en-Santerre
Kg 2	Do 17Z	U5	Stab/St Leger, I/Cambrai, II/St Leger, III/Cambrai
KG 3	Do 17Z	5K	Stab/Le Culot, I/Le Culot, II/Antwerp-Duerne, III/St Trond
KG 4	He 111	5J	Stab and I/Soesterburg, II/Eindhoven
	Ju 88		III/Schiphol
KG 26	He 111	1H	Stab and II/Gilze-Rijen, I/Courtrai and Moerbeke
KG 30	Ju 88	4D	Stab and I/Brussels Evere, II/Gilze-Rijen
KG 40	Ju 88	F8	Stab/Bordeaux-Merignac
KG 53	He 111	A1	Stab/I/II/III Lille complex
KG 76	Do 17Z	F1	Stab and III/Cormeilles, I/Beauvais-Tille, II/Creil
KG 77	Ju 88	3Z	Stab and I/III/Laon, II/Asch
KGr 126	He 111	1T	Minelayers
StG 1	Ju 87/Do 17	J9	Stab/St Pol
	Ju 87		Pas de Calais complex
StG 2	Ju 87/Do 17	T6	Stab/Tramecourt
	Ju 87		II/St Omer, St Trond
LG 1	Ju 87	L1	IV/Tramecourt
	Bf 109E		II/St Omer

FIGHTERS

JG 1	Bf 109E		Stab/Pas de Calais complex
JG 3	Bf 109 E		Stab, I, II, III/Pas de Calais complex
JG 26	Bf 109E		Stab and I/Pas de Calais, II/III/north-east France
JG 27	Bf 109E		Stab and I/Etaples, II/Montreuil, III/Sempy
JG 51	Bf 109E		Stab, I, II/St Omer and St Inglevert, III/Pas de Calais
JG 52	Bf 109E		Stab and I/Laon-Couvron, II and III/Pas de Calais
JG 53	Bf 109E		Stab and III/northern France, II/Wissant
JG 54	Bf 109E		Stab/I/II/III/Netherlands
JG 77	Bf 109E		I/northern France
ZG 2	Bf 110	25	I/Amiens and Caen, II/Guyancourt and Caudran
ZG 26	Bf 110	U8	I/Abbeville and St Omer, II/Crecy, III/Barley and Arques
LG 1	Bf 110	L1	V/Ligescourt, Alençon
Erprobungsgruppe			
210	Bf 109 and 110	S9	Denain

Luftflotte 2

RECONNAISSANCE

1(F)/22	Do 17/Bf 110	4N	Lille
1(F)/122	Ju 88 F6	S6	Schiphol
2(F)/122	Ju 88/He 111		Melsbroek
3(F)/122	Ju 88/He 111		Eindhoven
4(F)/122	Ju 88/He 111/Bf 110		Melsbroek
5(F)/122	Ju 88/He 111		Haute-Fontaine

COASTAL PATROL/MINELAYER

1/ and 2/106	He 115	M2	Brest-Poulmiac
3/106	He 115		Borkum

Luftflotte 3

BOMBERS

LG 1	Ju 88	L1	Stab, I, II/Orleans-Bricy, III/Chateaudun
KG 27	He 111	1G	Stab and I/Tours, II/Dinard and Bourges, III/Rennes
KG 40	Fw 200	F8	I/Bordeaux-Merignac
KG 51	Ju 88	9K	Stab, II/Paris-Orly, I/Melun, III/Etampes
KG 54	Ju 88	B3	Stab and I/Evreux, II/St André
KG 55	He 111	G1	Stab and III/Villacoublay, I/Dreux, II/Chartres
KGr 100	He 111	6N	Vannes
KGr 606	Do 17	7T	Brest, Cherbourg
KGr 806	Ju 88	M7	Nantes, Caen/Carpiquet
StG 3	Do 17/He 111	S7	Brittany
	Ju 87		Brittany

FIGHTERS

JG 2	Bf 109		Stab/I/II/Beaumont-le-Roger, III/Le Havre
JG 53	Bf 109		I/Brittany
ZG 76	Bf 110	M9	Stab
	Bf 110	2N	II/Le Mans and Abbeville, III/Laval

RECONNAISSANCE

Aufklärungsgruppen

7(F)LG 2	Bf 110	L2	
4(F)/14	Bf 110/Do 17	5F	Normandy
3(F)/31	Bf 110/Do 17	5D	St Brieuc
3(F)/121	Ju 88/ He 111	7A	North-west France
4(F)/121	Ju 88/Do 17		Normandy
1(F)/123	Ju 88/Do 17	4U	Buc
2(F)/123	Ju 88/Do 17		Buc
3(F)/123	Ju 88/Do 17		Buc

Luftflotte 5

II/JG 77	Bf 109E		Southern Norway
(F)/22	Do 17	4N	2, 3/Stavanger
1(F)/120	He 111/Ju 88	A6	Stavanger
1(F)/121	He 111/Ju 88	7A	Stavanger, Aalborg
KF1Gr 506	He 115	S4	1/Stavanger, 2/Trondheim and Tromso, 3/Lyst

Chapter 14

Is London burning?

S ooner or later it was bound to happen to such a near and tempting target. Morning on 7 September brought mainly fighter forays to Folkestone and Hastings and Bf 109s dive-bombing Hawkinge in two lines, killing six civilians with a direct hit on a shelter, then striking at Dover. Not until about 16.30 did the big action begin, when six formations, 160 aircraft, passed over Deal and Dover heading north, followed soon by a second wave of more than 200. Was the Safety Curtain preceding the invasion about to be lifted? Was London about to be destroyed?

Although seen as a tactical blunder in British minds, the destruction of central government, civilian morale and the breakdown of order in London were considered by the Germans to be an essential invasion prerequisite. As for the desecration of London's huge dockland, that came to be viewed as an early shot in the Battle of the Atlantic, which it may well have been. London was most certainly neither bombed in error nor pique, but because of its importance as a sea port, industrial and communications centre, seat of government, and in an attempt to demoralise its population.

The shocking news that the capital had come under harsh attack came on the 6 o'clock news. About an hour and a half later there was a heavy banging on our front door. A neighbour was on a train coming to Cambridge from Liverpool Street and he had witnessed the docks beginning to burn, had seen so much smoke. He was in a very disturbed state because he had heard that the invasion fleet had sailed, and that we should expect anything in the night. It was indeed alarming, even more so when

The tide of battle turned when the enemy shifted its attention to Britain's ports. This reconnaissance photograph shows the Indies Docks, which were easy to find on a bend of the river Thames.
Bundesarchiv

a Home Guard sergeant living nearby went rushing by to his post alongside a viaduct over the river, calling, as he quickly cycled away, 'Cromwell, I think.' Our train traveller had told us that smoke from the bombing was visible many miles away, so my father and I decided to cycle to Hills Road bridge, the highest easy place to reach, in order to see if anything was visible.

Dusk fell around 20.00 and when we reached the bridge many others were there. As darkness closed in we could see, 60 miles away, the sky fluctuating in colour between deep red and quite bright yellow. It was very disturbing because everyone was saying that this was the start of the invasion. Once home we had the arsenal to look to, and it seemed likely we might soon be using it.

Tempestuous, horrific ... not since the 1666 Great Fire had London been subjected to such terrible destruction. Fires started by the Luftwaffe around tea-time on Saturday afternoon, 7 September, were long visible over 60 miles away. So thick and black was the smoke that it delivered darkness to London's East End long before night was due. Soon it smothered the sky over a third of the world's greatest city. Ironically, the conflagrations kindled not the alarm intended, but even greater determination to beat the Nazis, to win through. Far from lowering morale as was intended, it boosted it throughout the land. No cowering, no failure by all to face and tackle horrendous situations, no ridiculous counselling or health and safety nonsense – just defiant desire to get to grips with 'that 'itler' and make him pay for the evil now being dispensed.

As 11 Group had scrambled fourteen squadrons, 12 Group another four, that giant German perpetrating swarm had swung north-westerly to approach London's East End along Old Father Thames. At 17.15 their first loads were released, on Beckenham. Next it was on Nunhead, hitting three factories and rail links. By 17.30 bombs from another group of bombers had smashed into Rochford, Brentwood, then

Dornier 17Zs crossing the Thames and heading for Woolwich Arsenal on 7 September. *IWM*

Dartford, and into Stone, where children became imprisoned when a shelter was hit. A few minutes later Anglo-American Oil Company installations at Purfleet were rent asunder, causing a colossal petroleum fire that engulfed the site. Nearby, Thamesboard Mills was soon blazing. High explosives fired Jurgen's margarine works, tore apart Cory's Wharf and battered a berthed vessel, although no ships were sunk. Shell-Mex and BP oil installations at Shorehaven were by then flaming fantastically, and casualties everywhere were mounting fast – and the Luftwaffe had barely commenced its angry orgy.

Massed in rectangular formations composed of vics three abreast, line astern, and surrounded by hosts of fighters in two or more layers above and to the rear, the armada approaching from north-east and south to bomb both shores of the Thames was an impregnable force. Neither Fighter Command nor the 1,026 rounds of heavy-calibre AA shells fired by the ZE, ZS and ZW batteries could prevent its intent or tear the formations apart.

By 17.50 bombs by the score were screaming down, tumbling closer to the centre of London, onto Woolwich, lighting an ominous thirteen fires at 'the Arsenal'. Siemens' factory (unlike its Berlin relation) was soon burning, sewers were torn and Harland & Wolff in North Woolwich was battered. In Plumstead station a train was hit, and at Falconwood carriages were derailed. More bombs fell at Crayford as the Luftwaffe pressed on towards its main target, dockland.

Try as it might, Fighter Command could not stop the firing of the docks. A No 615 Squadron Hurricane is seen returning from an engagement. *IWM*

Small groups of bombers that had earlier left the main groups were meanwhile pounding Camberwell, Croydon, Putney and Kensington. A feint towards the Solent had turned back now that the main force was closing in upon the biggest prize.

Before 6 o'clock Goering's bomb-aimers had the warehouses of the Royal Albert Docks, East and West India Docks, London Docks and Surrey Commercial Dock in their sights and they unleashed horrendous terror upon them. Upper Quebec Shed and others in the Surrey Docks erupted into masses of flame, which soon covered a square mile. Mammoth explosions shattered Millwall Dry Dock, and so enormous were the blast storms that huge pieces of masonry floated around, producing terrifying sounds. For many, many hours tiny fragments of glass danced around, some hideously scratching the eyes of the unfortunate. Serious fires engulfed the East India Dock, Whitechapel's London Docks and Royal Victoria Dock, mercifully killing but four and wounding fifty-eight people. An enemy aircraft was said to have plunged into the heart of the South West India Dock, where there had been an instant inferno. King George V Dock's vital entry lock gate was battered, and within just a few minutes the entire dock area and a very large number of homes were within a mass of smoke and fire. Terrible was the weeping, for many had lost their dearest old and young, and all too many were trapped beyond hope of recovery, including some in West Ham's public shelters, of which there were too few. Indeed, many hurried to take shelter in railway tunnels or viaducts, which offered little protection. That long-awaited attack had, in the end, come so suddenly, so unexpectedly, and was judged so serious, that an hour later the Army was indeed warned 'invasion imminent'.

Bombing of the Royal Victoria Dock caused huge fires there and across the Thames. *Bundesarchiv*

By early evening the docks were burning fiercely behind the Tower of London.

From 7 and into 8 September huge fires raged in the Royal Docks and by the Thames, where they were fought from the river as much as the land. .A burning barge has been towed into midstream while warehouses not far from Tower Bridge are being gutted. *IWM*

Serious fires had taken hold in Barking, and the major Beckton gasworks had received such a heavy pasting that supplies to much of East London were seriously reduced. A potentially highly explosive situation there was narrowly averted. Extensive damage had been done to the railway system of East and South East London. In Bermondsey, where eleven had soon died and thirty-five were injured, two giant fires were reclassified as 'conflagrations'. Southwark had immediately reported forty-three casualties, and there were forty-six in the Canal Bridge area of Camberwell. In many parts there was less certainty, but thousands had received a wide assortment of injuries.

As the fires raged, some consuming mills and many quite out of control as darkness spread over the surreal scene, widespread diversionary bombing of Kent took place. It was far worse than anything ever experienced in the British Isles – and much more was soon to follow.

Surviving raiders homed to their lairs at around 18.30-19.00. An hour and a half later, radar detected fresh activity, this time in the Fécamp-Caen area, Luftflotte 3's region, from which tracks were soon crossing the coast near Shoreham before more were spotted heading for Beachy, Dungeness, Sussex, Kent, Essex – and all bound for Greater London.

At 20.50 the first bomber entered the IAZ, whose guns commenced firing at 21.06. Continuously the raiders came, three to eight at a time, to deposit their torment upon London's fires in the most intensive bombing of any British city so far. They stoked and extended earlier conflagrations, lit huge new fires, and brought grotesque and unimaginable horror and grief to shattered lives, homes and livelihoods, particularly in the poorest parts of the East End. In Bethnal Green a large shelter in Columbia Market received a direct hit. A train in Victoria station was hit too and the driver killed. Silvertown became 'a raging inferno' when it was overtaken by possibly the most horrific event in hours of horror. As Tate & Lyle burned furiously, sugar and molasses burst out of containers and slowly oozed into the streets, then sneaked into homes like glowing molten lava. So terrible was the situation that Silvertown had to be completely evacuated, mainly by boat, which gave its people a view of their homes being incinerated and an image surely unimaginably bad and never to be forgotten.

During the night phase many incendiaries had been dropped, particularly on the docks at West Ham, on Poplar, Liverpool Street station, Stepney and other areas on the north side of the river. By dawn, with more than 500 HEs reported as well as UXBs, 600 fire appliances had been in operation. Confirmed casualties totalling 292 killed were nowhere near as high as feared, but 1,285 had been seriously injured and not all would pull through. Estimates were for 320 and 1,349 respectively.

At 22.00 11 Group had agreed for AA gunners to commence firing at fixed azimuth targets, and 10 minutes later a raider was brought down west of Barking, possibly by Site ZE2 or Cheshunt gunners. A second bomber, an He 111 of KG 4, crashed at 23.18 in the Thames at Ref Q9897, off Purfleet. The Luftwaffe had acted almost with impunity.

Not until 04.30 did the last bomber leave London, which had thus endured 10 hours of bombardment. A handful of attackers had also visited Birmingham, Liverpool and South Wales, and mined off Norfolk. At Waddington aerodrome an intruder engaged a landing Hampden bomber before strafing the airfield.

London's defenders, 16.00-18.30 7 September 1940

According to the relevant squadron Operations Record Books, the aircraft used were as follows:

No 1 Squadron Hurricanes: V7379, P2548, V7301, V7258, P3395, V7377, P5199, V7256, P3318 V7376, P3396, P2751, P3406

No 19 Squadron Spitfires: P9386, P9546, K9967, N3199, P9431, X4059, P9391

No 41 Squadron Spitfires: X4345, P9500, R6697, N3059, R6756, N3266, X4318, V5346 No 43 Squadron Hurricanes: V6541, P3466, P3386, others uncertain

No 46 Squadron Hurricanes: V7360, V6582, V7438, R4074, P3525, V7409

No 66 Squadron Spitfires: X4320, N3225, X4321, L1083, X4376, R6925

No 72 Squadron Spitfires: i) K9847, X4254, K9841, R6710, R7022, X4252, P9460; ii) second response by R6710, K9841, X4337, P9460, X4252

No 73 Squadron Hurricanes: identity uncertain

No 79 Squadron Hurricanes: six aircraft of 'A' Flight, identities uncertain

No 111 Squadron Hurricanes: identity uncertain

No 222 Squadron Spitfires (with No 603): N3169, P9364, X4058, P9324, X4024, N3203, X4249, L1031, X4089, P9397, X4275

No 234 Squadron Spitfires: X4009, P9319, R6959, P9320, N3057, N3191, X4251, R6957, X4036, P9466, R6986

No 242 Squadron Hurricanes: P2967, P3087, P3281, P3090, P3054, V7203, 2884, P3207, P3061, P3715, P3718, P3048

No 249 Squadron Hurricanes: V6559, V6610, V6574, P3594, V7313, R4230, V6534, R4114, P3579, V6614, V6628, P5206

No 253 Squadron Hurricanes: i) P5172, P2883, P2865, P5179, V6637, P3551, P3580, P5184, P3537;' ii) second response by P2883, P5172, P3580, 2686, V6637, P5184, V7441, P2865, V6683, P5179

No 257 Squadron Hurricanes: P3893, P3620, V7298, V7254, 4088, P3049, P3775, P3776

No 303 Squadron Hurricanes (with No 1 Squadron): V7290, V6605, V7242, V7244, R2685, V7235, R4127, P3975, R4173, P3890, V7289

No 1 Squadron RCAF (with 303 and 1 Squadrons): P3859, L1973, P3670, V6671, P3081, V7228, V6603, P3534, V6609, P3647, P3876, V6670

No 501 Squadron Hurricanes: P3397, P5193, R4105, V6545, V7403, V7357, P2760, P2329, L1572, V6645, P3605

No 504 Squadron Hurricanes: P3614, N2481, P3429, P2987, P3774 all made two sorties; L1945 operated on first response only

No 602 Squadron Spitfires: L1040, N3198, N3228, R4162, P9515, X4270, P9510, K9839, N3282, P9446, R6965, X4256

No 603 Squadron Spitfires: X4250, X4259, K9963, X4274, L1057, X4324, P9499, N3267, P9440, X4323, N3196, X4263

No 609 Squadron Spitfires: X4107, R6915, R6961, N3223, K9841, N3280, L1096, R6691, X4234, K9997, N3113

Night bombing 7-8 September: main incidents

County Hall

Crayford: gas main fired

Dagenham: Ford Company

Erith: services hit

Edmonton: Grosvenor Bridge

Falconwood: railway station

Finsbury

Greenwich: Vacuum Oil Co

Islington: public shelter

King George V Dock

Lewisham

London Dock No 10 Warehouse

London Hospital

Minories

Nine Elms goods yard

Plaistow

Royal Albert Dock: No 25 Shed

Royal Victoria Dock: three warehouses gutted

Premier Empire and Vernon Mills

Poplar: LNER bridge and Bow Road

Rotherhithe Tunnel

Stepney

St Thomas's Hospital

Whitechapel Fire Station

Battersea Power Station: major damage

Bermondsey: Bricklayers Arms Southern Railway depot

Bethnal Green: Hackney Road, Columbia Market shelter

Paddington: Harrow Road

Shadwell: Badger's Highway

Twickenham: timber yard fire

Waterloo Bridge

Wapping: Colonial Wharf

Wimbledon: train set on fire

Woolwich: Royal Dockyard

Westminster: Victoria Street, Vauxhall Bridge Road, Victoria station

Railways blocked: London Bridge-New Cross; Waterloo-Clapham junction blocked by UXBs; Borough High Street (bombs near gunpowder factory)

Throughout the night the whole country was held on high alert, the invasion expected to start at any time. In a few country parishes church bells were rung in expectation after 'Cromwell' was signalled. Alert State No 2 required all Service personnel to be recalled from leave. At 00.10, under Alert No 1, 'imminent action' was now signalled. Of our Home Guard neighbour there was no sign: he was guarding the bridge and watching out for Nazis parachuting in dressed as nuns!

We were up very early in the morning in case there was news of invasion. Instead there was nothing to report, no news of any barges arriving and no Ju 52s on the local common.

An important question was would the scale, success and low cost of the London night raid cause the enemy to reduce or increase his daylight effort? Daylight on the 8th witnessed two attacks on South East England. In the first a formation attacked the coastal area around North Foreland-Rye in what looked like an invasion softening-up raid, while small numbers made for Sheppey and the London area. Not until 19.30 was the next raid mounted, and by only thirty aircraft, which crossed

Beachy towards London while reconnaissances were flown to Bedford and Hornchurch. With only limited daylight activity, it seemed certain that London was going to suffer another night of pounding. Around 19.45 came the first representatives of Luftflotte 3, heading in from the Le Havre area. An hour later a steady stream was overflying Selsey and Shoreham, and soon a continuous average of five raiders passed across the IAZ until 05.00 – except for a brief lull around 01.00. Every Metropolitan borough and sixty local authority areas reported bomb damage. Large fires overtook Berger Paints in Homerton, Madame Tussauds and premises in Baker Street. Three hospitals were hit, Fulham Power Station was set on fire and many bombs dropped indiscriminately fell close to the Thames. Major incidents occurred at Acton, Leyton, Poplar and Broad Street station. The Embankment was flooded at Chelsea. Yet still there was no sign of the invasion.

A new pattern of attacks was clearly evolving, for on 9 September there was again little enemy activity until late afternoon, when a large formation bombed London suburbs south of the river as well as targets in Kent, including Canterbury. Behind them they left small fires in Barnes, Epsom, Maldon, Purley and Richmond and blocked roads in Kingston. Wandsworth, Surbiton, Lambeth, Fulham and Chelsea had also been hit.

As dusk settled, London braced itself for what was becoming a nightly event. Clearly, all means of transport were under attack and communications were prime targets, suggesting that the invasion build-up was continuing. Private houses also suffered badly. Major fires took hold at the Barbican, in West Ham, at Woolwich Arsenal and Greenwich, where a cordite shop at Batley's exploded. Ludgate Hill,

Plan 'Banquet Light' – or
'How to gently Devour the Invaders'

One of the ideas for utilising every available resource to counter invading forces was Plan 'Banquet Light', for which the Air Ministry authorised (only) offensive use of Flights of five Tiger Moth and Magister elementary trainers, each armed with eight 20lb F (fragmentation) bombs. Each flown by an instructor, these trainers would have given HQ Home Forces an additional strike force whose role was to dive- or level-bomb troops trying to disembark or land and to attack initial inland penetrations. Attached to and controlled by army co-operation Lysander squadrons, the light aircraft would have operated from their aerodromes or advanced landing grounds. Each pilot would have taken a passenger to his operational base, the latter's task being preparing and bombing-up of the aircraft by drawing upon 4,800 gallons of petrol, 240 gallons of oil and the 2,000 F bombs specially available at each Lysander base.

These unarmed, unarmoured trainers would have depended upon their manoeuvrability to survive. While pilots were authorised to commence their dives at 1,500 feet at up to 60 degrees, their bombs could not safely be dropped from below 650 feet, although plans were for a developed weapon to be delivered from a mere 50 feet! In any case, getaway was, for safety's sake, to be at very low level. Bombing practice was undertaken at the home training school.

Schools and their designated operational stations as on 13 August 1940

Command EFTS/Base	No of Flights*	Lysander Squadron/Base affiliation
Southern		
No 2 Staverton	1	No 225 Tilshead
No 3 Watchfield	1	No 225 Tilshead
No 10 Weston-super-Mare	2	No 16 Weston Zoyland
No 13 White	2	No 110 Canadian, Waltham Odiham
Eastern		
No 1 Hatfield	2	No 239 Hatfield
No 6 Sywell	2	No 2 Sawbridgworth
No 8 Woodley	1	No 26 Gatwick
No 18 Fairoaks	1	No 26 Gatwick
No 22 Cambridge	2	No 268 Bury St Edmunds
Northern		
No 4 Brough	2	No 4 York
No 9 Ansty	2	No 613 Firbeck
No 21 Desford	2	No 4 York
Western		
No 14 Elmdon	2	No 13 Hooton Park
Scottish		
No 11 Perth	2	No 241 Inverness
No 12 Prestwick	2	No 614 Grangemouth

* each Flight had a reserve of at least two aircraft

Cheapside, Fenchurch Street and Cannon Street, all were hit, together with parts of Bow, Lambeth and Southwark during bombing that still concentrated on the East End. At Charing Cross station a bomb spectacularly penetrated a platform and closed the Embankment. Many bombs acted unpredictably, often causing damage unrelated to their size and type, or failed to explode for a host of reasons. Detonations above ground were particularly terrifying. Some even slipped in through small toilet windows, then bounced downstairs. Others exploded high in trees or low in sewers and mains. Fractured sewers and water pipes brought health alarms. Shattered gas mains erupted with mighty flashes and incredibly loud bangs followed by masses of fire. Luckily, many Londoners had corrugated iron Anderson shelters in their gardens, and there were public shelters. Some sheltered in basements, which in a number of instances – like the public shelters – received direct hits with consequences too bad to relate. Probably the safest of all places were underground stations, where increasing numbers spent the night. They then had uncertainties to face at dawn.

Night bombing of London, 8/9 September 1940

Acton marshalling yards

Bank of England

Bushey School

Chelsea Embankment

Deptford Royal Victualling Yard

Hackney: two factories seriously damaged

Holborn

Homerton: Burger Paints

Poplar: Green & Silley Weir Ltd, Institution, District Railway

Mansion House

Metal Box Factory

Lindley Aircraft Co

Shoreditch Road: blocked, shelter hit, fires

St Pancras: blocked

Stepney: British Oil Cake Mills, Sutton's Wharf

Stoke Newington: serious flooding

Broad Street station: all lines cut

Fulham Power Station

Baker Street: Chiltern Court, Madame Tussauds

City: Great Arthur Street, King William Street, Lombard Street to Adelaide Place, London Bridge, near Bank of England and Mansion House

Islington: services and sewer cuts

Westminster: Odhams Press

Law Courts

Knightsbridge Barracks

Green Park and St James's

Constitution Hill: UXBs, also in Buckingham Palace Gardens

Natural History Museum: fire

Desoutter Co: fire

Battersea: railway between Queen's Road and Clapham Junction

Bombing of London, 9 and 9/10 September 1940: main incidents

Surbiton: Kingston Bypass

Barnes station: No 1 Platform

Stainer Road, Heston: military training centre

Hounslow Heath

Silley Weir, Poplar: second fire

Shoreditch: near St Leonard's Hospital

West Ham: LNER station

Greenwich: Deptford Bridge

Camberwell: LCC Estate

Bow High Street

Southwark: St George's Road and New Kent Road

Bloomsbury: Guildford Street

Woolwich: Rochester Way and roundabout blocked

Charing Cross: No 2 track

Stepney: rail bridge

Nine Elms goods yard

Greenwich: Royal Naval College

Crayford: Vickers

East Ham: power station

Somerset House

Fenchurch Street station

Westminster Embankment

Something to sing about?

Relatively few songs of 1940 have achieved lasting success, and in any case few were recorded in British studios that year. Little of the sheet music, 6d for a large format copy, has survived. How many of these songs can you recall?

Let the people sing; It's a lovely day tomorrow; I'm nobody's baby; Memories live longer than dreams; Can't get Indiana off my mind; Arm in arm; My sister and I; Careless; No, mama, no; I hear a dream; Where the blue begins; We'll go smiling along; I'm in love for the last time; You made me care; Get happy; It's a blue world; In a little rocky valley; Sing a round-up song; Too romantic; Moonlight avenue; They call me a dreamer; With the wind and the rain in her hair; The memory of a rose; Faithful, forever; There'll come another day; Our love affair; You gorgeous, dancing doll; If I only had wings; I've got my eyes on you; There goes that song again; I was watching a man paint a fence; Fools rush in.

There was just a handful of lasting songs: *Deep purple; Over the rainbow, When you wish upon a star; Blueberry Hill; If I should fall in love again;* and *A nightingale sang in Berkeley Square.*

Some 1939 titles were very popular in 1940, among them: *There'll always be an England; We'll meet again; Moonlight serenade; Little brown jug; Stairway to the stars; In the mood; My prayer;* and *Indian summer.*

The bombing of London quickly brought an enormous change to the progress of the campaign. There were fresh variations including increased night-intruder operations against British bomber bases. On 9/10 September alone intruders fired upon a Blenheim over Alconbury, a Hampden over Scampton and a Wellington landing at Marham. By Cambridge airport incendiaries burned near squadrons of anti-invasion Lysanders, and over the next few weeks night intrusions directed against bomber stations showed a steady increase. Events quite different from those commonly recalled were widely occurring.

Daylight operations on the 10th began in the now traditional way with lone armed reconnaissance flights. Convoy attacks off East Anglia followed, as well as sharp raids on coastal towns including Great Yarmouth and Hastings, and raids on West Malling and Woolwich. Was this activity preluding the invasion? The Southern Railway power station at Newhaven was also hit, before late afternoon saw a build-up begin over France. About 300 aircraft crossed at about 16.55 between Dover and North Foreland. 'Six were reported to be four-engined bombers with strong fighter escort,' read the official summary, most swinging west to stream across south London, bombing here and there while another group of about thirty entered the IAZ. A small diversion was mounted west of Salisbury. Opposing the Kent incursion were twenty-four RAF fighter squadrons, a far cry from the 'Few' of recent days, for Fighter Command was fast recovering strength. Night brought the usual streams from Cherbourg and the Somme, with about four raiders being over the capital at any one time. Around 02.30 more began arriving from the Low Countries, while Luftflotte 3 attacked Cardiff. It was 04.55 when the 'All Clear' sounded in London.

This effort of the Germans to secure daylight mastery of the air over England is, of course, the crux of the whole war. So far it has failed conspicuously ... to try to invade this country without having secured mastery in the air would be a very hazardous undertaking... If this invasion is going to be tried at all, it does not seem that it can be long delayed ... Therefore, we must regard the next week or so as a very important period in our history.

Winston Churchill, 11 September 1940

The events of 11 September brought reminders of earlier days of the Battle. Small-scale attacks involved Portsmouth, Tangmere, Poling and Weymouth. Port Victoria on the Isle of Grain was struck mid-afternoon, by which time about 300 enemy aircraft were heading towards London. Most of them were fighters or fighter-bombers, of which only thirty-six proceeded to bomb the capital before a second, smaller group flew over South East London. Several serious incidents occurred, fires again being started in Woolwich and the Surrey Docks. A public shelter was hit in Lewisham High Street, 100 casualties resulting, and rubble buried fifty people when Deptford Central Hall was hit. UXBs rested at Paddington and Islington. Meanwhile, eight Bf 110s dive-bombed the Cunliffe-Owen aircraft works at Eastleigh, Southampton, killing twenty-eight and injuring seventy when another shelter was hit.

A further reminder of days gone came after convoy CW 11 sailed from Southend Roads at 01.20 on the 11th. Its seven colliers carrying about 10,000 tons of coal and three merchant vessels were being escorted by two destroyers, three armed trawlers and four balloon ships, each with its charge flying at around 1,400 feet. By 16.00 the convoy was provocatively in the Straits, which prompted Cap Gris Nez guns to unsuccessfully blast it. Their shells also pounded Dover, where many houses were damaged. At 18.23 three Bf 109s attacked Dover balloons, then a few minutes later bombers attempted a level attack from 4,000 feet on the convoy. Ten minutes later, near the Goodwins Light Vessel, about twenty enemy aircraft started dive-bombing the escort ships using HE and fire bombs and holing HMS *Atherstone*. The most serious action took place at 19.10 when thirty-four dive-bombers pressed home a daring onslaught on a destroyer. They had scored hits amidships on its engine room before RAF fighters arrived in strength. A trawler towed the destroyer safely to port in another episode reminiscent of weeks ago. But still there was no indication that invasion was near.

Nine hours of night attacks on London by KG 4, KG 27, KG 51, KG 54 and KG 55, although spasmodic, left much major damage. A blaze at St Katherine's Docks raged out of control, and a fire float was sunk at London Dock. Greenwich's Telcon Works was set on fire, and Thomas de la Rue's Star Works gutted. At Poplar the Manganese, Bronze & Brass Company wharf was hit, the rail link south from Holborn was cut, and there were serious factory blazes in Camberwell. Bombs also fell on Aldgate, and at Shadwell, where the east end of the Maternity Hospital was hit. At Stepney two warehouses were incinerated, and a huge timber fire illuminated

Bombing of London, 11 and 11/12 September: main incidents

Smithfield Market

Metropolitan Tea Warehouse, India Street

Southwark: Great Dover Street

Borough High Street, Old Kent Road

Shoreditch: Widlock Brewery, Tapton Street

Holborn Viaduct

Islington: rail lines

Woolwich: Commonwealth Buildings, Arsenal

Hackney: Stamford Hill

Tottenham: Haveley Park to High Road

Deptford: Central Hall, cattle market

Greenwich: Telcon Works

Clapham Junction and Battersea

Central Telegraph Office, St Martins le Grand

Thornton Heath: London Road

Thomas de la Rue Ltd, Bunhill Row, and Star Works

City: Littlebrook and adjoining hospital, St Paul's, Blackfriars

Charing Cross Road

Lambeth: Stockwell Road

East Dulwich: Police Station, Camberwell

Lewisham: Park Hospital

West India Dock: Paddington Basin

Beckenham: Burroughes Welcome Ltd

Deptford Wharf: cattle market, supply depot

Finsbury: Allman Engineering Co

Camberwell: railway arches

Poplar: Manganese, Bronze & Brass Co

Brickley station

Crystal Palace station

London Dock

Mile End. More than 1,000 incendiaries set fire to Woolworths and a convent in Brentwood. Bombing was smashing the lives of many, but not the morale of Londoners. Many minor raids also took place in Lancashire, South Wales, Devon, Cornwall, Buckinghamshire and Hampshire. All the pointers were towards a Luftwaffe conserving strength for the still expected invasion.

On 12 September, HEs exploded around Harrogate's Majestic Hotel, injuring fifteen during an attack on an area where the Ministry of Aircraft Production had offices. GWR main-line services to Reading were interrupted, but an attacker failed to score a hit on Northern Aluminium's Banbury factory. Late afternoon Tunbridge Wells was sharply raided, incendiaries causing house fires and destroying the ambulance station when it was most desperately needed. Seven HEs fell at Hornchurch where the emergency operations room and nearby dwellings were damaged.

At night, widespread bombing of London again was thought to be intended to spread alarm preceding the invasion. London had a 7-hour raid involving about 120 enemy bombers. An Fw 200 attacked a ship off the Isle of Man, and KG 54 mounted a small raid on Rugby. As well as many country areas, Liverpool was bombed but little damage caused. Blackpool North station suffered, and Fulham's telephone exchange received a direct hit. An exploding bomb hurled a water tank onto the track at West Brompton station. In the 24 hours to 06.00 on the 13th listed casualties totalled 168 killed, and 689 seriously injured.

Shipping in Belfast Loch came under attack at 07.00 on the 13th and incendiaries fell on Bangor. Over the 2 hours beginning at 07.30, six single aircraft operated over southern England before raiders arrived at about 8-minute intervals over London. At 11.10 bombs fell at Buckingham Palace – on the quadrangle, at the Chapel, outside the forecourt – injuring four and slightly damaging the Victoria Monument. West Ham's Ravenshill School, where homeless were being accommodated, was hit mid-morning and fifty casualties caused. Ten bombs in Eastbourne's centre started large fires and resulted in twenty casualties. Between 13.00 and 15.00 Biggin Hill and Maidstone attracted scattered raids, one bomber later starting a fire in London's Great Titchfield Street, blocking Euston Road and causing fifty-nine casualties.

The now customary 8-hour night raid on London commenced at 20.45. Although only five night-fighter sorties were flown, Flying Officer M. J. Herrick in ZK-A of 25 Squadron managed to bring down He 111H 5J+BL of 3./KG 4 near North Weald. During the night Lavender Hill GPO sorting office, Wembley's Carrier Engineering Co, Victoria station, Battersea Public Library and many houses in Hammersmith and Mitcham were among places damaged.

Switching to night bombing meant that the Luftwaffe's day raids were often carried out by aircraft with black undersurfaces, like these He 111s including G1+ES of KG 55 which survived the battle to participate in raids on the USSR in 1941. *Bundesarchiv*

Night operations were undoubtedly straining Luftwaffe crews. That became clear when on 14 September, after a quiet morning, two main attacks on London were mounted by high-flying escorted fighter-bombers. The first developed around 15.30 with waves coming in fast between Dover and Ramsgate. About 100 comprising Raid 11 concentrated in the Maidstone-Biggin Hill area, leaving about fifty to bomb London. Into the IAZ flew twenty-five of them, keeping (as Raid 11J) to the south of the river. All had cleared the country by 16.30. Repelling these nuisance raids was demanding, 11 Group fielding twenty-four squadrons and 12 Group four. While the loads they could drop were not all that great, they were a threat that could not be ignored. After bombing, the aircraft reverted to being fighters – and that was an alarming aspect. A similar, smaller operation developed around 18.00 with about sixty bombing in the IAZ. About eighty bombers, fewer than usual, operated against London, suggesting that something big was being prepared.

Luftwaffe losses during operations 1-7 September 1940

a = failed to return/shot down, b = written off, c = seriously damaged

September	1			2			3			4			5		
Type	a	b	c	a	b	c	a	b	c	a	b	c	a	b	c
Do 17Z	1	–	2	1	1	1	1	–	–	–	–	–	–	–	–
Do 18	–	–	–	1	–	–	–	–	–	–	–	–	–	–	1
He 59	–	–	–	–	–	–	–	–	–	–	–	–	–	–	–
He 111H	–	1	4	–	1	2	1	–	5	1	3	4	3	1	3
He 111P	–	–	–	–	–	–	–	–	–	–	–	–	1	–	–
He 115	–	–	–	–	1	–	–	–	–	–	–	–	–	–	–
Ju 87	–	–	–	–	1	–	–	–	–	–	–	–	–	–	
Ju 88	–	1	–	1	1	–	–	–	–	–	1	2	–	–	–
Bf 109	5	1	1	16	4	6	2	2	2	4	4	3	14	3	2
Bf 110	1	–	–	6	1	4	6	3	–	15	1	1	–	–	–
Totals	7	3	7	25	9	11	9	6	4	20	6	6	20	4	6

September	6			7			Total loss in period		
Type	a	b	c	a	b	c	a	b	c
Do 17Z	–	–	–	4	–	2	7	1	5
Do 18	–	–	–	–	–	–	1	0	1
He 59	–	–	–	–	1	–	0	1	0
He 111H	3	4	13	9	14				
He 111P	–	–	–	1	1	–	2	1	0
He 115	–	–	–	1	–	–	1	1	0
Ju 87	–	–	–	–	–	–	0	1	0
Ju 88	2	–	2	2	–	1	5	3	5
Bf 109	15	2	2	14	1	1	70	17	18
Bf 110	4	–	–	8	–	–	40	5	5
Totals	25	5	5	33	6	9	139	39	48

RAF losses during operations 1-7 September 1940

September	1			2			3			4			5		
Type	a	b	c	a	b	c	a	b	c	a	b	c	a	b	c
Blenheim F	–	–	–	–	–	–	1	1	1	–	–	1	–	–	–
Defiant	–	–	–	–	–	–	–	–	–	–	–	–	–	–	–
Hurricane	9	–	6	8	1	10	9	1	9	5	1	7	5	2	9
Spitfire	3	2	5	3	2	8	3	1	1	7	2	8	7	6	7
Blenheim B	–	–	–	2	–	1	1	–	1	2	–	2	2	–	2
Hampden	–	–	–	1	–	–	–	–	1	–	1	–	–	1	1
Wellington	–	–	–	2	1	1	–	–	–	–	–	–	–	–	–
Whitley	–	–	–	1	–	–	1	–	2	1	1	1	–	–	1
Coastal Cmd	1	–	–	3	–	–	–	–	–	–	–	–	–	–	–
Totals	13	2	11	20	4	20	15	3	15	15	5	19	14	9	20

September	6			7			Total loss in period		
Type	a	b	c	a	b	c	a	b	c
Blenheim F	–	–	–	–	–	–	1	1	2
Defiant	–	–	–	–	–	–	0	0	0
Hurricane	13	2	10	13	2	13	62	9	64
Spitfire	5	–	4	8	–	17	36	13	50
Blenheim B	–	1	–	–	–	–	7	1	2
Hampden	5	1	6	1	–	1	7	3	8
Wellington	1	–	1	–	–	–	3	1	5
Whitley	1	–	–	–	–	1	3	1	5
Coastal Cmd	1	1	–	–	–	1	5	–	1
Totals	26	4	21	22	2	33	124	29	137

Chapter 15

Are they coming yet, Dad?

The intensity of the German air assault over the past week had generally been assumed to mean that the invasion was imminent. The question still was 'When?'

At the beginning of September twenty-seven infantry divisions formed the protecting Home Force. Although a dozen were fairly well equipped, the rest were half trained. None of the Mobile Brigades had experienced 'blitzkrieg' warfare. Main reserves in the Midlands were to be drawn upon as forward troops engaged any landing. The RAF would attack support and supply forces. About 500 light tanks, 500 anti-tank/light guns and 350 heavier-type tanks were operational, so the Army was far from well supplied. The LDV – which had become the Home Guard on 31 July – was half a million men strong and was designed to hamper enemy movement. Its younger members had been formed into mobile brigades of a sort, reliant upon motor cycles, commandeered vans and bicycles. Shades, indeed, of a familiar 'Dad's Army', although in reality it was a far better force than is often portrayed. It certainly was not laughed about in 1940, but viewed as a force of faithful men, many men with front-line battle experience, prepared to lay down their lives just like Regular soldiers. By September 1940 many had useful weapons, our neighbours having been supplied with rifles and grenade-launching rifles captured from the Italians in North Africa.

Off the East Coast a mine barrage had been sown, and small minefields barred approaches to many southern ports. Taken all round, the defences were not insignificant. Beaches were mined in likely landing places between The Wash and the South West. Barbed-wire barriers in increasing numbers and varieties decorated the shores.

Composition of RAF Bomber Command by aircraft types, 15 August 1940

Composition of RAF Bomber Command by aircraft types, 15 September 1940

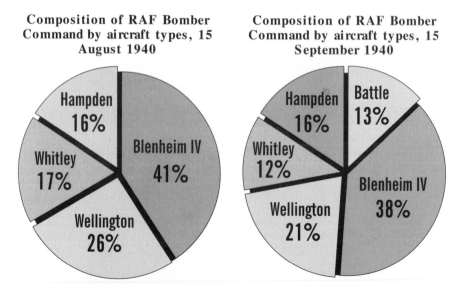

Aircraft available in RAF bomber squadrons, 15 September 1940

A = established, B = serviceable

		Total
Battle	A	96
	B	79
Blenheim IV	A	208
	B	224
Wellington	A	128
	B	119
Whitley	A	80
	B	72
Hampden	A	96
	B	92

By early September the first assault wave was moving into place across the Channel. In ports between Flushing and Le Havre, ships, including motor boats, inland waterway barges and their tugs, had been assembled, a German manifest of 4 September listing 168 transports, 1,600 motor boats, 419 tugs and 1,910 large 'Rhine-type' barges, many stolen from their rightful owners. There were, according to the German Navy, more than enough ships for the task. Everything was to be in place by 19 September, the Navy adding that it would take ten days to lay minefields to prevent flank attacks and generally to prepare for sea. Hitler would therefore need to have given the executive command on 11 September for the assault intended to be launched on the 21st.

For him there were three little snags. The Luftwaffe had still failed to destroy Fighter Command and he did not control the sky over the English Channel. Nor had his forces disposed of the Royal Navy. Hitler therefore advanced the command decision date to 14 September, which gave the Luftwaffe three more days to act decisively. Instead, both 11 and 12 September brought indecisive action, so on the 13th the Navy told Hitler that an invasion was not yet feasible. On 14 September Hitler, on staff advice, postponed authorisation to the 17th. On the 15th senior naval officers rated the event a 'dangerous gamble' after the Luftwaffe was given a hiding on Battle of Britain Day.

Bad weather then rolled in to interfere with minelaying. Even had the go-ahead been given on the 17th – when the RAF was proving itself very much intact and effective – no invasion launch would have been possible before 8 October, due to the need for suitable tidal conditions. There was also the assumption that on the selected day the sea state would allow towed inland watercraft to complete a Channel crossing. Bearing in mind the enormous amount of training and preparation needed to mount the 1944 Allied Normandy landings, one cannot but question the readiness of the Germans to have achieved a successful sea crossing, get ashore, advance, and be capable of supporting such a huge, difficult and hazardous venture.

A German photograph of preparations aboard barges – possibly at Antwerp – and including the *Ascenseur* of Antwerp, the *Ben-Hur* and the *Lea*. Square bows allowed several to be pushed, the straight sides permitting grouping. *Bundesarchiv*

They had made some preparations for air support. The Stuka force had been positioned close to the Dover Straits, and more Bf 109s were available. Luftflotte 5 had been deprived of the He 111s of KG 26 and Ju 88s of KG 30, which were now based in Belgium and the Netherlands. That freed Scotland and its naval anchorages from their unwanted attention. On the morning of 7 September, the day of the first huge London raid, there were serviceable about 600 bombers and 700 fighters in Luftflotte 2 available for independent operations or supporting the 16th Army in its invasion attempt. To its west, Luftflotte 3 held about 350 bombers and 100 fighters. They all needed control of the air over southern England and the Channel; they had neither.

Gazing greedily northwards, the Germans must surely have wondered how Churchill's wretched 'Few' had managed to thwart the vaunted Luftwaffe. The latter's main fault remained their inability to overcome Dowding's skilfully prepared policy and brilliantly conceived defence plan for the United Kingdom. Undoubtedly, they imagined that they could generate enough force and terror to destroy the fighter force and demoralise the most stout-hearted. Their inept intelligence deductions misled them into wasting time and effort attacking the wrong targets. They had not planned their air campaign, whereas the British had. Worse was eventually to come, for a handful of new aircraft designs were well under way.

Not the image one had at the time of German troops training to overcome us. Still, they are showing great spirit – and enjoying themselves. The tug would have been used to push some barges to England – hopefully! *Bundesarchiv*

With the Rolls-Royce Vulture engine in trouble, A. V. Roe during February 1940 reviewed a four-motor version of its Manchester, first considered in 1937. It looked to be a promising idea and in May 1940 the newly formed Ministry of Aircraft Production asked for the project to be fully explored. A new scheme was completed in June 1940, and in July development of a four-engined version of the Avro Manchester bomber was given the go-ahead – but with many official reservations. During the second half of 1940 the prototype was built of what became the Lancaster, so superior to any German bomber. Had the effort directed upon Manchester in December 1940 been directed onto the local A. V. Roe factory the Germans would have very much helped themselves. Instead, the Lancaster first flew a fortnight later, on 9 January 1941.

On 7 May 1940 the first production Short Stirling four-engined bomber flew, and during summer Stirlings underwent trials at Boscombe Down. The first to enter squadron service arrived at Leeming for No 7 Squadron on 3 August. Ten production Stirlings were flying by 15 September, sixteen by the end of December 1940. Unfortunately, the aircraft's weight had dramatically increased and specified engines were still awaited. It did not become operational until February 1941.

During the summer the second prototype Stirling long-range bomber underwent performance trials at Boscombe Down. On 3 August N3640, Bomber Command's first Stirling, arrived at Leeming where 7 Squadron had reformed. Not until February 1941 did the new bomber fly operationally.

Also flying by 1940 was the Handley Page Halifax, the first production example of which flew on 10 October. The design had undergone considerable change, which had delayed development. Only five production Halifaxes had been delivered to the RAF by the end of 1940. Delivery of the third new bomber type, the Avro Manchester, started in November 1940.

Hawker Aircraft had begun work on a new fighter design in 1937, the first version of which, called the Tornado, flew in October 1939. It had the same troublesome Rolls-Royce Vulture engine as Avro's Manchester bomber. On 24 February 1940 another version powered by a 2,200hp Napier Sabre first flew. Both types were developed throughout 1940, the Sabre version emerging as the Typhoon in 1941.

The second prototype Handley Page Halifax L7245 first flew on 16 August 1940. Could this have been misreported as a Junkers four-motor bomber? The first production Halifax was delivered on 12 October, two days after its first flight. Only five had been delivered by the end of 1940.

Big Wing

By the official closing date of the Battle of Britain (31 October) 2,698 German aircraft were claimed as destroyed. Post-war examination of Luftwaffe records suggested 1,733. Comparative German claims amounted to 3,058 British aircraft; 915 fighters is the British official figure. Would the British have scored higher using different tactics?

Dowding sited half his effective fighter force in 11 Group and the South East, relieving squadrons when they tired. There had, however, been smouldering criticism that he should have held more squadrons in 11 Group and adjacent 12 Group Sectors, for the short range of the Bf 109 limited it to day-fighting thereabouts, and the criticism was to flare up after the Battle was won.

Dowding's aerodromes had insufficient room for more squadrons and would have easily become congested, ideal targets, and would have left other parts of Britain wide open to attack. Supporting, maintaining and operating more squadrons would not have been easy. Coastal convoys, highly vulnerable to attack, had to be covered, even escorted. Fighter conservation was essential too, for there was no early indication of the length of the campaign. In consequence Park had to field small responses during much of the Battle.

Both Dowding and Park were criticised for their work, particularly by the rather forceful Air Vice-Marshal Trafford Leigh-Mallory, No 12 Group commander. When called upon to aid 11 Group by guarding its territory north of the Thames, 12 Group fielded from Duxford a formation of three, four, even seven squadrons. Usually leading the 12 Group contribution was Squadron Leader Douglas Bader, who had lost both legs as a result of a flying accident in 1931. By 'stealth', together with courage, tenacity and the skilful use of his two metal legs, he had managed to resume flying duties on the outbreak of war and spent a while at Duxford in 1939 before in the summer of 1940 taking command of Coltishall's 242 Squadron, which generally led Leigh-Mallory's formation.

There was considerable support in the Air Ministry for the 'large formation' and when the differences of opinion began to be strongly aired the Air Staff ordered an enquiry. The heart of the matter was that the two Group commanders faced very different threats. Park, often receiving only a few minutes warning of attack, had to respond fast, his squadrons sometimes taking off as bombs fell on their airfields. They rarely had time to unite prior to combat, whereas 12 Group had ample warning time, allowing its squadrons to formate prior to engaging. It was paramount for 11 Group squadrons to guard their bases as well as engage incoming raids, and difficult even for squadrons to pair off in time for action. Initial interception by 11 Group squadrons undoubtedly raised 12 Group's success rate. The 12 Group squadrons could not resist the temptation to score more by chasing raiders well into the 11 Group area, thus leaving northern 11 Group stations unprotected. The size of 12 Group formations confused the raid reporting and controlling system into mistaking them for enemy forces, resulting in wasted and dangerous effort. So went the arguments.

The outcome was undoubtedly harsh, for in November 1940 both Dowding and Park were 'rested', the former joining the British Mission in the USA and Park being given a post, albeit important, in Training Command, before he distinguished himself yet again in Malta. Doubtless they had earned a period of respite after their outstanding, unequalled efforts. Perhaps Leigh-Mallory was a very suitable choice to head 11 Group when it gradually switched to an offensive role requiring large formations. Maybe Air Chief Marshal W. Sholto Douglas, Deputy Chief of the Air Staff, was a sound choice as Dowding's successor. Nevertheless, the changes shocked many at the time and were made in a most ungenerous manner. The British have a poor record in rewarding successful leadership, tantamount to almost punishing it, as in the removal of Dowding and Park after proving such brilliant leaders.

Withdrawal of German bomber units from Norway was soon discovered, which indicated that an invasion of Scotland need no longer be feared. The strength of invasion forces in France and the Low Countries was not precisely known. Discovering it was placed in the hands of RAF Bomber Command, Coastal Command and in particular the Photographic Reconnaissance Unit (PRU), an organisation that has already been referred to.

On 1 July 1940 'A' Flight of the PRU formed and was immediately ordered to Wick to watch from there for movements in Norwegian ports. Its 'B' Flight shifted to St Eval to observe Brest and the west and north-west coasts of France.

Both Flights dispatched their first operational sorties on 3 July. Fine photographs of the Channel ports and French coastal areas taken from Spitfires, flying high and coloured pale pink, cream or light blue, were being secured. Two more Flights, 'C' and 'D', formed on 24 July using Spitfires operated from Heston from where they concentrated upon photographing the Channel ports.

By the end of July seventy-eight sorties had been flown from Heston, fifty-seven of them securing photographs. Another ninety-three were flown in August. Although there were signs of invasion preparations, none appeared far advanced. No barges were evident on photographs produced after a sortie to Ostend by Spitfire R6879 on the 28th, but three days later eighteen had arrived. Within hours, fast build-up of ships and barges was recorded. Between 1 and 4 September about 100 barges arrived at Flushing, and on the 6th and 7th many reached Calais and Dunkirk. On 4 September cameras in the first production Spitfire, K9787, secured pictures of Boulogne, and those in N3117 recorded 270 in Ostend alone on 7 September. This suggested that the invasion was soon to be launched.

Early that evening, while fires raged in Woolwich and London's dockland, the Combined Intelligence Committee met and informed the Chiefs of Staff that tidal conditions favoured an invasion between 8 and 10 September. Invasion believed near, Alert No 1 was signalled widely and at 19.07 on the 7th the codeword 'Cromwell' was flashed to Eastern and Southern Army Commands and GHQ Reserve, but not to the Home Guard. The codeword implied 'imminent action', and when some Home Guard units discovered the alert had been signalled they rang the

Did they really mean to invade us aided by mules? In the highly mechanised, mighty Wehrmacht, horses and mules were used extensively. *Bundesarchiv*

Jacketed troops in bathing attire practice getting a gun ashore as a friend shoots some holiday snaps using his Leica.

Spitfire N3117 of the PRU was very busy spying upon the invasion preparations. Eventually converted into a PR Mk IV, it was lost on operations 9 December 1941. *Bruce Robertson*

church bells to warn their areas. A stop had to be quickly put to that, and next day Home Guard members were told not to ring the bells unless they had actually set eyes upon at least twenty-five German paratroops. Among the PR flyers taking a look along the French coast on 8 September was, again, Spitfire K9787 (virtually 'the first of the few'), which between 10.00 and 11.30 operated between Zeebrugge and Calais. That month 100 out of 126 sorties from Heston were effective, as well as eight from Wick and thirty from St Eval.

Alert No 1 meant that the Navy, its capital ships sailing south, would need to be ready to react rapidly. The RAF, expecting the landing within three days, placed twenty-four bombers at 'readiness', and ordered half of the remainder to be prepared to attack German forces at sea. All troops were ready between dusk and dawn and at 8 hours readiness in daylight. The situation was then far from eased when four spies, caught after rowing across the Channel and landing on the South Coast, admitted they had come to report upon movements of the reserve forces.

While no details of these matters were revealed, there was much public awareness of impending invasion. The situation was not helped when alarming rumours quickly spread that an invasion attempt had been made, and that many bodies were being washed ashore in Hollesley Bay and at Shingle Street on the Suffolk coast, some horribly burned, from sunken ships. There was little truth in these tales, although some burned bodies were washed ashore as a result of action and sea and air battles.

Late in June 1940 Bomber Command's invasion task was outlined – the sinking of ships in their ports and during their invasion voyages. The Fleet Air Arm would assist. On 4 July invasion ports and barges were added to Bomber Command's target listing, but in August 1940 the targets were deemed still not ripe for massive attention, although 2 Group Blenheims frequently attacked barges on Dutch and Belgian waterways. The Hampden raid of 12 August on the Dortmund Ems Canal undoubtedly delayed barge assembly.

During the first week of September Bomber Command continued attacking industrial targets, utilities and communications, and carried out small-scale penetrations to Berlin, Magdeburg, Stettin and Munich, and sent a few Whitleys to Italy. On 2/3 September twenty-nine Wellingtons carrying, among many other incendiaries, fifteen examples of the 250lb light case fire bomb, set out to light fires in Germany's Schwarzwald and Thuringerwald forest areas. The Bosch works at Stuttgart, oil plants at Ossage and Rheinmettal Borsig's Berlin factory were all targeted by Hampdens, Wellingtons and Whitleys. Blenheims intruded on airfields and big guns at Cap Gris Nez. That was until 7 September when, invasion alert effective, the bombers began destroying the assembled vessels in the Channel ports.

On that first night twenty-six Hampdens called at Ostend, dropping 194 250lb HEs and 360 4lb incendiaries onto loading vessels, while thirteen Blenheims dealt with Dunkirk's assembly and eleven Battles of 1 Group delivered seventeen 250lb and 153 40lb HEs, and ten 25lb incendiaries. In daylight next day Blenheims attacked destroyers off the Dutch coast; at night eighteen Blenheims raided Ostend, repeating that attack twenty-one-strong the next night, while Battles called on Calais. On 10/11 September fourteen Hampdens and six Blenheims bombed Calais and fifteen Hampdens and nine Blenheims Ostend, while more Blenheims tackled invasion shipping in Boulogne and Flushing. There was even more bombing of the invasion fleet on the 11/12th, including twenty Wellingtons that joined eleven Blenheims raiding Ostend.

Throughout each day PRU's Spitfires repeatedly photographed the invasion ports, bringing back vital evidence of the build-up – and destruction. Nine such flights were made on the 9th and again on the 11th, and five on the 13th. That night ninety-one bomber sorties were directed against the invasion fleet. Thereafter, until a return to industrial targets on 23/24 September, most of the night effort was directed at the Channel ports. By 17 September in Dunkirk alone eighty-four barges had been sunk or damaged, 200 by two nights later. Photo reconnaissance on 20 September surprisingly showed ships leaving the ports and heading for Germany. On 18 September 1,004 barges had been visible between Flushing and Boulogne – but only 691 by the end of the month. Initially it was thought that they had been dispersed to protect them from air attack. On 31 October PR flights revealed only 448 barges still in their ports, a mere forty-five in Flushing.

John Hannah was 18 years old when, during a raid on Antwerp on 15 September, he extinguished a fire in the Hampden in which he was a wireless operator/air gunner. Two other crew members had baled out. Hannah's courage earned him a Victoria Cross. *IWM*

Blenheim IV s of 2 Group's No 40 Squadron at Wyton. *IWM*

'Bombing-up' a Blenheim of No 40 Squadron at Wyton. *IWM*

PR sorties were also flown by Blenheims and Hudsons, among them was this Blenheim shot down in the Netherlands. *G J Zwanenburg*

An oblique shot from a PR sortie showing 'Rhine barges' assembled for the invasion attempt. *IWM*

Hitler – with the air war not won, his landing craft nightly bombarded and his Navy warning of the hazardous nature of the venture – had on 17 September decided to postpone Operation 'Sealion' until October. By 21 September a tenth of the fleet had been dispersed. Constant movement makes the number of vessels committed variable, but German figures for 21 September list:

	Assembled	Lost/damaged
Transport vessels	170 + 4 in transit	21
Barges	1,918 + 424 in transit	214
Tugs	386	5

British reliance for up-to-the-minute news on the composition of the invasion force depended very much upon Heston's PRU and its London photo interpretation unit. The enemy, clearly aware of this activity, on 17 September laid a stick of HE bombs across Heston, one bomb falling on the tarmac by the main hangar. On 18 September HEs and fire bombs dropped on Heston's eastern end, then came next night's big trouble. At 22.48 a raider circled the aerodrome before carefully placing a parachute mine on the tarmac by the main hangar which was blown apart, together with its contents. Blast, the weapon's main feature, tore through the Operations Block and badly damaged a small hangar's roof. Five Spitfires and ten other aircraft were variously damaged. Next day Air Marshal Sir Arthur Bowhill, AOC-in-C Coastal Command, hurried along to view the very serious damage.

For the Luftwaffe, while an invasion intention remained, the wearing down of Fighter Command continued. The loss of so many bombers and skilled crews with vital invasion tasks could not, however, be brushed aside. Although on 12 October Hitler decided to postpone the invasion, it was not until January 1941 that Operation 'Sealion' was finally abandoned. On that basis it might be argued that the Battle of Britain continued long after October, although the postponement of the invasion on 12 October could be a suitable date to chose to mark the end of the Battle of Britain.

Reinforced concrete 'pillboxes' proliferated. Many were quickly built to afford protection to valued sites, in this case, RAF Martlesham Heath.

Assessment of invasion barge build-up from Spitfire PR photographs

September														October
	1	**3**	**5**	**6**	**7**	**8**	**9**	**11**	**14**	**16**	**18**	**23**	**27**	**31**
Beveland canal	71	240	40											
Hanasweert	80		80					38	38					
Ghent/Terneuzen	200		200		120									
Terneuzen														
Ostend		+50	+110	273	302	300		250	250	250	250	227	170	65
Boulogne			+50	61	11	65	70	90	90	102	150	230	230	125
Flushing			+100		130	200		200	150	145	145	140	75+	15
Middleburg			70										50	18
Le Havre				15					34		205	200	220+	54
Calais				53	85	86		140	120	120	266		140	160
Gravelines								40	40	40	15	36	51	40
Dunkirk				65	97			110	110	100	140	220	220	130
Dunkirk Canal				100							80			
Ghent					120									
Delfzyl							150	150	150	150	150	150	240	
Ijmuiden									20				62	62
Antwerp									625	625	625	600		500
Emden									65	75	133			
Amsterdam												300	300	180
Rotterdam												650	400	446

Bomber Command raids on invasion ports, 13/14-22/24 September 1940

Date	Antwerp	Boulogne	Calais	Dunkirk
13/14	15 Wellingtons	9 Hampdens	9 Whitleys	9 Whitleys
		–	11 Blenheims	8 Blenheims
14/15	10 Whitleys	10 Battles	–	3 Blenheims
15/16	–	11 Blenheims	27 Wellingtons	23 Blenheims
16/17	24 Hampdens	–	–	–
17/18	20 Hampdens	20 Battles	22 Wellingtons	27 Blenheims
		13 Blenheims		
18/19	5 Whitleys	7 Battles	11 Blenheims	9 Blenheims
19/20	–	–	–	–
20/21	10 Hampdens	10 Battles	19 Wellingtons	25 Blenheims
		7 Hampdens		
21/22	–	21 Whitleys	16 Wellingtons	21 Blenheims
			6 Battles	14 Wellingtons
22/23	3 Hampdens	8 Hampdens	8 Wellingtons	5 Blenheims
		4 Wellingtons	12 Blenheims	–
23/24	–	9 Battles	26 Blenheims	–
			2 Battles	

Date	Flushing	Le Havre	Ostend
13/14	–	–	10 Hampdens
	–	–	10 Blenheims
14/15	–	–	4 Blenheims
			17 Wellingtons
15/16	–	–	–
16/17	4 Hampdens	–	8 Wellingtons
17/18	8 Hampdens	–	15 Wellingtons
			10 Whitleys
18/19	6 Wellingtons	22 Wellingtons	16 Blenheims
		25 Hampdens	
19/20	4 Hampdens	–	5 Hampdens
20/21	10 Wellingtons	– 14 Wellingtons	–
21/22	–	–	– 8 Hampdens
			5 Blenheims
22/23	5 Hampdens	10 Hampdens	10 Blenheims
		11 Wellingtons	3 Hampdens
23/24	–	–	13 Blenheims

Additional attacks:

17/18	Terneuzen: 7 Hampdens
18/19	Terneuzen: 7 Whitleys
22/23	Terneuzen: 6 Whitleys
25/26	Ostend and Dunkirk: 16 Battles
25/26	Boulogne and Calais: 18 Blenheims and 27 Wellingtons
26/27	Le Havre: 13 Wellingtons and 15 Whitleys

Chapter 16

Battle of Britain Day, 1940

Aircraft in Fighter Squadrons
09.00 hrs 15 August 1940

A = established, B =serviceable

		0	100	200	300	400	500	Total
Blenheim 1F	A							96
	B							61
Spitfire	A							328
	B							233
Hurricane	A							568
	B							351
Defiant	A							32
	B							25
Gladiator	A							8
	B							2

09.00 hrs 15 September 1940

A = established, B =serviceable

		0	100	200	300	400	500	Total
Blenheim 1F	A							96
	B							47
Spitfire	A							304
	B							192
Hurricane	A							528
	B							389
Defiant	A							32
	B							24
Gladiator	A							8
	B							8

Sunday 15 September 1940 must always be remembered, for it was one of the greatest days in our history. Besides marking the zenith of the Luftwaffe onslaught, it proved beyond any doubt that the German Air Force was incapable of smashing Fighter Command. With a hoard of splendid Messerschmitt 109s, many soon to become bombers, the enemy would subsequently maintain pressure upon Fighter Command, though no longer for the assumed reason. Hitler and his chums had postponed the invasion of Britain without telling any of us. Their decision

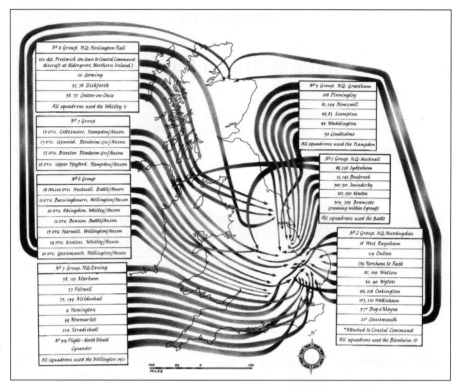

Bomber Command operational layout, 15 September 1940

resulted from the realisation that the air defence of the UK had not been smashed, a fact made abundantly clear on what has become the hallowed Battle of Britain Day.

Not since 7 September had the Luftwaffe mounted so massive a conventional bomber onslaught in daylight. In the meantime Fighter Command had seized the opportunity to invigorate 11 Group by bringing back rested squadrons and reintroducing some, like Nos 46 and 229. As part of 12 Group they had not experienced much fighting but were well staffed. In the miraculous and incredible gift of a pause, Fighter Command worked up the newcomers. Such an activity had been impossible for many weeks past.

It was one of those lovely, clear, sunny, early autumn days. Small puffy clouds dawdled across the wide blue yonder, encouraging the better memories to surface from the passing summer. If the enemy was going to resume massed raids, then this day was ideal for the purpose. Dowding's men and women were accordingly up early, waiting, ready. Maybe he had advance warning, or knew from his clever intuitive mind that something special was certain to have been dreamed up across the Channel. If so,

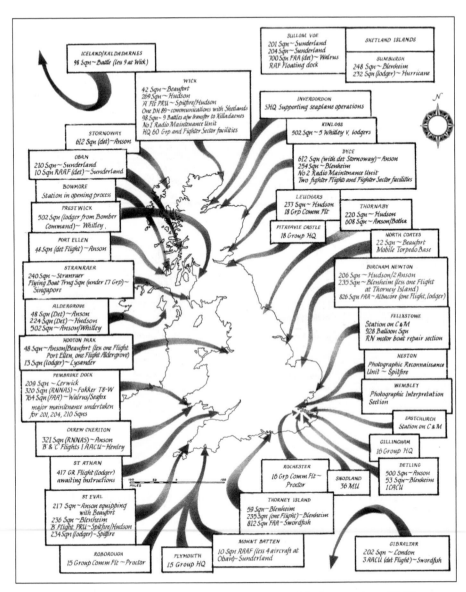

Coastal Command operational layout, 15 September 1940

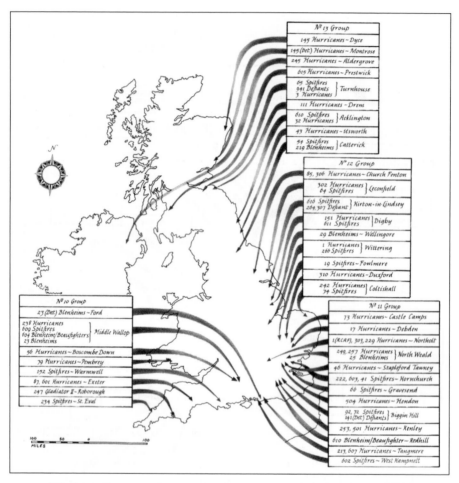

Fighter Command operational layout, 15 September 1940

it was shortly before 11.00 that he received confirmation from radar stations in Kent, which reported that enemy forces were assembling, as so often, inland of Boulogne.

HQ Fighter Command told Park to prepare his squadrons for action, and warned 10 and 12 Groups that a large attack looked to be pending. Almost immediately Nos 72 and 92 Squadrons scrambled from Biggin Hill, performing an act now symbolic. Coming their way was most of Kampfgeschwader 3 and other bomber formations. After leaving their Belgian bases, they had quickly formated with their huge fighter screen awaiting them over France, and headed for Dungeness. Around 11.30 a score of Biggin's Spitfires presented an unwanted greeting. Pressing on towards London the raiders were harassed by ever more British fighters. Shortly before reaching the capital they received a hammer-blow. Four Hurricane squadrons launched head-on assaults, then it was that Squadron Leader Douglas Bader's 'Big Wing' (two Spitfire and three Hurricane squadrons) forced their ways through the flanking escort to deal with the Dorniers. Within a few moments more 150 fighters were running amok among the bombers. With no concentrated attack upon central London now possible, KG 3 made a curving midday pass across its southern and south-western districts, dropping bombs at random as they fled for home as fast as possible. Losses on both sides were considerable, individual combats many, the pain, the sorrow, the carnage plentiful. Bombs exploded over a wide area, two unexploded HEs lodging at Buckingham Palace. Sergeant R. T. Holmes of newcomer 504 Squadron became involved with a Do 17Z of 5./KG 3, which exploded so violently that it hurled his Hurricane P2725 into a spin. Holmes baled out, landing in a Chelsea back garden while his Hurricane came down in Buckingham Palace Road. Remnants of the Dornier Do 17Z–3, W Nr 1176, 5K+DN, fluttered onto Victoria station and its surrounds.

By then the 'first up' British fighters were undergoing turn-round at their bases. Their pilots, aware of considerable success, also refuelled and prepared for another very likely round. It was not long in coming, and this time it was the turn of more than 150 Dorniers of KG 2 and KG 76, with KG 26's and KG 53's Heinkels depending for their safety mainly upon the Messerschmitt 109s of JG 26 and JG 54.

At 14.00, as the raiders crossed the Kent coast on a broad front, the RAF response was quite incredible. Despite morning losses, there was already a sense of grand success. Most squadrons somehow managed to field full strength, and groundcrews, worn out by the August campaign, suddenly acquired new life. They had all been rejuvenated as a result of the German switch largely to night-bombing in early September.

Heading for London the Germans met some 170 eager, refreshed British warriors out to kill and avenge the misery being cast upon Londoners. At first the fight was tough, for the German fighter pilots were highly skilled. As the raiders neared East London they ran into Duxford's 12 Group 'Big Wing', half-a-dozen 11 Group squadrons and two reinforcing squadrons from 10 Group. The Hurricanes and Spitfires ferociously tackled the invaders, forcing the bombers to jettison their loads, this time over South East London. As they ran for home the Bf 109s did their best to save the bombers – and themselves.

Casualties on both sides were high, but in the RAF fighter squadrons there was jubilation. Who, even a few days ago, would have imagined that such resounding success was possible? Among German bomber crews there must have been an ever-increasing fear as more and more RAF fighters fought through to them. So much for the 'four days' to annihilate Fighter Command! As for the German fighter pilots, they had constantly to bear in mind that their small fuel loads would quickly be used during high-speed manoeuvres. Once home they might well have demanded the truth, for yarns about the RAF being down to its last few aircraft were obviously ridiculous. Add to this Bomber Command's hammering of the invasion fleet and presence over Berlin and all was suddenly less encouraging.

As the afternoon wore on, more German fighters arrived over Kent to provide withdrawal support for what had become little better than a rabble.

At Cherbourg/Maupertus in September we see the Bf 109E of JG 2 flown by Helmut Wick when leading the first Gruppe. Note the double Winkel marking, blue pennant of his former Staffel (No 3) on the cowling, and the armoured windscreen. *Michael Payne*

The tail of Wick's aircraft with its kill tally. A Ju 34 communications aircraft stands by the trees; behind the tail is a visiting Bf 109 of JG 53 wearing a red band around its cowling and unusual Stab marking. *Michael Payne*

For twenty-seven He 111s of III/KG 55 heading for Portland via the Solent, the day's fighting was also far from over. They were engaged en route by 152 Squadron Spitfires, which shot down a bomber and probably forced the inaccurate bombing. Now, a far more serious threat developed, and in roughly the same area.

It is reasonable to assume that KG 55's raid was intended to divert attention from Bf 110 fighter-bombers of Erpr 210 skirting fast by the Isle of Wight. They were making direct for Supermarine's Woolston works at Southampton, where Spitfires were still being built. Why was such a venture not carried out many weeks previously? It is said that, incredibly, the Germans confused work at Woolston with activity at the Hamble aircraft factory, where the Albemarle bomber was under way. They must have known that Spitfires were produced at Woolston long before Castle Bromwich began churning them out very fast. Where did they suppose they came from, other than the Southampton region where Supermarine had been active since the 1920s? If they had made a fundamental error in the Battle it must surely have been their failure to destroy the supply of Hurricanes and Spitfires. This attempt came too late, and in any case the Solent guns drove the Bf 110s away on this glorious day.

By late afternoon the southern sky had clouded due to the huge number of high-flying aircraft producing sufficient vapour to entirely hide the blue. The nights were already closing in, but darkness came a trifle sooner on the 15th.

During the great day Churchill unexpectedly visited HQ 11 Group Uxbridge to watch the state boards and plotting tables as squadrons responded to a massive advancing armada. When he asked Keith Park about his reserves, Park said to the PM, 'There are none.' It sure was a close-run affair. In the evening Churchill sent a congratulatory note to Dowding when the extent of the day's victory was clear. He included the words 'aided by Czech and Polish squadrons, and using only a small proportion of their total strength, the Royal Air Force cut to rags and tatters separate waves of murderous assault upon the civil population of their native land.' Did he, in the evening, think to himself, 'Never in the field of human conflict was so much owed by so many to so few'? He must sometime have felt very satisfied with his compilation of that famous phrase.

We must take September 15th as the culminating date of the air battle. On this day the Luftwaffe made its greatest concentrated effort in a resumed daylight attack on London. It was one of the decisive battles of the war and, like the Battle of Waterloo, it was on a Sunday. I asked if early results had come to hand. The attack appeared to have been repelled satisfactorily. It was evident that the enemy had everywhere pierced our defences. Many squadrons of German bombers with their fighter escort had been reported over London. Although post-war information has shown that the enemy's losses on this day were only fifty-six, September 15th was the crux of the Battle of Britain. On September 17th, as we now know, the Führer decided to postpone the invasion indefinitely. Thus perished Operation 'Sealion', and September 15th will stand as the date of its demise.

Winston Churchill, post-war recorded recollections

Late on 15 September, with the nation's ears tuned to the BBC, the Air Ministry issued a communiqué announcing that, 'In today's air battles 185 enemy aircraft have been destroyed.' It fostered jubilation throughout the land on this, the best Sunday of the war so far. Just as 'Winnie' had encouraged us to believe, victory might be possible. That total, given in good faith, was far in excess of reality, for fifty-four

Where had the bombs fallen?

First attack, circa midday

About seventy-five enemy aircraft penetrated to central London. Two UXBs fell at Buckingham Palace. Damage overall was quite slight

No 5 CD Region (London)

Battersea 12.10: Pouparts Junction bridge and Longhedge bridge, also on the West London Extension line

Camberwell 11.15: Minor damage

Lambeth 12.15: Norwood Road and Brixton Hill blocked. UXB near Telephone Manufacturing Co

Beckenham 12.00: Electricity station hit, road near Birbeck station blocked

Second attack, afternoon

Barking: Longbridge Road blocked. Cape Asbestos Co hit

Battersea 14.46: Minor incidents

Beckenham: Private dwellings, forty-six casualties

Bexley: Two trolleybuses damaged, some casualties

Camberwell 15.00: Gas and water mains hit

Crayford 14.30: Minor incidents

Croydon: Private dwellings, some casualties

Dagenham: Several fires soon extinguished

East Ham 14.50: delayed-action HE at Plaistow motive power and engineer's depot. Direct hit derailed train, blocked line Upton Park-London. Direct hit on Grangewood Telephone Exchange, destroyed, also cutting electricity supplies. Fire at Power and Ammonia works at Beckton gasworks

Erith 14.43: Ten HEs Erith oil works. One week production delay

Ilford: Eight killed in direct hit on Anderson shelter, seven other casualties

Penge 14.55: HEs/UXHEs near flyover bridge, London Bridge-Crystal Palace line. Lines blocked, Sydenham and Penge West. Bomb fell through tunnel near Penge East station. Platform damaged. Some casualties.

Poplar 14.45: Damage to dwellings

West Ham 15.15: Direct hit on electricity transformer, sub-station destroyed. Extensive damage to Generating Station, fire soon under control. Forty-eight casualties and nineteen people trapped in district

Numerous UXHEs: Battersea Gas Light & Coke Co, near Clapham Junction; Buckingham Palace (one on lawn, one through King's apartment into basement); rail lines near Barnhurst station, Crayford; near searchlight site off Elmstead Lane, Bromley; Greenwich, blocking London rail route

No 6 CD Region (Southern)

Lingfield, Surrey, 15.00: HEs

No 7 CD Region (South Western)

Portland 15.00: Many HEs, ibs. Four houses damaged, eighteen evacuated due to UXHEs. Telephone lines cut, several small fires. HEs on dockyard, little damage. Few casualties

No 12 CD Region (South Eastern)

Many fires caused by crashed aircraft during the day.

11.50: aircraft crashed on booking office and waiting room, Staplehurst station, two killed, one injured

12.30: crash damage at three farm sheds near Ashford, child killed, two people injured

The prototype Miles M.20 'utility' fighter. *Miles Aircraft*

enemy aircraft were variously destroyed for a loss of twenty-seven British fighters written off. It wasn't just those numbers that mattered, it was the manner by which the rejuvenated Fighter Command had risen in such strength to repel the intruders.

Amid all the satisfaction there might have been disappointment at Philips & Powis, Reading, commonly called Miles Aircraft, for on 14 September 1940 they flew their M.20 utility fighter. They had converted twenty-six Master 1 trainers into rudimentary fighters by fitting three machine guns in each wing, but these aircraft had a top speed of only 200mph. Earlier in 1940 the company fast designed a wooden single-seat eight-gun fighter powered by a Merlin XX. Of rugged design, it prominently featured a fixed undercarriage. Testing showed its creditable top speed to be 345mph. When the RAF rejected it the Navy showed interest, although it never entered production. There will always be winners and losers.

The Fighters in the Battles, 15 September 1940

According to the relevant squadron Operations Record Books, the aircraft used were as follows. Many squadrons were in action twice, i) between 11.00 and 12.30 and ii) between about 13.45 and 16.00.

No 17 Squadron Hurricanes: ii only) P2794, V6553, V7416, V7408, P2972, P3033, P3027, V7888, P3894, P3536, P3878

No 19 Squadron Spitfires: i) X4336, R6991, X4179, X4070, X4237, X4352, X4351, X4353; ii) X4170, N3199, X4070, X4336, X4179, P9431, R6991, X4237, X4353, X4352, X4351, X4173, X4331

No 41 Squadron Spitfires: i) X4343, P9324, X4068, X4338, X4344, R6687, R6619, X4409, P9427, R6605; operated again, X4345 replacing X4068

No 46 Squadron Hurricanes: i) V7438, V6852, P3066, R4182, V7442, V7443, P3816, N2497, N2599, V6550; ii) all operated again except N2497 and N2599, replaced by P2968 and V6582

No 66 Squadron Spitfires: i) X4322, X4020, R6800, R6927, X4253, X4326; ii) X4302, N3029, X4176, R6925, R6603, R6771

No 72 Squadron Spitfires: i) X4337, R6881, X4416, N3068, K9940, X4340, X4063, P9460, X4252, K9989; ii) all operated again except K9940 and X4063

No 73 Squadron Hurricanes: i) Aircraft 'J', 'B', 'K', P2975, L2036, P3868, P3785, P8812, P3226; ii) 'B', 'N', P2975, P3785, L2035, P3226

No 74 Squadron Spitfire Mk IIs: i) P7363, P7364, P7312; ii) P7368, P7367, P7329

No 92 Squadron Spitfires: P9371, X4038, R6767, R6606, R6616, N3248, P9544, R6760, R6622, X4051; ii) all flew second sorties except R6767, P9544 and R6622; also K9998 and P9513

No 152 Squadron Spitfires: six of 'B' Flight operated off Portland

No 222 Squadron Spitfires, afternoon only: K9939, L1089, X4341, P9878, P9469, N3202, K9993, P9397

No 238 Squadron Hurricanes: P2836, P3920, P3426, P2983, P3219, P3920, P3618, P3836, P3230, P3611, P3833, P2681, P3178

No 242 Squadron (led Nos 19, 302, 310 and 611 Squadrons of 12 Group): i) V6576, 2982?, V7467, V6576, P3151, R4385, V6578, V7203, P3054, 2884, R4115; ii) all flew second sorties except V6576, R4385, V6578, R4115, replaced by P3048, P3458

No 249 Squadron Hurricanes: i) V6559, V6683, P3834, V6556, V6622, V6685, P3579, V6594, V6635, V6680 and one unknown; ii) V6559, V6683, P3834, V6566, V6622, P3615, V6693, V6617, V6635, V6680 and two unknown

No 253 Squadron Hurricanes: i) P2958, R2686, V7466, P5179, V6637, N2588, P3609, P3537; ii) P5172, P2865, P2958, N2455, P5179, N2588, R2686, V6637, V6698

No 257 Squadron Hurricanes: i) V6557, V7357, P3705, P3776, V7254, P3642, R4190, P3893; ii) R4190, P3898, P3705, P2835, V6557, V7351, P2960, P3775, V6555 (Stanford Tuck)

No 302 (Polish) Squadron Hurricanes: i) R2684:B, P3935:D, P2954:E, P3867:T, V6569:K, R4095:M, P3812:L; ii) 'B', 'F', 'L' with V6571:Q, P2752:R and P3812:Z

No 303 (Polish) Squadron Hurricanes: i) P3089, V6665, P3939, R2685, P3120, P3577, V7244, V7235, V7289, P2903, V6673, V7465; ii) P3089, V7465, V7235, V6673, L2099, V6684, P3577, R2685, P3120, P3939

No 310 (Czech) Squadron Hurricanes: i) R4089, V7304, L2713, R4087, V6619, P3612, R4085, V6608, P3143, P3056, V6542, V6556; ii) R4085, V6608, P3143, P3056, V6556, V6579, P3887, L2713, R4089, R4087, V6619, P3612

No 1 Squadron RCAF Hurricanes: P3859, L1973, P3080, '323', V6669, P3672, V7288, P3647, V6605, V6609, P3876, V6603; ii) V6603, V6609, P3647, L1973, P3859, V6671, P3672, V6669, V6605

No 501 Squadron Hurricanes: i) P3397, V7403, V6545, P3820, L1572, P5193, V6600, V6672, V6570, P2760, V7357, V6645, P5194, V7433, '2760'; ii) V6672, P5193, V6545, P3820, V7357, V6645, '5494?', L1657, V6600

No 504 Squadron Hurricanes: P3415, P3774, P2987, P3388, P3614, N2705, N2481, L1913, P3414, L1583, N2725, P2908; ii) P3429, P3774, P2987, P3388, P3614, N2705, P2908, P3414

No 602 Squadron Spitfires, afternoon only: X4411, X4414, N3242, X4382, X4389, R6780, X4269, R6601, X4412, R6839, X4390, X4160

No 603 Squadron Spitfires: i) R7019, X4359, N3267, X4324, X4323, X4348, P9440, P9499, X4274, R6836, X4394, X4250; ii) R7019, X4359, N3267, X4323, X4324, R6836, P9499, K9803, X4274, X4378, P9440, X4250

No 605 Squadron Hurricanes: i) P3580, V6699, P3583, P3677, P3832, L2018, P3308, N2352, P2589, P3737, P3828, L2122; ii) P3677, L2012, P3583, P3832, P3965, P2589, P3737, P3828, L2122; iii) P3677, L2012, P3583, P3832, P3965, P2589, P3107, P3737, P3828

No 607 Squadron Hurricanes: aircraft used in the two operations uncertain, combats in second scramble only, serial numbers uncertain

No 609 Squadron Spitfires: i) R6691, N3133, L1096, X4107, K9997, R6922, R6979, N3223, R6961, R6631, R6699, R6690, X4165, R6922; ii) N3280, X4107, L1096, R6691, N3113, R6979, R6922, X4165, N3223, R6961, R6631, R6699, X4234

No 611 Squadron Spitfires: i) P7291, P7305, P7283, P7383, P7354, P7302, P7303, P7314, P7322, P7322, P7323, P7299, P7284, P7282; ii) P7284, P7323, P7282, P7291, P7283, P7302, P7303, P7305

No 615 Squadron Hurricanes: operated in afternoon only, Brooklands area, aircraft used uncertain

Sorties flown by Fighter Command and Luftwaffe during and related to operations against the United Kingdom, 13 August-15 September 1940

Fighter Command listing includes all types of operational sorties flown. Luftwaffe sorties marked * are British official approximations, and often quite inaccurate

Date (to period ending 06.00) August	Patrols	Fighter Command Sorties		Luftwaffe Sorties	
		Day	Night	Day	Night
13	192	889	27	1,485	?
14	132	494	26	489	?
15	227	974	?	1,786	?
16	163	895	?	1,715	?
17	100	288	15	560*	?
18	155	766	?	650*	72*
19	130	403	?	600*	150*
20	166	477	1	120*	50*
21	181	620	10	120*	50*
22	?	?	44	190*	250*
23	200	507	?	?	120*
24	187	936	45	1,030	170
25	150	481	43	730	150
26	197	787	42	1,088 (total)	
27	?	288	47	225(total)	
28	187	739	22	636	340
29	125	498	28	720	220
30	208	1,054	–	1,345	260
31	192	978	29	1,450	170
September					
1	?	661	29	640	180
2	100	751	29	972	75
3	123	711	34	586	90
4	123	677	20	750	197
5	121	672	50	685	218
6	144	987	44	722	75
7	143	817	44	400*	260
8	65	215	23	170*	200*
9	68	441	25	400*	?
10	?	?	41	?	?
11	114	637	58	?	125*
12	81	190	5	50*	120*
13	98	209	?	90*	?
14	?	?	28	400*	140*
15	115	705	68	930+*	175*

Luftwaffe losses during operations 8-15 September 1940

a = shot down, b = crashed during sortie, c = seriously damaged

September	8			9			10			11			12		
Type	a	b	c	a	b	c	a	b	c	a	b	c	a	b	c
Do 17P	–	–	–	–	–	–	–	–	–	–	–	–	–	–	–
Do 17Z	3	2	–	–	–	–	1	–	–	–	–	–	–	–	–
Do 18	–	–	–	–	–	–	–	–	–	–	–	–	–	–	–
He 59	–	–	–	–	–	–	–	–	–	–	–	–	–	–	–
He 111H	–	–	–	2	–	1	–	–	–	9	1	3	–	–	–
He 111P	–	1	1	–	–	–	–	1	–	–	1	–	–	1	–
He 115	1	–	–	–	–	–	–	–	–	–	–	–	–	–	–
Hs 126	–	–	–	–	–	–	–	–	–	–	–	–	–	–	–
Ju 88	1	3	2	5	2	–	1	1	–	–	–	–	1	2	1
Bf 109	–	2	–	12	1	1	–	–	–	6	1	1	–	–	–
Bf 110	–	–	–	3	–	1	–	–	–	6	1	1	–	–	–
Totals	5	8	3	22	3	3	2	2	–	21	4	5	1	3	1

September	13			14			15		
Type	a	b	c	a	b	c	a	b	c
Do 17P	–	–	–	–	–	1	–	–	–
Do 17Z	–	–	–	–	–	2	16	–	4
Do 18	–	–	–	–	–	–	1	–	–
He 59	–	–	1	–	1	–	1	–	–
He 111H	–	1	–	3	–	–	9	1	2
He 111P	1	1	–	–	–	–	1	–	–
He 115	–	–	–	–	–	–	–	–	–
Hs 126	–	–	–	–	–	1	–	–	–
Ju 88	–	1	1	–	–	1	2	–	2
Bf 109	–	1	–	3	–	2	18	1	1
Bf 110	–	–	–	–	–	–	–	–	–
Totals	1	4	2	6	1	7	48	2	9

RAF losses during operations 8-15 September 1940

a = failed to return/shot down, b = battle casualty, c = seriously damaged

September	8			9			10			11			12		
Type	a	b	c	a	b	c	a	b	c	a	b	c	a	b	c
Blenheim F	–	–	–	–	–	–	–	1	–	–	–	–	–	–	–
Beaufighter	1	–	–	–	–	–	–	–	–	–	–	–	–	–	–
Defiant	–	–	–	–	–	–	–	–	–	–	–	–	–	–	–
Hurricane	3	–	–	14	2	2	–	–	–	18	–	3	–	2	–
Spitfire	–	–	–	5	1	1	–	–	–	13	–	3	–	2	–
Battle	–	–	–	–	–	–	1	–	–	–	–	–	–	–	–
Blenheim B	–	–	–	–	–	–	–	–	–	–	–	–	–	–	–
Hampden	–	–	–	–	–	–	–	–	–	2	–	–	2	1	–
Wellington	–	–	–	–	–	–	–	–	–	–	1	–	1	1	–
Whitley	–	–	–	–	–	–	1	–	–	3	–	–	–	–	–
Coastal Cmd	3	–	–	–	–	–	1	–	–	5	–	–	–	–	–
Totals	7	–	–	19	3	3	3	–	–	41	1	6	3	4	–

September	13			14			15			September Total		
Type	a	b	c	a	b	c	a	b	c	a	b	c
Blenheim F	–	–	–	1	–	–	–	–	–	1	1	0
Beaufighter	–	–	–	–	–	–	1	–	–	2	0	0
Defiant	–	–	–	–	–	–	–	–	–	0	0	0
Hurricane	1	–	–	7	–	1	19	1	4	62	5	10
Spitfire	–	–	–	6	1	2	6	–	3	31	2	8
Battle	–	–	–	–	–	–	–	–	–	1	0	0
Blenheim B	–	–	–	1	–	–	–	–	–	1	0	0
Hampden	–	–	–	1	–	–	–	–	–	5	1	0
Wellington	–	–	–	–	–	–	–	1	–	1	3	0
Whitley	–	–	–	–	–	–	2	–	–	6	0	0
Coastal Cmd	2	–	–	1	–	–	–	–	–	12	0	0
Totals	3	–	–	16	1	3	28	2	7	122	12	18

Chapter 17

You've forgotten us

'Last night, Anson bombers of Coastal Command attacked the docks at Brest, and yesterday Hudsons bombed shipping off Norway. Blenheims of Coastal Command bombed the docks at Le Havre and engaged enemy aircraft over the Channel. Three oil tankers bringing petrol vital for our fighters were escorted into port by Sunderlands and Ansons, while high-flying PR Spitfires photographed the enemy coastline from Bergen to Bordeaux. Blenheim fighters escorted an Empire flying boat safely during the last stage of its flight to Britain. Over the Channel an Anson escorting a convoy fought off attacks by four Messerschmitts. A Beaufort torpedoed a 6,000-ton vessel in Calais roads. Whitleys, manned by Bomber Command crews, Stranraers, Blenheim fighters, Hudsons and Ansons again escorted convoys approaching our north-west ports. From these operations three of our aircraft are missing.'

Numbers of serviceable Aircraft in RAF Coastal Command squadrons

	0	50	100	150	200	250	Total
1.7.40							201
12.7.40							215
22.7.40							223
12.8.40							240
21.8.40							255
30.8.40							240
7.9.40							232
15.9.40							246
18.9.40							244
29.9.40							261

Sad that the heroism of those who served with Coastal Command throughout the 1939-45 war has received such scant attention. Their contribution to the winning of the Battle of Britain has gone almost unnoticed, maybe due to its complex and extensive nature. (A detailed survey of the work of the Command, its squadrons and aircraft can, incidentally, be found in *Aircraft for the Few* (Patrick Stephens Limited).

'Ansons bombing Brest?' you may question. It certainly seems unlikely, yet three times in September 1940 217 Squadron's 'faithful Annies' did just that. Ansons are thought of as trainers and light transports, but they performed well, operationally, in Coastal Command.

From 26 August 1939 to beyond the end of the European war, Coastal Command's squadrons were fully operational. It was a Coastal Command Anson crew of 608 Squadron that, early on 1 July 1940, spotted a half-submerged He 59 floatplane off West Hartlepool, an item some rate as the first fighter success of the

Ansons of 217 Squadron really did bomb Brest! Two of the squadron's aircraft, N9742 and K6285, are seen here earlier in September 1940 in the hands of No 321 Dutch Squadron. *IWM*

Battle. In direct contrast, Hudsons of 220, 224 and 233 Squadrons next day carried out typically hazardous daylight attacks on MVs and destroyers sailing in convoy off Lotbrerg, in the face of flak and fighters and at a time when invasion from Norway was thought feasible. After dark, a dozen Swordfish of 825 Squadron Fleet Air Arm (among those seconded to work with the Command) set out to bomb barges in the River Maas. Only three were successful, 'B' and 'H' failing to return and three others crashing – 'R' near Harwich, 'L' at Birchington and 'M' on Harrocks Island, Suffolk – in a venture typical of many. That same night another six, of 812 Squadron, set off from North Coates to the same target area, which only one crew located and in the face of intense flak. Their companions in five Fairey Albacores of 826 Squadron, Bircham Newton, attacked a ship off the Hook. Such operations by the FAA were

A flight of Ansons of No 48 Squadron. The Ansons kept watch over East Coast north-south convoys.

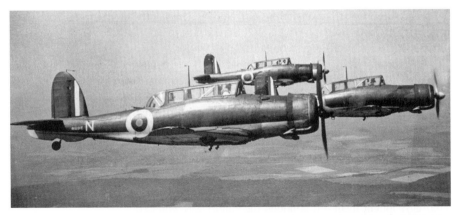

The Fleet Air Arm was ready to tackle an invasion with a few Blackburn Skuas – L2934 is
seen here – as well as its Swordfishes.

many times repeated, together with mining, often from dangerously low levels and in
heavily defended areas of the Maas, the Scheldt, the Ems Estuary and Hubert Gat. The
Fleet Air Arm's part in the events of 1940 is scarcely remembered.

Bircham Newton's Blenheims, and Hudsons of 206 Squadron, long active
against shipping, were allocated search and strike areas off the Dutch and Belgian
coasts. As early as 6 July their low- and medium-level reconnaissance flights –
supporting the Command's high-flying spies – were watching barge movements.
Leuchars-based Hudsons of 220 and 224 Squadrons conducted their anti-invasion and

The Roc was the turreted version of the Skua. Its turret added firepower but too much
weight. What part if any the Roc played in the Battle is uncertain, but an operational
Flight was based for a short time at Cambridge, possibly there to strafe any East Coast
landing? Illustrated are L3114-E and L3119-0.

merchant shipping strike operations off Norway, frequently bombing harbours and fringe targets, and, aided by Wick's 269 Squadron, typically attacked an ammunition dump at Faltoens, near Bergen, on 9/10 July 1940.

An ever-increasing part in the fighting was soon taken by Blenheims after two squadrons, Nos 53 and 59, which had specialised in reconnaissance for the BEF, joined Coastal Command on 3 July. No 53 moved to Detling, No 59 to Thorney Island, and both began attacking shipping in the Channel and its ports, together with coastal aerodromes and other fringe targets. On 11 July three crews of 59 Squadron searching for E-boats south-west of Selsey Bill engaged instead a Do 17, which retired behind a smoking engine. Such confrontations became commonplace. Next day a 59 Squadron crew discovered two ships in Cherbourg harbour and, in the face of heavy AA fire, tried to sink them. A dozen Me 109s were soon engaging the Blenheim, whose crew amazingly fought them off, although the gunner was wounded.

Although strike operations formed the more spectacular part of Coastal Command's war, most of the flying at this period involved the protection of coastal convoys. Only the score or so of Sunderlands in hand had sufficient endurance for prolonged ocean patrols. Most escort duty was carried out by the Command's 'inshore' Anson squadrons, and for Detling's No 500 (County of Kent) Squadron that meant having its 'Annies' in the thick of the summer fighting – and bombing – along a lengthy front from Sussex to Essex. 'L' Love was on 12 July escorting East Coast convoy FS19 (twenty-one MVs and two destroyers) when at 07.40 nine He 111s attacked. Pilot Officer Pain and crew tackled them, claiming a Heinkel just before fighters arrived. Three survivors were rescued, although the MV *Hornchurch* (2,162grt) was bombed and sunk off Aldeburgh LV. Another incident involved Sergeant Barr and crew in G/500 Squadron escorting thirty-four ships forming convoy FS24 on 18 July when, at 11.03, four Bf 110s dashed in and began strafing the vessels. Again, an Anson crew decided to engage raiders, one of which soon plunged into the sea with a burning engine. By that time RAF fighters had arrived, but 500 Squadron maintained that the victory was theirs. Attacks on U-boats brought usually brief, exciting but often unrewarding moments during many, many hours of monotonous patrolling. Even when submarine attacks were accurate, the results were usually indecisive, for the bombs used simply did not have sufficient charge needed to sink a U-boat. One such attack was made on 12 July by Fokker T8-W floatplane 'P' Peter. Before the Netherlands fell, a handful of these seaplanes escaped to Britain and, manned by Dutch Navy personnel, operated out of Pembroke Dock along the Welsh Coast, and on this occasion the crew attacked a U-boat 40 miles north of Holyhead without success. The weapon needed was the depth charge, which Sunderlands of No 10 (RAAF) Squadron began using in July.

Throughout their long service career Sunderlands performed with distinction, and far from home, for the aircraft's operational radius was more than 500 miles. On 2 July Sunderland H/210 Squadron managed to sink U-boat U-246 with a direct hit using a 250lb AS bomb – luck indeed – after which the Navy picked up forty-one survivors. The tables were soon turned when, that morning, K/204 Squadron reported the sinking of the 15,501grt SS *Arandora Star* at 55°20N/10°33W. Several

The Ministry Says...

The Anson machine is not itself for fighting, but the fact has not deterred Anson crews from entering a scrap with enemy fighters. Last month three Anson machines engaged on reconnaissance engaged no less than nine Messerschmitts over the Channel. They destroyed two and crippled another without loss.

Air Ministry communiqué, 17 July

lengthy flights by Sunderlands included a reconnaissance flown by Pilot Officer Lindsey in L5802 'U' of 201 Squadron. Operating from Sullom Voe, he flew to Narvik then to Harstaad, where, although most of his bombs hit an oil storage area, none exploded. Chagrin all round! By touch-down the sortie had lasted some 15 hours. Another long flight had been undertaken on 12 July when Squadron Leader Pearce took N9049 of No 10 (RAAF) Squadron for a midday reconnaissance of Bordeaux and St Nazaire, a journey of 12 hours, in very dangerous air space.

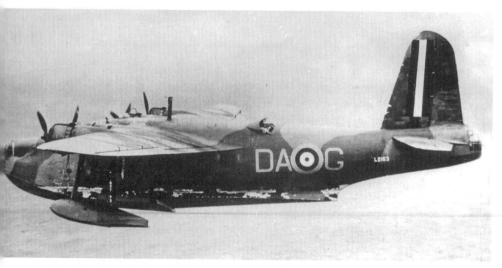

Sunderland L2163 joined 210 Squadron in June 1938 and remained with them until December 1941. *Shorts*

The Sunderland's manoeuvrability came in very useful when on 15 July Flight Lieutenant Birch in H/10 (RAAF) Squadron battled with He 111s attacking the convoy over which he was patrolling, and on 2 August when V/201 Squadron fought a Do 17 north of the Shetlands. Close to the *Britannic* on 14 August J/210 Squadron battled with an Fw Condor, was damaged and forced to make for home.

Shots in the hull of a flying boat could indeed bring a particularly alarming homecoming... The common idea that a flying boat might readily land on the open sea was often proved wrong, and when Sunderland B/10 (RAAF) Squadron off Slyne Head came across a lifeboat from the 11,081grt SS *City of Benares*, sunk on 17 September at 56°43N/21°15W when it was carrying many children, the sea state prohibited putting down. A total of thirty-nine Sunderlands and crews served in four squadrons during the Battle, and acquitted themselves with great distinction. Three were posted missing on operations and another three crashed.

The Ministry Says...

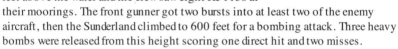

The performance of the Sunderland flying-boat which went to Tromso during Sunday is one of the most spectacular flights of the war. It represents a direct flight of longer than from London to Rome and back. It came down to 50 feet above the water and the crew saw eight He 115s at their moorings. The front gunner got two bursts into at least two of the enemy aircraft, then the Sunderland climbed to 600 feet for a bombing attack. Three heavy bombs were released from this height scoring one direct hit and two misses.

Air Ministry Bulletin, 27 August

One of Coastal Command's main tasks was to watch for indications of invasion activity by flying a variety of patrols over a host of specified sea areas. It was also responsible for the observation of the movement of barges to be used in the expected invasion. Prominent in this and many other activities were Blenheims of 53 and 59 Squadrons, which were particularly active against airfields when fighting was at its most intensive. On 21 August 53 Squadron raided Abbeville airfield and 59 Squadron bombed Caen/Carpiquet. Earlier the same day Blenheim fighters of 236 Squadron, St Eval, had protected a civilian Empire flying boat heading westward from the Scillies, and six Hudsons of 206 Squadron tackled two large merchant ships. No 236 Squadron, which received Blenheim IVs on 13 July 1940 when it joined the Command, operated them in both low attack and escort duties, and engaged enemy raiders when opportunity arose. No 236 was dealt a harsh blow on 21 August when, at 13.52, three Ju 88s attacked St Eval, badly damaging the squadron's hangar and five Blenheims therein and three men were wounded. By chance another six Blenheims had just left to escort a Sunderland along the Channel when their crews spotted the Ju 88s, one of which some chased to Land's End but without scoring a kill.

Opposite top: Lockheed Hudson Mk 1 T9303 VX V of 206 Squadron, Bircham Newton. Received late July 1940, it failed to return on 15 October 1940.

Bottom: Typically dressed for flying in a multi-engined aircraft, the crew board Hudson T9303.

Also very active at this period was Thorney Island's 235 Squadron. It mounted defensive patrols over the aerodrome on most days between 13 and 30 August as well as escorting British minelayers. On 22/23 August six Blenheims of 53 Squadron carried out one of the earliest intruder raids, engaging a German bomber landing at St Omer while other Blenheims of 59 Squadron attended to Dinard. On 24/25 August thirteen Blenheims delivered raids on Flushing and oil tanks at Cherbourg. At the same time four Fairey Albacores of 826 Squadron, FAA, set off from Bircham Newton for Vlaardingen. Flak was intense, target location in a friendly nation's territory difficult, and only 'C' Charlie attacked, gliding quietly down from 13,000 to 5,000 feet to drop six 250lb GPs and eight 25lb incendiaries, a fair load from a biplane.

Strike and escort squadrons were now very busy, and on 1 September Blenheims from Bircham Newton were covering a naval force, while three Ansons together with three Beauforts of 22 Squadron searched for any U-boats nearby. During the evening Blenheims bombed Lorient, then on 3 September the Thorney squadron raided Ostend. Next afternoon three crews of 235 Squadron discovered a Do 18 seaplane some 18 miles off the North Foreland, but it escaped before they were in a position to engage. On 11 September five Beauforts of 22 Squadron mounted a late afternoon strike against four large MVs in Ostend Roads, getting hits on one in the face of murderous fire from five escorting flak ships. Equally eventful was the activity produced when, after reconnoitring Texel, 235 Squadron escorted naval Albacores bombing shipping off Calais. Pilot Officer Coggins claimed two intercepting Bf 109s, but a Blenheim was also shot down and another lost to intercepting Bf 109s, when others of the squadron escorted 59 Squadron raiding Boulogne.

'Battle of Britain Day 1940' also saw the Blenheims in action, five of 53 Squadron attacking shipping off Sangatte during the late afternoon. After dark thirteen crews of 53 and 59 Squadrons visited Le Havre and six naval Swordfish from Thorney Island mined off Flushing. The air maritime forces were very active indeed throughout the fight. It was, however, far from plain sailing for Coastal Command, as August was also the month when difficulties with its equipment and manning levels began producing serious problems.

High hopes, soon brutally dashed, were directed towards long-awaited new types of aircraft. One was the mixed-role Blackburn Botha, the intended Anson replacement that, in the hands of Thornaby's 608 Squadron, began coastal escort duties on 10 August. Even before its operational debut it had been roundly condemned due to its inability to maintain height on one of its unreliable Perseus engines, and also because of the very poor view, which rendered it useless as an observation platform. Coastal Command persevered with it, but the Botha's career was brief and the squadron was relieved to re-equip fully with Ansons.

Another new type was the Bristol Beaufort torpedo bomber, initially viewed as a standby aircraft in case the Botha failed, and originally intended for use only in the Far East. Problems with its Taurus engines caused it to be switched to Home Service. About 100 had been built by mid-1940, many of which had to be returned to the manufacturer for major modifications. That meant that the Command had no reliable torpedo bomber to fight any invasion shipping, although a few Beaufort and Swordfish sorties were operated with the prime weapons just before the Battle ended. Usually, both types bombed and mined, roles they were also intended for. Against large ships the torpedo was a necessary prime but costly weapon.

Ill-fated and very unpopular among fliers was the Blackburn Botha. *Blackburn*

A third disappointment was the small Saro Lerwick inshore flying boat, whose troubled history rivalled that of the Botha. In this case the failings were mainly aerodynamic. Until 26 July No 209 Squadron persevered with the aircraft, flying anti-submarine patrols off the West Coast. Operations ceased, then on 3 August all flying was stopped until modified engines, floats and controls were fitted. Meanwhile, the Supermarine Stranraer biplane flying boats, which the Lerwick was intended to replace, soldiered on with 240 Squadron and into 1941, performing very reliably.

Aircraft problems were paralleled by another – the lack of sufficient crews to man the Command. The problem did not escape the notice of the Prime Minister, who seemed convinced that poor serviceability and not bad management and crew shortage were responsible for reduced levels of aircraft available for operations. He pressed Air Chief Marshal Sir Frederick W. Bowhill, AOC-in-C Coastal Command, for explanations. Nothing could be done to improve the situation until Coastal OTUs provided the necessary output. Mid-August brought a boost to the Command's strength when two squadrons of Fairey Battles were seconded to it and initially placed at Thorney Island before settling at Eastchurch for operations. The inadequate range of the Battle rendered it useless to Bomber Command, except in an anti-invasion role for which Battle squadrons trained. Nos 12 and 142 Squadrons were, however, lent to

The only biplane flying boats operational with the RAF in summer 1940 were nine Supermarine Stranraers including K7298 BN-P of 240 Squadron. They flew shipping protection duties off Scotland's west coast and from the aptly named Stranraer seaplane station. *A S Thomas collection*

Torpedoes were the prime and very expensive anti-shipping wartime weapons. Delivery was never easy, as 22 Squadron's Beaufort crews found. L4516 OA-W operated with the squadron between April and December 1940. In the distance is a Swordfish that the Fleet Air Arm courageously operated from North Coates. *IWM*

Perhaps an unkind view, but the Saro Lerwick was certainly a troubled seaplane. L7251 is pictured partially sunk at Stranraer on 21 November 1940. It was later recovered.

Coastal Command specifically to stop Boulogne's E-boats interfering with Channel shipping. Those operations commenced on 13 August, and four days later, escorted by Coastal Command's Blenheim fighters, both squadrons bravely carried out an evening raid on Boulogne. When the possibility of invasion much increased, both squadrons returned to Bomber Command to join No 1 Group's night attacks, mainly on Calais and Boulogne, as the invasion force prepared itself for action.

By the end of the Battle of Britain Coastal Command's future campaign was very evident. The U-boat menace was becoming a major and alarming threat to all supplies, not least oil. The Battle of Britain, with ample justification, may be viewed as an early part of the Battle of the Atlantic. That became evident when long-range Blenheim escort fighters were switched to operate off Northern Ireland to scare away KG 40's Fw 200 Condors, increasingly harassing shipping entering the north-west approaches to Liverpool and Glasgow, ports already being bombed. Hudsons moved from Leuchars to assist by patrolling from Aldergrove. Also available was a detachment of 102 Squadron Whitleys, Prestwick-based in October, which used their considerable duration to protect convoys. Coastal Command was the most ubiquitous of all RAF Commands.

Coastal Command operational strength, 18.00hrs

a = number of squadrons, b = squadron establishment, c = total aircraft establishment, d = number of aircraft serviceable

	1 July				31 August				29 September			
	a	b	c	d	a	b	c	d	a	b	c	d
Anson	2	18 ⟩92		73	6	21	126	68	6	21	126	58
Anson	4	14										
Botha	–	–	–	–	–	–	–	–	–	–	–	10
Blenheim	3	16	48	15								
Blenheim F	–	–	–	–	2	24	48 ⟩40		2	24	48 ⟩47	
Blenheim F	–	–	–	–	2	16	32		2	16	32	
Blenheim GR	–	–	–	–	2	18	33	24	2	18	36	28
Fokker T8W	–	–	–	3	–	–	–	3	–	–	–	–
Hudson	5	21	105	56	5	21	105	44	5	21	105	46
Beaufort	1	21	21	–	1	21	21	–	1	21	21	14
Battle	–	–	–	–	2	16	32	22	–	–	–	–
Sunderland	1	6 ⟩22		12	4	6	24	15	4	6	24	16
Sunderland	3	4										
Lerwick	1	6	6	0	1	6	6	0	1	6	6	0
London/Stranraer	1	6	6	4 Str	–	–	–	–	–	–	–	–
Stranraer	–	–	–	–	1	6	6	3	1	6	6	4
Wellington	1*	3	3	3	1*	3	3	0	1*	3	3	0
Whitley	–	–	–	–	–	–	–	–	–	–	–	12
FAA attached:												
Albacore	1	–	–	7	1	–	–	5	1	–	–	8
Swordfish	3	–	–	24	1	–	–	8	1	–	–	8
Walrus	–	–	–	1	–	–	–	3	–	–	–	5
PRU Spitfire**	1	?	?	?	1	?	?	?	1	?	?	?
Totals	26	115	303	198	29	158	436	235	27	142	407	256

* One Flight only
** Full details unknown   ⟩combined figures

Coastal Command operational strength, 18.00hrs

a = number of squadrons, b = squadron establishment, c = total aircraft establishment, d = number of aircraft serviceable

31 October

	a	b	c	d
Anson	6	21	126	43
Anson				
Botha	–	–	–	6
Blenheim				
Blenheim F	2	24	48	⎫46
Blenheim F	2	16	32	⎭
Blenheim GR	2	18	36	19
Fokker T8W	–	–	–	–
Hudson	5	21	105	50
Beaufort	1	21	21	4
Battle	–	–	–	–
Sunderland	4	6	24	10
Sunderland				
Lerwick	1	6	6	0
London/Stranraer	–	–	–	–
Stranraer	1	6	6	5
Wellington	1	3	3	0
Whitley	–	–	–	6
FAA attached:				
Albacore	1	–	–	0
Swordfish	1	–	–	2
Walrus	–	–	–	2
PRU Spitfire**	1	?	?	?
Totals	27	142	407	193

** Full details unknown

Chapter 18

Safer at night

As the nation celebrated the glorious victory of the 15th, Hermann Goering was still voicing crazy notions about destroying Fighter Command in four days. A long four days! At night, however, his bombers were inflicting fearsome damage as on 15/16 September.

Typifying activity during many nights to come, the vanguard of bombers arriving from Le Havre caused London's sirens to warn at 20.09 and at 20.14 the guns to start firing the first of the night's 8,937 rounds. Two hours later more raiders started heading in from over Dieppe. Between 01.00 and 03.00 a contingent travelled from Dutch and Belgian bases via Essex or the Thames Estuary. All were surely eager to avenge the losses during the day. They managed to wreck the central tower of the prominent Shell Mex building in the Strand and damage London's Gaiety Theatre, together with St Thomas's, Guy's and Lambeth Hospitals. Bursting shells wrenched the sky apart until 04.30, and searchlights prodded it almost continuously from 23.15 until the 'All Clear' sounded at 05.36. By that time Liverpool, the Midlands and South Wales had also been raided. Although London was the main target on forty-two consecutive nights, other areas frequently came under night attack.

Throughout 16 September Fighter Command reviewed the claims made on the 15th. *If* 185 German aircraft had been brought down, where were the wrecks? Proven reports soon suggested the score to total about one-third of the original claim. Fighting was intense, confused, and it appeared that pilots had often concentrated upon ensuring one kill. Even if the score was lower than originally believed, the 15th had seen the Luftwaffe well and truly thrashed, and next day's poor weather provided a good excuse for it to avoid more harsh treatment. Six shells were hurled towards Dover during the morning, and more than 300 German aircraft ventured high over Kent without brazenly flaunting their presence in the face of twenty-one RAF squadrons. Low clouds soon rolled in, cloaking lone callers at many RAF stations. Besides the five German aircraft destroyed during the day, a captured, inverted He 115 floatplane was towed into Eyemouth by fascinated fisherfolk.

Nightfall saw the return of the London bombers, which started seven huge fires that brightly lit much of the East End. At West Smithfield alone, eighty fire pumps were needed. Parts of Birmingham were also hit, and at Wakefield Prison incendiaries resulted in a fire.

On 17 September lone bombers caused incidents in Caterham, Portsmouth and Speke. Mid-afternoon saw a large formation mainly of Bf 109s progressing over Kent, the strong top cover hoping to pounce upon any British fighters responding. JG 53 crippled 501 Squadron with a lightning strike before the day's losses became about equal – except that every German airman coming down on land was a loss to his side, while an RAF pilot baling out might be able to fight again soon. High aircraft production rates and the ample stored reserve made that increasingly feasible.

London's underground station at Piccadilly Circus provided excellent night shelter. *IWM*

It was after dark that a new, vicious obscenity first descended upon London, the 1,000kg parachute mine blast weapon. The Government at once declared it to be an 'indiscriminate form of aerial attack against the morale of the people'. An adaptation of the sea mine, and originally thought erroneously to still be magnetic, these cylindrical objects were about 8 feet long and 2 feet in diameter. Each Luftminen

After leaving any shelter one always
wondered what familiar old friend might
be no more. In this incident on 22
August it was a cinema in Edmonton,
north London. *IWM*

The King and Queen survey the damage
on one of the occasions that
Buckingham Palace was hit, while Mr
Churchill, ever the politician,
contemplates the photographer! *IWM*

descended suspended from a 27-foot-diameter green artificial silk parachute, and drifted down making a 'swishing sound' at about 40mph to ensure a soft landing. The thin case and high charge/weight ratio combined to produce a colossal hollow bang, tremendous shock waves and extensive blast damage reaching even to a radius of 2 miles – assuming the weapon's fusing worked. Often it did not. Quite soon there were a number of versions of the weapon.

The first drops had been reported from the East Coast after cylindrical shapes were seen descending. By early 18 September twenty-one incidents had been reported, some referring to a pair of mines. They were believed to have been sown by Heinkels of KG 4 and Kgr 126. Extensive serious damage and giant craters resulted after nine mines exploded, the first two at Petts Wood and Rochester. Another dangled alarmingly from a pawnbroker's symbols in Shoreditch High Street. While no official announcement was made concerning the introduction of mines, their arrival was soon general knowledge. Secrecy induced fear, and rumour gave them a 'spooky' aura. Anger greeted the news widely spread that among a dozen huge fires that night were those consuming famous stores in Oxford Street, among them D. H. Evans and John Lewis. That demanded attention from hundreds of firemen, whose hoses seemed to snake everywhere. Ten extensive fires also blazed in the East End.

Three multi-wave operations mounted on 18 September and against the South East had a ratio of about four fighters to one bomber. They either crossed Kent or rounded the Foreland into the Thames Estuary to attack riverside targets. The first was Tilbury, the second Gillingham, attacked at 12.55 and leading to twenty-eight casualties. The third involved a high-speed dash by Ju 88s of KG 77 to the Medway Oil Company's Port Victoria store on the Isle of Grain. In another phase of this last operation Chatham, Tilbury/Gravesend and Maidstone came under attack. Fighters making up half the enemy force flew high over Kent hoping to surprise RAF interceptors. Inexperienced crews of III/KG 77 flying Ju 88s hurrying along the south side of the Thames were pounced upon by fourteen RAF squadrons, including the 12 Group Wing, which disposed of five bombers. Reports relating to the first part of this operation refer to the inclusion of two four-engined bombers within a diamond formation of fifteen He 111s. If true they would have been Fw 200s.

Whatever the study of paper returns may have shown, the fact is that the situation was critical in the extreme. The majority of squadrons had been reduced to the status of training units, and were fit only for operations against unescorted bombers. The remainder were battling daily against heavy odds. The indomitable courage of the fighter pilots and the skill of their leaders brought us through the crises, and the morale of the Germans eventually cracked because of the stupendous losses which they sustained.

Air Chief Marshal Sir Hugh Dowding
Commander-in-Chief Fighter Command

A staggering 13,000 rounds of discouraging AA shells were hurled aloft during the following night from sixty-one IAZ sites firing almost continuously for 3 hours. Flames consumed Plessey's main works, the cordite section of ICI's Waltham Cross factory and a 30-inch gas main at Southall. At 23.30 a parachute mine exploded near Westminster's County Hall and thirty fire pumps rushed to the scene. Among five other huge blazes was that which overtook Taylor's Depository in Pimlico.

Events during the last few days must surely have increased Hitler's belief that an invasion would be a risky venture, and might even end in disaster for his forces. That was not view of the British Government, but on 19 September and without telling us, the Führer postponed the launch of the invasion. Single aircraft raided London, killing four in Croydon with an oil bomb, and machine-gunned Hackney from low level. A mine exploded at Barnes while attempts were being made to defuse it, and Clifford Bridge was destroyed.

Small-scale activity on the 19th preluded central London's worst night raid so far. For the first time bombs fell in Whitehall near the Scottish Office and the War Office. Gunners naturally hastened to its defence and some of the 2,418 rounds fired from forty-nine sites at last clouted the foe. The first success came to ZE6 or ZE11 when the tail was shot off an He 111P of 3./KG 55, which at 23.05 crashed at Spellbrook, north of Harlow. The second victory came at 00.17 to ZS18 Raynes Park, whose victim, a Ju 88 of KG 51, smashed into nearby houses and the garden of Blinchley House, Merton. Potentially terrible incidents that night came when UX mines landed at St Stephen's Church in East Ham and on the LMS line near Leyton. An horrific incident involving a mine at Tilbury's Ladywell Institution was averted by evacuating the inmates. Less fortunate were sixty who suffered when a direct hit wrecked a trench shelter in Lordship Lane, Tottenham. Among well-known places that suffered during the night were the Inner Temple hall and library, Senate House and London University building in Holborn, Westminster's County Hall and Peter Robinson's store in Oxford Street. By dawn London's fatalities totalled 390. Again, it was not only London that was being dealt with, for one bomb exploded in a Lyneham hangar on the 20th. In daylight a two-raid fighter sweep over Kent cost the RAF seven Spitfires and four pilots killed when the top cover bounced them. Unrecognised by the British, the German invasion force was starting to disperse.

While Bf 109s roamed very high over the South East on the 21st, small numbers of Ju 88s carried out nuisance attacks, one of Lehr 1 flying low-level to Brooklands where three bombs exploded on the landing ground and one entered the Hurricane assembly shop. Before it could explode it was courageously taken from the building. It was fortunate, too, that after the ninety-third parachute mine floated down it rested in a stonemason's yard in Cemetery Road, central Ipswich, and failed to explode. An ARP team using a stirrup pump bravely extinguished its burning harness. Impossible to defuse, it had to be blown in situ, the controlled explosion producing a crater 50 feet wide and 25 feet deep. Some ninety-five houses were demolished, 750 damaged and windows smashed as far away as 650 yards. Parachute mines – not to be confused with land mines – were very frightening to gaze upon and most potent area destruction blast weapons.

Night raiders penetrating a hail of 4,124 AA shells over London on the 21st/22nd dropped a mine on Hornchurch's landing ground. It failed to detonate. Serious damage was caused to Allen & Hanbury's Bethnal Green medical works. A fire started in Howard's timber yard, Poplar, was attended by eighty pumps. On 22/23 September a parachute mine exploding at Ilford demolished 100 houses and damaged many more, while in Poplar and Lambeth direct hits killed more than fifty in shelters. The British Museum's King Edward buildings were damaged, and Mile End 'tube' station was closed by a direct hit.

On the 23rd/24th London was under Red Alert from 19.56 to 05.27. Fire engulfed Clarnico's, trapping more than 100 in the factory's basement shelter. By midnight twenty-four serious fires were burning in West Ham. Searchlights were exposed 220 times, seven times illuminating raiders for the forty-two AA sites, which loosed off 5,565 rounds. Fire from a Vickers Twin Mk 8 at Waltham Cross exploded a descending mine, and SM11 guns brought down He 111H-3 1H+GP of 6./KG 26 at Q3981, Chobham, and three men became PoWs. Heavy night raids employing from around 150 to 230 bombers against London, daylight forays by fighters intended to wear out RAF pilots, and a few bombers carrying out cloud-cover attacks formed the backbone of activity while the Germans formulated new means of reducing British resistance. Far too late to influence the Battle came concentration upon flattening fighter production sources.

Numbers of guns and searchlights deployed

Date	Heavy guns	Bofors guns	Searchlights
31 July	1,267	390	4,193
28 August	1,327	447	4,242
28 September	1,378	479	4,278
26 October	1,405	542	4,524

The gunners' success, 30 September
About 250 rounds of AA fire were needed to bring down an enemy aircraft by day. At night 20,000 rounds were expended to bring down one raider, 11,000 rounds by 31 October.

The gunners' claims – much inflated

Total	In daylight	At night
To 31 August	178	28
For September	122	23
For October	21	18

Two groups of bombers operating on 24 September over the Medway area – one entering over Dover and the other by way of the River Crouch – were challenged by eighteen fighter squadrons. Soon after 13.00 there came from the Cherbourg direction eighteen Bf 110s of Erpr 210. ZG 76 provided top cover to the fighter-bombers making direct for Supermarine's Woolston works. Each dived upon the factory area to deliver a 250kg bomb; five scored hits on the factory area but they did not cause serious damage. One bomb, however, killed and wounded skilled and senior staff in a shelter, for the loss – south of the Isle of Wight – of only one bomber. Higher-level raiders also tried unsuccessfully for Woolston. After dark London suffered yet again, while Berlin was bombed and a Wellington delivered 91,500 propaganda leaflets to residents there and at Hanover and Hamburg.

Too late, the Luftwaffe attacked Southampton's Supermarine works, seen by the river at the top of the photograph (the topmost 'C'). As here, concentration was mainly on the dock area. *Bundesarchiv*

London was under a long Red Alert – from 20.10 to 05.30 – on 24/25 September, some raiders over the IAZ chancing their luck by trying to fire the colours of the day. That did not stop AA gunners from firing another 5,480 rounds. Very heavy bombing that commenced at midnight caused incidents in Camberwell, Chelsea, Islington, Kensington, at St Mary's Hospital, in Chancery Lane, Queen's Hall, University College, Lambeth, Marylebone Road, St Pancras, Waterloo station, Wormwood Scrubs, Earl's Court station, Kew Bridge and *The Times* building in Queen Victoria Street. Over North Woolwich there was an air burst of a parachute mine, and more mines fell at Mitcham and Luton. In dealing with the London fires, fifty-eight pumps were needed in Hampstead, forty-eight at the Southampton Buildings in Bloomsbury, and twenty at Maple's Tottenham Court Road furniture store.

Dispersal of the invasion assembly now released reinforcements for Luftflotte 3. That allowed it to resume large-scale daylight operations on 25 September with a morning attack by He 111s of KG 55 on the Bristol Aeroplane works at Filton. No 10 Group, after incorrect intelligence indications, had reacted to Raid 22H attacking Yeovil and positioned its squadrons accordingly. As a result, 90 tons of HEs and twenty-four oil bombs caused serious damage to Filton's aero engine and airframe works, as well as nearby villages and communications. Casualties amounted to sixty dead and 150 injured before Nos 152 and 238 Squadrons struck down at least three of the withdrawing Heinkels. AA gunners claimed another, and two escorting

Ju 88 As of 8.Staffel, III Gruppe of KG 77 based at Laon/Athies.

Bf 110s were also destroyed. Several Ju 88s of LG 1 later dive-bombed oil installations at Portland, and at Plymouth, where a crane was battered. Next day No 504 Squadron moved to Filton for local defence.

Encouraged by its achievements, KG 55 repeated the success on 26 September. Shortly before 16.00 Raid 20H, a group of about sixty enemy aircraft, was discovered by radar. Proceeding along the west side of Southampton Water, it then turned north-east, hiding behind large, elongated clouds, and was clearly heading for Southampton. At 16.28 twenty-seven Bf 110s attacked the Itchen and Woolston Vickers-Supermarine works, six dive-bombing, and the remainder attacking from 14,000 feet. A quarter of an hour later, tracking in over the New Forest, came thirty-five Heinkels escorted by fifty fighters to attack the Spitfire factory. Some of their 70 tons of bombs strayed onto Dawks gasworks, killing eleven and injuring sixteen. Another eleven were killed at the docks. Twelve squadrons of fighters ordered to intercept mostly flew too high, and it was Solent guns that challenged the raiders. Four fighter squadrons went into action after the bombing and shot down an He 111, and two ZG 26 Bf 110s on the Isle of Wight. The fight cost six RAF fighters and two pilots killed. Casualties at Supermarine were serious, nearly 100 dying in and around the factory, where Spitfire production and Supermarine's B.12/36 heavy bomber prototype were devastated. As a result, Spitfires were soon being completed widely over the area to prevent a repeat attack.

Air-bursting mines prompted immediate interest in the possibility of gun-laying radar detecting a slowly descending mine, allowing gunners to destroy the obscenity. Forlorn that hope, for when a Lysander flew over Richmond Park and released four canisters simulating mines, only gun site ZS20 located them. On the 25/26th, after the London sirens wailed at 20.44, gunners fired another 7,714 rounds, and the next night, settling for 4,418 shots, failed to prevent mines landing in Uxbridge and Hornsey, and damage to the west frontage of the House of Commons building.

On 26/27 September German bombers operated widely south of a line from Liverpool to Hull causing very many incidents. Standard Motors at Coventry was considerably damaged, and one of eight HEs that hit RAF Northolt struck a barrack block so steeply that it passed through two reinforced floors. Serious damage was also caused in Birkenhead and Liverpool.

By day the Luftwaffe was still trying in vain to exhaust Fighter Command. Bf 109s and 110s repeatedly rode over Kent to lure RAF fighter pilots into tiresome and wasteful high-altitude combat. In Phase One on the 27th the Observer Corps reported six large bombers circling Kenley. The only bombs to fall were reported in the Dover area. Ju 88s of KG 77 attempted two raids on London and lost thirteen of their number to British fighters, which forced back the rest. Bf 110s of LG 1 fared little better, losing seven of their number over Kent and Surrey. Mid-morning saw other Bf 110s of ZG 26 heading inland towards Bristol. Fighters, particularly of 504 Squadron, forced them to jettison their loads outside the city, and five were shot down. It turned out to be a day of mutual heavy losses.

On 28 September the Luftwaffe mounted two main attacks employing Bf 110 and Ju 88 fast bombers protected by masses of Bf 109s flying high over the South East. From four large morning raids, only six enemy aircraft managed to penetrate to central London after twenty-four RAF squadrons reacted. Afternoon activity aroused a twenty-five-squadron response to deal with about forty bombers and 120 fighters, again flying high. Other fighters engaged about fifty Bf 110s off Portsmouth. After dark 121 raiders approached London, sixty-five crossing its heart between 18.46 and 07.12, causing the guns to fire for 9 hours. Major incidents occurred at Lambeth and Nine Elms goods yards, on the Albert Embankment, and in Southwark, where three HEs destroyed St Peter's Crypt shelter, killing eighteen outright and trapping many. Difficult, isn't it, to believe such things really happened in familiar places?

On 30 September another four operations were mounted over the South East, the third involving Ju 88s of KG 30 and KG 51. Aimed at Kingston and apparently RAF Uxbridge, six Ju 88s dive-bombed Greenford in error, dropping about 100 bombs in that area, severely damaging more than 400 houses and causing widespread disruption to electricity supplies. Weybridge and Slough were listed for a fourth assault. Two operations were also mounted against Portland, and considerable damage was caused by two raids on Bexhill. Bombing operations were attempted widely over the South East and London, and a Bf 109/110 feint off Dorset, before forty escorted He 111s of KG 55 headed towards Yeovil. This time 10 Group's intelligence learning was right. Four squadrons engaged the intruders, Nos 56, 152 and 504 Squadrons very ferociously. They shot down four, but the rest, on being turned back, jettisoned their loads around Sherborne. In a hectic day's fighting the Luftwaffe lost in combat twenty-four Bf 109s together with five very seriously damaged and five more put out of action. Four Ju 88s and a Do 17Z were destroyed, and eight more bombers were very seriously battered. RAF fighter losses amounted to twenty-six aircraft destroyed, five badly damaged and fifteen pilots killed.

A contrast in camouflage is shown between two Bf 110Cs of ZG 26 the Horst Wessel
Gruppe. *Bundesarchiv*

September's night raids had seen 5,300 tons of bombs aimed at the capital,
whose proximity to so many new German bases, and its size, made it an easy night
target. Its defence mainly rested with blind-fired gun barrages. Dowding, despite his
protestations, was instructed to switch some Hurricanes to night-fighting, despite
his accurate forecast that only radar-equipped night-fighters were likely to make
many night kills. By 30 September in the IAZ alone there were 196 guns – 145
3.7-inch and forty-eight 4.5-inch and 6 3-inch. Numbers increased, and by 31
October the IAZ was holding a total of 233. Fighters patrolled, whenever possible,
but interceptions were a matter of chance. Little wonder that the Luftwaffe was now
putting much effort into the night sky.

Day raids had not been entirely abandoned. On 1 October a Portsmouth raid was
intercepted and next day, with Bf 109s plentiful over the South East, only Spitfires
tried to challenge them. That involved wearisome battle climbs to 25,000 feet above
which the two-stage supercharger in the Bf 109s' engine gave the German fighters a
good advantage. At more than 20,000 feet they could also easily avoid accurate
detection. Flying fast, they took only 20 minutes to reach London, giving British
fighters little time to react. Since it was impossible to distinguish fighters from
fighter-bombers at high altitude, and with the latter equipping or about to equip one
gruppe of each Jagdeschwader, reaction was needed in nearly all cases.

To improve detection a special unit, No 421 Flight, was formed. Its task was to
operate high observing and identifying enemy activity. Single Spitfires were initially
fielded, but after four were shot down pairs were substituted. In the tough, bright
conditions of the high combat zone, pilots easily tired, giving credence to German

belief that Fighter Command could still fail through exhaustion. October's weather prevented any likelihood of that possibility by producing many days when operations were impracticable except by single bombers selecting key targets. Even so, 100 RAF fighter pilots were killed and sixty-five injured during October, and the Luftwaffe had aimed 7,160 tons of HE and dropped 4,735 canisters of incendiaries upon London.

Luftwaffe losses during operations 16-30 September 1940

a = shot down, b = crashed during sortie, c = seriously damaged

September	16			17			18			19			20		
	a	b	c	a	b	c	a	b	c	a	b	c	a	b	c
Do 17P	–	–	–	–	–	–	–	–	–	–	–	–	–	–	1
Do 17Z	–	–	–	–	–	–	–	–	–	–	1	2	–	–	1
Do 215	–	–	–	–	–	–	1	–	–	–	–	–	–	–	–
He 111H	–	–	–	–	–	–	–	–	–	–	–	–	–	–	–
He111P	–	–	–	–	–	–	–	–	–	1	–	–	1	–	–
He 115	1	–	–	1	–	–	–	–	–	–	1	–	–	–	–
Ju 88	2	2	–	3	1	1	10	1	–	6	–	2	–	1	2
Ju 88C	1	–	–	–	–	–	–	–	–	–	–	–	–	–	–
Bf 109	2	–	1	3	–	–	6	1	1	–	–	–	–	2	1
Bf 110	–	–	–	–	–	–	–	–	–	–	–	–	–	–	–
Totals	6	2	1	7	1	1	17	2	1	7	2	4	1	3	5

September	21			22			23			24			25		
	a	b	c	a	b	c	a	b	c	a	b	c	a	b	c
Do 17P	–	–	–	–	–	–	–	–	–	–	–	–	–	–	–
Do 17Z	–	2	–	–	–	1	–	–	–	1	–	1	–	–	–
Do18										–	–	–	1	–	–
Do 215	1	–	–	–	–	–	–	–	–	–	–	–	–	–	–
He 59										–	–	–	–	–	–
He 111H	–	–	–	–	–	1	–	2	–	1	–	–	4	1	1
He111P	–	1	–	–	–	–	–	–	–	–	–	–	1	–	1
He 115	–	–	–	–	–	–	–	–	–	–	–	–	–	1	–
Ju87										–	–	–	–	–	–
Ju 88	2	2	–	1	1	–	1	1	–	1	1	1	–	–	–
Ju 88C	–	–	–	–	–	–	–	–	–	–	–	–	–	–	–
Bf 109	–	–	–	–	–	–	8	1	3	–	–	2	1	1	–
Bf 110	–	–	–	–	–	–	–	–	–	3	–	–	2	–	1
Totals	3	5	–	1	2	1	11	2	3	6	1	4	9	3	3

Luftwaffe losses during operations 16-30 September 1940

a = shot down, b = crashed during sortie, c = seriously damaged

September	26			27			28			29			30		
	a	b	c	a	b	c	a	b	c	a	b	c	a	b	c
Do 17P	–	–	–	–	–	–	–	–	–	–	1	–	–	–	–
Do 17Z	–	1	–	–	–	–	–	1	–	–	–	–	1	1	2
Do 18	–	1	–	–	–	–	1	–	–	–	–	–	–	–	–
Do 215	–	–	–	–	–	–	–	–	–	–	–	–	–	–	–
He 59	–	–	–	–	–	–	–	–	–	–	–	–	–	–	–
He 111H	1	–	–	–	–	1	–	3	–	–	3	2	–	–	1
He 111P	–	–	1	–	–	–	–	–	–	–	3	2	–	–	1
He 115	–	–	–	–	–	–	–	–	–	–	–	–	–	–	–
Hs 126	–	–	–	–	–	–	–	–	–	–	–	–	–	–	–
Ju 87	–	–	–	–	–	–	–	–	–	–	–	–	–	–	–
Ju 88	–	2	–	15	–	–	i	–	1	–	3	–	5	2	2
Ju 88C	–	–	–	–	–	–	–	–	–	–	–	–	–	–	–
Bf 109	1	–	–	14	2	3	2	–	1	1	–	2	26	3	5
Bf110	3	–	–	18	–	2	–	–	–	–	–	–	–	–	1
Totals	5	3	1	47	2	6	4	7	2	1	10	6	32	6	12

Luftwaffe losses during operations 16-30 September 1940

a = shot down, b = crashed during sortie, c = seriously damaged

September	Grand total		
	a	b	c
Do 17P	0	1	2
Do 17Z	29	9	17
Do 18	4	1	3
Do 215	2	0	0
He 59	1	2	1
He 111H	33	20	33
He 111P	7	10	6
He 115	4	3	0
Hs 126	0	0	1
Ju 87	0	1	0
Ju 88	81	29	21
Ju 88C	1	0	0
Bf 109	182	37	47
Bf110	75	5	9
Totals	419	118	130

RAF losses during operations 16-30 September 1940

a = shot down, b = crashed during sortie, c = seriously damaged

September	16			17			18			19			20		
	a	b	c	a	b	c	a	b	c	a	b	c	a	b	c
Blenheim F	–	–	–	–	–	–	–	–	1	–	–	–	–	–	–
Beaufighter	–	–	–	–	–	–	–	–	–	–	–	–	–	–	–
Defiant	–	–	–	–	–	–	–	–	–	–	–	–	–	–	–
Hurricane	1	–	–	4	1	–	4	–	1	–	–	–	–	–	1
Spitfire	1	–	–	1	–	3	6	–	2	–	–	–	7	–	1
Battle	–	–	–	–	–	–	–	–	–	–	–	–	–	–	–
Blenheim B	–	–	–	–	–	–	–	–	–	2	–	–	–	–	–
Hampden	–	–	–	–	–	–	1	–	1	2	–	2	–	–	1
Wellington	–	–	–	–	–	–	–	–	–	2	–	–	–	–	–
Whitley	–	–	–	–	–	–	–	–	–	3	–	–	–	–	–
Coastal Cmd	–	–	–	–	–	–	1	–	–	2	–	–	1	–	–
Totals	2	–	–	5	1	3	12	–	5	11	–	2	8	–	3

September	21			22			23			24			25		
	a	b	c	a	b	c	a	b	c	a	b	c	a	b	c
Blenheim F	–	–	–	–	–	–	–	–	–	–	–	–	–	1	–
Beaufighter	–	–	–	–	–	–	–	–	–	–	–	–	–	–	–
Defiant	–	–	–	–	–	–	–	–	–	–	–	–	–	–	–
Hurricane	–	–	–	–	–	–	6	–	–	2	1	–	2	–	–
Spitfire	–	–	1	–	–	–	3	1	–	4	–	1	1	–	–
Battle	–	–	–	–	–	–	–	–	–	–	–	–	1	–	–
Blenheim B	–	–	–	–	–	–	–	–	–	1	–	1	2	–	–
Hampden	–	–	–	–	–	–	–	–	–	1	–	–	–	–	–
Wellington	1	–	1	–	–	–	–	–	1	3	–	3	–	–	–
Whitley	–	–	–	–	–	–	–	–	–	2	–	1	–	–	–
Coastal Cmd	1	–	–	–	–	–	–	–	–	–	–	–	3	–	–
Totals	2	–	2	–	–	–	9	1	1	13	1	6	9	1	–

September	26			27			28			29			30		
	a	b	c	a	b	c	a	b	c	a	b	c	a	b	c
Blenheim F	–	–	–	–	–	–	–	–	1	–	–	1	–	–	0
Beaufighter	–	–	–	–	–	–	–	–	–	–	–	–	–	–	0
Defiant	–	–	–	–	–	–	–	1	–	–	–	–	–	–	0
Hurricane	6	–	1	11	–	4	10	1	–	5	–	–	14	1	5
Spitfire	2	–	–	16	1	1	4	1	2	–	–	–	3	–	3
Battle	–	–	–	–	–	–	–	–	–	–	–	–	–	–	1
Blenheim B	1	–	–	–	–	–	–	–	–	–	–	–	–	–	6
Hampden	1	–	1	2	–	–	1	–	–	–	–	–	–	–	8
Wellington	–	–	–	–	–	1	2	–	3	–	1	–	–	11	0
Whitley	–	–	–	–	–	–	–	–	–	–	–	–	–	–	5
Coastal Cmd	1	–	–	1	–	–	2	–	–	2	–	–	10	–	
Totals	11	–	2	30	1	6	19	3	3	10	–	2	27	1	8

RAF losses during operations 16-30 September 1940

a = shot down, b = crashed during sortie, c = seriously damaged

September	Grand Total		
	a	b	c
Blenheim F	0	1	3
Beaufighter	0	0	0
Defiant	0	1	0
Hurricane5	65	4	12
Spitfire	48	3	12
Battle	1	0	0
Blenheim B	6	0	1
Hampden	8	0	5
Wellington	11	0	7
Whitley	5	0	1
Coastal Cmd	24	0	0
Totals	168	9	43

The shapely body, unmistakable wing and obvious agility coupled with a unique whistling signature tune, made the Spitfire star of the show to which Hurricanes contributed in far greater numbers.

American aircraft lacked the performance needed in the 1940 European war. North American, answering British needs, quickly designed the P-51 Mustang which first flew on 26 October 1940. Others first flown in 1940 were the Italian Caproni Campini N-1 turbine test aircraft (28 August), German Bv 222 six-motor seaplane (7 September), Martin B-26 Marauder (25 November) and Henschel Hs 293A radio-controlled glider bomb (16 December).

Very effective raids making good use of cloud and rain cover were increasingly practicable now that the weather was generally deteriorating. Some fifty raiders employing such tactics on 2 October crossed London's IAZ and not all escaped. One was Do 17Z U5+FA of KG 2, which was shot down near RAF Pulham. Hurricanes of 17 Squadron involved were so short of fuel that two (V7241 of Pilot Officer F. Fajtl and V7650 of Flying Officer H. P. Blatchford) had to force-land. Pilot Officer J. K. Ross, who delivered the coup de grâce to the bomber, landed P3536 alongside his quarry just for the satisfaction of seeing its crew taken prisoner. He then took off for Debden, only to find his fuel state so low that he was lucky to reach Martlesham for refuelling. What that bomber's crew might have achieved was displayed at Banbury's gasworks, and more importantly at Hatfield next day. Ju 88A 3Z+BB of Stab I/KG 77 set out from Laon to bomb Jacob's biscuit factory in Reading. Poor conditions prevented the crew finding their objective and, in seeking another, they came across the de Havilland factory at Hatfield. Small arms fire encountered as they ran in low set light to their starboard engine. Undaunted, they made a second run to drop four HEs, killing twenty-one workers and wounding seventy before crashing at Hertfordbury. They had, without realising it, destroyed 80% of the raw materials gathered for Mosquito production and much work in progress.

At night on 3/4 October London was hit again. Damage was caused to the main hangar at General Aircraft's Feltham works, where Hurricanes were repaired. A single raider started a fire at Hawker's Kingston factory on the 5th, and New Cross telephone exchange was hit. Better weather allowed Bf 109s and 110s to operate high over Kent and the London area before KG 77s afternoon raid on Southampton.

Prominence is naturally awarded to large-scale raids, but lone aircraft sorties by day and night – daily events – were often memorable, as on 5 October. At around 23.45 four oil bombs and some 300 1kg incendiaries fell near Reach, Cambridgeshire, close to the Devil's Ditch and on Slade Farm. Needing to ensure that in future all bombs were accounted for, a Civil Defence officer next morning visited the local school where it transpired that an amazing 213 bomb tails had been harvested by the children and many by adults who, using spades, had extinguished bombs by throwing soil upon them from about 5 feet away. One bomb, which penetrated a roof and set fire to bedding, was extinguished by the house occupant who climbed onto the rafters and put out the fire using his garden hose, one end of which his wife was holding on an outside tap. Another incendiary crashed through a roof but failed to penetrate the ceiling. The woman householder, aided by two friends, climbed onto the rafters then pushed the burning bomb through the ceiling and into a large dish held by two men who daringly took it into the garden, where it burned itself out. It later transpired that several live incendiaries were being locally used as door stops!

My father called, 'I've got a job, boy. Near Burwell, have to pick up some things. Do you want to come?'

At 10:30 on 3 October Ju 88A 3Z+BB of Stab I/KG 77 set out from Laon to bomb Reading. Visibility was poor and instead a damaging attack was made by chance on de Havilland Hatfield where 21 died and 70 were injured. The raider was shot down nearby. About 80% of raw materials for the Mosquito were lost and much completed work too. The attack could so easily have destroyed the prototype seen here on 19 November about to start pre-first flight engine running.

Although he didn't explain what, I was only too pleased to go, and true to expectation some ARP chaps and a 'bobby' greeted us. 'They're in the shed – we'll bring them to your car. Hold this,' said one of them, passing me a live 1kg 'ib'. We put six of them in the boot. Then a far more menacing object appeared. Very dark grey, about 3 feet long and almost cylindrical, it was an unignited parachute flare. 'Whatever you do, don't pull the string – it might make it go off!' said a cheery soul. I did *not* pull the string. I did wonder, though, who and what had dropped it, and where it has come from.

'Hang on,' one of the locals called, 'here's another one.' I told Dad to drive home very carefully, not too much bumping and no speeding, please. My father's local authority work, and the fact that his brother was the area Civil Defence Officer, led him/us to sometimes gather supposedly 'safe' items, which were taken usually to Cherry Hinton Hall for safe disposal by the Army, as in this case. Flares were alarming, spooky, hovering heralds of doom. Nursing a couple of parachute flares across one's lap when sitting in the back seat of a family Hillman was not a funny experience.

Another formation day raid, this time by Ju 88s of II/KG 51 covered by Bf 110s of ZG 26, penetrated to Westland's Yeovil works on the 7th, despite the attention of British fighters, which shot down seven of ZG 26 and two Ju 88s before Bf 109s at the Dorset coast offered withdrawal support to their comrades. Four small day raids against London left fires in dockland and Rotherhithe. On 9 October it was Maidstone that particularly suffered, eighty-seven buildings being damaged by fighter-bomber attack. Using cloud cover a single raider managed to damage English Electric's Stafford factory. On the 11th Bf 109s gave cover to fighter-bombers flying at almost 30,000 feet. It was a misty day and their bombs fell over Kent. Later, similar formations bombed Biggin Hill and Kenley. At night Liverpool and the Midlands came under attack.

A compressed paper parachute flare case 3ft 3 in long (left) and the metal base of the four 3-inch diameter candles. A 14 foot diameter parachute was packed in a domed lid (missing). It was best to handle one of these objects with care…and resist the temptation to pull the string and see the firework display!

October became 'Messerschmitt month' because their dual fighter-bomber role was hard to deal with. One target was North Weald where Hurricanes like V6728 GN-Z of 249 Squadron were based. Free Frenchman Flt Lt Georges Perrin stands in his distinctive uniform. *Michael Payne*

By now it looked certain that very large-scale, conventional, escorted bomber operations against Britain were all but over. Far, far more effective it had become to employ high-speed fighter-bombers protected by fighters, and all soon equally furious. Although their bombing from high altitudes was inaccurate, that was true of many heavily escorted conventional bomber raids. On 12 October, the date when Hitler finally abandoned a 1940 invasion of Britain, a 250kg bomb dropped by LG 2 from a great height exploded in Piccadilly Circus, killing five. Fighter Command would have difficulty in combating such activity. It would be costly, but in no way could break the Command. Instead, resolve to hold on would strengthen – like the demand to hit back.

The use of Bf 109s as fighter-bombers (a Bf 109E-4 is seen here) radically changed the campaign. These high-fliers came in fast, bombed, and became excellent fighters. *Bundesarchiv*

Two days later fighter-bombers penetrated as far as North Weald. On 14/15 October an assault was mounted on industrial Coventry by sixty Do 17s while, making maximum use of bright moonlight, some 200 Heinkels and Ju 88s rained some 1,000 HEs and fifty mines upon London, killing 591 and injuring nearly 2,300 people. Wood Green underground station was hit as well as an adjacent tunnel, killing fourteen and seriously injuring fifty-one people. Unbelievable, isn't it, that where one passes, maybe waits for a bus, chats to a girlfriend, awful events have occurred like the one that overcame a block of flats at Stoke Newington, where 150 were sheltering in basements, two of which were destroyed. The other was flooded.

The fighter-bombers found London once more for, on the 15th, they placed a 250kg bomb at the entrance to Waterloo station. A decision was now made: No 11 Group would have to regularly fly at high altitude despite it being wasteful, expensive and with a quite high attrition rate.

A night painted Ju 88 A of KG 30 shelters under camouflage nets.

Not since June had the Luftwaffe concentrated on night bombing operations. Heavy losses in daylight, the onset of inclement weather, long hours of darkness and the success of fighter-bomber operations, all led to a switch to night raiding. Airfields captured in France and the Low Countries allowed Luftflotten II and III to readily operate short-range bombers, and when the weather over the UK was bad for its defenders but not the attackers. Radio and visual beacons, homing equipment, target finding relying upon radio beams, all were now in use, enabling a force of about 700 bombers each carrying a modest load nevertheless to pack a hefty punch. Lightly defended, they had been designed to rely more on speed than gun defence, but by 1941 were clearly too slow. During the period from 7 September to the end of that month, about 5,300 tons of HE bombs were unleashed upon the London region, four times as much as in daylight.

Immediately following the 7/8 September London raids, the number of heavy AAQ guns in the IAZ was increased from 92 to 190 by transferring them from smaller south coast ports and the Midlands. From 11 September, the gunners no longer relied upon prediction and produced undirected barrages, a kill by chance and not by aim. Although the intense noise from constantly bursting shells was for many a morale booster cloaking the sound of enemy aircraft and bursting bombs, the barrage produced shoals of fragmented hot shrapnel.

By October 1940 80 Group RAF had in place fifteen very secret installations to counteract *Knickbein*, equipment to interfere with German M/F beacons, with *X-Gerät* and to re-radiate radio signals. Dowding had only eight dedicated night-fighter squadrons, six flying Blenheims too slow for the role. They were divided among the four fighter Groups, Nos 11 and 12 Groups each holding two squadrons. In 12 Group there was No 264 Defiant Squadron, the others split to serve Nos 11 and 13 Groups. Single-engined day fighters could be called upon at night, but without guidance and homing aids their pilots had an almost impossible and quite hazardous task. A handful of airborne interception (AI) radar sets being tested by the Fighter Interception Unit's Blenheims and Beaufighters had teething problems. Without direction towards the foe, AI radar projecting a wide search 'beam' was of little use. Gun laying and searchlight guidance radar had been developed, and was being tried. London's balloon barrage kept the enemy high. Radio transmissions to mislead the enemy were tried with some success, but London was too big to miss.

Switching to night operations brought various problems, lit runways inevitably attracting RAF attention.

Damage had become widespread in London, and most severe in dockland and river side. Many warehouses holding highly combustible contents and much food were destroyed. Gasworks and power stations were disabled, rail traffic was severely interrupted, unexploded bombs caused much chaos. The extent of fatal and serious civilian casualties was lower than forecast pre-war, but interruption of daily life was very extensive, and especially when public transport was hit.

On 15th October, after 400 bombers attacked, London Transport's District and Metropolitan line was left seriously disrupted. Baker Street and Moorgate stations were out of use, and no trains ran between South Kensington and Edgware Road stations. Liverpool Street, Paddington and Waterloo stations were hit along with Beckton gasworks and Battersea power station. A burst main sewer flooded the tunnel linking Farringdon Street with King's Cross. Delayed action bombs and parachute mines caused damage to two underground stations, and the City was badly hit. Road closures due to UXBs were widespread and included Oxford Street and London Bridge. Three large water main pipes were fractured causing flooding and loss of water for fire fighting. That was very serious because there were over 600 fires, six classified as 'major', nine as 'serious'. Resulting from bombing lasting from soon after dusk to 05:55 next day, 512 civilians were killed outright and almost 1,000 were seriously injured and 11,000 were left homeless, mainly in London's East End. Around 200 people had died while trying to find shelter. Serious incidents were widely occurring outside London too. On the 17th, while the capital was bombed, a parachute mine exploded on a hangar at RAF Ternhill and destroyed twenty aircraft within.

By October 1940 intense night bombing of London resulted in many Londoners sleeping not just on the underground station platforms but, as here at Aldwych, on newspaper laid over the greasy tracks. *IWM*

Despite the prolonged period of night attacks on London, results although serious were not catastrophic. Damage to the dock warehouses was extensive, but rail links, quays and locks survived. Trade was eventually restored in the Port of London, and public utilities and the transport system were quite soon repaired. Food loss was reduced as result of widespread storage. Delayed action and UX bombs were courageously attended to very effectively, naval parties dealing with UX parachute mines.

Very large numbers of homeless Londoners were short of sleep and toilet facilities, needed hot drinks and somewhere to escape. Move outside and they entered a frightening world where total darkness was punctured by land and air explosions, brilliant flashes, fearsome fires and terrifying looking skies or a most unwelcome moon. Although they experienced Hell on Earth, the resolve of the great Prime Minister helped morale to remain high. Of great importance was widespread bizarre humour, also new levels of friendship which crossed class divides as much as age groups. Self sacrifice in the face of great peril – ever present – strengthened the national backbone. In the poor boroughs of the East End as much as in the West End there was grim determination never to waver. Many would have said 'Maybe it's because I'm a Londoner'.

What might have changed the outcome of the entire campaign, even the war, would have been ample long-range drop tanks for Bf 109s, as fitted to this Bf 109E-7. *Bundesarchiv*

Had the Germans otherwise devoted the effort spent on the Bf 110, their success might have increased. This Bf 110, 2N+ET, was of I/ZG 26, Stavanger. *Michael Payne*

Much 'Jabo' (ie fighter-bomber) activity occurred on 20 October, a day that also saw an unbelievable event. With a four-man crew, Dornier Do 17Z, W Nr 2783, 7T+AH, of 1./Ku Fl Gr 606, departed late afternoon from Poulmiac to photograph damage at Liverpool. After turning in from the Irish Sea too soon, heavy storms encountered around Shrewsbury put the radio out of action. They headed south and near Chippenham their compass was put out by storm action. In error they made what they believed was a 180-degree turn. With the aircraft short of fuel they baled out when near Salisbury. Amazingly, the Dornier flew on easterly and next day was discovered belly-flopped, intact and lying in the mud of Ness Creek, Erwarton, 7 miles south-east of Ipswich.

Most attention was being paid to the heavy night raids upon London, but at sea there were equally terrifying events. Operating out of Norway and north-west France was KG 40, partly equipped with a handful of Fw 200 Condor long-range bombers. On 26 October, about 150 miles north-west of Ireland, a Condor of 2./KG 40 came upon the 42,000 grt CP liner *Empress of Britain*, which was bombed and set on fire. As the ship limped towards safety with limited fighter cover it was torpedoed by a U-boat. Soon after, the huge ship exploded and sank.

It was late afternoon on 27 October, a day that saw Fighter Command fly 1,007 sorties against the Jabo nuisance, and when extensive operations against RAF bomber stations in eastern England were ending, that a low-flying Do 17Z slipped in at 18.23 to cross south Ipswich at dusk and in drizzle. A considerable number of small unusual objects were seen to fall from it. Soon came reports of damage to assorted overhead wires following small explosions. Then, on Poplar Farm, Sproughton, five unexploded objects were discovered, small cylinders with vanes attached to a rod. One was dropped by police examining it, the small resultant explosion killing one officer and badly injuring three others. Very soon it became clear that a shoal of vicious small anti-personnel weapons had been sown along a 2-mile corridor about a quarter of a mile wide. Search for more continued through the night, then next day the main fear was realised. Two children found one in a wood and were badly injured when it exploded. By then more had been discovered at Kelsale, near Saxmundham, and several had apparently been discovered and unidentified two days previously in Blyth RD. On 14 October different small bombs later identified as Type SD1 had been dropped on Luton, further research leading to the conclusion that twenty-three (probably intended for RAF

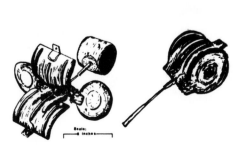

To have dropped SD 2 butterfly anti-personnel bombs over populated areas was a dastardly deed. Weighing 2kg the little cylindrical bomb 3.5in long and 3.25in in diameter was delivered in an AB 23 container which carried 23 of them. Upon ejection four wings encasing the bomb unfolded and began twisting a five inch arming cable which variously activated the fuse making the small bomb lethal – especially to inquisitive children.

Night raids brought great chaos to many parts of London, including streets such as this in the West End.

Cunliffe-Owen's major repair works at Eastleigh, near Southampton, are under attack on 13 October 1940. *Bundesarchiv*

Coltishall) had fallen near Aylsham on 31 August from an AB23 container. By 1 November fifty-four of the small bombs, commonly known as 'butterfly bombs' and officially as Type SD2, had been dealt with by the Navy at Ipswich. The Ministry of Home Security, which told the BBC to issue suitable warnings on 30 October, reckoned that 165 SD2s had so far been dropped/exploded and another sixty were unexploded, in addition to ten believed to have fallen in Samford RD on 27 October.

Gradually the weather was generally deteriorating, which was to halt the high-level Jabo raids. One of the last was one of the most memorable. Bf 109s of 3./Erpr 210 dive-bombed North Weald at 16.45, dropping 100kg HEs just as Nos 249 and 257 Squadrons were responding to their threat. A fight ensued during which the Staffelkapitan was shot down. At North Weald nineteen were killed and forty-two injured, in a very effective operation.

As the hours of darkness lengthened, and the mists of autumn further reduced daylight, the cost of achieving victory beyond doubt in what later came to be so well known as the Battle of Britain was very evident. Few pilots of pre-war days had survived, and many of the youngest perished within hours of joining a squadron. There was now more time to contemplate upon a love lost so soon, cruelly, suddenly. For many, all that remained were dreams, poignantly featured in a haunting song of the time:

'In the still of the night once again I hold you tight,
Though you're gone, your love lives on when moonlight beams.
And as long as my heart may beat,
Lover, we'll always meet here in my deep purple dreams.'

While deep emotion laced many lonely hours, there was still a need to brace oneself for certain, terrible storms ahead. Safely stowed for winter was the precious harvest, amid fears that the Luftwaffe might determinedly incinerate the grain. Every apple, including all the fallen, was safely gathered in, ere the winter storms began. Plums and greengages had been bottled or converted into jam made possible by a special sugar allowance. Even countryside verges were changing into profitable, cultivated strips, like every portion of garden plot. Going were the iron railings from the front garden, together with aluminium objects, although their recycling value for weapons was minimal. Everything that could be done to help win through was being done, and in an ideal atmosphere of community cooperation.

Going down, too, were many merchant ships, which resulted in rationing fluctuations, yet nobody seemed to feel hungry. The leaner nation was probably a fitter nation. Long nights in the shelters, and the intense cold of dawn upon emerging often presented homelessness far removed from any present-day variant. To find a home gone, changed into a pile of rubble, or to have the front blown off and a private world displayed for all to see, such were the experiences of many thousands. When a bomb burst it produced powerful shock waves that moved the air away from the explosion. Almost immediately the vacuum was filled and in the process millions of doors and windows were shattered, and sometimes people. Throughout the land there had been terribly difficult days, and for many far worse was soon to overtake them.

The Battle of Britain was waged at increasing altitude which generated amazing contrails
– particularly during Messerschmitt month. Ironically it was also Messerschmitts which
heralded the switch to low-level, under the radar hit and run raids.

Chapter 19

Nightmare visitations

The night bombing of London continued into November, for which ten Kampfgeschwaderen based in France and the Low Countries (KG 1, 2, 3, 26, 30, 51, 54, 55, 76 and 77) generated a nightly average of 200 sorties.

On 1-2 November KG 55's He 111s raided the capital while KGr 100 led others to Birmingham. More than 230 aircraft crossed the coast between Portland and Brighton on 4/5 November, before dividing into two streams. One headed for London, the other Liverpool. Between them they released forty-one parachute mines and 103 tons of incendiaries. While the Luftwaffe prepared on the 5th for the next night's activity, the RAF's No 35 Squadron reformed at Boscombe Down. A month later it would proceed to Linton-on-Ouse to equip with Handley Page Halifax four-engined bombers.

After dark 126 German aircraft operated, KG 77 bombing London, leaving the Midlands to KG 55. Daylight raids had not stopped entirely, and on 6 November seventy-one Ju 88s attacked Southampton. At the same time No 207 Squadron at RAF Waddington was eagerly examining another new British bomber, its first example of the Avro Manchester. The first production example had flown in July 1940 and twenty-five were complete before the year ended. Whereas the British were rebuilding their bomber force, the Germans would mainly soldier on with the same aircraft types or later variants of them.

On the 6/7th KGr 100 headed trains of forty Heinkels to Birmingham, and Ju 88s of Ku Fl Gr 606, the latter to position eleven large delayed-action bombs in Liverpool's dockland. At the same time seventy Ju 88s of KG 51 kept up the pressure by concentrating their effort upon north London.

An unusual event, a reminder of the past, evolved on 8 November. Ju 87s, long driven from Britain's skies, unexpectedly attacked a convoy in the Thames Estuary.

While London was nightly pounded RAF Bomber Command began re-arming with the Avro Manchester. It was ruined by its troublesome Rolls-Royce Vulture engines. L7277, the second production example and built in August 1940, was used at Boscombe Down before joining No 1654 Conversion Unit.

Day raids by Ju 88s brought formation raids to an end. Most of the 88s were by then wearing night camouflage like the KG 30 example here.

For Stukageschwader 77 this would be a last, expensive show. Six Stukas were shot down, two by the destroyer HMS *Winchester*. After dark, KG 1 and KG 77 dropped twenty-two parachute mines on London together with the normal weapons, which resulted in 300 casualties. Although destroying night raiders was difficult, the AA barrage involving the firing of more than 22,000 shells brought down three German bombers and seriously damaged another three. On 10/11 November twenty-two Ju 88s of Ku Fl Grp 606 visited Liverpool again while KG 54 attacked specified targets in London. Quite often particular places were targeted, but a near miss was equivalent to and regarded as an indiscriminate attack.

By now there had come a novel interjection into the fight, the Corpo Aereo Italiano. Signor Mussolini, El Duce, ever an opportunist, on 10 June had declared war on the Allies – after France had been subdued by Germany. Thinking the British much occupied with their home defence, he ordered his army in Libya to take the Suez Canal zone. Britain, determined to maintain its oil supplies and Far East links, resisted the Italian attack, easily driving back the invaders and capturing many together with their equipment. RAF Whitleys upset Benito by making very long night sorties to northern Italy, causing unwanted excitement among the Italian public.

Mussolini, not amused and certain that Britain was doomed, was eager for his air force to attack the seat of its Empire so that he might obtain some of the spoils from British defeat. There was German unease with those notions, but in September they relented, and forty Fiat BR 20M bombers of the 98th and 99th Gruppo, 43rd Stormo, moved into Melsbroek and Chievres. In support came fifty Fiat CR 42 270mph biplane fighters of the 55th and 56th Stormo, 18th Gruppo. Those settled at Eech/Charleroi while forty-eight Fiat G.50s of the 20th Gruppo also moved to Belgium and made Ursel their home. A few Cant Z.1007bis transports supported the force.

After dark on 25 October the Italians set forth with Harwich as the target for sixteen BR 20s. One crashed on take-off and two crews lost their way. The townsfolk of Harwich had little bother with the remainder. Next day Italian bombers were active off Kent, unsuccessfully on 5 November, trying for Harwich. On 11 November when the Fleet Air Arm slaughtered the Italian fleet in Taranto Operation No 8, the climax to the northern excursion evolved.

At 13.30 radar detected forty Fiat CR 42s escorting two formations of BR 20s, each aircraft carrying three 550lb bombs. They were heading for Convoy *Booty* off Harwich. Scrambled to greet them were thirty Hurricanes of Nos 17, 46 and 257 Squadrons, which tore apart the Italian formations. In the confusion six bombers were claimed shot down; final analysis showed three fighters and three bombers destroyed. One BR 20 crashed at Bromeswell, near Woodbridge, the only Italian bomber ever brought down on UK soil. Martlesham's Hurricane pilots went to look it over. The crew had brought along bottles of wine to enjoy as they returned from their successful sortie. Instead, it was mean local Customs men who enjoyed a celebration. There was chocolate aboard, and children were warned not to eat as it was 'probably poisoned'. Consumed by adults, it produced no undesirable effects.

Two CR 42s had crashed on land, one near Corton, the other on Orford Ness. The latter, test-flown in 1941 by NAFDU Duxford as BT474, now resides in the RAF Museum, Hendon. The Italians appeared over the Thames Estuary on 17 November, and attempted seven more night raids on East Coast targets, the last on 5 January 1941, before returning to warmer climes.

The largest Italian assault on Britain ended badly for the Romans, this being one of two Fiat CR 42s brought down. MM6976 crashed near Corton railway station. *Ford Jenkins Photography*

By November 1940 mist, rain and fog were making target-marking harder and homing difficult for the Germans, even when using radio aids. On 13/14th seventy-seven He 111s of KG 26 attacked London, dropping twenty parachute mines and many incendiaries, while sixty-three crews of KG 55 bombed Birmingham. Greater London had now been subjected to forty-two consecutive nights of aerial bombardment. Now, a dramatic operational change came into play.

'Ultra' intercepts during November revealed special activity indicating that KGr 100 was to lead and mark up to four selected industrial areas for very intensive, concentrated assault. It was essential that the enemy knew nothing of the British discovery. Nevertheless, Bomber Command was told to institute patrols over German bomber bases, and night-fighter squadrons were discreetly alerted. The first raid in the series, codenamed 'Moonlight Sonata', was found to be scheduled for 14/15 November. The chosen target was unknown. For the thousands on the receiving end the intensive bombing was never forgotten.

Brilliantly shone the moon, excellent the visibility, which made for easy marking by eighteen He 111 crews of KGr 100, who passed over Lyme Bay at 18.17 and flew directly to Coventry (which the enemy codenamed KORN). All went according to plan.

British interference with *Knickebein*, intended for daylight use and daytime cloud conditions, had rendered it of little value. In use for night-bombing since mid-August was its sophisticated replacement, *X-Gerät*, a superior radio beam system (known as Ruffians to the British), more suitable for a night offensive now directed against aircraft and aero-engine factories. On a chosen frequency, an extremely narrow radio beam with a rage of about 200 miles was precisely directed at the target. A receiver in the aircraft enabled it to be flown along the beam. Two other beams were projected across the main beam, one intersecting 15km from the target, the other at 5km. The aircraft's ground speed could be calculated from the time taken to fly between the intersections, making weapon release quite accurate, particularly since the direction beam was narrow.

Heinkel He 111H 1H+BN of 5./KG 26 beneath camouflaged protective netting features aerials associated with beam riding.

At first the necessary equipment was carried in a few aircraft of KGr 100, which began using it for flare-dropping. Later, some elements of KG 26, Poix-based, used *X-Gerät,* which guided the KGr 100 fire and marker raisers, who reached Coventry at 20.20. Using sixty-four Leuchtbomben LC 50 marker flares they marked the city centre and dropped forty 50kg H E bombs aimed at utilities, perchance close to the cathedral.

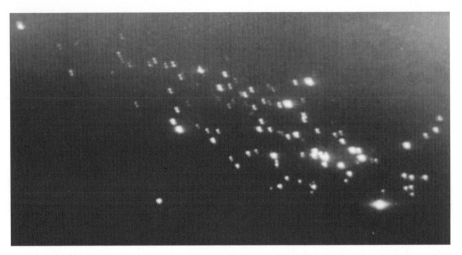

Early fires in Coventry seen from a Heinkel He 111 of KG 100.

Three Main Force elements followed. One was routed in between Selsey Bill and Portland, another between Selsey Bill and Dungeness. A third stream, presumably relying on DR navigation, processed north-westerly across East Anglia on a path about a mile wide. At 19.45 a Do 17Z of either I or III/KG 2 from Cambrai, I/KG 3 Le Culot or II/KG 3 Antwerp/Duerne led around 50 Dorniers northwesterly over Cambridge. Their contrails drenched the clear, cold moonlit sky. At about 21.30 I heard them returning on reciprocals. I had not long been in bed when more flew over, heading inland. Later, they too returned. The Red Alert lasted 9 hours. Nothing like that had happened before.

Far from being an indiscriminate attack, this, like many night raids, was directed at very specific targets including the ancillary and municipal services that could nullify its effectiveness. For the citizens of Coventry their torture was due in particular from the positioning of industrial undertakings throughout the city. For more than 10 hours they endured the bombing, which reduced central Coventry and much more to ruins.

Between 20.20 and 06.35 449 bombers in all dropped 503 tonnes of high-explosive bombs on Coventry. Luftlotte 3 alone distributed 881 BSK containers which opened to shower 28,960 x 1kg incendiary bombs upon on the city.

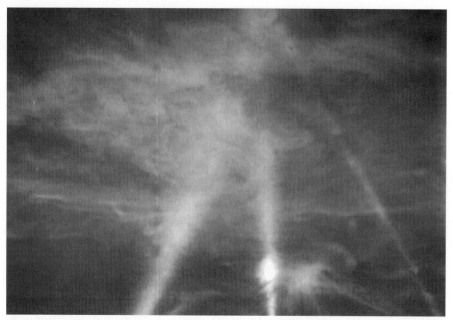

Trios of searchlight beams were a very familiar 1940 winter sight.

Bomb Loads Carried By Luftlotte 3 During 'Moonlight Sonata'

Unit of aircraft	No	SC/D -50kg	SC -250kg	SC -500 kg	SC/D -1000kg	SC -1400kg	SC -1800kg	F-250	F-500	1kg Brandbomben
I./LG 1	12	120	36	–	–	–	–	–	–	–
II. /LG 1	12	–	13	12	–	–	–	–	–	–
III. LG 1	8	50	14	5	–	–	–	–	–	–
I. /KG 27	20	375	20	1	–	–	–	–	–	–
II. /KG 27	14	224	14	–	–	–	–	–	–	–
III. /KG 27	13	200	12	–	–	–	–	–	–	–
Kgr.100	13	40	–	–	–	–	–	–	–	10,224
KFGr.606	5	90	–	–	–	–	–	–	–	540
I. /KG 51	16	10	17	18	–	–	–	14	–	360
II. /KG 51	10		4	10	3	–	–	–	–	1,368
III./KG 51	10	10	11	4	3	–	–	2	5	360
I./KG 54	11	90	22	2	–	–	–	–	–	–
II. /KG 54	7	–	–	9	–	–	–	–	9	–
KFGr.806	12	–	8	16	–	–	–	8	–	–
Stab. KG 55	2	40	–	–	–	–	–	–	–	–
. I./KG 55	13	156	–	2	11	–	–	–	–	1,872
II. /KG 55	16	64	–	5	–	11	5	–	–	2,412
III. /KG 55	9	144	–	–	–	–	–	–	–	3,888
KG 26	28	196	65	7	8	–	3	2	–	1,872
KG 76	20	296	–	5	—	–	–	2	5	1,944
KG 77	25	186	81	–	–	–	–	–	–	1,512
KG 1	24	24	49	7	1	–	–	–	–	2,176

Additional to Do 17s, Luftlotte 2 operating about 150 aircraft sent He 111s of I/KG 4 Soesterberg, II/KG 4 Eindhoven, II/KG 26 Gilze Rijen and III/KG 4 Lille/Nord, weapon loads uncertain.

A British official source reckoned that 437 aircraft attacked, dropping fifty-six tons of incendiaries and 394 tons of HE bombs, the latter a low estimate possibly influenced by the number of unexploded weapons. Also recorded was the attempted delivery of 127 Luftminen or parachute mines 104 of which were thought to have been effectively sown. They could not be directly aimed, but were parachuted onto Coventry to drift down quite slowly as they were carried along by the wind. A German survey listed forty-one LMA and eighty-six LMB weapon scarriers unknown.

Weapons dropped on Coventry were chosen for their special effects. The Brandbomben-Schuttkasten BSK-36 aluminium container weighing forty-two kg and carried on many 1940 raids contained thirty-six 1kg Elektron incendiary bombs. At the other extreme was the SC-1800 weighing around 4,000 lb containing 1,000kg of explosive for use against large buildings. Its effectiveness resulted from extreme air pressure which caused extensive damage. The smaller SC-1400 equivalent weighed around 3,000lb. Able to penetrate strong roofs of buildings was the Flammenbombe C-500, a development of the small Flam 250 'oil bomb'. The larger weapon carried 846 lb of a petrol/oil mix and relied upon a fast acting electric fuse. SD weapons had thick cases which shattered into over 1,000 splinters. The high charge content represented half the weight of the SC 500.

Among specific targets allotted to I/LG 1 were the Standard Motor Co works and Coventry Radiator & Presswork Co. II/KG 27 were given the Alvis aero-engine factory, I/KG 51 the British Piston Ring Co, using fifteen SC 500s, three LZZ 500s, seventeen S C 250s, fourteen Flam 250s ten SC 50s and ten BSK loads. Nine He 111s of II/KG 55 55 unloaded 144 SD 50 HEs and 118 BSK containers onto the Daimler works. Eighteen aircraft including those of Ku Fl Gr 606 had as their target Cornercroft gas-holders in Hill Street. The Humber Hillman works were attacked by sixty aircraft which aimed four SC 1000s, five SC 250s, four Flam 250 oil bombs, 318 SC 50s, 495 SD 50s as well as fifty-six BSK containers. The General Electric Company in the same sector of the city was raided by twenty aircraft dropping 22 SC 250s, 105 SC 50s and 105 SD 50s.All targets were variously damaged, and the entire city centre was burning within the first hour. Roads leading to it were quickly and intentionally made impassable by fallen masonry and UXBs. More than 200 major fires were raging by the early hours. Gas and water mains were badly damaged very soon after commencement of the bombing, and rail links were cut.

All bombers were vulnerable as, like these Ju 88s, they queued for take-off.

Hollow bangs from firing then bursting AA shells were an unforgettable feature of night attacks on Britain. Some batteries, like this 3.7in gun, had to be positioned in built-up areas to be effective.

Unimagined horror and terror rapidly overtook the city's population. Gas mains horrendously erupted, and water cascaded from broken pipes. Loud explosion after explosion caused thousands of homes to shudder. Adding to the cacophony was the sound of AA fire hurled into a hideous burning panoply. Many sheltered within their houses because no other refuges were available. Tested to the extreme were Civil Defence and police forces, aided by others from adjacent areas. Great courage was shown by those rescuing the many afflicted as fires raged and bombs continually fell, and over an ever-widening area. No precise record of casualties was possible to produce, but official listing showed 554 as killed outright, and 865 seriously injured, many of whom died later. Of the thousands less seriously and variously injured, and those suffering mental distress and anguish, no tally could be kept.

Although advance warning of a fearsome assault had been obtained, there was insufficient detail to allow any precise defensive measures to be taken. Fighter Command interception sorties amounted to twelve by Beaufighters, thirty by Defiants, forty-three by Hurricanes and five by Roborough/Plymouth-based 247 Squadron using Gladiator biplanes. Only one raider was destroyed, by AA fire as it approached Loughborough; it crashed in a field near Prestwald Hall. When the bombers arrived back at their bases, thirty-five Bomber Command Blenheims were awaiting them. Little was achieved, although ten crews claimed to bomb airfields at appropriate times.

It was 06.35 when the last enemy aircraft departed from Coventry. By then, much of this important provincial and industrial centre was in ruins so severe and extensive that rejuvenation seemed impossible. Yet, and quite soon, the mighty blow began to be seen as not mortal. True, central Coventry was totally smashed, together with other areas. Fresh fires had repeatedly broken out, yet all were under control by daybreak. Some 400 to 500 highly combustible retail outlets had suffered

Night fighter Defiants operated on the night of the Coventry raid.

badly, and plentiful UXBs added to extensive hazards. The city centre was closed to all but essential traffic. Mobile canteens and field kitchens were set up for CD rescue forces, and the thousands whose homes had been destroyed or made uninhabitable. Troops and additional rescue workers were brought in to commence a clear-up, and within four days there was an excellent transport service conveying workers to factories. Many of the latter suffered far less than expected, for their metal frames were less combustible than the wooden structures of shops and warehouses.

By evening on the 18th all rail routes had reopened except that to Nuneaton, which remained closed for a further three days. Highways leading out of Coventry were also open, but the local transport system had been very badly hit. Plans were made for the evacuation on the 15/16th of no fewer than 10,000 people, but only 300 accepted the offer, which, for the authorities, was extremely good news. If the torture they underwent failed to break their resolve, then nothing would, and visits from Mr Churchill and HM King George VI greatly increased morale.

Of Coventry's twenty-one main factories – a dozen aviation-orientated – most had been seriously battered or fire-damaged. Major worries concerned all water supplies. Almost 200 gas mains had been broken and electricity lines were seriously damaged. Production at nine major factories was halted due to lack of power, yet only one electric power plant was hit. A big surprise was the high proportion of workers arriving on the 16th at the badly damaged Standard Motors factory where a major building had been destroyed. Even the most seriously damaged factories were back in production within a few weeks. There were serious setbacks to production, but Coventry's industries were reparable and recoverable.

The logical assumption was that the Luftwaffe would return to Coventry in force the following night, but, as was often the case with the German war effort, someone decided to 'miss the bus' to Coventry. Only eighteen bombers attempted a follow-up raid and half of those aborted, leaving the others to tip a mere 7 tons of HE and thirty-two incendiary canisters onto the city. On the next two nights the Luftwaffe returned to London.

Of all the destruction in Coventry, that of the cathedral by fire almost immediately became the iconic representation (and propaganda coup) of the raid. Within hours a large charred, rakish main altar cross was erected and became symbolic of Coventry's torture. Melted lead from the roof trickled down the cathedral's walls and solidified to resemble lengthy grey tears shed for all who, like the precious irreplaceable building, had died in the most intense, ferocious assault ever carried out upon a British city.

Smoke and heat have produced the haze surrounding remnants of central Coventry.

What of the British bomber offensive at this period? Night operations were on a far smaller scale than the Luftwaffe's, and involved forces of around 100 aircraft. Blenheims flew day and night operations. While the Luftwaffe was raiding Coventry, RAF Bomber Command had eighty-two aircraft operating, fifty of which had been dispatched to Berlin. Only half reached the city, their bombs doing little harm. Other aircraft patrolled over Schiphol and Soesterberg to interrupt German bomber operations. The loss of ten aircraft was the heaviest yet during night operations. Next night, the 15/16th, sixty-seven bombers carried out a two-phase raid on Hamburg and caused damage to the Blohm und Voss shipyards. Casualties

The death of Coventry Cathedral and the curly smoke from its pyre were surely one of the war's most tragic and memorable events. To have released 127 parachute mines to drift at will onto Coventry was an appalling deed.

Rubble and the destroyed roof fell and covered the cathedral nave's floor. The symbolic charred cross had yet to be erected.

on the ground were low by comparison with the German raids, the city records listing twenty-six killed, 102 injured and more than 1,600 homeless. In anticipation of a second heavy night raid, Blenheims had patrolled over enemy airfields.

What was on the wireless while Coventry burned?

Home Service		Forces	
6.00pm	News	5.00pm	English Songs (records)
6.30pm	News in Norwegian	5.55pm	Ack-Ack, Beer-Beer
6.45pm	Farming Today	6.00pm	Dutch and French News
7.00pm	Howdy Folks (revue)	6.30-7.00pm	Sandy Calling (requests)
7.40pm	At the Armstrongs	7.40pm	Geraldo's Open House
8.00pm	Tantivy Towers (light opera)	8.20pm	Fred Hartley and his Quartet
9.00pm	Time and News	9.00pm	German News
9.30pm	War Commentary by Air Marshal Sir Philip Joubert	9.20pm	Good Old Timers – Jenny Hill
9.35pm	Schubert: String Quartet in A Minor	10-11.00pm	Time, Dance Orchestra
10.15pm	Service		
10.35pm	Sir Roger de Coverley		
11.15pm	Scottish Orchestra		
12-12.20am	Time and News		

While Coventry blazed 25/50 RAF bombers ineffectively raided Berlin. The loss of 10 bombers was the heaviest yet at night. One was Hampden X2996 which had joined 44 Squadron on 8 October.

Daylight raids by the Luftwaffe had not ended, but mostly they involved single aircraft using cloud cover for precise attacks or flying a roving commission. On 17 November fighter-bomber Bf 109s of Erpr 210 carried out a low-level strike on Ipswich, with more Bf 109s giving top cover. The operation came to be regarded as the first fighter-bomber 'hit and run' raid on a town. That night London and Southampton were the main targets.

On 19 November Birmingham suffered heavily, for more than 360 bombers drawn from KG 26, 54, 55 and Ku Fl 606 were used, led, as usual, by KGr 100. One of five raiders shot down fell to a sector controller and searchlight-aided airborne-interception-radar-equipped Beaufighter of 604 Squadron, which engaged its quarry over the Dorset coast. Still few in number, they became a scourge of the night-bombers in 1941. On the 22/23 Birmingham was again subjected to heavy bombing by KGr 100 and KG 76, more than 900 being killed and more than 2,000 people seriously injured. Smaller raids, each comprising some sixty aircraft, were directed at Southampton and London on 23/24 November, Bristol and Avonmouth being bombed by fifty Heinkels of KG 55 while one Gruppe, drawn from KG 26, targeted London during the night of the 24/25th. An official statement revealed that during the past three weeks 4,720 people had been killed, 6,100 seriously injured and 22,000 made homeless. Then came the unbelievable.

On 25 November, after all that he had so brilliantly achieved, and the great burden of responsibility that he shouldered so well, Air Chief Marshal Sir Hugh Dowding, now aged 58, left his post as AOC-in-C Fighter Command after ten brilliant years of leadership. His replacement was Air Chief Marshal William Sholto Douglas. To many this seemed an appalling way to treat Dowding, who had devised the means of shielding us and the civilised world from tyranny. With his very shrewd mind and strong personality he was considered aloof, and commonly called 'Stuffy' Dowding. His views sometimes conflicted strongly with members of the Air Staff. He also had

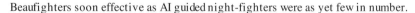

Beaufighters soon effective as AI guided night-fighters were as yet few in number.

Many smaller cities of Britain also suffered badly from bombing, Southampton included. This picture of smashed homes typifies scenes which could be viewed in many places.

to cope with differing views of his two main Group Commanders. Park favoured small formations of fighters able to respond fast, adapting their tactics to deal with approaching enemy forces, while Mallory favoured the 'Big Wing'. Dowding's problem was possibly that he did not suffer fools gladly, and was too successful among the less successful! Whatever the reasons for his departure, it was not for another three years that his contribution to victory was rewarded with a Peerage.

Meanwhile there was no let-up in the pounding of British cities. Bristol, Portsmouth and Southampton were heavily bombed for towns of their size. Most of the bombs were directed at Birmingham, Manchester, Merseyside and Sheffield. In addition there were many small-scale operations by day and night directed at airfields, ports and mixed industrial targets. Since deep and widespread penetrations of UK air space were involved, much of the country was held under 'red' warning for many hours, particularly at night.

December 1940 was a month when rain, snow, fog, ice and ample cloud interfered with the enemy's offensive to such an extent that there were fifteen nights when no major operations were attempted. On the remainder, eleven major raids and five at moderate strength were undertaken. London had to endure three heavy and a dozen smaller attacks.

Southampton was hard hit on 1/2 December, Birmingham on the 3rd/4th, Bristol by KG 27 on the 6/7th when, using intelligence information, RAF Bomber Command had fifty-five aircraft patrolling enemy bomber airfields. When KG 77 visited London on the 8/9th it cruelly unloaded many parachute mines, causing great swathes of damage. In a block of flats forty-five died, seven hospitals and four churches, two hotels and many shops being damaged or destroyed. On the 11/12th Birmingham and its people again underwent a heavy battering by more than 200 raiders, while eighty others focused their attention on Coventry. Next night Sheffield received attention from 150 aircraft, while another seventy-five of KG 3 were programmed to bomb Birmingham.

High calibre, large H E weapons were carried externally, and in 1940 usually on Heinkel He 111s. The photograph was possibly taken at Poix.

An RAF attempt at retaliation came on 16/17 December when 134 bombers were sent to incinerate the centre of Mannheim. Fire-raising Wellingtons in the lead lacked radio aids such as the enemy used and failed to locate the city centre. The following bombing was widely scattered, and possibly as few as eighty-five aircraft bombed some part of the city. Casualties amounted to thirty-four people killed and eighty-one injured, while 1,266 were made homeless, low figures compared with those resulting from German raids.

On 21/22 and again on 22/23 December, Liverpool was the target for Ku Fl Gr 606, which dropped parachute mines. Night-fighter kills were still rare, but the downing over Lincolnshire on the 21st/22nd of an Fw 200 Condor by a Beaufighter was indeed unusual. Next night five Liverpool attackers were brought down, three falling to fighters. An attack on Leicester by thirty-one Dorniers of II/KG 2 resulted in the loss of two of their number.

On 22/23 December Manchester endured its heaviest raid, large fires in particular causing most damage. Buildings hit included five hospitals, twenty churches, a theatre and a public shelter. A smaller force repeated the raid the following night. Would there be an attack on Christmas Eve, everyone seemed to ask?

The Lancaster prototype BT308 which was complete when the Luftwaffe raided Manchester in December 1940. Its destruction could have been a major coup and a hefty blow to Britain.

Since the age of four I had been to the Christmas Festival of Nine Lessons and Carols in King's College Chapel, Cambridge. This time, as Mum and I queued, I remember praying that 'Kings' – surely the world's most beautiful building – would never succumb. If destruction could overtake Coventry Cathedral, might 'Kings' be taken, sometime, in revenge and rage? I recall saying to myself, 'Please, don't let them...'

Unheated inside the chapel, how cold my hands and feet became! The myriad of candles providing the only lighting always added to the magic of Christmas that, in 1940, seemed so very important. Intense cold was the only thing by then not in short supply. The very little meat and no ham had, sadly, to be enhanced from the squadron of back garden chickens. The 'Dig for Victory' campaign, which led to lawns and flower beds becoming small small-holdings, was yielding carrots, potatoes, Brussels sprouts and cauliflowers, together with proper, well-soil-encrusted Fen celery. Home brews replaced the absent wine, while oranges and bananas were memories. It was still possible to obtain assorted ginger products, chocolate was not yet rationed, and Christmas cakes embraced ample carrots and parsnips in lieu of currants and raisins. The Ministry of Food issued useful recipes in those 'TV chef-less' times. In 1940 proper home cooking was the norm, like brown paper wrapping. Paper chains made from newspapers and magazines, silver furlongs of lametta from Woolworth's and folding paper decorations were available, although they increased the chance of fire raid damage.

Surprisingly, details of shipping losses were still issued. In the week ending 23 December fifteen British vessels (22,845 gross tons in total) had been sunk, and three neutrals. In 1940 the total loss of merchant shipping (excluding those attending Dunkirk) amounted to 63,287grt, so it was little wonder that food and materials were in short supply. Lord Woolton, the Food Minister, kept telling us to eat less meat, more potatoes, and more porridge from local oats. Making pastry was not a good idea, he said, because it used precious fats.

Unlit streets seemed so incongruous with Christmas. Although it retained its basic elements, with lots of families fractured and many never going to see their loved ones again, it was a subdued affair. What of the future, many asked? Will they invade? Will America join us? Can we beat the U-boats? What about the Balkans? Can we blockade Germany? What about Spain, Portugal and Switzerland? There were so many 'What ifs?'

Mercifully there were no night raids at Christmas, but we knew that it was only a brief pause allowing, folk said, for 'the other lot' to celebrate. Nights away from home brought considerable worry, and if undertaken were accompanied with a little leather attaché case containing valuable papers, cash and National Savings Certificates – for those able to save. Income tax taking was high, although the Government promised that, once we'd won the war, some of it would be given back. What better incentive to fight for victory? As expected, the bombing pause was brief. When it resumed the last big raid of 1940 lit probably the most spectacular fires ever witnessed in Britain.

On 29 December, a very dark night, the main *X-Gerät* beam was set in a south-west to north-east direction across London, including a line extending from Battersea Reach to Bloomsbury. A last-minute correction to account for wind direction and speed moved the very narrow track about five-eighths of a mile to the west. Ten He 111s of KGr 100, loaded with incendiaries, the marker force, crossed the coast soon after 18.00. Being Sunday evening, few people were in the target area.

A high proportion of the 135 Heinkels involved and setting out from France were packed with incendiaries. Just after 19.00 the markers' fire bombs ignited in the centre of the City of London, which the Luftwaffe had chosen to incinerate during a 9-hour raid.

Standard high explosive bombs heading for Heinkel He 111H 1H+EP possibly at Poix.

What was on the wireless that Christmas Day?

Home Service

7.00am	News
7.15am	Christmas in Song
7.30am	A Merry Christmas, Children, Everywhere, with Uncle Mac's Christmas carols
8.00am	Theatre organ
8.30am	Military band
9.00am	News
9.15am	The Kitchen Front
9.45am	Theatre organ
10.00am	From the children – Christmas Greetings from evacuated children
10.30am	Christmas morning service
11.30am	Records
12.00pm	BBC Orchestra
12.35pm	Snapdragon
1.00pm	News
1.15pm	Light music
2.00pm	Christmas Under Fire
3.10pm	National Anthems of the Allies
3.30pm	Children calling home
4.00pm	Teatime teasers
4.15pm	Music for Christmas
5.00pm	Studio service in Welsh
5.15pm	Children's Hour
6.00pm	News
6.30pm	News in Norwegian
6.45pm	Children's Half Hour from South Wales
7.15pm	Christmas Star Variety
8.15pm	John McCormack with Gerald Moore at the piano
8.50pm	Wireless for the blind
9.00pm	News
9.20pm	Think on these Things
9.25pm	Transatlantic Rhythm
10.00pm	*The Squeaker* by Edgar Wallace
11.00pm	Billy Cotton and his band
Midnight	News

Forces

6.30am	Merry Christmas (records)
7.00am	News
7.15am	Roland Powell Octet
10.30am	Music While you Work
11.00am	Time, Foden's Motor Work's Band
11.30am	Christmas Morning Service
12.00pm	Accent on Rhythm
12.15pm	News in French
12.30pm	Snapdragon
1.00pm	News in Dutch
1.15pm	Sandy MacPherson at the organ
1.40pm	Swansea and District Male Voice Choir
3.30pm	Floor Show cabaret entertainment
4.15pm	Fred Hartley and his Music
4.45pm	Grand Children's Party
6.00pm	News in Dutch and French
6.15pm	News in German
6.20pm	Vocal Jazz
6.40pm	Sports News from Canada
6.30pm	The Signalman
6.45pm	Stars in the Shelter
8.15pm	Victor Sylvester and his Ballroom Orchestra
9.00pm	News in German
9.25pm	Savoy Minstrel Songs
10.00pm	Time, Christmas Cabaret
10.40pm	Theatre organ
11.00pm	Closedown

By chance it took place when the ebb of the Thames was at its greatest. That and icy conditions were hardly conducive to fire-fighting in a large area of aged, highly combustible buildings.

Very soon, all-consuming conflagrations spread fast, but the procession of Heinkels lasted for 3 and not the intended 9 hours. Deteriorating weather was overtaking their bases. Although hundreds of incendiary canisters fell to the east of the display main beam, most incendiaries cascaded within a 2½-mile radius centred on St Paul's Cathedral. High explosive bombs fell mainly in riverside boroughs between Westminster and Poplar, and many south of the river in Lewisham and Camberwell.

In the City, Bermondsey and Southwark, fires rapidly became uncontrollable. More than 1,500 were started, of which fifty-two were listed as serious, twenty-eight were major fires and six designated as conflagrations, of which the two largest covered half a square mile and a quarter of a square mile respectively. Six vast areas of fire had been started in the City, around which another sixteen major fires burned.

Rising dominant from the flames that surrounded it like a halo, soaring above the inferno majestically, mightily, symbolically, was the dome of St Paul's Cathedral. Below, huge chunks of burning wood, embers and shoals of sparks raced around in the wind storm created by the fires. Yet the great church did not surrender. As if by a miracle, it defied the all-engulfing evil, although eight other Wren churches suffered badly. Cheapside was soon a charred ruin, and the Central Criminal Court was damaged.

From the Cathedral to the Guildhall the entire area was alight, and little could be done to save anything. Within the area Moorgate-Aldersgate-Old Street-Cannon Street there was one huge blaze. Around 20.00 a shoal of sparks from the nearby church of St Lawrence Jewry, settling upon the roof of the Guildhall, were sufficient to set light to the roof above the Lord Mayor's screen. Attempts to save the precious building were abruptly thwarted when water ran low and wind strength increased. The interior was soon burning, and just after 20.30 the roof, in flames, crashed to the floor. Fortunately, some of the special items within had been removed for safety, but the Council Chamber and Banqueting Hall were soon gone. Only the walls survived, fortunately well enough to allow eventual restoration. Just as in the Great Fire of London in 1666, explosives were used to produce fire breaks to prevent fires extending. There was considerable damage outside the City, nine hospitals being hit as well as the Tower and County Hall.

At the start of the attack the wind was a fresh south-west-to-westerly. It increased to 50mph at 6,000 feet during the evening and the weather steadily deteriorated, especially over France. At 22.00 the attack was called off and the bombers were ordered back to their bases; as a result the Whitehall area of London escaped incineration.

Next day the entire City could be seen to have been incinerated, the acrid smell of burnt buildings pervading for many days. Walking through the area was a disturbing experience. Six churches had been all but destroyed, and of Wren's St Brides, Fleet Street, only part of the spire and the walls were left. Of St Lawrence Jewry, where Dick Whittington was said to have prayed, and attended by the Lord Mayor of London prior to his election, not much remained. Its roof had fallen in, the pews were burnt and the organ area was a charred ruin. Incendiaries that had burned through the lead roof of St Paul's had been extinguished by the courageous Cathedral ARP force using stirrup pumps.

A novel development was the anti-balloon fender fitted to a few He 111s as on this example.

It was now certain that fire-raising on a grand scale was new part of the night-bombing campaign as in the pre-Christmas Manchester raids. Many buildings in both cities might have been saved had there been firemen close by, or people staying overnight within premises to deal immediately with penetrating incendiaries.

The grand totals of casualties between September 1939 and May 1945 were 60,595 killed and 86,182 seriously injured. Of the overall total of 146,777, 80,397 occurred in the London Civil Defence Region. All such figures – these are based upon Ministry of Home Security records – include some element of estimation. They cannot include those seriously injured who died from wounds during and after hostilities.

Civilian casualties caused by air raids, 1 July-31 December 1940

	Male		Female		Children under 16		Total	
	Killed	Injured	Killed	Injured	Killed	Injured	Killed	Injured
July	178	227	57	77	23	17	258	321
August	627	711	335	448	113	102	1,075	1,261
September	2,844	4,405	2,943	3,807	1,167	2,403	6,954	10,615
October	2,791	4,228	2,900	3,750	643	717	6,334	8,695
November	2,289	3,493	1,806	2,251	493	458	4,588	6,202
December	1,838	2,962	1,434	1,775	521	307	3,793	5,044
Totals	10,567	16,026	9,475	12,108	2,960	4,004	23,002	32,138

On 21 December Fighter Command added dedicated night intruding over enemy airfields to its repertoire when six Blenheim 1(f) night-fighters of 23 Squadron patrolled over six airfields in Normandy and Artois. Four German bombers were seen. More patrols were flown on the 22nd and the 29th

MARTLET (CYCLONE or WASP)

| Purpose : **Single-Seat** **FIGHTER (FLEET).** | Dimensions : **Span 38 ft. 0 in.** **Length 28 ft. 10 in.** | Performance : Maximum Speed **330 m.p.h.** Cruising Speed **304 m.p.h.** |

Noisy and tubby, the Grumman Martlet gave the impression of being a fast mover when it provided me with an interesting Boxing Day treat.

At 13.50 on Boxing Day an unusual, noisy engine enticed me into the garden. Passing over was a tubby little monoplane, a Grumman Martlet 1. If proof were needed, here it was. American aircraft were here, this one from Duxford wearing Fleet Air Arm colours.

Since July the US had been sending aircraft to the UK. Their origins were mixed, for some were leftovers from orders by defunct European air forces. A few were direct British purchases such as Lockheed Hudsons, some of which, like Catalinas, were already serving in Coastal Command. Although the US industry was highly innovative, most of its good ideas had yet to be applied to their military designs.

The most useful item the British had so far acquired from the US was the .303in Colt Browning machine gun, standard fit in Spitfires and Hurricanes. Unfortunately, the considerable number of US fighter aircraft arriving were designed to defend the Panama Canal. Far too slow for combat use in Europe, their performance also peaked too low. Curtiss P-36s and Brewster Buffaloes were therefore moved to the Far East. Curtiss P-40 Tomahawks, after much modification, would later serve in a fighter-reconnaissance role. The most useful arrivals were the Douglas DB-7 Boston and Martin Maryland bomber-reconnaissance aircraft, taken over from French orders. The French operated the former type during May-June 1940, but its nosewheel undercarriage meant special training for pilots. In October 1940 the intent was for 2 Group to explore the Boston. Instead, on 8 December the decision was taken to modify them into night-fighters because they could easily carry AI radar. Creature comfort was high in the US types, but the trimmings brought weight penalties. Special tools (in short supply) were needed for the newcomers, which arrived with extensive maintenance documentation. Many needed extensive modifications to fit them for RAF service. Between July and the end of 1940 the following had that year reached Britain:

Northrop A-17A Nomad	61
Buffalo	33
Douglas DB-7 Boston I	153
Douglas DB-7A Boston II	3
Curtiss Cleveland	5
Consolidated 'Guba'	1
Harvard II	24
Hudson I	97
Hudson II	17
Hudson III	54
Hudson IV	7
Maryland	87
Martlet	71
Mohawk	204
Tomahawk	21

Not all were uncrated before dispatch overseas. En route/at sea to the UK on 1 January 1941 were twelve Boston IIs, three Hudson IVs and 152 Tomahawk Is.

For me, 1940 had provided all that any aviation enthusiast might desire, and as a bonus it donated one more special sighting. It was 30 December, 13.57, when friend Ken hammered on the back door shouting, 'Come out, Mike, you'll never guess what's about!'

I grabbed the binoculars, rushed into the garden and – I was too late. Or was I? A few moments later *it* appeared low, retracting its main gear. Throughout the Battle of Britain RAF pilots persisted in shooting down 'Do 215s' when in reality they were Dornier 17s. Not this one though, for in my sights there really was a rare, strange-sounding Dornier 215 with DB 601 engines clearly in view. I noticed some little flashing lights.

'It's firing, Mike!' called Ken, and a few bullets struck the tiles on the roof of the school opposite our house. After joining the circuit it had strafed Cambridge aerodrome.

Not only had Fighter Command survived the summer fight, it did so to flourish. At the close of 1940 its six Groups, seventy-one squadrons strong, held 1,467 operational aircraft. Six night-fighter squadrons were flying the excellent

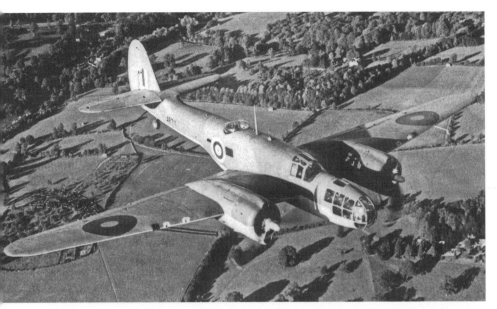

The best American so far around was the Glenn Martin Maryland. Several were tested in Britain, including a pair at the NAFDU Duxford. Their long range led to their employment from Hatston for naval reconnaissance purposes. France received a few but they never operated.

Dornier 17s rattled their way along. I remember the one Do 215 I saw not by its shape but by its unusual, smooth engine note.

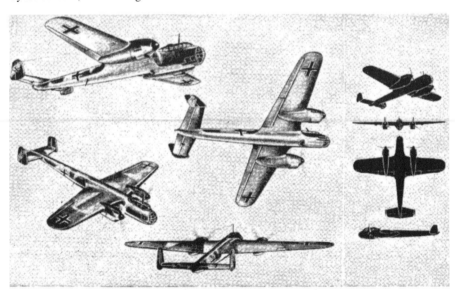

DORNIER Do. 215 (D.B. 601).

A measure of its excellence was the Spitfire's suitability for development into the 1950s. Much was expected from the 1940 devised Mk III seen here. A Merlin XX series engine increased the speed, clipped wing tips improved the rate of roll, but before its assets were exploited the Merlin XLV engine came along and the Mk V was born eclipsing the Mk III.

Beaufighter. Bomber Command, too, was beginning to rearm. When Luftflotte 2 and 3 counted their assets on 31 December they found a total of 1,214 aircraft – they had 1,291 at the end of September. Many of their aircraft needed repair, and on 4 January 1941 only 551, or 45%, of their combined forces were serviceable. In September 1940 the average serviceable had been around 800, or 61%.

Just before darkness fell on a dreary, chilly final day of the most fateful of years, a sort of rushing, whispering sound heralded the enormously thrilling sight of low-flying MG:H, a four-engined Stirling bomber from Oakington's 7 Squadron. Far, far more thrilling even than that Dornier 215 was this and the other new heavy bombers filtering into Bomber Command's currently forty-five squadrons. They would, but not for some time, give the enemy a taste of his medicine. Britain had survived all that the enemy could direct upon her, and soon it would be their turn to feel the pain.

Since then I've many times been to Germany and often lingered in Cologne Cathedral which, contrary to general belief, was very badly damaged by bombing. I always ask myself how could the world's two most sophisticated and talented nations have allowed crazy politicians to talk us into doing such awful things to one another, destroy wonderful things and lovely places? What a relief that 'Kings' survived, complete with Bach's 'In Dulci Jubilo' to still bring such delight on Christmas Eve.

For all its pathos, terror and evil, that fighting summer, the fearsome winter, of 1940 was a tremendously exhilarating time that brought all so close, for bombs, unlike awful politicians, were not class-conscious. The possibility of instant annihilation or serious injury seemed not to cause as much concern as might be expected. It took second place to the overriding determination never to surrender, to achieve total victory. There was no missing work because the bus was late, buildings were burning, streets flooded and covered with hosepipes likely to cause one to trip over, or because there was only 6 inches of snow and plenty of ice. Mercifully, nothing like today's instant media expert was on hand to analyse matters and give plentiful advice without the necessary years of insight. There was usually an effective, self-devised way round every problem. Self-sufficiency was essential and satisfying, while the actual fighting was left to wonderfully brave people being enveloped in so many fearsome situations, and whose courage you admired whether it be close by or miles above.

Does that perilous summer have any messages for the 21st century? Certainly it reminds us of how absolutely essential it is for nations to base their actions upon good, accurate intelligence material – emphasised during the Falklands conflict and even more so in the case of the foolish and erroneous Iraq excursion. Doubtless the German High Command must, after reflection, have thought along similar lines, and appreciated the importance of never underestimating a foe. History does not repeat itself – that is impossible. Events are merely new versions of old activities.

Changing tactics were certainly an interesting aspect of the 1940 fighting. Large formations of bombers would always be very vulnerable without fighter cover. Flying above the level of anti-aircraft fire was necessary, although by so doing the accuracy of bombing was reduced. That meant carrying out area-bombing involving attacks on civilians. But what was a civilian? Were the many among the latter employed upon 'war work' of no direct threat to the enemy?

The introduction of fighter-bombers was clever, and using them as low-level attackers even more so, although their value for 'under the radar' activity had yet to be appreciated.

From the story of the big battles of 1940 one name surely stands way above all others, that of Lord Dowding. It was he who fashioned the air defence of Britain; it was he who directed the air defence at the most crucial time. We should honour him, always. How fortunate, too, that our political leader was the greatest of all time. Without them ... but that is too terrible to contemplate!

What remains of those days that one can actually touch? Surprisingly little, apart from buildings, museum trophies, a Hurricane and the famous Spitfire P7350, which really did take part in the fight. Weary pillboxes can be found often braving onslaught by vandals and health and safety souls. Incongruous slates and tiles can still be detected on once-stricken roofs, and a few walls are still supported by gaunt buttresses rearing from the place of a vanished companion. At Duxford garden seats have replaced Spitfires and Hurricanes, and the shelter where I used to hide from KG 2 has fallen to something less spectacular called a 'developer'.

And what of the 1940 people, now quite aged or just memories? Recently crossing the Kiel Canal by train, an aged unknown foreign companion tried hard to communicate with me. Surely he wasn't the guy who, ordered by an awful fellow, dropped the bomb that uprooted Aunt Emily's lovely Victoria plum tree, and placed it superbly inverted in her neighbour's garden. It *is* all a long, long time ago, that most memorable of all years, and, as the great man told us, it really was our Finest Hour.

Luftwaffe night attacks on London, 7 September-31 October 1940

Raid commencing September	Aircraft claiming to attack London	HE used (tons)	Incendiary containers
7	247	335	440
8	171	207	327
9	195	232	289
10	148	176	318
11	180	217	148
12	43	54	61
13	105	123	200
14	38	55	43
15	181	224	279
16	170	189	318
17	268	334	391
18	300	350	628
19	255	310	533
20	109	154	79
21	113	164	329
22	123	130	476
23	261	300	611
24	223	256	384
25	219	260	441
26	180	218	224
27	163	167	437
28	249	325	303
29	246	294	136
30	218	287	104
Totals	4,405	5,361	7,499

Raid commencing October	Aircraft claiming to attack London	HE used (tons)	Incendiary containers
1	214	250	115
2	105	130	300
3	44	61	Nil
4	134	190	236
5	177	242	176
6	7	8	Nil
7	179	211	143
8	208	257	264
9	216	263	245
10	222	269	718
11	132	213	126
12	119	148	24
13	211	249	131
14	242	304	299
15	410	538	177
16	280	346	187
17	254	322	134
18	129	172	132
19	282	386	192
20	298	356	192
21	100	115	52
22	82	98	40
23	64	65	Nil
24	64	75	Nil
25	159	193	193
26	203	253	176
27	114	127	40
28	146	176	111
29	186	236	109
30	125	178	92
31	67	48	83
Totals	5,173	6,479	3,208
Grand totals	9,578	11,840	10,707

Luftwaffe losses during offensive operations, and RAF losses during defensive operations, 1-31 October 1940

By the end of September, and with the immediate prospect of invasion fast waning, Bomber Command reverted to its strategic bombing campaign and Coastal Command, too, had largely switched to 'non-invasion' operations. A more direct comparison between British fighter and German attack losses therefore becomes more feasible.

a = shot down, b = crashed and written off during/as a result of operational sortie, c = seriously damaged

October	1			2			3			4			5		
	a	b	c	a	b	c	a	b	c	a	b	c	a	b	c
Luftwaffe															
Do 17Z	–	–	–	1	1	–	1	1	–	1	–	i	–	–	–
He 111H	1	–	–	2	–	–	1	–	1	2	–	–	1	–	–
He 111P	–	–	–	–	–	–	–	–	–	–	–	–	–	–	–
Ju 88	–	–	–	1	–	–	3	–	–	2	2	–	2	–	–
Bf 109	2	–	–	4	–	–	–	–	–	–	–	–	6	1	–
Bf 110	1	–	–	–	–	–	–	–	–	–	–	–	2	–	–
Totals	4	–	–	8	1	–	5	1	1	5	2	1	11	1	–
RAF															
Blenheim	–	–	–	–	–	–	–	1	–	–	–	–	–	–	–
Hurricane	3	1	2	–	–	–	–	–	–	–	–	6	4	–	1
Spitfire	1	–	–	1	1	–	–	–	–	2	–	2	1	1	1
Totals	4	1	2	1	1	–	–	1	–	2	–	8	5	1	2

October	6			7			8			9			10		
	a	b	c	a	b	c	a	b	c	a	b	c	a	b	c
Luftwaffe															
Do 17Z	2	–	–	–	–	–	i	–	–	1	–	–	–	–	–
He 111H	–	–	–	–	–	–	–	1	–	–	1	–	–	–	–
He 111P	1	–	–	–	–	–	–	1	–	–	2	–	–	–	–
He 115	–	–	–	–	–	–	–	–	–	–	–	–	–	–	–
Ju 88	2	–	–	2	–	–	2	–	1	3	–	–	–	–	–
Bf 109	–	–	–	8	4	–	–	–	–	3	2	1	–	–	1
Bf 110	–	–	–	7	–	1	–	–	–	–	–	–	–	–	–
Totals	5	–	–	17	4	1	3	2	1	7	5	1	–	–	1
RAF															
Blenheim	–	–	–	–	–	–	–	–	–	–	–	–	–	–	–
Hurricane	–	2	–	5	4	1	1	–	–	1	–	–	2	–	–
Spitfire	–	1	–	5	–	–	–	–	–	–	2	1	1	2	–
Totals	–	3	–	10	4	1	1	–	–	1	2	1	3	2	–

October	11 a	b	c	12 a	b	c	13 a	b	c	14 a	b	c	15 a	b	c
Luftwaffe															
Do 17Z	2	–	–	–	–	–	–	–	–	–	–	1	–	–	–
He 111H	–	–	–	–	–	–	–	–	–	–	–	–	–	–	–
He 111P	–	–	–	–	–	–	–	–	–	–	–	–	–	–	–
He 115	–	–	–	–	–	–	–	–	–	–	1	–	–	–	–
Ju 88	1	–	–	–	–	1	–	1	–	–	–	–	1	–	–
Bf 109	1	–	–	1	–	–	1	–	2	1	–	–	7	–	1
Bf 110	–	–	–	–	–	–	–	–	–	–	–	–	2	–	–
Totals	4	–	–	1	–	1	1	1	2	1	1	1	10	–	1
RAF															
Blenheim	–	–	–	–	–	–	–	1	–	–	–	–	–	–	–
Hurricane	2	–	–	7	–	–	–	1	–	–	1	–	12	–	1
Spitfire	4	3	–	1	1	2	1	–	1	–	1	–	4	–	–
Totals	6	3	–	8	1	2	1	2	1	–	2	–	16	–	1

October	16 a	b	c	17 a	b	c	18 a	b	c	19 a	b	c	20 a	b	c
Luftwaffe															
Do 17Z	–	2	–	–	1	–	–	–	–	–	–	–	1	–	–
He 111H	1	–	1	–	–	–	–	–	–	–	–	–	–	–	–
He 111P	–	–	–	1	2	1	–	–	–	–	–	–	–	1	–
He 115	–	–	–	–	–	1	–	–	–	–	–	–	–	–	–
Ju 88	1	5	1	2	5	3	–	1	1	–	1	1	–	1	1
Bf 109	–	–	–	3	1	–	–	–	–	–	–	–	5	–	1
Bf 110	–	–	–	–	1	–	–	–	–	–	–	–	1	–	–
Totals	2	7	2	6	10	5	–	1	1	–	1	1	7	2	2
RAF															
Blenheim	–	–	–	–	–	–	–	–	–	–	–	–	–	–	–
Hurricane	1	1	–	2	–	–	–	–	–	–	–	–	–	–	3
Spitfire	–	–	–	2	–	–	–	–	–	–	–	–	2	–	–
Totals	1	1	–	4	–	–	–	–	–	–	–	–	2	–	3

October	21 a	b	c	22 a	b	c	23 a	b	c	24 a	b	c
Luftwaffe												
Do 17Z	1	–	–	–	–	–	–	1	–	–	–	3
Do 215	–	–	–	–	–	–	–	–	–	1	–	–
He 111H	–	1	1	–	2	–	–	–	–	–	–	–
He 111P	–	–	–	–	2	–	–	–	–	–	–	–
He 115	–	–	–	–	–	–	–	–	–	–	–	–
Ju 88	1	–	–	–	1	–	1	1	–	–	–	1
Bf 109	–	–	–	3	–	–	–	–	–	–	1	–
Bf 110	–	–	–	–	–	–	–	–	–	–	–	–
Totals	2	1	1	3	5	–	1	2	–	1	1	4
RAF												
Blenheim	–	–	–	–	–	–	–	–	–	–	–	–
Hurricane	–	–	–	2	–	–	–	–	–	–	–	–
Spitfire	–	–	–	2	–	–	–	–	–	–	–	–
Totals	–	–	–	4	–	–	–	–	–	–	–	–

October	25			26			27			28			29		
	a	b	c	a	b	c	a	b	c	a	b	c	a	b	c
Luftwaffe															
Do 17P	–	1	–	–	–	–	–	–	–	–	–	–	–	–	–
Do 17Z	1	–	–	–	–	–	1	–	–	1	–	–	–	–	–
He 59	–	–	–	1	–	–	–	–	–	–	–	–	–	–	–
He 111H	–	2	–	2	–	–	1	–	2	1	–	–	1	–	–
He 111P	–	–	–	–	1	1	–	–	–	–	–	–	–	–	–
He 115	–	–	–	1	–	–	–	–	–	–	–	–	–	–	–
Ju 88	2	–	1	–	1	–	2	–	–	1	–	1	1	–	–
Bf 109	11	–	–	3	–	–	7	–	–	4	1	–	14	–	1
Bf 110	1	–	–	–	–	–	–	–	–	–	–	–	–	1	–
Totals	15	3	1	7	2	1	11	–	2	7	1	1	16	1	1
RAF															
Hurricane	4	4	–	4	–	–	3	–	–	–	–	–	3	1	2
Spitfire	2	–	–	1	–	1	6	–	–	–	–	–	1	–	–
Blenheim	–	–	–	–	–	–	–	–	–	–	–	–	–	–	–
Totals	6	4	–	5	–	1	9	–	–	–	–	–	4	1	2

October	30			31			Grand totals for October			
	a	b	c	a	b	c	a	b	c	
Luftwaffe										
Do 17P	–	–	–	–	–	–	0	1	0	
Do 17Z	–	–	–	–	2	–	14	8	5	
He 59	–	–	–	–	–	–	1	0	0	
He 111H	–	–	–	–	–	–	14	10	6	
He 111P	–	–	–	–	–	–	1	6	2	
He 115	–	–	–	–	–	–	1	1	0	
Ju 88	1	1	–	–	–	–	31	20	6	
Bf 109	4	–	–	–	–	–	88	10	7	
Bf 110	–	–	–	–	–	–	14	2	1	
Totals	15	1	–	–	2	–	164	58	27	
RAF										
Hurricane	4	1	–	1	–	–	–	57	15	17
Spitfire	6	–	1	–	–	–	43	12	9	
Blenheim	–	–	–	–	–	–	0	2	0	
Totals	7	–	2	–	–	–	100	29	26	

Sorties flown by RAF Fighter Command, 16 September-31 October 1940

Date	Day		Night	
	Patrols	**Sorties**	**Patrols**	**Sorties**
September				
16	78	428	?	?
17	121	544	44	45
18	200	1,210	63	65
19	108	237	12	16
20	124	540	40	46
21	118	563	43	46
22	65	158	46	50
23	116	710	70	70
24	126	880	46	50
25	137	668	37	39
26	120	417	34	34
27	138	939	27	27
28	110	770	53	65
29	121	451	25	25
30	168	1,173	48	50
October				
1	122	673	29	29
2	125	807	35	35
3	68	138	–	–
4	61	171	1	1
5	136	1,074	4	4
6	67	181	3	3
7	129	822	77	78
8	203	639	33	33
9	115	439	42	42
10	133	712	49	49
11	154	900	41	41
12	144	756	30	39
13	121	552	?	?
14	?	?	42	45
15	106	598	40	41
16	73	234	5	5
17	100	563	9	9
18	36	135	2	2
19	63	286	15	18
20	87	457	12	13
21	113	262	24	24
22	70	360	9	11
23	32	79	11	11
24	119	463	33	33
25	131	775	54	54
26	134	678	40	40
27	166	967	33	33
28	117	606	20	20
29	148	649	44'	45
30	91	535	6	6
31	53	145		

Total numbers of aircraft available on fighter squadrons at 18.00 on given dates

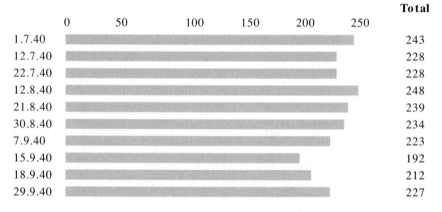

Date	Total
1.7.40	618
12.7.40	635
22.7.40	669
12.8.40	699
21.8.40	729
30.8.40	717
7.9.40	694
15.9.40	660
18.9.40	655
29.9.40	697

Hurricanes available

Date	Total
1.7.40	282
12.7.40	316
22.7.40	357
12.8.40	363
21.8.40	400
30.8.40	410
7.9.40	398
15.9.40	389
18.9.40	362
29.9.40	387

Spitfires available

Date	Total
1.7.40	243
12.7.40	228
22.7.40	228
12.8.40	248
21.8.40	239
30.8.40	234
7.9.40	223
15.9.40	192
18.9.40	212
29.9.40	227

Appendix 1

Serial numbers of aircraft flown during operations

Listed here, and linked to the superscript numbers in the text, are airframe serial numbers of aircraft used in many of the engagements – according to the relevant squadron Operations Record Books.

1   Hurricanes N2461, N2463, N2532, N2588, N2724, P3481, P3522, P3677, P3679

2   Hurricanes L1824, L1849, N2621, N2665?, P3484, P3788

3   Hurricanes P2955, P2957, P3400

4   Hurricanes P2920, P3393

5   Spitfires L1004-H, L1009-B, P9495-K, R6694-F, R6695-P, R6765-T

6   Spitfires K9905, K9909, K9915, L1094, N3101, N3128, P9436, R6618, R6619 and two more abortive

7   Spitfires N3173, P9387, P9549, R6707, R6708, R6709

8   Spitfires N3223, L1069, L1095, R6637, N3023, P9322

9   Spitfires P9503-D, R6629-E, R6630, R6694-F, K9931-R, N3284 J, P9545-Q, P6765-T, R6695-P

10 Hurricanes L2075, P2755, N2588, N2524, N2670, P3679

11 Spitfires P9393, P9399, P9398 (Mungo Park), P9379, K9951, L1089

12 Spitfires R6700, L1075, N3230?, K9991, N3293, K9795

13 Spitfires L1069 (Barren), L1095 (Mitchell), N3223, R6699, P9322

14 Hurricanes N2486 (Dixon), P2691, P3082

15 Hurricanes P3681, 2435, L1670, P3363, P3302, P2753

16 Hurricanes P3124, P3872?, P3617, P2948, P3599, P2978

17 Hurricanes P2753, P2690, P3302, P3363, L1670, P3681

18 Spitfire 1bs R6625, R6770, R6688, N3234, K9944, R6882

19 Hurricanes P3152 (Sqn Ldr Donaldson), P3316, P3312, L1750, P3320, L2005, P3275, P3304, P3301, P3307

20 Hurricanes N2402, P2970, P3479, P3473, P3356, P2985, P2922, P3587, P3612, P3354, P2970

21 Spitfires P9549, P9387, R6708, N3173, R6893

22 Spitfires P9450, L1035, L1073, N3230, P9507, P9447, R6694, N3293, K9991, P9369, R6975

23 Hurricanes including P3273, P3065, P3882

24 Hurricanes including P2966, P2963, P2768, P3109, P3160, L1584

25   Spitfires L1045-G (Sqn Ldr A. T. Smith), R6976-A, P9503-D, R6694-F, N3284-J, P9495-K, P9540-M, R6806-N, R6695-P, P9545-Q, R6621-S, R6765-T

26   Hurricanes P3164 (Sqn Ldr J. R. Peel), P2955, P2957, P3521, P2770, P3391

28   Defiants L6974, L6983, L6995, L6999, L7001, L7009, L7014, L7015, L7016

29   Hurricanes N2461, P3522, P2921, P3144, P3936, N2458, P3481, P3677, N2671, P3112, P3679

30   Hurricanes P3410, P3781, P3468, P3327, P3351, P3964

31   Hurricanes P3122, P2921, N2524, P3679, N2461, N2458, P3481, N2670

32   Hurricanes N2337, P2963, P3380, P2768, P3160, P3487, P2801, P3162?, P3151, P3158, P2966, P3161

33   Spitfires R6621-S, L1044-H, R6986-A, R6595-0, P9495-K, P9496-L, R6806-M, R6695-P, P9330-V

34   Spitfires R6812, N3192, R6710, R6899, R6816, P9549, R6707, N3173, R6893

35   Spitfires R6799, R6620, R6712, N3164, P9516, R6617, N3101, K9915, R6777

36   Hurricanes N2458, P3146, P3481, N2596, P2921, P3112, P3936, N2671, P3677

37   Hurricanes P3109, P3487, P3158, P3111, P2801, N2587, P3160, P3380, P2768, N2337, N2328, P3109

38   Spitfires R6893, N3173, R6707, P9387, R6899, R6895, R6814, P9367, R6913, R6816, N3097

39   Spitfires L1055, P9421, R6865, N3293, L1073, L1039, P9447, N3231

40   Hurricanes P2980, P3047, P3170, P3172, P3395, P2686, P3396, P3684, P3296, P3678

41   Hurricanes P3618, P3819, P3702, P3219, P3617, P3823, P3462, P3402, P2827, P2947, P2983

42   Spitfires R6692, P9322, N3023, R6690, R6699

43   Spitfires N3091 (Malan), P9336, P9380, R6779, R6706, P9306, P9398, P9397, L1001, K9878, R6772 (Park), P9547

44   Spitfires P9428 (Sqn Ldr Hood), P9429, N3038, N3163, N3132, N3234, P9430, N3126, N3264, N3112, K9890

45   Hurricanes P3704, P3776, P3709, P3705, P3706, P3775

46   Spitfires as note 44

47   Spitfires K9991, R6688, R6975, P9569, R6645, L1029, R6659, P9540

48   Hurricanes P3547, P3612, P3879, P3587, P3153, P3579, P2977, P3473

49   Hurricanes P3816, P3059, P3141, P3646, P3397, P3820, P3083, P3041, L1868

50   Spitfires R6976-A, P9503-D, R6629-E, L1004-H, N3284-J, P9496-L, P9495-K, R6806-N, P9545-Q, R6765-T, R6963-W, R6630-X

51   Spitfires K9991, N3293, R6700, R6995, P9369, L1029

52   Hurricanes L1750, P3310, P2826, L2005, P3301, P3940, P3312, L1975, P3065, P3271 (Wg Cdr Beamish)

53   Hurricanes VY-Q (Allard), VY-W (Marshall), VY-M (Ellis)

54 Hurricanes P3164 (Sqn Ldr Peel), P3896, P2955, P3391, V7294, P3163, P3221, P3736, -?-, P2951, P2918, P2696, P3381

55 Hurricanes P3971, V7221, P3386, P3216, P3267, P3460

56 Hurricanes P3164 (Sqn Ldr Peel), P3163, P3896, P3521, P3391, P2957, P3221, P3736?, P2951, P2918, P2696, P3167

57 Hurricanes P3823, P3462, P3664, P2827, P2989, P3223, R4097, P3819, P2978, P3617, P3767, P3222

58 Hurricanes P3058, P3775, P3662, P3078, P2981, R4091?, P3620, P3642, P3623, R4088 and -?-

59 Spitfires P9322, R6699, R6977, R6986, R6979, N3024, R6691, R6769, L1082, K9841, R6986, R6690

60 Hurricanes P3164, P3896, P3163, P3521, N2496, P2957, P3221, P3736, -?-, P2951, P3545, P2918

61 Hurricanes P3202, P3781, P3786, P3468, P3527, P3214, P3971, V7221, P3386, P3216, P3267, P3466

62 Hurricanes N2921 (Brothers), P3679, 2755, P3956, 2524, P3147, P3146, N2458, N2596, V7223, P3522, P3481

63 Spitfires R6683, X4018, R6975, R6623, N3293, P9450, N3230, X4060, R6991

64 Spitfires R6840, R6839, P9306, R6773, R6757, R6772, K9871, P9951, R6759, R6962, P9492

65 Hurricanes P3598, V7233, P3593, P3387, V7231, P3404, P3389

66 Hurricanes P3164 (Sqn Ldr Peel), P3391, V7294, P3521, 2495, P3896, R4177, P3221, P3736, P2951, P3167, R4176, P2918

67 Hurricanes P3402, P3462, P3664, P2827, P2989, P3226, R4097, P3819, P2978, P3176, P3222, P3124

68 Hurricanes P3363, R4092, P3885, P3382, P2960, L1917, P8818, P3393, P3383, P3783, L2057

69 Spitfires P9322, N3223, N3024, N3113, L1082, R6769, L1096, K9841, R6915, R6977, R6896, K9997

70 Spitfires R6976-A, P9553-E, X4028-F, K9818-H, R6599-J, X4067-K, K9947-M, N3124-N, R6891-Q, K9975-S, K9970-V

71 Hurricanes P2587?, P2801, L1983, L1992, P3162, P3109, P2966, P3160, N2328, P2768, L2075, P2871

72 Spitfires K9997, N3223, N3113, L1008, L1096, R6915, K9841, R6699, R6692, R6977, N3024

73 Spitfires R7017, R7019, N3097, R6814, R6981, X4019, R6898, R6892, R7015, R6893, R6708

74 Spitfires R6975, X4067, R6623, R6683, R6605, L1038, P9447, N3230, R6990

75 Hurricanes R4109, P3786, P3527, R4102, P3202, R4107, P3971, P3386, V7221, P3972, V7206, L1739

76   Hurricanes N2602, P3886, L1917, P3363, 2690, P3382, P2920, P3358, P3884,
      P3383, L1990

77   Spitfires K9953, N3091, R6840, K9878, R6716, X4061

78   Hurricanes R4109, P3786, P3527, R4110, R4107, P3220, R4108

79   Hurricanes P3232, P3228, 2690, P3363, P3382, P3886, P3884, L1990, L1951,
      P3393, P3383, P3358

80   Spitfires R6975, X4067, R6623, R6683, R6605, L1038, P9447, N3230,
      R6990

81   Hurricanes P3402, P3462, P2983, P3177, P3223, R2681, P3176, P3219,
      P3804, R2680, L2089

82   Hurricanes P3232, P3228, P3363, L1670, N2602, L2102, P3358, P3393,
      L1951, P3230, L1990, P3263

83   Spitfires R6986, R6690, N3024, L1065, N3113, L1008, L1096, R6915, N3223,
      R6977, R6699, L1082

84   Hurricanes P3479, N2429, P3587, N2440, P3384 and others

85   Spitfires R6803, R6610, R6884, K9915, N3101

86   Hurricanes 2459, 2458, P3481, P3171, V7223, P3146

87   Hurricanes P2587, L1983, P3161, P3162, P3158, L1992, P3380, L2075,
      P2871, P3109, P3160, N2328

88   Spitfires also scrambled were R6961, N3024, N3113, R6915, N3223, R6699,
      L1082, R6986, L1008

89   Spitfires X4201, N3108, N3123, N3126, N3162, N3266, P9428, P9430,
      R6603, R6605, R6756, R6885, R6611

90   Hurricanes P3580, P3650, L2012, P3832, L2018, P3583, N2557, P2717,
      P3308, P2994, L2122, P3827, L2014

91   Three Blenheims of 235 Squadron were about 150 miles out to sea heading for
      the Danish coast when they met about forty He 111s. Plt Off Jackson-Smith and
      his gunner in T1803 shot down one. The others, L9404 (Fg Off Laughlin) and
      T1804 (Sgt Hall) damaged another before the trio continued their sorties.

92   Blenheims 1F L1236, L8699, L1128, L1113, L1374, L1229, L1240, L8724,
      K7118, L1261, L8698, L6624

93   Hurricanes N2359, P3891, P2558, V7408, up 15:00; P3673, P3892,
      N2674 up 15:20

94   Hurricanes P3276, P2686, P3678

95   Hurricanes P3871 (Wg Cdr Beamish), P3490, V7411, P3065, V7410, L1975,
      P3309 included

96   Spitfires K9964, R6990, N3230, X4067, N3293, R6623, P9554, L1068,
      R6683, P9964

97   Hurricanes V7207, P3394, P3215, 2687, V7285

98   Spitfires N3242, R6985, N3277, P9466, R6988, R6896, P9363, N3239,
      N3279, P9320, R6967, N3191, P9494, X4016

99   Hurricanes R4109, P3527, P3786, P3202, P3220, R4107, P3971, P3386, V7221, V7206, P3466, V7366

100 Hurricanes L1951, P3263, P3358, P3884, L1990, P3393, P3232, P3228, P3363, V7253, P3836

101 Hurricanes P2910 (Sqn Ldr J. Grandy), P2866, P3660, P3376, P3316, P3870, P3656, P3655, P3123, L1595, P3615, P3855, P3866

102 Spitfires R6708, R6709, R6893, R6898, R7021, R7017, P9389, P9367, L1042

103 Spitfires K9895, L1038, L1068, N3230, N3293, P9450, P9554, R6975

104 Spitfires R6987, X4059, R6712, R6618, R6620 (Fg Off 'Paddy' Finucane), R6982

105 Spitfires R6768, P9312, R6920, K9864, N3095, R6762, R6861, N3240, N3127, X4030

106 Hurricanes N2461, P3481, P3900, P3112, N2524, P3936, P3679, N2755, N2921, P3205

107 Hurricanes including R4193, P3029, V7222, N2482

108 Hurricanes P2548, P3170, P3169, P3042, P3653, P2751, P3396, P2686, P3276, P3173, P3784

109 Hurricanes L1742, N2621, P3202, P3216, P3220, P3386, P3466, P3971, R4109, V7221, V7366

110 Hurricanes L1951, L1990, P3228, P3232, P3263, P3358, P3363, P3393, P3884, V7253, V7305

111 Spitfires K9839, K9881, K9969, L1002, L1005, L1019, L1040, N3227, P9381, P9463

112 Hurricanes reinforced by P3655, P2910, P2866, P3660, P3870, P3123, N2986, L1595, P3855, P3861

113 Hurricanes P3276, P3782, P3396, P3229, P2548, P2980

114 Spitfires K9895, L1068, N3293, P9540, P9554, R6700, R6975, X4067

115 Hurricanes L1992, L2075, P2587, N2768, N2871, N2963, P2966, P3111, P3158, P3161, R4192, R4194, R4221

116 Hurricanes 2921, P3112, 2461, V7363, 2524, P3679, P3481, V6535, R4106, P3147, P3900, V6536

117 Hurricanes P2760, N2617, P8816, P3803, N2329, L1865, P3059, P3208, R4105, P3815, L2038, V7234

118 Spitfires X4166-B, X4028-F, K9818-H, R6599-J, P9311-L, K9947-M, N3128-N, X4011-O, P9451-P, R6891-Q, X4064-T, R6802-Z

119 Hurricanes 'A', 'K', 'L', 'R', 'T', 'X'

120 Spitfires X4108, R6901, R6973, L1042, R7017, R6709, R6899, R7021, R6989, R6893, R6701, X4163

121 Hurricanes P2921, N2524, P3936, P3147, P3112, P3679, V7363, V6536, V6535, R4081, P3481, P3900

122 Hurricanes R4220, P2966, R4192, P2871, R4221, P3231, P2768, L1592, P3161, P3811, P3901, P3111

123 Spitfires R6623, R6975, X4067, N3293, R6990, P9450, P9596, P9557

124 Hurricanes R4109, P3786, P3627, P3202, R4107, P3466, P3386, P3179, P3903, V7366, V7208

125 Hurricanes P8818, P3263, P3393, P3230, L1990, P3228, P3886, V7303, N2602, V7253

126 Spitfires L1019, K9969, X4160, K9839, N3223, X4161, X4110, N3198, P9381, L1040, L1005, K9910, N3228, L1002

127 Spitfires P9466, R6957, X4036, N3283, X4035, X4023, N3280, X4035, X4023, N3280, P9494, X4009, N3279, N3239

128 Spitfires R6899, R7021, R6893, R6709, R6898, R6973, P9367, L1042, R6901, X4108

129 Hurricanes L2005, L1750, P3306, P3320, P3940, P3312, V7411, R4181, R4182, R4183, R4184

130 Hurricanes R4220, P2871, P3231, R4192, V7339, R4116, P3811, V7314, R4119, R4194, P3901, P3111

131 Spitfires K9909, R6775, (Fg Off J. K. Quill), N3101, N3163, R6683, R6803, R6982, X4059, R6712, R6818, R6714, N3164

132 Spitfires R6969, R7021, R6898, R6899, R6708, X4163

133 Hurricanes including VY-H, VY-E, VY-F, VY-KK, VY-G, VY-B

134 Defiants L7025, L6985, L7005, L7003, N1536, L7024, L6967

135 Hurricanes V7380, P3309, P3739, P3119, 2826, V6537, R4185

136 Spitfires R6919, R6917, R6776, R6889, R6958, R6923, R6833, R6761, X4231, R6888, R6897, R6890, R6770, R6882

137 The three aircraft involved, of 235 Squadron, were T1804, shot down, L9261-P and Z5736, which crash-landed

138 Hurricanes P3194 (Wg Cdr Dewar), P3594, N2798 (Flt Lt Gleed), V7225, P3993, P3755, P3118, V7307, P3404, P3174 (Plt Off Beamont), P3389, P3394, P3593

139 Spitfires R6986, X4165, R6631, N3223, R6915, P9661, L1082, R6769, X4104, R6691, L1008, K9997, X4107

140 Hurricanes P3788, P3878, P3536, P3168, P3894, P3027, P3168, P3033, V7416

141 Hurricanes N2755, N2920, V6547, N2433, P3936, V6546, P3679, V7425, V6547

142 Defiants L6985, L7028, L7005, L7026, L7024, L7025, N1536

143 Hurricanes R4089-R, P3889-S, P3156, P3142-M, P8809, R4087-X, P3887, P3143, P3157, R4184, P3159, P3960

144 Hurricanes V6549, V6542, P3466, -?-, P3386, V7308, V6548, V7303, V7306, P3903, P3179

145 Spitfires L1027, K9910, X4162, P9381, N3228, L1040, P9411, R6834, P9446, N3226, K9839, X4256

146 Spitfires X4009, P9494, N3279, X4l82, X4183, R6959

147 Hurricanes P3102, P2760, L1578, P5194, R4223, V7234, P3397, V6545, R5193, R4105, L2038

148 Hurricanes V7314, P3162, R4194, V7239, R4119, R4220, P3231, P2871, R4116

149 Defiants L7021, L7028, N1576, N1574, N1672, N1569, N1673, N1556, L6957, L7026, L7018, L6963

150 Defiants N1672, N1576, N1556

151 Spitfires R6899, R6709, R6892, R6893, X4163, R6898, X4053, X4054, X4108, X4235, R6973, R6832, N3110

152 Hurricanes P2751, P3042, V7379, V7258, P2548, V7302, P3044, P3396, P3276, V7377, P3019

153 Hurricanes P3150, V7349, V7343, P3467, V7350, also VY-Q (Sqn Ldr Townsend), VY-A, VY-G, VY-H, VY-K, VY-M

154 Hurricanes V7342, P3384, N2668, N2402, R2689, R4124, P5190, R4198, N2523, P3579

155 Spitfires R6899, R6898, X4053, R6892, X4163, R6973, R6974, P9367, N3110, X4054, X4235

156 Hurricanes P3150, N2645, V7343, V6581, L2071, also VY-A, VY-B, VY-D, VY-G, VY-K, VY-M, VY-Q (Sqn Ldr Townsend)

157 Spitfires N3267-S, L1021-M (Fg Off R. H. Hillary), L1024-R, R6808-Z, P9459-N

158 Spitfires R6993-W, X4028-F, K9974-M, N3124, P9433-E, R6976-A, X4064 T, R6891-Q, K9818-H, X4011-O, also DW-X and DW-Y

159 Hurricanes P3150, N2645, V7343, V6581, L2071, also VY-D, VY-G, VY-K, VY-L, VY-M, VY-Q (Sqn Ldr Townsend)

160 Spitfires R6735-W, R6753-G, L1021-M (Hillary, force-landed), L1040-R

161 Spitfires X4064-T, K9818-H, P9433-E, R6976, X4028-F, R6891-Q, P9311-L, X4239-R, X4966-B, N3124-N, DW-X and DW-Y

162 Hurricanes L1750, P3301, R4184, R4182, V7369, P3813, P3119, V7384

163 Hurricanes P3150, V7343, N2645, V7349, L2071, also VY-D, VY-G, VY-H, VY-K, VY-M and VY-Q

164 Hurricanes P5179, P3213, P3537, V6640, P5188, P3551, P3032, P3115, P3717, P3804, P3921, P2883, L1965

165 Spitfires K9947, P9492, P9469, X4321, P9878, R6773, N3119, L1031, X4067, P9434

166 Hurricanes P3061, P2961, P2982, P3207, P3715, P2831, P3084, P3090, P3218, P3814, P2884, P2967, P3864, P3087

167 Hurricanes R4088, P3620, R4094, P3890, P3643, L1706, N7296, V7250, P3705, P3706, P3049, P3708, P3709, R4189, V7298

168 Hurricanes V7332, P2863, V7378, P3384, R4197

169 Hurricanes V7302, P3395, P2548, P3042, V7375, P2751, V7251, V7376, P3396

170 Spitfires R6888, R6912, R6890, R6882, X4231, R6924, R6958, R6809, R6923, R6833, R6917

171 Hurricanes V7343, N2645, V7349, L2071, V6581, P3150, also VY-G, VY-H, VY-K, VY-M, VY-P, VY-Q

172 Hurricanes P3032, P3115, P2883, P3804, V6640, P3537, P3551

173 Hurricanes P3312, V6537, V7384, P3739, P3813, V7630, R4184, R4185

174 Hurricanes R4089, P3156, P3142, P3889, P3888, P8810, R4084, P8811, P3159, R4085, V6621, P3268

175 Spitfires R6899, X4238, R6892, X4163, R6898, R6709

176 Spitfires N3056-B, R6752-E, R6754-F, L1020-L, X4264-M, X4273-K, X4271-N, X4274-P, X4264-R, N3267-S, X4250-X, R6626 Y, R6853-W

177 Spitfires K9940, K9935, K9938, P9338, X4013, P9460, X4241, P9958, X4105

178 Spitfire 1bs R6888, R6924, X4159, X4059, R6776, R6917, R6923, R6833

179 Hurricanes V7408, V7416, P3673, P3539, P3033, R4122, P3027, P3892, P2741, P3878, P3536, P3023

180 Hurricanes P3756, P3114, N2599, V7201, P2965, P3066, P3063, P3062, P3053, P3094, P3064, P3024

181 Hurricanes P3049, V7298, P3704, P3705, P3708, P3735, L1703, P3645, V7254, L1706, P3578, R4088

182 Hurricanes P3143, V6556, R4085, P8811, V7436, P3056, P3142, V7304, P8809, P3148

183 Hurricanes P5179, V6637, P2588, P2686, P3032, P5181, P5172, P2865, P2883

184 Hurricanes V7360, V7202, P3756, P3066, V6531, P3201, P2599, P3053

185 Hurricanes R4175, R4179, V7243, V7284, V7290, V7289, P3974, V7242, P3700

186 Hurricanes R4229 (Sqn Ldr Grandy), V6610, V7313, V6559, P3594, P2863, V6628, V6534, V6614, P5206, P3088, P3579

Appendix 2

High-scoring RAF fighter pilots, 1 July–31 October 1940

The RAF generally avoids establishing small, elite groups within its ranks. Many interception successes during the Battle resulted from teamwork; some pilots were individually very successful in combat. Certain success is nevertheless often difficult to confirm. Where a victory was shared it is here shown as '1/2'. While few pilots used only one aircraft, quite a number flew the same machine many times. Likely scores, listed here, are based upon surviving combat reports, ORB listing and surviving relevant Luftwaffe and Fighter Command records. Likely scores of five or more 'kills' are listed.

Rank	Name	Sqn(s)	Score	Examples of aircraft flown	Remarks
Sgt	Allard, G.	85	9, 2 x 1/2	N2477, VY-L	
Plt Off	Atkinson, H. D.	213	6	P3200, R4099	KIA 25.8.40
Sqn Ldr	Badger, J. V. C	43	4, 2 x 1/2	P3971	
Plt Off	Barclay, R. G. A.	249	5	P3807	
Sgt	Beard, J. M. B	249	5	P2866	
Plt Off	Beaumont, W.	152	5, 3 x 1/2	R6829, R6831	
Plt Off	Bennions, G. H.	41	8	R6684, X4343	
Plt Off	Berry, R.	603	8, 3 x 1/2	P9459-N, R6626 -Y	
Fg Off	Blair, K. H.	151	4, 1/2	P2826, P3309	
Sub Lt	Blake, A. G.	19	6, 1/2	P7423	KIA 29.10.40
Sgt	Boddington, M. C. B.	234	5, 1/2	N3057, P9494	
Plt Off	Bodie, C. A. W	66	8, 2 x 1/2	P3029, X4321	
Flt Lt	Boitel-Gill	152	8	K9954	
Flt Lt	Boyd, A. D. McN.	145, 600	6, 3 x 1/2	P3381 (145 Sqn)	
Flt Lt	Brothers, P. M.	32, 257	5, 1/2	N2921 (32 Sqn), V7254 (257 Sqn)	
Fg Off	Carbury, B. J. G.	603	15, 1/2	R6835, X4263	
Plt Off	Carpenter, J. M. V.	222	5	P9378	
Fg Off	Clyde, W. P.	87, 601	5, 1/2	P3389 (87 Sqn), P3230 (601 Sqn)	
Flt Lt Sub	Connors, S. D. P.	111	5	V7222	
Lt (A)	Cork, R. J.	242	5	P2831, P3515	
Flt Lt	Crossley, M. N.	32	9, 1/2	N2461, P3146	
Plt Off	Cunningham, W.	19	5, 2 x 1/2		
Plt Off	Curchin, J.	609	7, 2 x 1/2	N3223, R6699	
Plt Off	Currant, C. F.	605	7, 3 x 1/2	P3580, V6783	
Fg Off	Count Czernin, M. B.	17	7, 5 x 1/2	V7408	
Flt Lt	Dalton-Morgan, T. F.	43	7, 1/2	P3784	
Plt Off	David, W. D.	87, 152	6, 1/2	P3405 (87 Sqn)	
Fg Off	Davis, C. R.	601	11, 1/2	P3363, P3382	KIA 6.9.40

Rank	Name	Sqn(s)	Score	Examples of aircraft flown	Remarks
Fg Off	Davis, C. T.	238	5, 2 x 1/2	P3462	
Flt Lt	Deere, A. C.	54	4	N3183, R6895	
Plt Off	Doe, R. F. T.	234, 238	15	V6814 and V6801 (238 Sqn), X4036 (234 Sqn)	
Fg Off	Dundas, J. C.	609	7	R6769, N3113	
Flt Lt	Dutton, R. G.	145	7, 3 x 1/2	P3521	
Flt Lt	Ellis, J.	610	6	R6806-N, R6993-W	
Fg Off	Eyre, A.	615	5, 2 x 1/2	P3151, R4194	
Sgt	Farnes, P. C. P.	501	6	P2760	
Sgt	Feary, A. N.	609	5	R6691, X4234	
Plt Off	Feric, M. (Pol)	303	7	V6681	
Flt Lt	Forbes, A. S.	303, 66	7	R4217 (303 Sqn), X4324 (66 Sqn)	
Sgt	Frartisek, J. (Pol)	303	17	R4175, P3975	KIA 8.10.40
Plt Off	Freeborn, J. C.	74	6	K9863, R6706	
Flt Lt	Gibson, J. A. A.	501	8	P3102	
Flt Lt	Gillam, D. E.	616, 312,	7, 1/2	X4181 (616 Sqn)	
Sgt	Glowacki, A.	501	8	P3815, P3820	
Plt Off	Goodman, G. E.	1	5, 1/2	P2686, P3678	
Flt Lt	Gracie, E. J.	56	5	P3554, P3570	
Plt Off	Gray, C. F.	54	14, 2 x 1/2	R6893	
Plt Off	Gribble, G. D.	54	5, 2 x 1/2	P9387, R6899	
Plt Off	Grier, T.	601	9, 5 x 1/2	P5208, P3393	
Fg Off	Haines, L. A.	19	5, 2 x 1/2	X4352	
Sgt	Hallowes, H. J. L.	43	9, 1/2	P3386	
Sgt	Hamlyn, R. F.	610	8	X4028-F, R6891-Q	
Sgt	Harker, A. S.	234	5	R6957	
Fg Off	Herneberg, Z.	303	8	V6684	
Plt Off	Hillary, R. H.	603	4	L1021-M	
Sqn Ldr	Hogan, H. A. V.	501	5, 3 x 1/2	R4228, V7433	
Flt Lt	Howell, F. J.	609	5, 1/2	R6769, X4104	
Sgt	Howes, H. N.	85, 605	6	P3107 and P3965 (605 Sqn)	
Flt Lt	Hughes, P. C.	234	14, 3 x 1/2	X4009	KIA 7.9.40
Sgt	Karubir, S.	303	5	P3901	
Sgt	Kilner, J. R.	65	5, 1/2	P9516, R6713	
Flt Lt	Kingcombe, C. B. F.	92	6, 2 x 1/2	R6622, X4051	
Sgt	Lacey, J. H.	501	15, 1/2	P8816	
Fg Off	Laricheliere, J. E. P.	213	6	-?-	
Plt Off	Lewis, A. G.	85, 249	9	V6617 (249 Sqn)	
Sgt	Llewellyn, R. T.	213	11	P3113	
Plt Off	Lock, E. S.	41	16, 1/2	N3152, X4409, R6610	
Fg Off	Lovell, A. D. J.	41	5	N3266, P9429, X4021	

Rank	Name	Sqn(s)	Score	Examples of aircraft flown	Remarks
Sqn Ldr	MacDonald, A. R. D.	64	5, 1/2	R6995, L1055	
Plt Off	MacKenzie, K. W.	501	5, 1/2	V6799, V6806	
Flt Lt	Malan, A. G.	74	6	R6773, K9953	
Plt Off	Mayers, H. C.	601	7	L1917, P2620, R4218	
Flt Lt	McArthur, J. H. G.	238, 609	6	R6915 and X4165 (609 Sqn)	
Sgt	McDowall, A.	602	11	K9910, L1040, N3228	
Flt Lt	McKellkar, A. A.	605	14, 1/2	P3308, V6878, V6789	
Fg Off	McMullen, D. A. P.	54, 222	10, 3 x 1/2	P9389 (54 Sqn), X4341 (222 Sqn)	
Plt Off	Meaker, J. R. B.	249	5, 2 x 1/2	P3123, P3834	KIA 27.9.40
Plt Off	Millington, W. H.	72, 249	9, 2 x 1/2	V6614	KIA 30.10.40
Fg Off	Mungo-Park, J. C.	74	6	K9878, R6772	
Plt Off	Neil, T. F.	249	7, 2 x 1/2	P3316	
Plt Off	Oxspring, R. W.	66	5, 2 x 1/2	R6800, X4052, X4421	
Fg Off	Paszkiewicz, L. W. (Pol)	303	6	V7235	KIA 27.9.40
Flt Lt	Rabagliati, A. C.	46	6	P3597, V6544	
Sgt	Rolls, W. T. E.	72	7	K9841	
Flt Lt	Sing, J. E. J.	213	6, 1/2	P3780	
Plt Off	Stapleton, B. G.	603	5, 2 x 1/2	L1040-R	
Plt Off	Stephen, H. M.	74	8, 2 x 1/2	P9492, P7361	
Fg Off	Strickland, J. M.	213	5, 1/2	P3979, V6544	
Sgt	Szaposznikow, E.	303	8	P3120, V7244	
Sqn Ldr	Townsend, P. W.	85	6	P2716 VY-F, P3166 VY-Y	
Flt Lt	Tuck, R. R. S.	92, 257	10, 1/2	N3268 (92 Sqn), V6555 (257 Sqn)	
F/Sgt	Unwin, G. C.	19	10	X4425, P9546	
Plt Off	Upton, H. C.	43, 607	10, 1/2	V7206 (43 Sqn)	
Fg Off	Urbanowicz, W. (Pol)	145, 303, 601	14	R4177 (145 Sqn), V7290 and R2685 (303 Sqn)	
Plt Off	Urwin-Mann, J. R.	238	8	P3226	
Plt Off	Vigors, T. A.	222	5	X4341, K9947	
Fg Off	Villa, J. W.	72, 92	10, 4 x 1/2	X4252 (72 Sqn), X4419 (72 Sqn)	
Fg Off	Weaver, P. S.	56	7, 1/2	P3554	KIA 31.8.40
Fg Off	Webb, P. C.	602	6	L1019, R6834	
Flt Lt	Webster, J. T.	41	8	R6635, R6661	KIA 5.9.40
Sgt	Whall, B. E. P.	602	6	K9969, R6601	KIA 7.10.40
Plt Off	Wlasnowalski, B.	32, 607, 213	5	V7223 and P3679 (32 Sqn)	
Plt Off	Woods-Scawen, C. A.	43	7	P3964	KIA 2.9.40
Plt Off	Zumbach, J. (Pol)	303	8	P3700, V7242	

Appendix 3

Pilots and aircrew of Fighter Command killed in action during the Battle

	Pilots	Other aircrew
RAF		
British	370	32
Belgian	5	–
Czechoslovakian	7	–
French	–	–
Polish	29	–
RCAF	3	–
RNZAF	–	3
Totals	414	35

Appendix 4

RAF personnel casualties,
1 July–31 October 1940

Bracketed figures = number of pilots.

All totals to noon on date listed.

Second line entries relate to casualties resulting from flying accidents.

Source: Returns to Air Ministry War Room, July–October 1940. Adjustments to the figures were to be repeatedly made, over a long period. No final summary along the lines of this seems to have been prepared.

Fighter Command	Killed	Wounded	Missing in action	POW
To 1.7.40	51 (42)	42 (36)	180 (151)	28 (26)
	120 (95)	31 (24)	3 (2)	
1.8.40	81 (67)	63 (57)	224 (182)	34 (31)
	141 (111)	39 (31)	6 (2)	
1.9.40	136 (114)	139 (129)	329 (269)	43 (38)
	157 (123)	46 (35)	8 (2)	
1.10.40	238 (204)	230 (223)	377? (315)	47 (42)
	171 (135)	50 (38)	10 (4)	
31.10.40	317 (278)	266 (256)	365 (305)	54 (47)
	207 (159)	55 (41)	14 (9)	

Bomber Command	Killed	Wounded	Missing in action	POW
To 1.7.40	233 (91)	68 (24)	656 (237)	139 (52)
	233 (101)	49 (22)	10 (2)	
1.8.40	331 (129)	84 (31)	747 (27)	219 (78)
	260 (110)	65 (27)	15 (3)	1 pilot interned
1.9.40	497 (189)	98 (39)	723 (270)	325 (120)
	332 (144)	73 (28)	35 (8)	2 pilots interned
1.10.40	539 (205)	108 (42)	878 (331)	407 (145)
	393 (169)	83 (32)	43 (10)	3 interned
31.10.40	616 (230)	134 (52)	945 (363)	438 (157)
	447 (197)	98 (37)	39 (9)	1 interned

Coastal Command	Killed	Wounded	Missing in action	POW
To 1.8.40	132 (55)	31 (10)	213 (93)	6 (4)
	44 (25)	23 (12)	16 (9)	
1.9.40	166 (68)	37 (12)	216 (93)	25 (12)
	80 (44)	27 (14)	16 (9)	
1.10.40	180 (75)	39 (14)	250 (107)	36 (16)
	82 (45)	33 (15)	21 (11)	
31.10.40	199 (82)	45 (16)	315 (133)	41 (18)
	87 (46)	38 (17)	20 (12)	

Grand total of personnel losses to noon 31.10.40

	Killed	Wounded	Missing in action	POW
	1,688 (667)	936 (387)	2,303 (940)	683 (270)
	1,194 (664)	329 (171)	103 (42)	31 (8) interned

Accumulated total as at noon on listed date.

Appendix 5

Main night attacks on British cities
14 November – 29 December 1940
(Data based upon surviving German records)

Date	Aircraft reaching target	Tons HE dropped	Incendiary containers dropped
November			
14 Coventry	449	593	881
15 London	358	414	1,142
16 London	87	104	68
17 Southampton	159	198	300
17 London	49	60	64
19 Birmingham	357	404	810
20 Birmingham	116	132	296
22 Birmingham	204	227	457
23 Southampton	121	150	464
24 Bristol	333	134	160
27 Plymouth	107	110	170
27 London	57	60	nil
28 Birkenhead/Liverpool	324	356	860
29 London	335	380	820
30 Southampton	128	152	598
December			
1 Southampton	123	147	586
2 Bristol	121	122	615
3 Birmingham	51	55	448
4 Birmingham	62	77	184
5 Portsmouth	74	88	148
6 Bristol	67	78	158
8 London	13	387	3,188
11 Birmingham	278	277	685
12 Sheffield	336	355	457
15 Sheffield	94	80	600
20 Birkenhead/Liverpool	205	205	761
21 Birkenhead/Liverpool	299	280	940
22 Manchester	270	272	1,032
23 Manchester	171	195	893
27 London	108	111	328
29 London	136	127	613

August

2	Bridge Blean RD 200 (4), ibs
11/12	Bristol 50
12	Folkestone 150 (1), ibs
12	Gosport 40 (1)
12	Portsmouth 21 (36), 3 ob
13	Ventnor 60 (18)
13/14	Birmingham CB 47
14/15	Bristol 50
15	Chatham 72 (6)
15	Malling RD, Kent, 150 (96), 1 ob
15	Reigate 158 (14)
15	Sunderland 71 (1)
15	Swale RD, Kent, 98 (8)
15/16	Birmingham CB 64 (1), ibs
16	Custon RD 53
16	Gosport 48 (5)
16	Malling RD 63 (3)
16	Northfleet 104 (2)
16	Sevenoaks 229 (30)
16	Strood RD, Kent, 84 (2)
18	Strood RD 69
18	Swale RD 75 (2)
20	Shardlow RD 38 (2), ibs
23/24	Birmingham 48, 250+ ibs
24	Bridge Blean RD, Kent 400 (29), 4 ob
24	Portsmouth 100
24	Ramsgate 500 (45), mainly in sea, a jettisoned load clearly overestimated, and ibs; also 60 HE and 6 ob around Broadstairs
25/26	Birmingham CB 96 (16), 1 ob, ibs
25/26	Rugby RD 56
26/27	Birmingham CB 152 (22), ibs
28	Rochford RD 78 (24)
29/30	Liverpool 49 (8), 1 ob, ibs
31	Birkenhead 35 (8), 1 ob
31/1.9	Bradford 41 (8), 10 ob
31/1.9	Strood RD (45)

September

1/2	Bristol 125, 1 ob, ibs
1/2	Swansea 84 (22)
3/4	Bristol 36 (4)
3/4	Liverpool 45 (4), 3 ob, ibs
4	Chatham 75 (6)
4	Rochester 55 (6)
4/5	Bristol 40, 5 ob, 1,000+ ibs
4/5	Liverpool 76 (3), 2 ob, ibs
4/5	Strood RD 43 (2), 2 PM, ibs
7	Dover and Deal 36 (5), ibs
8	Dover and Deal RD 159 (24), 1 ob, ibs

15	Dover and Deal RD 77 (17), ibs
15	Portland 70 (10), 4 ob, ibs
15	Tonbridge RD 77 (30), ibs
16	Dover and Deal RD 31 (10)
17	Thurrock 44 (1), 1 ob, ibs
25	Bristol 300
29	Bagshot RD 39 (1)

October

8	Eastleigh 20 (27)
12/13	Coventry 98 (1), 1 ob, ibs
14/15	Coventry 94 (40), 2 ob, ibs
15/16	Birmingham 73 (9), 3 ob, ibs
19	Battle RD, Kent, 61 (5)
19/20	Coventry 94 (34), ibs
21/22	Coventry* 100 (35), ibs
25/26	Birmingham 78 (3), 1 ob
26/27	Birmingham 108 (5), 2 ob, ibs
29/30	Birmingham 39 (3), 1 ob

Raids to 31 October 1940 involving 30-39 HEs = total 17; 20-29 HEs = 45

* By way of comparison, in the well-known heavy Coventry raid of 14/15 November 1940 the dropped loads were assessed officially as 50 PMs, 1,120 HEs, 280 UX and unknown incendiary load. German listing shows 503 tonnes of HE and 31.716 tonnes of incendiaries. London's heaviest raid during the Blitz period came on 16/17 April 1941 according to the Germans – a total of 890 tonnes of HE and 151.20 tonnes of incendiaries. The heaviest fire raid came not as generally supposed on 29/30 December 1940 (22.248 tonnes of incendiaries) but on 8/9 December 1940 (114.768 tonnes of fire bombs).

Night Attacks on London
7 September – 13 November 1940
(Data based upon surviving German records)

Date	Aircraft reaching target	Tons HE dropped	Incendiary containers dropped
September			
7	247	335	440
8	171	207	347
9	195	232	289
10	148	176	318
11	180	217	148
12	43	54	61
13	105	123	209
14	38	55	43
15	181	224	279
16	170	189	318
17	268	334	391
18	300	350	628
19	255	310	533
20	109	154	79
21	113	164	329
22	123	130	476
23	261	300	611
24	223	256	384
25	219	260	441
26	180	218	224
27	163	167	437
28	249	325	303
29	246	294	136
30	218	287	104

Date	Aircraft reaching target	Tons HE dropped	Incendiary containers dropped
October			
1	214	250	115
2	105	130	300
3	44	61	–
4	134	190	236
5	177	242	176
6	7	8	–
7	179	211	143
8	208	257	264
9	216	263	245
10	222	269	718
11	132	213	126
12	119	148	24
13	211	249	131
14	242	304	299
15	410	538	177
16	280	346	187
17	254	322	134
18	129	172	132
19	282	386	192
20	298	356	192
21	100	115	52
22	82	98	40
23	64	65	–
24	64	75	–
25	159	193	193
26	203	253	176
27	114	127	40
28	146	176	111
29	186	236	109
30	125	178	92
31	67	48	83
November			
1	181	227	130
2	102	117	126
4	157	184	16
5	119	139	–
6	192	223	4
7	193	242	9
8	125	133	–
9	125	124	–
10	171	212	7
11	23	17	16
12	126	165	92
13	25	28	–
TOTALS	**11,117**	**13,651**	**12,586**

Appendix 6

Tonnage of bombs
dropped on the United Kingdom

British assessment German listing

	Tonnes	Percentage of German figures	HE tonnes	Incendiary tonnes	Total
August	6,770	257.7	2,462	165.456	2,627.456
September	9,975	111.4	8,528	429.336	8,957.336
October	6,910	74.5	9,027	252.432	9,297.432

British over-assessment was due to the belief that many bombs fell at sea. The 'Ramsgate incident' highlights that. There was also great difficulty in locating unexploded bombs, particularly in rural areas, where some unquestionably remain.

London's heaviest raids – British assessment

15/16 October 1940	1,186 HE bombs, the most up to 31 October
20/21 October 1940	691 HE bombs, the second heaviest raid
16/17 October 1940	535 HE bombs, one 1,800kg bomb reported

Appendix 7

Estimate of the number of bombs dropped – British figures

1940	HE	Oil	Parachute mines*
June (night)	1,388	14	9
July	1,921	162	19
August	5,103	318	45 (9)
September	18,327	688	122
October	476 50kg bombs, 280 250kg plus 17,550 unclassified HE 1,253 113 = 5,845 MT		

* Prior to 17 September, when the dropping inland of parachute mines began on a major scale, these weapons were almost all sea mines; some are known to have been dropped in error on coastal regions. Prior to October no regular attempt was made by the Ministry of Home Security to record the calibre of HE weapons.

The *Luftminen* known to the British as the parachute mine. The top picture shows the basin attached in which the parachute – deployed in the lower illustration – was carried.

Appendix 8

Strength and Availability of Allied Aircraft
– 10 May, 1940

When at daybreak German forces launched their blitzkrieg they faced air forces diversely armed with aircraft types intended mainly for army co-operation. The French Armée de l'Air with a considerable number of air defence aircraft and a few strategic bombers was re-equipping with new types, some from the USA others from home manufacturers. They were integrating with French designs little changed from the 1920s and early 1930s. The Belgian Air Force mainly had biplanes - Gloster Gladiators, Italian-built Fiat CR42s as well as licence-built Fairey Fox variants derived from a mid-1920s design akin to the British Hawker Hart and Fury. A few Fairey Battles were also available for the mainly army support role. The Netherlands air forces relied almost entirely upon home-built Fokker fighters, bombers and army support aircraft, the best of which were the twin-boom Fokker G-1As. Douglas 8A support bombers were fielded on the day as fighters. The Marine Luchtvaartdienst, the MLD, using Fokker designs, was ordered to France from where their Fokker C XIV and T-8W floatplanes moved to the UK.

The RAF in France consisted of the Air Component of the BEF and an Advanced Air Striking Force, previously No 1(Bomber) Group. Home-based No 2(Bomber) Group was a Blenheim IV equipped second echelon of the AASF. The AASF in France was unfortunate enough to be armed with the cumbersome Fairey Battle bomber. It had a wing span of 52 feet, and was poorly defended. It had been designed to be powered by either a Rolls-Royce engine (tentatively called the Griffon) based upon that used in the Supermarine S.6B Schneider Trophy winner, or the powerful P.24 engine Fairey were working upon. Instead, it had one Rolls-Royce Merlin giving little over 1,000 hp, far too little for this hefty machine. Ironic, for sure that the Merlin which, along with Mr Churchill and Sir Hugh Dowding, did as much as any towards ultimate victory, was also the Battle's Achilles heel. A daily return of RAF aircraft held by squadrons showing strength (basically 12 each) and aircraft availability (around 60-70% usually) at 09:00 was usual, but the fluidity of the situation on 10 May 1940 renders that of limited value. Listed are the squadrons and their positioning which very soon changed.

Internal civilian, political and military wrangling overawed the French Air Force which, in May 1940, held over 4,000 good aircraft, almost 1,000 more than the German Luftwaffe. Many were the equal of the foe, but only about a quarter were committed to front line units. The Army, which for historical reasons many politicians feared, still wanted to control and direct the air arm despite its acquired independence in 1928. It was also fear of land attack that influenced many in the French Air Force, but some encouraged a strategic long-range bomber force whose eight squadron Amiot 143M force in 1940 managed 551 operational night sorties before 16 June for a loss of 12 aircraft. Amiot's of the 34th and 38th Escadres on 14 May made one courageous daylight attack at a mere 800m on the Sedan bridgehead, their escort keeping losses from the 13 aircraft force to only four. Push and pull four-engined Farman 222 bomber squadrons made 71 night sorties to German targets.

Such operational records as survive suggest the LeO 451 bombers managed 392 sorties but lost 98 of their number, the fast Breguet 693s 484 sorties for a loss of 47, the new Glenn Martin 167Fs which began operations on 22 May managing 385 sorties for a loss of 15 aircraft and the Douglas DB-7F – which entered the arena on 23 May flying 69 sorties for a loss of 9 aircraft. High altitude reconnaissance could have been well performed by the Bloch 174 which had just entered service. Instead there was a very low utilisation rate. Tactical reconnaissance was performed by a considerable number of the large heavily defended Potez 63.11 unsuitable for tactical warfare and too slow to escape Bf 109s, and there were no strike aircraft suitable for attacking German armour. Organised air defence of the country having been very neglected, it was easy for the Luftwaffe to bomb vital targets. Better organised, the French aviators whose courage was much to the fore might well have curtailed the German venture.

Outlines of the Air Forces on 10 May 1940

Belgian Air Force

Formation	Aircraft type	Strength	War station
No 1 Air Regiment (Army close support)			
1re Escadrille	Fairey Fox II/III	10	Hingene
3e Escadrille	Fox II	12	Glabeek
5e Escadrille	Fox III	10	Jeneffe
7e Escadrille	Fox VI	9	Lonzee
9e Escadrille	Renard 31	11	Wilderen
11e Escadrille	Renard 31	8	Hannut
No 2 Regiment (Fighter)			
1e Escadrille	Gladiator	15	Beauchevain/Bevekom
2e Escadrille	Hurricane	11	Beauchevain/Bevekom
3e Escadrille	Fiat CR 42	10	Brustem
4e Escadrille	Fiat CR 42	14	Brustem
5e Escadrille	Fox VI	15	Vissenaken
6e Escadrille	Fox VI	15	Vissenaken
No 3 Regiment (Bomber-reconnaissance)			
1re Escadrille	Fox III	15	Neerhespen
3e Escadrille	Fox III	15	Neerhespen
5e Escadrille	Fairey Battle	14	Belcele
7e	Fox VIII	9	Belcele

Armee de l'Air

Formation/Unit	Aircraft type	Strength	Base
Northern Zone			
Groupement de Chasse 21			
HQ	Morane 406	2	Chantilly-les-Aigles
GC I/I	Bloch 152	15	Chantilly-les-Aigles
GC II/I	Bloch 152	18	Buc
GC III/3	Morane 406	23	Beauvais/Tille
	Dewoitine D.520	2	Beauvais/Tille
GC II/10	Bloch 151	14	Rouen/Boos
	Bloch 152	6	
GC III/10	Bloch 151	5	Le Harve/Octeville
Groupement de Chasse 23			
HQ	Curtiss Hawk-75C	2	Laon/Chambry
GC II/2	Morane 406	22	Laon/Chambry
GC III/2	Morane 406	28	Cambrai/Niergnies
GC I/4	Curtiss Hawk 75C	30	Wez/Thuisy
GC I/5	Curtiss Hawk 75C	25	Suippes
ECMJ 1/16	Potez 631	10	Wez/Thuisy
Groupement de Chasse 25			
GC III/1	Morane 406	20	Norrent/Fontes
GC II/8	Bloch 152	11	Calais/Marck
Groupement de Chasse de Nuit			
ECN 1/13	Potez 631	8	Meaux/Esbly
ECN 2/13	Potez 631	7	Melun/Villaroche
ECN 3/13	Potez 631	10	Le Plessis/Bellevile
ECN 4/14	Potez 631	7	Betzx/Bouillancy
Groupement de Bombardement 6			
GB 1/12	Liore et Olivier LeO 451	9	Soissons/Saconin
GB II/12	Liore et Olivier LeO 451	13	Persan/Beaumont
Groupement de Bombardement 9			
GB I/34	Amiot 143	10	Mointdidier
	Amiot 354	2	
G B II/34	Amiot 143	9	Roye/Amy
	Bloch 131	1	
Groupement de Bombardemont 18			
GB 1/54	Breguet 693	13	La Ferte/Gaucher
GB II/54	Breguet 683	10	Nangis
Reconnaissance			
GR II/	Potez 637	6	Laou/Athies
	Potez 63 11	5	
	Bloch 174	1	

Formation/Unit	Aircraft type	Strength	Base
Army co-operation squadrons and associated Armée formations:			
1st Armée			
GR 1/14	Potez 63.11	7	Clastres/ St Simon
GAO 502	Potez 63.11	3	La Fere/Courbes
	Mureaux 115	4	
GAO 503	Potex 63.11	3	Valenciennes
GAO 504	LeO C 30	28	Denain/Prouvy
	Potez 63 11	3	
GAO 505	Potez 63 11	4	Le Qesnoy/Vertain
GAO 545	Potez 27	4	Denain/Prouvy
GAO 4/551	Potez 63 11	2	Le Quesnoy/Vertain
	Mureaux 117	3	
GAO 544	Potez 63 11	4	Villers les Guise
	Mureaux 115	4	
2e Armee			
GR II/22	Potez 63 11	7	Chatel/Chéhéry
GAO 507	Potez 63 11	4	Attigny
	Mureaux 115	5	
GAO 510	Potez 63 11	6	Attigny
	Potez 39	3	
GAO 518	Potez 63 11	6	Challerange
	Breguet 27	5	
Ga 2/520	Potez 63 11	4	Challerange
	Mureaux 115	5	
7e Armee			
GR 1/35	Potez 63 11	11	St Omer/Wizernes
GAO 501	Potez 63 11	3	Dunkirk/Mardyck
GAO 516	Potez 63 11	4	Calais/St Inglevert
GAO 552	Potez 63 11	5	St Omer/Wizernes
9e Armee			
GR II/52	Potez 63 7	5	Couvran
	Potez 63 11	6	
GAO 511	Potez 63 11	2	Villers-les Guise
	Potez 39	2	
GAO 545	Potez 27	4	Denain-Prouvy
GAO 547	Potez 63 11	6	L Malmaison
	Potez 27	5	
GAO 2/551	Potez 63 11	2	Tournes/Belval
	Mureaux 117	5	

Formation/Unit	Aircraft type	Strength	Base
Eastern Zone			
Groupement de Chasse 22			
HQ	Morane 406	2	Velaine-en-Haye
	Curtiss Hawk 75	1	
GC I/2	Morane 406	27	Toul/Ochey
GC II/4	Curtiss Hawk 75	29	Xaffevillers
GC II/5	Curtiss Hawk 75	14	Toul/Croix de Metz
GC II/6	Morane 406	20	Anglure-Vouarces
GC III/7	Morane 406	23	Vitry le Francois
GC I/8	Bloch 152	20	Velaine-en-Haye
Groupement de Bombardement 10			
GB I/38	Amiot 143	9	Troyes/Barberey
	Bloch 200	2	
GB II/38	Amiot 143	10	Chaumont/ Chemoutiers
Groupement de Bombardement 15			
GB I/15	Farman F222	2	Reims/ Courcy
GB II/15	Farman F222	4	Reims/ Courcy
Army Co-operation Squadrons and Associated			
3e Army			
GR 1/22	Potez 637	6	Metz/Frescaty
GAO I/506	Potez 63 11	4	Doncourt-les-Conflans
	Mureaux 113/115	4	
GAO 2/506	Potez 63 11	5	Chambley/Bussieres
	Mureaux 117	4	
GAO 2/508	Potez 63 11	6	Mars-la-Tour
	Potez 27	5	
GAO I/551	Potez 63 11	5	Etain/Buzy
	Mureaux 117	4	
GAO 3/551	Potez 63 11	4	Senon/Spincourt
	Mureaux 113/117	3	
4^e Armee			
GR I/36	Potez 63 11	7	Martigny-les-Gerbonvaux
GAO 2/509	Potez 63 11	4	Delme/ Essey-les-Nancy
	Breguet 27	2	
GAO I/520	Potez 63 11	4	Morhange
	Mureaux 115	5	

Formation/Unit	Aircraft type	Strength	Base
5ᵉ Armee			
HQ FA 105	Curtiss Hawk 75	1	Neufchateau
GR II/36	Potez 63 11	6	Neufchateau
	Bloch 174	2	
GAO 512	Potez 63 11	3	La Perthe
	Potez 39	7	
GAO 517	Potez 63 11	5	Neufchateau
	Potez 39	3	Baume
GAO 548	Mueaux 115	5	Dogneville
GAO 553	Potez 63 11	6	Nancy/Azelot
	Mureaux 115	2	
Southern Zone			
HQ	Morane 406	1	Dijon/Longvic
Groupement de Chasse 24			
HQ	Morane 406	2	Dijon-Longvic
GC III/6	Morane 406	30	Chissey sur Loue
GC II/7	Morane 406	24	Luxeuil/ St Sauveur
	Dewoitine 520	1	
Reconnaissance			
GR I/33	Potez 637	2	Dole
	Potez 63 11	1	
	Bloch 174	1	
Army Co-operation Squadrons			
8e Armee			
GR I/55	Potez 63 11	8	Lure-Malbouhans
Alpine Zone			
HQ	Morane 406	7	Valence Gal Laurens
GC 1/6	Morane 406	12	Marseilles/ Marignane
GC III/9	Bloch 15	9	Lyon/Bron
ECN 5/13	Potez 631	11	Loyettes
GC 1/3	Morane 406	14	Cannes/Mandelieu
	Dewoitine 520	34	
GC II/3	Morane 406	14	Le Luc
	Dewoitine 520	4	
GR II/14	Potez 637	1	Valence/Chabeuil
GAO	Potez 63 11	5	Geoirs
	Mureaux 115	3	

In addition to these listed, operational units were converting to Glenn Martin 167F, Bloch 210, Liore et Olivier 451, Amiot 354, Breguet 691 and 693

Militaire Luchtvaart – Royal Netherlands Air Force
1^e Luchtvaartregiment(Luchtverdediging}
Strategic Group

Formation	Aircraft type	Strength	War station
Strat. Ver VA	Fokker C – X	10	Bergen
Bomva	Fokker T – V	9	Schiphol
Jachtgroep			
1^e Java	Fokker D – XXI	11	De Kooy
2^e Java	Fokker D – XXI	9	Schiphol
3^e Java	Fokker G-1A	11	Waalhaven
4e Java	Fokker G-1A	12	Bergen

2e Luchtvaartregiment (Legervliegdienst)

*te Verk,Gr. Hilversum	1 Fokker C-x, 4 Fokker C-V, 4 Koolhoven FK-51
*ne Verk Gr. Ypenburg	7 Fokker C-V, 5 Koolhoven FK-51
*me Verk. Gr. Ruigenhoek	9 Fokker C-v, 4 Koolhoven FK-51 1 Fokker C-x, 3
Fokker **F-VIIAs**	
*ive Verk Gr Gilze Rijen	7 Fokker C-v, 3 Koolhoven FK-51

Jachtgroep Veldleger

1e Java	Ypenburg	8 Fokker D XXI
3e Java	Ypenburg	11 Douglas 8-A3N

The Elementaire Vligschool at Vlissingen also held 11 Fokker S-IV and 15 Fokker S-IX
The Vliegschool at Hamstede had 10 Fokker C-V, 10 Koolhoven FK-51 3 Fokker F VIIAs
and one Fokker S-IV. The fighter school on Texel held 7 Fokker D XVII, 2 Fokker D –
XXI, 1 Fokker G- 1A, 1 Fokker T –V, 7 Koolhoven FK-56 and six diverse types

The Royal Air Force based in France

Formation	Aircraft type	War station
No 14 Group, Air Component of the British Expeditionary Force		
No 60 (Fighter) Wing		
No 85 Squadron	Hurricane	Lille/Seclin
No 87 Squadron	Hurricane	Lille/Marcq
No 61 (Fighter) Wing		
No 607 Squadron	Hurricane	Vitry-en-Artois
No 615 Squadron	Hurricane	Abbeville
No 70 (Bomber Reconnaissance) Wing		
No 18 Squadron	Blenheim IV	Meharicourt
No 57 Squadron	Blenheim IV	Rosieres-en-Santerre
No 52 (Bomber) Wing		
No 53 Squadron	Blenheim IV	Poix
No 59 Squadron	Blenheim IV	Poix
No 50 (Army Co-operation) Wing		
No 4 Squadron	Lysander	Monchy-Lagache
No 13 Squadron	Lysander	Mons-en-Chaussee
No 16 Squadron	Lysander	Bertangles
No 51 (Army Co-operation) Wing		
No 2 Squadron	Lysander	Abbeville/Drucat
No 26 Squadron	Lysander	Dieppe
No 81 (Communications) Squadron	Tiger Moth	Amiens/Mountjoie
Advanced Air Striking Force		
No 71 (Bomber) Wing		
No 105 Squadron	Battle	Villeneuve-les-Verrus
No 114 Squadron	Blenheim IV	Conde-Vraux
No 139 Squadron	Blenheim IV	Plivot
No 150 Squadron	Battle	Ecury-sur-Coole
No 75 (Bomber) Wing		
No 88 Squadron	Battle	Mourmelon
No 103 Squadron	Battle	Betheniville
No 218 Squadron	Battle	Moscou Ferme
No 76 (Bomber) Wing		
No 12 Squadron	Battle	Amifontaine
No 142 Squadron	Battle	Berry-au-Bac
No 226 Squadron	Battle	Reims/Champagne
No 67 (Fighter) Wing		
No 1 Squadron	Hurricane	Berry-au-Bac
No 73 Squadron	Hurricane	Reims/Champagne

Nos 3 and 79 Hurricane squadrons joined the Air Component and No 501 the AASF on 10 May, No 504 the Air Component on 12 May and Nos 17 and 242 joined the AASF on 8 June.

Appendix 9

Battle of Britain Treasures

The 1968 film 'The Battle of Britain' attracted Heinkel 111s to our shores, albeit strange sounding for these Spanish examples were powered by Rolls-Royce Merlin engines. One – in parts – has in recent years resided at Duxford and, parts of others exist, awaiting an entrepreneur with money!

Spanish 'Buchon' fighters pretending to be Messerschmitt Bf 109s resting at Duxford in August 1968 during the making of the Battle of Britain film.

Spitfire 1 K9942 served with 72 Squadron 24 April 1939 to 7 June 1940 when it suffered battle damage. After repair by General Aircraft at Hanworth, 7 OTU used it from 17 August 1940 to 17 July 1941. It also served with Nos 57 and 53 OTUs. On Royal Navy charge 17 March to 6 April 1944, it was earmarked for preservation on 28 April 1944 and resides in the RAF Museum, Hendon.

Spitfire Mk II P7350, rescued just in time from a northern scrap metal merchant, is now top star of the Battle of Britain Memorial Flight. P7350 participated on Battle of Britain Day 1940 flying from Duxford in Leigh Mallory's Big Wing. An early Mk II, it joined No 611 Squadron at Digby on 6 August. Slightly battle damaged on 21 August, it stayed with No 611 until 16 November 1940. Struck off charge on 30 May 1941 due to battle damage, P7350 had managed only 75.35 flying hours. It is pictured passing Duxford tower in July 2008.

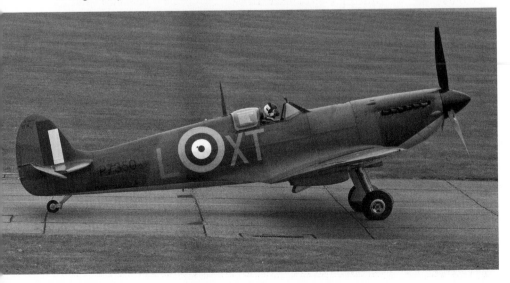

On 23 December 2007, Merlin III-engined Hurricane R4118, genuine 1940 survivor superbly re-engineered by Hawker Restorations, Ltd, took-off from Marshall Aerospace, Cambridge Airport to resume a flying career after waiting for an astonishing 64 years! R4118 joined No 605 (County of Warwick) Squadron at Drem on 17 August, 1940. Operating from Croydon, it was battle damaged on 22 October, 1940. Subsequently, 'Treble-One' Squadron flew R4118, also Nos 59 and 56 OTUs. Packed at Cardiff in December 1943, it was shipped to India staying crated until 1947 when it was struck off charge. Peter Vacher, its saviour, found it in 1982, but it was 2001 before R4118 returned to the UK. It is a remarkable 1940 treasure.

Making the Battle of Britain film brought a mixed assortment of Spitfires and Hurricanes to Duxford including this Hurricane.

One of two Duxford based 'Heinkel 111s' in the summer of 1968. Pity about the engines and the wrong engind sound!

Select Index